Why Europe Grew Rich and Asia Did Not

Why Europe Grew Rich and Asia Did Not provides a striking new answer to the classic question of why Europe industrialized from the late eighteenth century and Asia did not. Drawing significantly from the case of India, Prasannan Parthasarathi shows that in the seventeenth and eighteenth centuries the advanced regions of Europe and Asia were more alike than different, both characterized by sophisticated and growing economies. Their subsequent divergence can be attributed to different competitive and ecological pressures that in turn produced varied state policies and economic outcomes. This account breaks with conventional views, which hold that divergence occurred because Europe possessed superior markets, rationality, science or institutions. It offers instead a groundbreaking rereading of global economic development that ranges from India, Japan and China to Britain, France and the Ottoman Empire and from the textile and coal industries to the roles of science, technology and the state.

PRASANNAN PARTHASARATHI is Associate Professor in the Department of History at Boston College. His previous publications include *The Transition to a Colonial Economy: Weavers, Merchants and Kings in South India, 1720–1800* (Cambridge, 2001) and *The Spinning World: A Global History of Cotton Textiles, 1200–1850* (co-edited with Giorgio Riello, 2009).

Why Europe Grew Rich and Asia Did Not: Global Economic Divergence, 1600–1850

PRASANNAN PARTHASARATHI

CAMBRIDGE
UNIVERSITY PRESS

University Printing House, Cambridge CB2 8BS, United Kingdom

One Liberty Plaza, 20th Floor, New York, NY 10006, USA

477 Williamstown Road, Port Melbourne, VIC 3207, Australia

4843/24, 2nd Floor, Ansari Road, Daryaganj, Delhi - 110002, India

79 Anson Road, #06-04/06, Singapore 079906

Cambridge University Press is part of the University of Cambridge.

It furthers the University's mission by disseminating knowledge in the pursuit of education, learning and research at the highest international levels of excellence.

www.cambridge.org
Information on this title: www.cambridge.org/9780521168243

First published 2011
3rd printing 2012

A catalogue record for this publication is available from the British Library

Library of Congress Cataloging in Publication data
Parthasarathi, Prasannan.
   Why Europe grew rich and Asia did not : global economic divergence, 1600–1850 / Prasannan Parthasarathi.
      p.   cm.
   ISBN 978-1-107-00030-8 (Hardback) – ISBN 978-0-521-16824-3 (Paperback)
   1. Economic development–Europe–History.   2. Economic development–Asia–History.   3. Europe–Economic conditions.   4. Asia–Economic conditions.   I. Title.
   HC240.P2485 2011
   330.94′02–dc22

                                                                        2011002484

ISBN 978-1-107-00030-8 Hardback
ISBN 978-0-521-16824-3 Paperback

To *Juliet*

Contents

List of figures   *page* viii

List of maps   ix

List of tables   x

Acknowledgments   xi

List of abbreviations   xiv

Maps   xv

1 Introduction   1

Part I Setting the stage: Europe and Asia before divergence

2 India and the global economy, 1600–1800   21

3 Political institutions and economic life   51

Part II The divergence of Britain

4 The European response to Indian cottons   89

5 State and market: Britain, France and the Ottoman Empire   115

6 From cotton to coal   151

Part III The Indian path

7 Science and technology in India, 1600–1800   185

8 Modern industry in early nineteenth-century India   223

9 Conclusion   263

Notes to the text   270

Bibliography   324

Index   353

Figures

2.1 Detail of an end-panel of a *pha-nung*, skirt cloth, Coromandel Coast for the Thai market, eighteenth century   *page* 28

2.2 Man's military coat or *Su'a senakut*, Coromandel Coast for the Thai market, eighteenth century   29

2.3 *Kain sambagi*, skirt or shoulder cloth, Coromandel Coast for the Indonesian market, late eighteenth century   30

5.1 Swatches of Blackburn cloth woven for the West Africa market, 1751   135

5.2 Exports of British cotton cloth to West Africa as a proportion of total cotton cloth exports, 1751–1807   136

6.1 Detail of a view of the coal depot at Ying-tih-heen, in Shaouchow foo (Guangdong), late eighteenth century   163

8.1 Distribution of British great inventors by level of education and birth cohort   260

Maps

1 India in the eighteenth century   *page* xv

2 Europe in 1815   xvi

3 The Middle East in the eighteenth century   xvii

4 China and Southeast Asia in the eighteenth century   xviii

Tables

2.1 Sales of cotton cloth by British slave traders in
West Africa by decade, 1699–1808   *page* 25

2.2 Slave purchases in West Africa by decade, 1698–1807   25

2.3 Average current and constant prices of selected
textiles in English retailers' inventories, 1660–1738   36

2.4 Grain earnings in the mid-eighteenth century   39

2.5 Daily grain wages in eighteenth-century South India   44

5.1 Cotton prices in Cairo, 1687–1797   120

5.2 An index of cotton and linen cloth prices in Cairo,
1700–1789   121

5.3 Distribution of cotton workers in Rouen, 1727   149

Acknowledgments

I have incurred many debts in the research and writing of this book. Grants from Boston College supported several research trips to Britain and India. Fellowships from the American Council of Learned Societies and the Dibner Institute and a sabbatical from Boston College freed me from my day-to-day academic responsibilities and gave me the time to write much of the book. The Dibner also provided wonderful space and congenial company for which I am grateful to George Smith, Bonnie Edwards, Trudy Kontoff and Rita Dempsey. While writing this book I was also a member of the Global Economic History Network (GEHN), which gave me many opportunities to present my ideas to gatherings of knowledgeable and engaged colleagues. I am grateful to Patrick O'Brien for including me in that enterprise.

I benefited from the comments of three anonymous readers for Cambridge University Press. William Ashworth, Robin Fleming, Kevin Kenny, Rebecca Nedostup, Sarah Ross, Subashree Rangaswami, Patrick O'Brien and Giorgio Riello read and commented upon portions of the manuscript. Juliet Schor gave a close reading to the whole work in its final stages.

I presented portions of the book at seminars, workshops or conferences where I benefited from the responses of participants at Boston College, the London School of Economics, the Dibner Institute, Cambridge University, the University of Pennsylvania, Istanbul University, Sussex University, the Indian Institute of Technology (Madras), the annual meeting of the Economic History Society at Leicester, the International Economic History Association Congress at Helsinki, the International Congress of Historical Sciences at Amsterdam, the Anglo-American Conference on History, and meetings in Oxford, Leiden, Padua and Pune. I thank the organizers of these events and am especially grateful to the helpful suggestions that I received from Aashish Velkar, Maxine Berg, Kent Deng, Ken Pomeranz, Tine Bruland, Beverly Lemire, Kapil Raj, David Ludden,

Bob Nichols, Robert Duplessis, Huw Bowen, Chella Rajan, Richard Grove, Vinita Damodaran, Filippo Osella, Jeff Horn, Şevket Pamuk, Giorgio Riello, Patrick O'Brien, the late Larry Epstein, Tirthankar Roy, David Washbrook, Gareth Stedman Jones, Norbert Peabody, Harold Cook, Dhruv Raina and Deepak Kumar.

The staffs of the British Library, the Manchester Central Library, the John Rylands Library (Manchester), the Bolton Central Library, the National Archives of the United Kingdom, the Archives of the Royal Society of Arts, the Tamil Nadu Archives, the Burndy Library and Houghton Library were of the greatest assistance. I owe a special thanks to Mary Ginsberg of the British Museum who tracked down "A view of the coal depot at Ying-tih-heen, in Shaouchow foo" for me to see and then sent me a photograph of it that she took herself. The staff of the Boston College libraries never failed me and I am deeply indebted to Anne Kenny and Daniel Saulean of the Interlibrary Loan Department who supplied me with copies of even the rarest publications.

At Cambridge University Press Michael Watson supported the project from its earliest days and his editorial hand improved the book enormously. For this I am deeply grateful. Chloe Howell and Jo Breeze made the process of production and publication a smooth one and Diane Ilott was an exemplary copy-editor. Pierce Butler and Susan Holbert compiled a superb index.

Thanks are due to Hidetaka Hirota of Boston College who translated materials for me from Japanese. I also benefited from the suggestions of undergraduates in my "Wealth and Poverty of Nations" and graduate students in my "Introduction to Global History" who read early versions of the manuscript. I am also grateful for the friendship and support of my colleagues in the history department at Boston College, especially Peter Weiler, Lynn Johnson, Jim Cronin, Rebecca Nedostup, Robin Fleming, Kevin Kenny and David Quigley. While at the Dibner Institute I learned a great deal from my almost daily conversations with David Cahan as well as from George Smith and Conevery Valencius. In London, the department of economic history at the London School of Economics welcomed me for two extended stays. I am grateful to Patrick O'Brien for making those visits possible and to Giorgio Riello for extensive intellectual engagement as well as continued friendship and support. I thank John Styles for showing me the cloth swatches in the London Foundling Museum. He and Beverly Lemire taught me a great deal about British cottons.

In Cambridge, I always received a warm welcome from Jennifer Davis and the late Raj Chandavarkar. I am sorry that I will not be able to share this work with Raj, who I still miss terribly.

Closer to home, many friendships sustained me during this project. Bernard and Louise Lown have been unflagging with their support and encouragement, as have Eric Fernald and Navjeet Bal. Vicky Steinitz, Elliot Mishler and others in the Biolab fight carried me through good times and bad, as have my friends in Boston Mobilization, Newton Dialogues and the 25% Solution. John Maher has been a good friend throughout.

My greatest debt is to my family. I am grateful for the love of my parents as well as that of my sister Ranja, Dan, Maya, Jimmy, Sharon, Oliver and Jon. Krishna and Sulakshana have made so many things worthwhile and they were always patient with my preoccupation. To Juliet, who is the love of my life, I dedicate this work.

Abbreviations

APAC	Asia, Pacific and Africa Collections
BL	British Library
CSSH	*Comparative Studies in Society and History*
IESHR	*Indian Economic and Social History Review*
JAS	*Journal of Asian Studies*
JEH	*Journal of Economic History*
MAS	*Modern Asian Studies*
P&P	*Past & Present*
PRO	Public Record Office
TNA	The National Archives of the United Kingdom

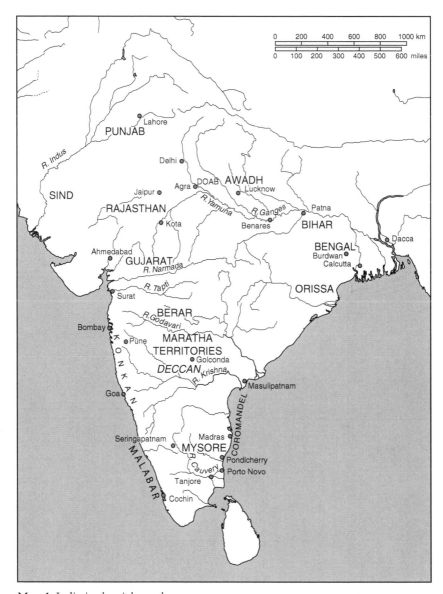

Map 1 India in the eighteenth century

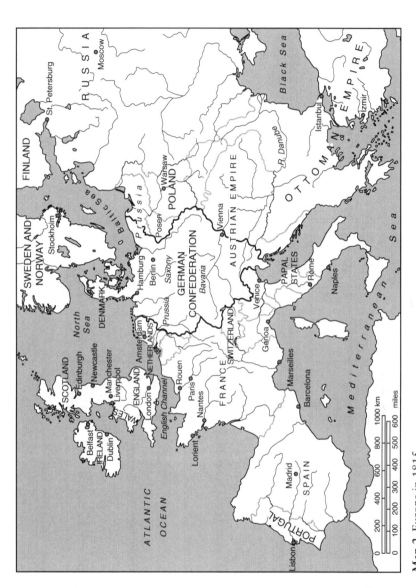

Map 2 Europe in 1815

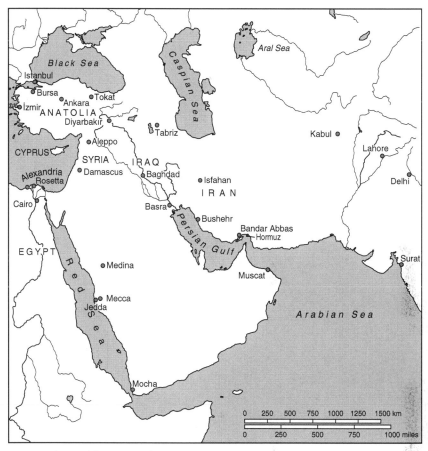

Map 3 The Middle East in the eighteenth century

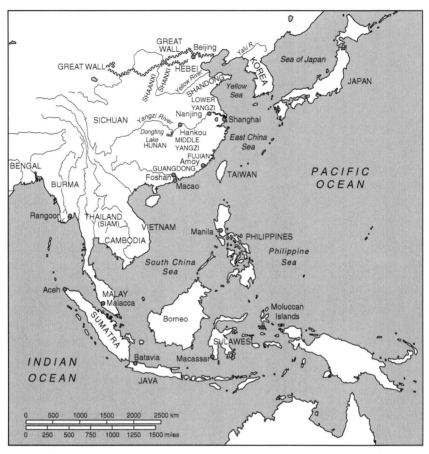

Map 4 China and Southeast Asia in the eighteenth century

1 | *Introduction*

Beginning in the late eighteenth century economic life in Western Europe was transformed. Revolutionary methods of manufacturing were developed and diffused. Inventors dreamed up new machines that increased by several hundred-fold the productivity of the human hand. New industries took root and expanded in Britain, Belgium, France and Germany. By the mid-nineteenth century, the scale of production in Europe was staggering. The decline in prices for cotton yarn and cloth, iron and other manufactures had no precedent in human history and the export of these goods led to deindustrialization in India, China and elsewhere. By 1850, Western Europe was the undisputed center of a new global manufacturing order.

Since the nineteenth century a number of explanations have been offered for why Europe industrialized and Asia did not. Advantages in markets, population, property rights, rationality, state systems and scientific life have all been invoked to account for Europe's exceptional path of development. While the differences between these explanations have been much discussed and debated, less examined is a striking similarity in method. For despite their disagreements, they explain divergence in the same way. They all identify something that made Europe different, to which Europe's divergent path is then attributed.

This book takes a different approach. Drawing on scholarship that points to profound similarities in political and economic institutions between the advanced regions of Europe and Asia, it rejects claims for European difference. This does not mean that these regions were identical. While there were some areas of economic life in which Europe was more advanced, in others the opposite was the case. However, the stark differences that were once believed to be plausible explanations for Europe's divergence are looking less stark and less plausible.

Narratives which attribute divergence to difference are also less credible because understandings of economic life have grown more sophisticated. A diverse body of economic theory argues that there is

1

no straightforward correspondence between economic variables and economic outcomes. "Economies with the same deep properties could have markedly different equilibria" is how Joseph Stiglitz has put it in a review of the economics of information.[1] More critical for the arguments of this book, however, are findings that the economic "situation" or context shapes the decisions, choices and actions of individuals.[2] These advances in economic thinking indicate that divergent paths of development need not imply – nor require – deep differences in economic institutions, for context matters.

The approach to divergence taken in this work moves away from seeing economic development in the eighteenth century in binary terms, as either leading to modern industry or its failure. Instead, it points to the existence of plural paths of change, which were the products of the pressures and needs that the dynamic and diverse economies of Europe and Asia faced. Since pressures and needs, as well as the political response to them, varied systematically across this vast geographical space, it is not surprising that in the eighteenth century there was no single path of development. Britain diverged from Asia, as well as other parts of Europe, not because it possessed rationality, science, markets, capitalism or anything else in greater abundance, but because the pressures and needs it faced – in combination with its state policies – produced a revolutionary response.

Two pressures were critical in generating British divergence. The first was the competitive challenge of Indian cotton textiles, which in the eighteenth century were the most important manufactured good in world trade and were consumed from the Americas to Japan. British efforts to imitate Indian cloth propelled a search for new techniques of production, which culminated in the great breakthroughs in spinning of the late eighteenth century. These new technologies transformed the world economy and shifted the center of global manufacturing from Asia to Europe. The second was shortages of wood, a consequence of deforestation. The British response was the substitution of coal for wood, which sparked the development of the steam engine, new techniques for the smelting of iron and eventually new means of transport, including the railway and steamship.

Neither of these pressures – shortages of wood and competition from global trade – was found in eighteenth-century India. From this perspective, British advances in cotton and coal were solutions to problems that did not exist in the Indian subcontinent. Only one, ecological problems due to deforestation and dwindling supplies of wood, operated in large parts of China. Although coal was being used on an expanding scale in a number of Chinese regions in the eighteenth and nineteenth centuries, including the Middle and Lower Yangzi, coal alone was not a sufficient solution to what were complex ecological problems. Far more radical action was required. In China, as in India, British technological breakthroughs in cotton and coal, while revolutionary, did not address major needs. Therefore, the British path of change was either unnecessary or inadequate for the pressing social, political and economic needs of the advanced parts of Asia in the eighteenth century.

On European difference

Classic texts of the nineteenth century – as well as modern historical writings – argue that there were three broad areas in which Europeans possessed an advantage over Asians. The first is in the realm of markets and property rights, under which may be placed approaches that are rooted in Smithian and neoclassical economics as well as writings that originate in Marxian political economy, for the latter also identify differences in property rights as critical to the exceptional European path of development.

For Smithians and neoclassicals, Europe possessed a more efficient market system because there were fewer restrictions on commerce and Europe was more likely to be home to states that respected property rights. These conditions allowed Europeans to deploy their resources of land, labor and capital to better effect, which raised output and productivity and yielded economic growth. Constraints on the market in Asia included Chinese bans on foreign trade, which blocked the benefits of overseas commerce, and Indian caste-based limits on occupational mobility, which impeded the operation of the market. Asian rulers were also less respectful of the rights of private property, which hampered investment, economic improvement and mercantile activity.[3]

Marxian accounts concur that at least some parts of Europe possessed more efficient and productive property regimes than any part of Asia. The most influential is the work of Robert Brenner, who argues that the British path of development emerged from an exceptional system of property rights, which was coupled with a favorable distribution of landed property. With this rural class structure, English agriculture underwent a revolutionary increase in productivity, which simultaneously released laborers for industry and supplied food to them. The agricultural producers of other parts of Europe, as well as the advanced regions of Asia, were unable to make such contributions, which blocked the emergence of modern manufacturing.[4]

The second area of European advantage has to do with population and is rooted in Malthusian arguments that Europe possessed superior methods for maintaining the balance between people and resources. Malthus argued that preventive checks, such as a later age for female marriage, limited fertility and thus population size in Europe, but were absent from Asia. As a result, Asian populations were larger, more likely to outstrip available resources and controlled through positive checks, such as famine, pestilence and disaster. Because of their better ability to limit their numbers, Europeans saved more and accumulated more capital, which led to higher rates of growth and eventually higher incomes.[5]

The third area of European advantage is in the realm of rationality. An influential line of thinking inaugurated by Max Weber argues that instrumental rationality, which has its roots in Protestantism, was unique to Europe and laid the foundations for a modern economy, polity and culture.[6] While Weber acknowledged that India and China displayed sophisticated forms of reason, their full development was blocked by clan and caste institutions which limited individual freedom and channeled the exercise of reason into traditional lines. The influence of Weberian arguments has waned, but the exceptionalism of European forms of rationality continues to have its adherents. The source of this exceptional reason is no longer Protestantism but the Enlightenment, however, and it has become a culture of reason which created a new scientific outlook on the world, which was essential for the technological breakthroughs of eighteenth-century Europe.[7]

Parallels in Eurasia

A substantial body of research on seventeenth- and eighteenth-century Asia challenges the above arguments for European difference. Consider the realm of markets and property rights. From the late sixteenth century, the Indian subcontinent entered a 200-year commercial boom in which the supply and use of money expanded, markets became a growing feature of daily life for much of the populace, and large merchant fortunes were built. In Bengal and other manufacturing regions, the rising demand for cotton textiles led to the reallocation and more efficient use of resources. Across the subcontinent, the production of cloth for export created a sizable long-distance trade in raw cotton, dyestuffs and the cloth itself. While data to assess the efficiency of markets are limited, in the late eighteenth century interest rates in North India and Britain fell in the same range, which, if the conventional assumption that equates high interest rates with a backward financial system is correct, shows that credit markets in Britain and India were at a similar level of development.[8]

Property rights were also not as insecure as many writers have imagined. Indian merchants operated vast empires that spanned the subcontinent as well as the Middle East, Central Asia, East Africa and Southeast Asia, which is indicative of the security of mercantile property. By the eighteenth century, the advanced areas of India possessed highly productive agricultural orders based on generations of investment, which is evidence that agrarian property rights were also well defined. In the eighteenth century, Bengal, Gujarat and South India not only fed their own substantial non-agricultural populations, but also exported grain to other parts of India and across the Indian Ocean, which points to the limitations of Brenner's arguments for the exceptionalism of English agriculture. Finally, historians argue that standards of living in Europe and India were more comparable than once imagined, which would mean that the economies of the subcontinent were more productive and advanced than has been long believed.[9]

Historians of China have identified similar parallels in the world of commerce. In his *China Transformed*, R. Bin Wong argues that early-modern China, as did Europe, experienced Smithian growth, which was propelled by the expansion of markets, the widening of trade and the extension of the division of labor. Kenneth Pomeranz builds upon this work and in his *The Great Divergence* demonstrates that the advanced regions of China and Europe were undergoing similar social and economic changes in the seventeenth and eighteenth centuries. In his words, it was a world of "surprising resemblances," including parallels in land and labor systems, luxury consumption and capital accumulation.[10]

In the realm of population, R. Bin Wong, James Lee and others challenge longstanding Malthusian arguments for demographic differences between China and Western Europe. Chinese and British fertility rates were not radically different, which suggests that preventive checks operated in both regions, for instance. Although the evidence for India is more limited, a variety of procedures to regulate fertility were practiced and these kept family sizes, and thus population, in line with land and food. The advanced areas of the Indian subcontinent were also relatively famine-free in the eighteenth century, which would suggest that Malthusian positive checks were not the method by which population was controlled.[11]

Finally, in the world of reason, Weberian arguments that the caste system in India created economic blockages are now seen as incorrect. Although in the nineteenth and twentieth centuries caste came to be a more rigid and more pervasive social institution, these modern developments should not be taken to be longstanding features of Indian society. In the centuries before 1800, caste had less social power and was more flexible, which translated into greater social and occupational mobility. Historians and anthropologists have also begun to recognize that caste helped to promote economic activity in a number of ways. Most importantly, caste connections were a source of mercantile trust, which was invaluable for commercial transactions that were conducted across large spaces and over long spans of time. Finally, Weberian arguments on the superiority of European commercial practices, as reflected in techniques of management such as accounting, have been widely criticized. In both India and China, there is plentiful evidence for the diffusion of a rational and methodical approach to the world, which was manifest in systems of bookkeeping and accounting.[12]

This book also challenges the still deeply held belief in the uniqueness of early-modern European scientific culture. In the period from 1600 to 1800, intellectual life in the Indian subcontinent was far from stagnant and there were intellectual shifts which led to self-conscious searches for new forms of knowledge. Indian thinkers also began to place a higher value on understanding the natural world for the economic and political utility of that knowledge. States and rulers sought to compile both European and Indian learning to put it at the service of political power. Indian artisans were also exposed to European technical developments through contact with skilled individuals and the products of Europe. While Indian manufacturers benefited from the encounter with European techniques and know-how, the flow of information was by no means one way. Europeans sought out both

Indian learned men and artisans to gain access to their technical and scientific knowledge. Therefore, any portrayal of Europe as uniquely scientific and technological rests on a misunderstanding of conditions in the seventeenth and eighteenth centuries or projects the backward conditions that emerged in nineteenth-century India into earlier periods.

From anachronism to context

Edward Said's *Orientalism* provided the inspiration for many historians, anthropologists and economists to reject the longstanding belief that Asia was essentially different from Europe.[13] Said demonstrated that the construction of the "Orient" as the other of Europe has a long history but became firmly entrenched in the nineteenth century with the establishment of European colonial rule in Asia, an insight which freed many thinkers from oppositions of East versus West and tradition versus modernity. Independently of Said, however, a number of scholars – some of whom were trenchant critics of his writings – were rethinking histories that relegated Asia to backwardness and stasis. In the study of the Indian subcontinent, perhaps not coincidentally, this shift in understanding began in the 1970s, at the same moment that *Orientalism* was published.[14]

Asia had long been portrayed as Europe's other, but this image was solidified and popularized in the nineteenth century. Marx, whose writings on India were read widely, no doubt had some influence on the matter. In 1853, for example, he famously declared that India "has remained unaltered since its remotest antiquity," a pointed contrast to the radical economic and political transformation of early nineteenth-century Europe.[15] The nineteenth century also gave rise to the method by which the problem of divergence is understood to this day, the essence of which is to identify the social, political or economic feature which made Europe different from Asia. This then becomes the explanation for divergence. For Marx, it was capitalism which produced Europe's divergence. Europe possessed capitalism, but Asia did not. For Weber, the answer was rationality, again, which arose in Europe but not in Asia.

This method assumes the same endpoint for economic development in all places and in all times. That end is modern industrial society. In the eighteenth century, the advanced areas of Europe followed the natural path to industry, while the economically developed parts of India and China were blocked, but they too would have taken that path if they had possessed the European features that they lacked. This method is anachronistic because it projects industrial society – an economic and social order which emerged in the nineteenth century and only then became universally desired – into earlier historical periods.

In *The Problem of Unbelief in the Sixteenth Century* Lucien Febvre cautioned that historians must resist the urge to "bring to bear . . . our ideas, our feelings, the fruit of our scientific inquiries, our political experiences, and our social achievements" on the past.[16] Febvre issued this warning in response to anachronisms in the study of religious ideas, but it is equally applicable to the world of economic action. When studying economic life in the centuries before 1800, historians must not "bring to bear" ideas and social categories that emerged in the nineteenth and twentieth centuries. Just as unbelief became possible only in the seventeenth century, industrial forms of production entered the economic lexicon only in the nineteenth. The term industrialism itself – "to indicate a new order of society based on organized mechanical production" – was first used in the 1830s, which betrays the nineteenth-century origins of the concept of industrialization.[17]

In the nineteenth century industrial society came to be seen as the end of economic development and became the measure of economic success. To assume that industrialization was the path in which economies were moving in earlier periods – unless it was blocked or the proper preconditions were missing – is anachronistic.[18] Marx, Weber, North and other writers on divergence project a nineteenth-century imperative, an industrial economy, into historical periods when such a mode of economic organization was not a category of thought. Even the leading economic thinkers of the eighteenth century, including Adam Smith, did not conceive of industrialization as the direction of economic change, as betrayed by Smith's failure to anticipate the industrial order that emerged within decades of the publication of the *Wealth of Nations*.

How can one construct comparisons that are not anachronistic? One possibility is the method of reciprocal comparison, which has been used by R. Bin Wong and Kenneth Pomeranz. According to Pomeranz, this method allows the historian to view "both sides of the comparison as 'deviations' when seen through the expectations of the other, rather than leaving one as always the norm." The task of the historian is "to look for absences, accidents, and obstacles that diverted England from a path that might have made it more like the Yangzi Delta or Gujarat, along with the more usual exercise of looking for blockages that kept non-European areas from reproducing implicitly normalized European paths."[19] This procedure has the great merit of denaturalizing the European path of development. It continues to operate, however, within the framework of presences and absences, of things that Europe possessed but Asia did not. It therefore conceives of economic development as following one of two routes – the European and the not European or the industrial and the not industrial. This retains the familiar nineteenth-century framework of industrialization as the universal path of development, unless it is blocked.

This book follows an alternative method of comparison which rests upon three principles. First, in the seventeenth and eighteenth centuries there were a variety of economic and political goals which produced plural paths of development. Second, different paths of economic change were the products of human agency and choice, and were shaped by social, political and economic context. Context refers to more than economic variables and institutions, such as prices, markets, property rights and population, or cultural qualities, such as reason and science, all of which have been invoked in the debate on divergence. The essential elements of the context are the specific conditions under which individuals operated and reshaped their economic lives. Since global competitive challenges and ecological pressures varied across Eurasia, it is not surprising that economic actors had different menus of choices. Finally, there is a political dimension to economic life. State actions were critical in determining paths of development in both Europe and Asia from the seventeenth to the nineteenth centuries. State actions encompassed more than enforcing property rights and maintaining the rules of the market. States in Eurasia shaped local, regional and long-distance trade, transformed the ecology, and pushed forward the scientific and technological frontier, among other things, and these actions were economically productive.

With hindsight one can conclude that industrialization produced the divergence between Europe and Asia, but neither Europeans nor Asians in the seventeenth or eighteenth centuries were attempting to develop an industrial society. Only from the nineteenth century did men and women make economic and political choices with that goal.

And from that moment, industry became the universal yardstick of economic development. Before then the advanced regions of Europe and Asia were following different paths of economic change as they each responded to their own economic, political and social pressures and needs. In the centuries before 1800, the paths of economic change were diverse and multiple.[20]

The Western European path of change was without a doubt extraordinary, but this was not because economic or technological dynamism was unique to that part of the world. Europe followed an exceptional path because it faced a set of pressures which were absent in India and only partly found in China. Therefore, India and China had no need to forge the economic and technological responses that emerged in Europe. India and China were not failures but took different routes which were shaped by their different contexts. By the nineteenth century, the European solutions became the basis for an industrial society, but industrialization in Western Europe did not emerge from an effort to industrialize. It was an unanticipated, unforeseen and unintended outcome of the economic and social needs that were found in that part of the world.

Two pressures loom large in this book. The first emanated from the global trading system, in which the position of Europeans was very different from that of both Indians and Chinese. In the world economy of the seventeenth and eighteenth centuries, silver flowed from west to east, balanced by an opposite flow of manufactured goods. And from the seventeenth century Europeans faced sustained competition from Asian imports, including cotton textiles, porcelains, ships, silks and even fans and furniture. Historians are beginning to recognize that some of the most dynamic sectors in eighteenth-century Europe were those that were seeking to imitate and compete against the products of Asia.[21] Of these, the European encounter with the cotton textiles of India would prove to be the most momentous for the divergence between Europe and Asia. Indian and Chinese manufacturers did not face such global competitive pressures, and, as a consequence, the powerful incentives for innovation that the global economy transmitted to Europe were absent.

The second pressure that differed across Europe and Asia lay in the realm of ecology, specifically in the supply of wood. While Britain and parts of France and central Europe faced shortages of wood, which was essential for fuel, building material and countless other uses,

Scandinavia and Russia had plentiful supplies. Similar differences existed in Asia. Much of the Indian subcontinent was heavily forested well into the nineteenth century and possessed abundant timber and wood. East Asia, on the other hand, faced greater pressures on its woodlands. In some regions, shortages of wood were growing from even the sixteenth or seventeenth century and by the eighteenth Japan and the Lower Yangzi delta suffered from severe deforestation.

In several parts of Europe and East Asia coal began to be used on an expanding scale as a substitute source of energy. These developments proceeded the farthest in Britain, where experimentation with the mineral fuel set in motion the development of new skills and new technologies, including advances in the steam engine and the substitution of coal for wood in many manufacturing processes, most critically in the smelting of iron. The rise of skills associated with coal date from at least the eleventh century in China and coal was consumed on a substantial scale in a number of areas by the eighteenth century, including in the north and along the Yangzi River. However, its use advanced farther in Britain than in China, in part due to different political priorities. While the British focused on provisioning London with coal, a decision which would prove to be of world historical importance, the Chinese focused on providing their populace with grain, which ensured the survival of millions in the eighteenth century but bore less technological fruit in the long run. Such an understanding of these choices can only be reached after the fact, however. No one in eighteenth-century Britain anticipated the energy revolution that would be wrought by coal. In India, the abundance of wood meant that there was no need to experiment with coal and the exploitation of its sizable deposits would await the nineteenth century.

The prominence given to cotton and coal accords with revised understandings of British industrialization in the late eighteenth and early nineteenth centuries. A longstanding view saw economic growth and technological change in Britain as proceeding on a broad front, spanning many areas of activity. However, a revisionist perspective, most prominently associated with Nicholas Crafts and C. Knick Harley, has shown that many technical advances made minimal contributions to British output and growth, and that in a number of trades, manufacturing methods remained largely unchanged well into the nineteenth century. In the Crafts–Harley interpretation, pride of place is given to cotton manufacturing, in which British cottons

supplanted Indian cottons, and iron smelting, which was revolutionized by coal. As Harley puts it, "Much of Britain's particularly industrial and urban character in the nineteenth century resulted from an
unusual technological history in cotton and iron."[22] Quantitative
estimates bear out this conclusion. In 1831, a sixth of the value added
in British manufacturing came from cotton textiles, the production
of which was mechanized as a consequence of global competitive
pressures. In another measure, cotton went from accounting for 1 percent of British manufacturing in 1770 to 10 percent in 1841.[23]

Given the different economic and ecological contexts, it is no surprise that the advanced regions of eighteenth-century Eurasia followed
divergent trajectories of change. The picture is not one of a dynamic
Europe and a stagnant Asia. Rather, contrasts in needs and imperatives led to a variety of paths of economic and technical development.
One of them, that of Western Europe, proved to be revolutionary,
but that is not because of a failure to change in Asia. What was
exceptional about Europe was not its economic and political institutions or cultural makeup but the pressures that it faced, which were
different from those in India and China.

Marx wrote in *The Eighteenth Brumaire*, "Men make their own
history, but they do not make it as they please; they do not make it
under self-selected circumstances, but under circumstances existing
already, given and transmitted from the past."[24] If historical change
is conceived as an interaction between structures and agents, then
economic, political, social and ecological structures define the range
of possibilities under which agents act. Because these conditions varied
widely in the eighteenth century – due to different positions in the
global economy and different ecological situations – individuals in
the advanced and populous regions of Europe, India and China
focused on different issues and made different choices.

It was not only the economic actions of individuals that shaped
paths of development in eighteenth-century Europe and Asia, however. State actions also influenced the path of change, and these
included provisioning, protectionism, patronage for scientific and
technological improvement, support for trade and investment, and
stabilization of forests. State policies took a variety of forms in Europe
and Asia due to differences in context and in political and economic
philosophies. In eighteenth-century Britain, the state was crucial
in shaping a response to the twin problems of global competition

and shortages of wood. The political exclusion of Indian imports and state mercantilist dominance of the Atlantic Ocean helped British cotton masters imitate and surpass Indian cloth. State support for coal – a commodity which was essential for the well-being of the population of London and, therefore, the political stability of the realm – helped to promote its mining and adoption.

State actions contributed to economic development elsewhere as well. In eighteenth-century Japan, political power, not increasing consumption of coal, was used to replenish wood supplies and stabilize the ecology of the archipelago, which shows that coal was not the only answer to deforestation. In the nineteenth century, state policies helped to produce a variety of responses to British industrialization. In France, Belgium and Germany state power was used to promote a new industrial order, but in India colonial officials subordinated the economy to that of industrializing Britain. As a consequence, the sizable reservoir of knowledge and skill that had been amassed in India over many years was dissipated, which produced a nineteenth-century divergence not only in income but also in skill.

The three pieces of the argument that follows are global competition, deforestation and state policy. Britain faced both an Indian competitive challenge and shortages of wood and possessed a powerful and activist state that helped to forge a response. China faced one of these challenges, the ecological, but not that of competition in the global economy. In the economically advanced regions of China, above all the Yangzi delta, deforestation created growing ecological difficulties for which China's political system was unable to formulate an answer, which hampered economic development into the nineteenth century. Finally, in the Indian subcontinent the prosperous regions of Gujarat, Bengal and North and South India faced neither global competition nor shortages of wood till the nineteenth century. Before 1800 there was no need for radical innovations to compete in the world trade in manufactures or to add to energy supplies.

New advances in economic theory stress the centrality of context. These contributions reject simple assumptions about rational agents and efficient markets as well as nineteenth-century universalisms of standard economic thinking and emphasize the complexity of individual decision making, the importance of institutions, and the political dimensions of economic life.[25] Of these advances, the study of institutions has had the greatest impact on the debate about divergence and on the writing of economic history more widely. From the classic works of Douglass North and Robert Paul Thomas and Eric Jones to others, superior institutions have been invoked to explain the exceptional path of Europe. New and more complex views of individual decision making are less in evidence in the debate on divergence, however.

The argument that individuals respond very differently to conditions of abundance from those of shortage can be seen as a case of loss aversion or status quo bias, a phenomenon described by pioneering behavioral economists Amos Tversky and Daniel Kahneman. Tversky and Kahneman found that in two scenarios in which the expected pay-off was the same – and for which standard economic models predict no difference in behavior – individuals were more inclined to take risks when they possessed nothing than when they possessed something.[26] They called this phenomenon loss aversion or status quo bias. This finding suggests that comparative economic development cannot be reduced to differences in prices, wages or efficiencies of markets because variations in economic situation can have a profound impact on economic action. Therefore, individual decisions must be understood in context and the direction of economic change cannot be predicted with reference solely to standard economic tools such as prices and supply and demand.[27] The interpretation of divergence in this book moves away from highly generalized and universal models of economic life and towards more detailed analysis of the particular problems that actors faced in specific situations.

On regions and comparisons

At the core of this book are a number of comparisons between Britain and the advanced regions of the Indian subcontinent. Britain was the most prosperous region in eighteenth-century Europe and the British path of economic development forged the divergence of Europe from Asia. It is therefore a logical pole of comparison. On the Indian side, no one region stands out in the eighteenth century as the most economically advanced. Gujarat on the west coast and Bengal and the Coromandel Coast in the east were thriving maritime regions with high levels of commercial activity and extensive local, regional and long-distance trade. They possessed sizable manufacturing capacity, sold their goods in distant markets, and had achieved high standards of living in the eighteenth century. In this mix must be included the heartland of northern India, from Delhi to Lucknow and even further east to Benares. This area had been the core of the Mughal Empire in the late sixteenth and seventeenth centuries. Even though it may not have exported on the same scale as the maritime regions of India, it was a highly commercialized region and its wealth and dense population created a large concentration of production and consumption.

Much of the material on Indian regions will be drawn from Bengal and South India. An abundant literature is available for these two regions and the author has collected a substantial body of archival material on South India which will be drawn upon. On a few occasions, however, when essential information is not available for Bengal and South India, one has to stray from them and draw upon evidence for Gujarat and the heartland of North India.

The Britain and Bengal/South India contrasts are central, but they by no means exhaust the comparisons that comprise the argument. There are a series of additional cases in which different regions are compared at different moments to unravel the causes of the divergence between Europe and Asia. Britain itself will be compared with other places in Europe (France, in particular) and elsewhere (the Ottoman Empire, for instance) to elucidate the impact of state policies on cotton manufacturing in the eighteenth century. Britain will also be contrasted with the Yangzi delta to explore the rise of coal and the latter will be put alongside Japan to understand how state actions shaped ecological change. Early nineteenth-century British India will be compared with Belgium, France and the German states of central Europe in order to explore different responses to new British technology. Therefore, in its discussion of Europe and Asia the text ranges beyond Britain and the Indian subcontinent in order to make several kinds of comparisons.

For some issues a larger geographical space than the region is necessary for both Europe and India. State systems and cultural mores must be included in this category and the most important for the concerns of this work are networks of learning and knowledge, which transcended political and regional boundaries. Knowledge, learned men and the written word circulated on a large European, Indian subcontinental and even intercontinental canvas. The discussion of science and technology in India will at times shift from the advanced maritime regions of Bengal and South India to the less economically advanced interior regions. More systematic research is needed, but the most technologically dynamic regions in eighteenth-century India appear to have been outside the highly commercialized coastal centers. Areas of the interior, including Mysore and the Maratha territories, were sites of great innovation, technical progress and scientific interest. Of course there were exceptions, the most prominent being Awadh, which was in the heart of northern India, and Tanjore, in the south, and the great shipyards on the western and eastern coasts.

A note on sources

The scholarship on divergence, and in global history, has been based largely upon the synthesis of secondary sources. This is understandable, given the large historical processes that are being examined, the scale of the comparisons and the number of world regions that often enter the analysis. This book is no different. An enormous quantity of secondary materials has been essential in the development and exposition of the arguments. At the same time, an exclusive reliance upon secondary works limits the scope of the contributions to the divergence debate and global history more generally, and makes it difficult to escape the biases and assumptions of existing historical writings. The new approach and the new answer to the problem of divergence contained in this book was made possible in large part because of an engagement with a number of archives for material on both eighteenth-century Britain and eighteenth- and nineteenth-century India.

Material from primary sources has been the inspiration for several major arguments, but two stand out in particular. The reconsideration of innovation in the British cotton textile industry, which is contained in Chapter 4, is the product of extensive research in the papers of early cotton manufacturers as well as in the pamphlet and other literature from the late seventeenth to the early nineteenth centuries. This research was conducted in several libraries and archives in northern England and the Midlands, as well as the British Library and the National Archives in London. The analysis of the Porto Novo Iron Works, which is central to the rethinking of manufacturing and industry in early nineteenth-century India found in Chapter 8, is based on a large body of documents on the enterprise available in the Asia, Pacific and Africa Collections at the British Library. This book also builds upon many years of archival research in the agrarian and manufacturing history of eighteenth-century South India.

The plan of the book

This book is comprised of three parts. Part I, which contains two chapters, sets the stage. The first examines India's place in the world economy between 1600 and 1800. Indian cottons achieved a global reach in those centuries, due to their great beauty, colorfulness and comfort. The chapter explores the factors behind the subcontinent's success as an exporter of cotton textiles and estimates the quantity of silver that flowed into India to balance this great export trade. The second chapter, "Political institutions and economic life," examines the economic and political institutions of Asia and Europe in the seventeenth and eighteenth centuries, with primary focus on the advanced regions of the Indian subcontinent and Britain.[28] The essence of the argument of this chapter is that the institutions of Britain, the most prosperous and dynamic area of eighteenth-century Europe, were neither profoundly different from nor superior to those of the advanced regions of India. While all was not the same, in some respects British economic institutions were more highly developed, in others it was the Indian ones that held the advantage, most strikingly in agriculture and in the global trade in textiles.

With this foundation, Part II turns to the divergence of Britain. The first of three chapters in this part, "The European response to Indian cottons," argues that the breakthroughs in spinning, which were the most significant textile inventions of the eighteenth century, emerged in Britain out of competition with Indian cottons. Since the early nineteenth century, the Indian dimension has been relegated to the background and replaced with stories of supply and demand for yarn, which was a revision of the history of innovation brought on by a theoretical commitment to Smithian political economy. The second chapter, "State and market: Britain, France and the Ottoman Empire," compares the responses in each of these places to the competitive challenge of Indian cottons. It argues that the British response emerged out of a combination of state policies that encouraged the development of local manufacturing in place of Indian imports and competition against Indian goods in the markets of West Africa. The cotton producers of France and the Ottoman Empire did not benefit from such state support and were less connected to African, as well as other Atlantic, markets. The final chapter of this part, "From cotton to coal," addresses the fact that while British textile innovations produced a divergence between Europe and Asia and moved the textile manufacturing center of the world from India to Western Europe, the economic transformation of Britain went much deeper. In the nineteenth century, Britain created a new energy complex, which was made possible by the greater use of coal. On the basis of a comparison of Britain and the Yangzi delta, the chapter argues that the endowment of coal is not an adequate explanation for its large-scale adoption in Britain and the support of the English and then British state also was essential to the development of the coal economy. Indeed the widespread use of coal was not the only response to growing wood shortages, as illustrated by Tokugawa Japan, where state policies forested and stabilized the ecology of the archipelago. Therefore, the pressures of competition against Indian cottons and shortages of wood were coupled with effective state policies to produce the divergence of Britain.

The final part of the book asks why nineteenth-century India did not follow the path of development laid down by Britain. The first of the two chapters examines science and technology in India in the seventeenth and eighteenth centuries and shows, in contrast to the conventional wisdom, that Europeans were not unique in their interest in these matters. The level of Indian technical skill and knowledge was not insignificant and in a number of areas it was comparable to that of Europe. The high level of Indian technical know-how receives further confirmation in the final chapter, which surveys a number of successful transplantations from Europe to India of machinery and industrial methods of manufacture in the early nineteenth century. As a consequence of British colonial rule, these enterprises faced an inhospitable political climate, in contrast to Belgium, France and the German areas of central Europe, where new forms of industrial manufacturing were nurtured and advanced. Despite impressive technical successes in British India, similar undertakings did not take root. This, coupled with deindustrialization and lack of British support for education, led to a sharp decline in the level of knowledge and skill in nineteenth-century India. Within a few generations of the establishment of British rule, the knowledge-poor India of the late nineteenth and twentieth centuries was in place. In the early nineteenth century, however, the Indian economy had the opportunity to keep pace with Europe, but as the following account will reveal, that path was not taken, and an opportunity was missed.

PART I

Setting the stage: Europe and Asia before divergence

2 | *India and the global economy, 1600–1800*

Introduction

Historians long thought it was self-evident that Europe lay at the center of the world economy of the seventeenth and eighteenth centuries. Immanuel Wallerstein summed up several generations of thinking when he wrote, "The modern world-system took the form of a capitalist world-economy that had its genesis in Europe in the long sixteenth century . . . Since that time the capitalist world-economy has geographically expanded to cover the entire globe."[1] This passage captures three assumptions that have informed decades of historical scholarship. Europe was dynamic while the rest of the world was static. Europe gave rise to capitalism and brought the rest of the world under its economic ambit. Europe was at the core of the early-modern trading system.

Flows of silver and manufactures between 1600 and 1800 present a different picture and reveal the key positions of India and China in the world economy. A rethinking of India's place in the global order began with the uncovering of the vibrant commercial world of the Indian Ocean. K. N. Chaudhuri provided an important statement in his *Trade and Civilisation in the Indian Ocean*, which showed that mercantile sophistication and commercial dynamism predated the arrival of European traders. He and others also demonstrated that Asian merchants did not fade away with the coming of the Portuguese, Dutch and English and subsequent research has shown that Asian mercantile capital was in a secure position into the nineteenth and even twentieth centuries.[2] On the Indian landmass itself, a number of historians have argued that European merchants and traders, rather than dominating their Indian counterparts, had to adapt and fit into the vigorous commercial order, which is testimony to the power and acumen of Indian merchants.[3] Similar research uncovered economic vibrancy in other parts of Asia. The substantial flows of rice, manufactures, spices, precious metals and other goods between Southeast Asia and China, for instance, comprised a dense network of exchange.[4]

Drawing upon this revisionist research, Andre Gunder Frank turned Eurocentrism on its head and argued that well into the eighteenth century Asia was at the center of the global system. According to Frank, "The two major regions that were most 'central' to the world economy were India and China," a status they claimed because of the volume of their exports of manufactured goods, which they exchanged for silver.[5] China exported porcelain and silk across the globe while the Indian subcontinent produced a seemingly endless variety of cotton textiles that "clothed the world," according to a title on the subject.[6] It is this structure of global trade in which silver flowed into Asia in exchange for manufactures that has produced a rethinking of the location of the center of the world economy in the seventeenth and eighteenth centuries. Whether from the Americas or Japan, silver entered the dynamic, commercial regions of India and China, where it fueled the expansion of economic activity, greased the heavy wheels of commerce, and produced greater economic specialization and sophistication.

Frank argued that China was more critical than India in the Asia-centered global economy because it possessed a greater capacity to export and, as a consequence, monopolized the bulk of the world's output of silver.[7] Frank, and others who share this opinion, underestimate the place of the Indian subcontinent in the world trading system of the seventeenth and eighteenth centuries. Blinded by the brilliance of the Chinese universe, they fail to appreciate the magnitude of the global trade in Indian cotton textiles, which had been the major export of the subcontinent for many centuries, and which were exchanged for silver, gold and other commodities that served as money. "Bullion for goods" is how Om Prakash labeled this trade.[8]

While this chapter argues that India was a major center in the early-modern world economy, it does not seek to replace Frank's Sinocentric global system with an equally incorrect Indocentric version. Although there were imbalances and inequalities in the global economy of the seventeenth and eighteenth centuries, there was no single center and it is more accurate to speak of a polycentric global order, but not all regions were equal in the system, as is strikingly illustrated by flows of silver and cotton textiles.

The global trade in cotton textiles

The cotton textiles of the Indian subcontinent were demanded across the world in the seventeenth and eighteenth centuries. Cotton reigned supreme because it yields a cloth that can be worn comfortably in a wide variety of climates. It suffices as the primary dress in the heat and humidity of the tropics and serves as a part of the repertoire of garments in colder climes. Cotton also takes and holds dyes and designs better than linen and wool, which allows for the manufacture of colorful and elaborately decorated cloths that maintain their finish even after repeated washings. The fabrics made from cotton were also lighter than even the lightest woolens, which added to their appeal, especially for many Europeans. Finally, the prices of cotton cloths were lower than those of silk, cotton's main competitor in terms of finish and color.

Before the seventeenth century the major export markets for Indian cotton cloth were in the Indian Ocean. The Red Sea and Persian Gulf were longstanding destinations for both Indian traders and Indian goods. Indian cottons were also exported to Southeast Asia, where they were exchanged for spices, and East Africa, where they were sold for slaves. The East African demand for Indian cottons made possible the slave armies that were fielded by the Islamic kingdoms of the Deccan in early-modern times. According to Richard Eaton, "African manpower was extracted and exported in exchange mainly for Indian textiles."[9]

The entry of European traders into the Indian Ocean opened three new markets for Indian cloth. The first was in Europe itself where from the sixteenth century small quantities of Indian painted and embroidered cloth were imported into Portugal. These textiles tended to be of very high quality, but they were distributed on a small scale to other parts of Europe. Most critically for future developments, these goods filtered into Holland and England, which became the leading trading nations of Europe in the seventeenth and eighteenth centuries. From these early luxury beginnings, Dutch and English traders, who had been selling Indian cloth in Southeast Asia to purchase spices, experimented with shipping cargoes of cloth back to Amsterdam and London. From the middle of the seventeenth century, these goods found a growing market in Europe, setting off what contemporaries labeled the "calico craze."[10]

Indian cotton cloths found ready buyers in Europe because they were light, colorful, colorfast, washable and available in a wide range of styles and qualities. The upper classes of Europe demanded fine cloth that was carefully painted with floral and other "nature" patterns. At the same time, Indian cottons made it possible for the poorer classes to have access to similar cloth, even though of a coarser weave and with more crudely printed rather than elaborately hand-painted patterns, but an exciting contrast to the limited designs of woolens and the drab browns and grays of linens. And to the casual observer, with the entry of cottons both rich and poor were dressed alike, producing a social leveling through consumption. For the poorer classes of Europe, Indian goods also made it possible for them to wear a lighter cloth that was less expensive than silk and far more comfortable than coarse linens or even the lightest woolens. By the end of the seventeenth century, the appetites of many Europeans for cotton cloth had been whetted.

The second major new market for Indian cloth in the seventeenth and eighteenth centuries was West Africa. East Africa had long been buying Indian goods and it is likely that some of this cloth made its way across the continent to the west coast via overland routes. European slave traders, however, began to sell Indian goods directly to West Africans from the sixteenth century, and cotton textiles became a linchpin in the Atlantic slave trade. In the eighteenth century, two-thirds of British exports to West Africa consisted of textiles. Indian cottons always loomed large in this trade and between 1720 and 1750 they accounted for about half of the textiles shipped from Britain to West Africa. After 1750, the Indian share in British textile exports fell to between 30 and 40 percent, but the quantity of Indian cloth increased sharply because the volume of British slave purchases took off, as can be seen from Tables 2.1 and 2.2. The prices of slaves also went up, which meant that more goods, including the cotton textiles of the subcontinent, had to be given in exchange for them.[11]

Indian cottons were also essential for the French slave trade. In the late 1760s and early 1770s, slavers from Rouen carried 1.4 million livres tournois (60,000 pounds sterling) worth of Indian textiles every year to West Africa, which was more than a third of their cargo.[12] These were the peak years for the French slave trade. (Three-quarters of French slave purchases in the eighteenth century were concentrated in the period from 1761 to 1792.) And in those decades, Indian cottons were an indispensable part of the goods with which French merchants obtained African slaves.[13]

Table 2.1 *Sales of cotton cloth by British slave traders in West Africa by decade, 1699–1808 (pounds sterling)*

Decade	Indian cloth	British cloth
1699–1708	128,752	79,359
1709–1718	101,586	9,216
1719–1728	493,580	75,331
1729–1738	775,805	40,848
1739–1748	627,171	13,887
1749–1758	481,196	329,654
1759–1768	762,427	817,513
1769–1778	1,258,738	797,295
1779–1788	1,166,079	1,098,402
1789–1798	2,404,492	1,847,032
1799–1808	3,207,133	2,895,036

Source: Johnson, *Anglo-African Trade*, pp. 54–5.

Table 2.2 *Slave purchases in West Africa by decade, 1698–1807*

Decade	British	Total
1698–1709	164,709	359,940 [1700–1709]
1710–1719	145,365	402,870
1720–1729	242,675	516,650
1730–1739	276,013	599,510
1740–1749	194,570	551,060
1750–1759	251,329	581,890
1760–1769	391,243	783,200
1770–1779	339,593	717,820
1780–1789	349,344	793,860
1790–1799	416,837	759,240
1800–1807	280,831	605,770 [1800–1809]

Sources: David Richardson, "The Eighteenth-Century British Slave Trade: Estimates of its Volume and Coastal Distribution in Africa," *Research in Economic History*, 12 (1989), p. 157; Klein, *Atlantic Slave Trade*, pp. 208–9.

The third and final new market for Indian cloth was the Americas, for which very little information is available. Indian cottons were exported to the Americas via two channels. The first was an export trade from northwestern Europe to the islands of the Caribbean and

North and South America. The plantation complex purchased some Indian cloth, especially for the dress of house slaves. In North America, the consumption of cottons grew in the eighteenth century, mirroring the broader European shift to the new fiber.[14] The second route for Indian cloth went across the Pacific from the subcontinent to Spanish America via Manila. Little is known about this trade, but there is scattered evidence for the sizable impact that Indian cotton cloth had in the Spanish colonies of the Americas, especially in the eighteenth century.[15]

The data to systematically compare the scale of demand for Indian cottons in different markets are not available. However, some figures from the 1780s show that longstanding markets in Asia remained more important than new ones in the Atlantic. According to a French report from 1785, 12.6 million livres tournois (550,000 pounds sterling) worth of Indian cotton textiles along with 1 million livres tournois (44,000 pounds sterling) of Indian cotton yarn were sold in the Levant (Iraq, Syria and Anatolia) every year.[16] In the 1770s, the French and British, who in that decade accounted for the bulk of the Atlantic slave trade, sold 185,000 pounds sterling of Indian cloth a year in West Africa. (The French quantity was given above; the British is contained in Table 2.1.) These figures show that the Levant alone purchased three times more cloth every year than West Africa, which was the largest market for Indian cotton goods in the Atlantic. While similar figures for other Asian markets are hard to come by, there is abundant evidence for a lively export of Indian cloth to both island and mainland Southeast Asia. One clue to the enormous volume of this trade comes from the Dutch East India Company, which in the second quarter of the eighteenth century had a stock of half a million to a million pieces of Indian cloth in its warehouse in Castle Batavia.[17]

Putting the above material together, by the eighteenth century Indian cottons found buyers in Southeast Asia, East and West Africa, the Middle East, the Eastern Mediterranean, Europe and across the Americas. The magnitude and reach of Indian cotton cloth has led several historians to call it the most important manufactured good in world trade in the seventeenth and eighteenth centuries.[18] The insatiable appetite for Indian cottons in markets around the world was also the reason why silver flowed from America, Europe and the Middle East to the Indian subcontinent. Since Indians had a limited demand for imports, Europeans and others had no choice but to bring silver and gold, as well as other commodities that were valued as money, to purchase cotton cloth. The trade in bullion will be taken up in the penultimate section of this chapter, but one must first explore in some more detail why Indian cottons were in such demand around the world.

The appeal of Indian cottons

Indian cottons were objects of desire because of their great beauty, their fashionability and their remarkable qualities of color and weave. The prices of these cloths also contributed to the demand for them, but in ways that are less straightforward than formerly believed. Consumers around the world demanded them for different combinations of these elements, and it is worth examining each in detail.

Aesthetics and fashion

In the seventeenth and eighteenth centuries, the bulk of the cotton textiles exported from India were printed and painted cloths, which came to be known as chintz in Europe. Smaller proportions of the Indian exports were plain cloths, typically dyed blue with indigo, or striped or checked cloths woven from dyed yarns. Aside from muslins, plain white cloth was not in great demand before the late seventeenth century when Indian printed and painted calicoes began to be banned in most European markets. From that point, white cotton cloth from India began to be used as the "raw material" for European printing industries, which grew rapidly in the eighteenth century.

In the nineteenth century the reputation of chintzes suffered as machine-printed cloth of low quality and poor design became ubiquitous. The coining of the term chintzy by George Eliot to mean cheap and gaudy is a sign of the low regard in which these cloths came to be held. Before 1800, however, the beauty of painted and printed calicoes from India – with their exquisite designs and deep colors – drew eager buyers from Japan to Europe. Not surprisingly, the cloths of highest quality must be ranked as great works of art. The designs on these high-end pieces were drawn by hand by the most talented painters. Figure 2.1, which is an end-panel from a skirt cloth produced for the Thai market, illustrates, in John Guy's words, "the consummate skill

Figure 2.1 Detail of an end-panel of a *pha-nung*, skirt cloth, Coromandel Coast for the Thai market, eighteenth century, Victoria and Albert Museum, London, IS.40–1991.

Figure 2.2 Man's military coat or *Su'a senakut*, Coromandel Coast for the Thai market, eighteenth century, reproduced with permission of the Royal Ontario Museum, Toronto, © ROM, ROM2010_11673_1.

of the cloth painters of the Coromandel Coast. The highly refined control of line, combined with a heightened sense of colour, achieves a vitality rarely seen, whether for the European or Asian market."[19] The highest-quality cloths often utilized several colors, which required an elaborate process of dyeing. Although the superb use of color cannot be seen in Figure 2.2, a coat manufactured in South India for the Thai market, the complexity of the design and the meticulous execution are evident. While these examples are of very high-quality cloths, even lower-quality goods reflected high aesthetic sensibilities. Figure 2.3 is a block-printed piece manufactured on the Coromandel Coast for the Indonesian market in the late eighteenth century. The colors have been restricted to two, for ease of dyeing and printing, and the weave of the cloth is coarse, but there is no denying the great beauty of the piece.

Because of their vibrant colors and vivid designs, these textiles served a variety of social purposes. John Guy observes that "the

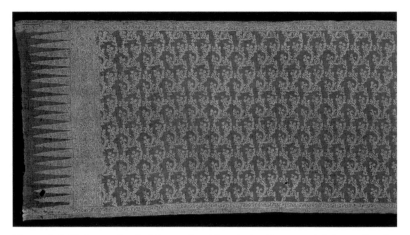

Figure 2.3 *Kain sambagi*, skirt or shoulder cloth, Coromandel Coast for the Indonesian market, late eighteenth century, Victoria and Albert Museum, London, IS.92–1990.

importance of the non-utilitarian uses to which Indian textiles were put in Southeast Asian societies is underscored by the sheer volume of the trade, which exceeded the needs of the region, given that much of the clothing of the people was provided by inexpensive locally woven goods."[20] For elites in Southeast Asia, costly Indian textiles served as markers of status and rank and they lent the wearer or bearer enormous prestige and high social standing. For those on the lower rungs of the social ladder, Indian cottons were no less desirable as they were associated with the rare and exotic, but in this case, the demand had to be satisfied with cloth of lower price and quality. Indian cottons conveyed status when used both as garments and as accessories in ceremonies and rituals. In many areas of Southeast Asia, Indian printed, painted and patterned cloths were prominently displayed as canopies, backdrops, awnings and floor coverings during birth, marriage and death rites. With these uses, according to Guy, Indian cloth came to be invested with spiritual power and authority. Whether as a marker of status or as a possessor of a spiritual force, the beauty of the cloth, both in design and execution, was of prime importance to buyers.

In several parts of the world, Indian cloth reshaped tastes, fashion and consumption, the best documented and perhaps the most striking case being that of Europe in the seventeenth and eighteenth centuries.

Some of the most detailed evidence for these changes in Europe comes from England, where Indian calicoes and muslins arrived in the seventeenth century, in the middle of a marked consumer shift in favor of lighter and more colorful cloth. The rise of the New Draperies in the late sixteenth century, which replaced heavier broadcloths, marked the first stage in this move. This was followed in the seventeenth century by a growing demand for French silks, which combined the desire for lightness with that for colorful and elaborate designs. French silks also made possible more flowing forms of dress that could only be achieved with lighter and more easily draped cloth. Silks were very costly, however, which limited their consumption to the upper classes. Nevertheless, the elites who consumed them popularized the styles and designs that silk cloth made possible.[21]

This was the context in which Indian cottons appeared in England. Middle and lower classes pioneered the use of Indian goods as they were less expensive substitutes for the brocades and flowered silks used by the wealthy. The Indian imports made it possible for "even the less affluent to own vivid, floral patterned, checked, or plaid clothing or soft furnishings."[22] In order to lend Indian cloths greater cachet, the English East India Company aggressively promoted them among the English upper classes. In 1683, in an effort to serve the elite market more effectively, the English East India Company instructed its servants to supply chintz on finer cloth because in Holland such printed and painted goods were "the ware of Gentlewomen," but in England their chief consumers were "of the meaner sort."[23] The Indian goods rose in esteem when leading figures in the realm adopted them. In the late seventeenth century, Charles II appeared in public in waistcoats made from Indian cloth. William and Mary also helped to popularize Indian cloth. Mary "had a fine apartment (at Hampton Court) with a set of lodgings for her private retreat only, but most exquisitely furnished, particularly a fine chintz bed, then a great curiosity," according to Daniel Defoe.[24]

The Company also popularized Indian goods by encouraging their servants in India to commission designs that would appeal to English tastes. According to Beverly Lemire, when buying cloth in India the Company had to conform "to the fashions of Europe," yet still retain an "aura of oriental exoticism."[25] Because of these efforts, from the late seventeenth century Indian cottons began to find growing favor among larger numbers of English consumers and they began to be a fixture of dress and fashion. "Nothing did more to change the way ordinary people dressed in the eighteenth century than the advent of cotton fabrics," John Styles has concluded.[26]

A similar rise of cotton driven by comfort, fashion and social pressure took place in eighteenth-century France where the consumption of cloth from the novel fiber grew dramatically. In 1700, household inventories indicate that clothing made from cotton accounted for 3 to 8 percent of wardrobes, the precise proportion varying by economic and social class. By 1789, this figure had increased to between 20 and 40 percent. Among the nobility and the middle classes of artisans, shopkeepers and the professions cotton replaced linen, but among wage-earners and domestics it displaced wool, which illustrates cotton's protean nature.[27] In France as well cotton became fashionable. "It is not their low prices," commented Jacob Nicolas Moreau in 1759, "it is fashion, and it is a certain vanity that makes the women of the lower classes so curious about calicoes. Dressed in light or printed cottons, they think themselves no longer at the same level of women of their social station . . . they think themselves superior to their social condition because ladies of quality too wear calicoes."[28]

With the spread of cotton, the mode of dress of all groups and classes in France, Britain and elsewhere in Europe became more alike. While the rich in France continued to wear more silks, the poor dressed in cottons and came to resemble their superiors far more than would have been possible with garments of linen or wool. The social hierarchy was upset when the lower and middling orders dressed like upper classes and from the late seventeenth century, the leveling that cotton created was widely criticized in Europe. One pamphleteer in Britain grumbled that it became difficult for men to "know their wives from their chambermaids."[29] John Pollexfen complained in 1700 that the "manufactured goods from India met with such a kind reception, that from the greatest gallants to the meanest cook-maids, nothing was thought to fit, to adorn their persons, as the Fabrick from India."[30]

Fashion is often taken to be unique to European social, cultural and economic life. Such a view, however, is being challenged by evidence from Asia and Africa, which shows that an association between Indian cotton cloth and fashionability was found widely, not only in Europe.[31] In the case of seventeenth-century Iran, Rudiger Klein has argued that the demand for colors and patterns in Indian cloth was not

fixed but changed regularly, which meant that merchants and manufacturers had to keep up with these shifts in taste. Similarly, Pedro
Machado has argued that the designs demanded in the markets of late
eighteenth-century Mozambique changed from season to season. Merchants probably used pattern books to show their African customers
what Indians could make and to send information on what was in
demand to the cloth manufacturers of the subcontinent. In Gujarat,
pattern books with designs for markets in Southeast Asia survive from
the late nineteenth century.[32]

Quality

The creativity and talent of Indian cotton cloth manufacturers were
unsurpassed in the world and they were highly skilled in creating cloths
of great beauty and developing new designs to satisfy shifts in tastes.
Indian textiles were not only beautiful and fashionable, however, but
also of high quality. When it came to colored cloths – whether painted,
printed or dyed by the piece or in the thread – the prime mark of
quality was the fastness of the colors. Indian cloth manufacturers had
mastered a variety of techniques with which coloring agents were
fixed, utilizing a variety of mordants for different shades and different
dyestuffs. Many Europeans in the seventeenth and eighteenth centuries
remarked upon this and saw it as one of the great appeals of Indian
goods. Europeans also marveled that repeated washings did not fade
the cloth but rather enhanced the brightness of the colors.[33]

In addition to their ability with dyes, Indian manufacturers were
unparalleled in the production of fine muslin cloths. These textiles had
long been famous around the world and they were in great demand in
the eighteenth century. The superfine varieties of Dacca are the best
known and the lightness of the cloth and fineness of the weave were
legendary. These qualities were captured in the names of the different
varieties, which included *subnam* (evening dew) because the cloth
resembled the dew on sand, *abraban* (running water) because it could
not be seen in water, *alaballee* (very fine), *tanjeb* (ornament of the
body) and *kasa* (elegant). Europeans gave them similarly whimsical
names, including *ventus textilis* (textile breeze), web of woven air and
cobweb.[34] Stories of the extraordinary lightness and fineness of
muslins circulated both inside and outside the Indian subcontinent.
There is, of course, the famous account of Aurangzeb, who became

angry with his daughter for wearing cloth so transparent that her skin could be seen. She protested that she was wearing seven jamahs or suits. In the seventeenth century, an Iranian ambassador to India returned home with a coconut in which a muslin turban that was thirty yards in length had been carefully folded. Dacca muslin manufacturers were famous for producing cloth that could be folded to the size of a matchbox. Anther test of fineness was to pass a piece of cloth through a ring, which could be done with pieces from Dacca that were twenty yards long and one yard wide.[35]

At times Indian cloths possessed qualities that appeared intangible, but nevertheless appealed to discerning buyers. A striking example comes from West Africa where the French exported blue cloth from South India in order to purchase gum Arabic, an essential thickening agent for the cloth-printing industry. In the early nineteenth century, French traders marketed a European imitation of the Indian cloth, but African buyers rejected it on the grounds that the smell and feel were not right. Because of the importance of gum Arabic, the French continued to procure the blue cloth in their South Indian possession of Pondicherry, from where they exported it to West Africa until the mid-nineteenth century.[36]

The question of price

It has been long assumed that Indian cloths were cheaper than cloth manufactured in Europe and elsewhere, but new evidence indicates otherwise. The belief that the prices of Indian textiles were low originated in the late seventeenth century when Europeans attributed the appeal of the Indian cloths to their cheapness, which they ascribed to the scanty level of wages in the subcontinent. Daniel Defoe was typical when he wrote, "The People who make all these fine Works are to the last Degree miserable, their Labour of no Value, their Wages would fright us to talk of it, and their way of Living raise a Horror in us to think of it . . . the Wages they get cannot provide better food for them; and yet their rigorous Task-masters lash them forward as we (cruelly too) sometimes do our Horses."[37] These late seventeenth-century arguments on the cheapness of Indian cloth and the lowness of Indian wages have been reproduced in the accounts of modern historians. The question of price is far more complex than this account would have it, however.

In many markets around the world Indian cottons were more expensive than locally made cloth. This was the case in Southeast Asia where low-quality cotton cloths were manufactured in large quantities, but higher-quality Indian cottons, despite being more costly, were in great demand. In 1700, a piece of Javanese cloth "may have been one-quarter to one-eighth as expensive as Indian equivalents" and in the 1770s "the average price of an Indonesian piece was a quarter to a third of an Indian one."[38] The same was true of Iran and the Ottoman Empire where by the seventeenth and eighteenth centuries local cotton weaving and printing works began to imitate Indian goods. The locally made imitations were less expensive, but of inferior quality, which led to the continued import of large quantities of Indian printed and painted cloth. Indian muslins were also in high demand in these markets because Iranian and Ottoman cotton manufacturers were unable to make this very fine cloth.[39]

In Europe as well, Indian cottons were by no means the lowest-priced cloths. Price information assembled by Carole Shammas, which is reproduced in Table 2.3, shows that in the final decades of the seventeenth century cotton calico was less expensive than most varieties of woolen cloth, but more expensive than all varieties of linen, except the finest Holland. By the early eighteenth century, the price of calico had increased relative to both woolens and linens and only broadcloth and fine Holland were significantly more expensive.[40] The price gap between cotton and other fabrics appears to have widened by the mid-eighteenth century. In the 1750s, a shopkeeper in Yorkshire sold worsted fabric for women's gowns at 10d. to 15d. a yard. His plain blue cotton sold at 13d. or 14d., striped cotton at 15d., printed cottons at 24d. to 28d. and chintz cotton, presumably a very fine variety, at 48d. a yard. John Styles has concluded that "the triumph of printed cotton as a gown material for plebian women resulted, therefore, from its superior appearance, not its cheapness."[41] Similarly, Styles notes that the delay in the substitution of cotton for linen for more utilitarian purposes such as shirts and household sheets – cotton did not triumph till the mid-nineteenth century – suggests that Indian cottons were more costly and less durable than many varieties of linen. He also observes that before 1800 cloth from cotton was rarely supplied by overseers of the poor to paupers, which suggests that it was more costly than other textiles. Cotton made more rapid inroads against linen as decorative fabrics

Table 2.3 *Average current and constant prices of selected textiles in English retailers' inventories, 1660–1738 (d. per yard)*

Type of cloth	1660–1699 (current and constant)	1700–1738 (current and constant)
Woolens		
Heavy broadcloths	56	54
Kerseys	21	25
Frieze	22	21
Serge	24	19
Baize	18	10
Flannel	10	15
Stuffs	9	9
Linens and cottons		
Fine Holland	41	32
Linen	11	13
Blue linen	10	10
Osnaburg	8	8
Fustian	8	10
Calico	12	24
Scotch cloth	13	10

Note: Constant prices were obtained by using the Phelps-Brown and Hopkins index with the base changed to 1660–99. The averages for the index in 1660–99 and 1700–38 were almost identical, so no adjustment was made for inflation in the later period.
Source: Shammas, "The Decline of Textile Prices," p. 484.

and as outer garments, which were more visible and where cotton's aesthetic properties made more of a difference.[42]

The consumption of Indian cottons in the seventeenth and eighteenth centuries, therefore, does not appear to have been driven by their low prices, but rather by their quality and the demands of fashion and social standing. This conclusion speaks to the fact that textiles are highly differentiated goods and their consumption is socially regulated. Nevertheless, the lower prices of Indian cottons were critical in two respects in seventeenth- and eighteenth-century Europe.

First, Indian cotton cloth was cheaper than the all-cotton goods that Europeans manufactured in the seventeenth and eighteenth centuries, especially in the higher-quality varieties. In Normandy, for example, a French firm successfully made muslins between 1753 and 1760 only because of a protective duty.[43] The manufacture collapsed when the protection was removed. Similarly, an attempt to make all-cotton muslins in Lancashire in the 1760s failed because of a lack of yarn "cheap enough to compete with Indian muslin."[44] And in African and Asian markets, European cotton manufacturers struggled to match Indian prices. Through much of the eighteenth century, Lancashire imitations of Indian goods found buyers in West Africa only when Indian goods were unavailable. The prices for Indian cotton cloth were to remain below those of European versions until the invention of machinery for spinning cotton in the 1760s and 1770s, in particular the water frame and the mule. Even then, it took some decades for British cloth to displace Indian goods. In 1788, the English East India Company sent cotton cloth manufactured in Manchester to Basra and Bushehr and discovered that "some of the qualities and colours were well adapted to the taste of the Persians; but the Invoice Price was so high that the loss must have been very considerable."[45]

Second, Indian cottons were less expensive than silk cloth, which in the seventeenth century became the fabric of high fashion in Europe. "When novelty was demanded, it was demanded first from the silk designers," Beverly Lemire has written.[46] The introduction of Indian cottons challenged the primacy of silk, which it replaced in the making of gowns as well as other garments. Initially, the "members of the middling and lower orders began to buy the vibrant cottons as a cheap facsimile of the brocades and flowered silks favoured by the aristocracy."[47] For the less wealthy, the lower prices of printed and painted cottons enabled them to imitate the silk styles of the elite. Given the threat that cottons posed, it is not surprising that the London protests of the 1690s against Indian imports were spearheaded by the silk weavers of Spitalfields who believed that they were being undercut by low-wage workers in the Indian subcontinent. "N. C.," a London weaver, for instance, criticized the English East India Company for "having their goods cheap wrought by the wretched poverty of that numerous people."[48] What should one make of such claims for low Indian wages?

Low Indian wages?

The silk weavers of London were not alone in their belief that the low wages of Indian workers accounted for the low prices of Indian cotton cloth. A number of pamphlets and books in the late seventeenth and early eighteenth centuries contrasted the well-paid laborer of Europe with his impoverished Indian counterpart, who was seen as a defense-less victim of merchant and state oppression. John Basset, for example, criticized in Parliament the importation of Indian cottons on the grounds that "people in India are such slaves as to work for less than a penny a day, whereas ours here will not work under a shilling."[49] The pamphleteers and writers of Europe may have drawn such bleak conclusions about the state of Indian laborers from the accounts of travelers to the subcontinent. Francisco Pelsaert, who journeyed through the Mughal Empire in the early seventeenth century, wrote: "For the workman there are two scourges, the first of which is low wages . . . The second is [the oppression of] the Governor, the nobles, the Diwan, the Kotwal, the Bakhshi, and other royal officers."[50] Even a relatively unknown traveler, a Mrs. J. Kindersley, wrote in 1765 that the poor of India "are poor indeed; scarce any covering, their food rice and water; their miserable huts of straw . . .; no liberty, no property, subject to the tyranny of every superior."[51]

Drawing upon these European sources, historians have concluded that wages and standards of living in India were far lower than in Europe. W. H. Moreland, the great economic historian of Mughal India, wrote that in the early seventeenth century India possessed a "very numerous lower class, living generally on the same plane of poverty as now, but on the whole substantially worse off." Tapan Raychaudhuri described the agricultural population of India as living in "great poverty" and attributed the competitiveness of Indian cloth in world markets to the "ruthlessly inequitable system of distribution." K. N. Chaudhuri opined that the Indian subcontinent in the seventeenth and eighteenth centuries was characterized by "surplus labour leading to low wages." And Eric Hobsbawm cautioned in his contribution to the debate on standards of living during the industrial revolution that British wages may have fallen, but they never approached "Asiatic" levels.[52] Arguments for Indian poverty and low wages were voiced with great conviction, but with little systematic comparison of incomes in the Indian subcontinent and Europe. When the evidence is examined, the conventional wisdom of high standards of living in Europe and impoverished conditions in India looks less plausible.

Table 2.4 presents estimates from the mid-eighteenth century of earnings converted to their food grain equivalents for weavers, spinners and laborers in agriculture for Britain, which was widely reputed to have the highest standards of living in Europe at the time, and for

Table 2.4 *Grain earnings in the mid-eighteenth century*

	Britain	South India	Bengal
Weaving (lbs/week)	40–140	65–160	55–135
Spinning (/lb)	4d.–2s.	7d.–2s.	5d.–2s.
Agricultural labor (lbs/week)	30–35	26–30	–

Note: The wages for weaving and agricultural labor are given in terms of pounds of grain per week, wheat for Britain and rice for South India and Bengal. For spinning they are given in terms of earnings per pounds of yarn spun but with correction for differences in grain prices. For further details, see Parthasarathi, "Rethinking Wages and Competitiveness."

Sources: Britain and South India: Parthasarathi, "Rethinking Wages and Competitiveness."

Bengal weavers' incomes: N. K. Sinha, *The Economic History of Bengal*, vol. I, *From Plassey to the Permanent Settlemen* (2nd edn., Calcutta, 1961), p. 176; D. B. Mitra, *The Cotton Weavers of Bengal, 1757–1833* (Calcutta, 1978), p. 123; P. J. Marshall, "The Company and the Coolies: Labour in Early Calcutta," in P. Sinha (ed.), *The Urban Experience, Calcutta: Essays in Honour of Professor Nisith R. Ray* (Calcutta, 1987), p. 28.

Bengal rice prices: Mitra, *Cotton Weavers*, p. 123; Marshall, "Company and the Coolies," p. 28; Rajat Datta, *Society, Economy and the Market: Commercialisation in Rural Bengal, c.1760–1800* (Delhi, 2000), p. 255.

South India and Bengal, which were highly commercialized, textile-manufacturing regions in the Indian subcontinent. The figures show that earnings for these occupational groups were comparable in these areas in the mid-eighteenth century. The numbers are rough measures of real well-being as they simply convert weekly earnings into their caloric equivalents. They exclude essential items of consumption, most importantly housing, clothing and fuel, but these exclusions should bias the results in favor of Britain where the colder climate required higher expenditures on all three. Nevertheless, these figures show that the longstanding conventional wisdom that in the eighteenth century Europe was far richer than the Indian subcontinent and that Indian workers were impoverished is a point of view in need of serious rethinking.

These kinds of calculations of earnings, whether nominal or real, are fraught with difficulties. The quality and reliability of the data pose significant problems. The existence of substantial non-monetary perquisites, the full extent of which is often unknown, means that the quantification of the wage is often impossible. And perhaps most importantly, even if weekly or daily earnings can be estimated with some degree of confidence, the number of days or weeks worked per year is often difficult to specify with precision. For these reasons, quantitative estimates of weekly earnings must be supplemented by additional, often qualitative, evidence wherever possible. By doing this, the numbers can be placed in a larger social, political and economic context and be given proper significance.[53]

The three most important determinants of earnings in the eighteenth century were the productivity of workers, their bargaining power vis-à-vis other claimants to a share of their output, and the level of employment. The qualitative evidence does not indicate significant advantages for British workers in any of these areas. If anything, the advantages lay on the side of workers in Bengal and South India.

First, on the question of the bargaining power, in the eighteenth century the political and economic order was far friendlier to laborers in India than to those in Britain. The customs of the contracting system in South India, for example, by which merchants financed the production of cloth, yarn and agricultural products, heavily favored weavers, peasants and other producers. Laborers were given rights and privileges of contract that allowed them to benefit from favorable price movements, deliver goods of substandard quality at high prices, and evade debt obligations to merchants. Because of this structure of contracts, laborers in South India were economically secure and possessed a solid claim to their incomes. Producers in South India and elsewhere were also the beneficiaries of a political system that limited the power of states to discipline them or to back merchant claims against them. The situation in eighteenth-century Britain was far different and state power was exercised routinely to defend mercantile and employer interests.[54]

Second, it appears that levels of unemployment and underemployment were lower in the Indian subcontinent than in Britain. The advanced regions of the subcontinent, including Bengal and South India, suffered from shortages of labor in the booming economic conditions of the eighteenth century. Demand for labor typically exceeded supply, which meant that weavers and other artisans as well as laborers in agriculture found steady and abundant work. Therefore, the comparable weekly real earnings given in Table 2.4 most likely translated into higher annual earnings in the Indian subcontinent.[55]

Finally, there is no evidence to indicate that the productivity of labor in the eighteenth century was higher in Britain than in the advanced regions of India, which means that there is little basis for large differences in earnings. In agriculture, which was the largest source of employment in both Britain and India, it is well known that the productivity of seed and land was higher in the advanced agrarian regions of the subcontinent than in Europe. While information to estimate the productivity of labor in Indian agriculture is not available, in Bengal and South India rice was cultivated using techniques that minimized the demand for scarce labor, the most important being methods of sowing that avoided the transplantation of seedlings, which required enormous inputs of time. In Bengal, rice was sown via broadcast. In the South, broadcast and seed drills were used for this purpose. With these methods the labor requirements in rice cultivation were substantially lowered.[56]

In the textile trades, which were the second largest source of employment for the labouring classes in Britain, Bengal and South India, the technologies that were used in spinning and weaving were similar across these regions.[57] For most counts of yarn, British and Indian spinners relied upon a basic wheel. For the finer varieties, spinners in both places used a distaff. In South India, some fine yarns were spun with a specialized spinning wheel, which was smaller and more delicate than the basic wheel, and more productive than a distaff. In Britain, Bengal and South India, almost all weaving was done on simple horizontal frame looms. More complex looms were found in Britain and the Indian subcontinent, particularly draw looms for the manufacture of complex, patterned cloths, but these accounted for a small fraction of total cloth production. The flying shuttle increased loom productivity in Britain, but did not penetrate very far before the late eighteenth century. Therefore, the technologies of spinning and weaving were more or less identical, which would have translated into similar levels of labor productivity, and therefore no productivity-driven differences in earnings. Of course, this situation changed from the late 1760s with the invention and diffusion of new technologies for spinning and weaving in Britain.[58]

Weekly earnings in Britain and the Indian subcontinent must also be placed in relation to working hours. There is much evidence that the eighteenth-century working day was far longer in Britain than in Bengal or South India. Therefore, roughly comparable grain wages were achieved with greater toil and trouble in Britain. According to John Rule, for London craftsmen in the mid-eighteenth century "a 14-hour day seems to have been usual." And Hans-Joachim Voth has documented extraordinary increases in working time in the late eighteenth and early nineteenth centuries for British workers.[59] There is no evidence for such prodigious work efforts and such long working days in either Bengal or South India in the eighteenth century and it is certainly not something that is remarked upon in the literature on weavers or other workers in the eighteenth century.[60]

This discussion has argued that the real standards of living for textile workers in Bengal and South India were comparable with those in Britain. Nevertheless, these regions in India possessed an important price advantage when it came to selling their cotton textiles in global markets. This advantage derived from differences in the price of grain, which in South India was one-half and in Bengal one-third the British level. (The comparison here is being made between rice and wheat bread.) The comparable grain earnings of Table 2.4 could, therefore, be obtained in South India with a half and in Bengal with a third of the silver that was needed in Britain, which translated into lower silver prices for cloth. Any price advantage that Indian textiles possessed may have had its origins in agriculture, which yielded lower prices for food in the Indian subcontinent.[61]

The estimates given in Table 2.4 for comparable weekly earnings in Britain and India have not gone unchallenged. Stephen Broadberry and Bishnupriya Gupta have argued that grain wages were comparable in the seventeenth century, but diverged in the eighteenth, when Indian wages fell to 30 to 40 percent of British levels.[62] There are a number of problems with the methods and procedures by which they have reached their estimates of earnings, however. Broadberry and Gupta obtained almost all their prices and wages from secondary sources, but with little critical evaluation of the reliability of the sources or the figures. They draw upon one primary text, the late sixteenth-century administrative manual, the A'in-i Akbari, for price and wage data on Mughal India, but Alan Heston cautioned that the A'in is of limited reliability because the prices and wages it contains appear to be nominal, not market, prices.[63] Broadberry and Gupta ignore other difficulties in the calculation of earnings in the eighteenth century, including the substantial non-monetary perquisites that workers in a variety of occupations received, such as meals, alcoholic drinks, housing and waste goods from the production process. While British sources typically include these non-monetary perquisites in the reported wage figure, those for India do not. Further complicating the calculation of earnings is that the incomes of many categories of workers did not consist of a simple wage payment. The earnings of weavers in India, for example, were the difference between the merchant price for the finished cloth and the weavers' costs. Weavers were capable of manipulating the production process to maintain or increase their incomes, which is reflected in a South Indian proverb: "When a merchant reduces his price, the weaver reduces his thread." Such methodological problems in the Broadberry and Gupta estimates lead them to some odd conclusions about incomes in India and Britain.

In Table 2.4, British and Indian earnings are classified by occupation, in this case weavers, spinners and laborers in agriculture. For all three types of workers, grain earnings fall in a similar range. Given the importance of these occupations, they provide a good guide to the standard of living for a sizable proportion of the population in both Britain and India. Broadberry and Gupta classify their wage estimates by skill level, not by occupation, and divide their estimates of earnings into unskilled and skilled. On this basis, they classify calico weavers as unskilled and reject the South Indian weaver earnings given in Table 2.4 as too high and give preference to their estimates. A closer examination of the Broadberry and Gupta figures points to some anomalies, however.

Table 2.5 presents daily grain earnings in South India by skill level, divided into low, medium and high skill. The figures are drawn from Broadberry and Gupta and from the calculations which were reported in Table 2.4. For low-skilled workers the two sets of earnings figures, which are for laborers in agriculture and scavengers, are compatible. (But oddly Broadberry and Gupta make no reference to the earning estimate for South Indian laborers in agriculture given in Table 2.4 and do not explain why they do not include it in their paper.)

When it comes to medium-skilled workers, in this case calico weavers, the Broadberry and Gupta figures are anomalous. Calico weavers were of middling skill, but according to Broadberry and Gupta their daily earnings were below those of low-skilled workers, which is unlikely. Not to receive any premium for work that was cleaner than scavenging or agricultural work and at the same time more highly skilled is implausible. Therefore, their calico weaver

Table 2.5 *Daily grain wages in eighteenth-century South India*
(lbs of rice)

Year	Low-skilled	Medium-skilled	High-skilled
1741–50	**4.6 (scavengers)**		
1750		9.3 (calico weavers)	23 (fine calico and muslin weavers)
1779		**2.4 (calico weavers)**	
1790		**4.0 (calico weavers)**	
1795	4.3 (agriculturalists)		

Source: The numbers in bold are from Broadberry and Gupta, "Early Modern Great Divergence." Others are from Parthasarathi, "Rethinking Wages and Competitiveness."

earnings figures, which are crucial for their argument that South India had lower standards of living than Britain, are problematic and appear to seriously underestimate the true earnings of these workers.

Some scattered information on consumption also indicates that calico weavers earned more than laborers in agriculture. Evidence from the 1790s on food consumption for a range of groups in the Baramahal, an area in the interior of South India, shows that weavers who were less skilled than the calico weavers discussed above had richer and more varied diets than occupational groups of low skill, including agriculturalists, as well as some of low- to medium-skill, such as pot-makers. Weavers in the Baramahal consumed more rice, more pulses and a greater variety of spices than every group in the sample except Brahmins, who would have had substantial rights in land and monopolized occupations that required literacy, and merchants and traders, who commanded capital and other resources. Weavers were even in a position to purchase a few luxury items such as ghee.[64] This material on consumption is powerful evidence that the Broadberry and Gupta earnings estimate for calico weavers is too low. Moving up the skill ladder, there are accounts from the late eighteenth century of fine muslin weavers of very high skill living in stone houses, some of them of two stories, in South Indian towns such as Kanchipuram and Arni.[65] The high grain earnings for the highest skilled weavers in Tables 2.4 and 2.5 are consistent with such a style of living.

Robert Allen uses a broader basket of consumption goods to compare standards of living in India and Britain, but concurs with Broadberry and Gupta that British real earnings were far above Indian. Allen argues that Indian incomes declined steadily from the seventeenth century and that by the early nineteenth century the standard of living of Indian workers was barely above subsistence. "In good years there was more than enough money to purchase the [subsistence] consumption basket, but in bad years there was not," Allen writes.[66] Allen's study has the merit of offering a broader measure of real earnings, but his wage and price data for India are drawn from secondary sources and therefore suffer from the Broadberry and Gupta problems of reliability.

Allen's conclusion that standards of living were lower in India has been challenged on the basis of voluminous data on prices and income collected by Francis Buchanan in his travels through the Mysore region of South India in 1800–1. Based on the Buchanan evidence, Sashi Sivramkrishna constructed a basket of consumption goods, much as Allen did, and concluded that in Mysore the average income was five times the subsistence level. (Mysore was by no means a particularly prosperous area of the South as its major food crop was millet which was less productive than rice.) For agricultural workers, if both husband and wife worked, household income could be as high as two-and-a-half times the subsistence level. For weavers, it could be as high as four times the subsistence level. Sivramkrishna concludes that "Buchanan's *Journey*, therefore, does seem to support the findings of Parthasarathi who argued that grain wages of weavers in India were on par and sometimes higher than weavers in Europe."[67]

The above discussion makes evident that the debate on comparative earnings in India and Britain is far from resolved. At the moment, the quantitative data are inconclusive, but the figures for India that have been obtained from primary sources are radically different from the scattered earnings data found in the secondary literature. This indicates that more research is needed on the basis of primary evidence for India. The quantitative material does not exhaust the evidence at hand, however, which is why qualitative findings on the place of laborers in the larger political economy are also essential to the discussion. And certainly more attention must be given to this evidence. Even more importantly, those who argue for higher British earnings must explain why there was such a gap with India. The evidence on productivity, levels of employment and the place of producers in the political and economic order does not suggest that British laborers were particularly favored in any of these respects. Thus there does not appear to be any compelling reason to believe that the laboring populations of Britain possessed a higher standard of living.

Bullion in the global economy

Between 1600 and 1800 Indian cotton cloth was consumed in markets around the world and in exchange enormous quantities of silver, gold, copper and other forms of money flowed into the Indian subcontinent. Despite the extensive evidence for sizable imports of silver into India, a number of historians have argued that most of the world's output of the precious metal in the seventeenth and eighteenth centuries made its way to China. Andre Gunder Frank declared that China was the "ultimate 'sink'" for the world's silver, echoing Dennis O. Flynn and Arturo Giráldez, who wrote, "All the great silver mines in both hemispheres sold ultimately to China."[68] These writers are not alone. Richard von Glahn has stated, "While we lack direct evidence to show that the bulk of New World silver entering the Asian market wound up in China, the premium value accorded silver in China certainly suggests that this was certainly the case."[69] According to Kenneth Pomeranz, "South Asian and other users who were often the initial purchasers of European silver [sent] much of it to China."[70]

These writers have misconstrued India's place in the global trading system and the place of bullion in the commercial world of the Indian subcontinent. A very conservative calculation reveals that between 1600 and 1800 about 28,000 tons of bullion in silver equivalents (and much of it actually silver), which represented roughly a fifth of the world's production of 142,000 tons, flowed into the Indian subcontinent. In this period, the major silver producers in the world were the Americas, which added 132,000 tons of bullion, in silver equivalents, to world supplies, and Japan, which accounted for about 10,000 tons.[71]

Bullion came into India via a number of routes in the seventeenth and eighteenth centuries. In the seventeenth century, the most important sources lay in the Middle East and silver and gold were carried from the Persian Gulf and the Red Sea. Central Asia, Southeast Asia and Europe were also sources of precious metals, the last especially in the eighteenth century when bullion carried on the Cape of Good

Hope route grew dramatically.[72] From a cursory examination of trade flows within Asia, Frank concluded that the bulk of the silver that was imported into India was re-exported to China. From the sixteenth century, China had a voracious appetite for the precious metal as it shifted from a disastrous late Ming experiment with paper currency to a monetary order based on silver. At the same time, there was enormous demand for the porcelains, silks and other goods for which China was renowned throughout the world, but little demand in China for imports from elsewhere. Therefore, foreigners had no choice but to bring silver to trade with the Chinese. Silver was also taken to China to be exchanged for gold, which had a lower price in China than in India or Europe. For these reasons, according to Frank, China absorbed half the world's silver, which made it the undisputed center of the world economy in the seventeenth and eighteenth centuries.[73]

Frank and others are mistaken in assuming that the bulk of the silver that entered India was re-exported to China. The figures available on this trade are fragmentary, but they do not suggest that it was conducted on a large scale. According to estimates from Richard von Glahn, between 1600 and 1640 the Portuguese carried less than four tons of silver a year from the Indian Ocean to Macao.[74] The English East India Company also entered this trade, but it appears to have been on a small scale before the British conquest of Bengal in the late eighteenth century.[75] The other route by which silver could have gone to China from India was via Southeast Asia for the purchase of spices, but the principal Indian medium of exchange for cloves, nutmeg, mace, cinnamon and other spices was not silver but cotton cloth.[76]

Even though some silver was taken from India to China where it was traded for gold, this did not mean a decline in the money supply of the Indian subcontinent. In contrast to China, gold was used as money in several parts of the Indian subcontinent. High-value gold coins, known as the *muhr* and *ashrafi*, were minted in northern India and used in large transactions and as stores of value. In southern India, gold coins, known to Europeans as the pagoda, were integral to the monetary system and set the standard by which silver and copper coins were valued. In the final decades of the seventeenth century, the English East India Company even exported substantial quantities of gold from Europe to India. The Company's expanding activities in the Coromandel Coast of southern India may have propelled this trade.[77]

There were additional routes, which Frank and others have missed, by which silver was brought to India, but the quantities of silver carried on these routes are not known. The Manila to India trade may have been the most important of these and via this path some of the silver carried across the Pacific from Acapulco made its way to the subcontinent. Om Prakash reports that in the late seventeenth century more than a million florins of silver, the equivalent of about nine tons, was transported every year from Manila to South India. According to K. N. Chaudhuri, in 1693–4 the price of silver dropped in Madras because of the "arrival of a considerable quantity of Spanish silver from Manila" and in 1712, 1715 and 1727 Madras suffered shortages because the Manila ships had brought very little silver. In the eighteenth century, Ashin Das Gupta has reported that the expansion of English private trade with Manila translated into considerable quantities of American silver entering the subcontinent via the Pacific route, but the magnitude of this trade is not known. This shows that not all silver carried to Manila went to China and that the Pacific was a regular source of bullion for South India, and perhaps other regions of the subcontinent. There is also evidence that silver made its way from both China and Japan to India. For instance, silver was exported from China to Central Asia from where some of it flowed to the Indian subcontinent. And the Dutch East India Company carried Japanese silver for sale in Bengal.[78]

Frank and others also ignore the evidence that vast quantities of silver were coined in the subcontinent where it entered into circulation in the seventeenth and eighteenth centuries. According to data compiled by Najaf Haider, between 1588 and 1602 an average of 136 tons of silver were imported every year into the Mughal Empire.[79] From 1630 to 1645 this figure fell to 93 tons per year, but from 1679 to 1685 increased to 145 tons per year. The larger import figures for the late seventeenth century are consistent with the great growth in Indian exports of cotton textiles in those years. Data on the silver rupee output of Mughal mints closely corresponds to these import figures for the first two periods, which indicates that much of the silver remained in the Mughal Empire and circulated as coins, according to Haider. (The quantity coined is lower than imports in the final period, perhaps because there was a limit to the speed at which the Mughal economy could absorb silver coins.) A weighted average of the above figures yields an average import into Mughal India of 120 tons of silver per year from the late sixteenth to the late seventeenth centuries. If this figure is projected to the seventeenth century as a whole, it yields a silver import total of 12,000 tons in those 100 years.[80] Najaf Haider's import figures exclude southern India and the important commercial centers of the Malabar and Coromandel Coasts. If we assume that the south imported about 15 percent of the quantity of the bullion that flowed into the Mughal Empire, which is consistent with its population relative to that of the empire, the average imports of silver into the Indian subcontinent come to 138 tons per year or 13,800 tons in the seventeenth century.

Neither silver import figures nor minting data comparable to those compiled by Haider are available for the hundred years after 1700 as minting became more decentralized. It is likely that even larger quantities of silver entered India in those years, however, given the abundant evidence for a great expansion of commercial activity, the rapid growth of marketplaces and the higher levels of exports. An eighteenth-century increase in silver imports into India is also suggested by Artur Attman's figures for both the quantity of silver mined in the Americas and bullion flows from Western Europe to Asia, both of which were significantly larger after 1700, as well as information on the bullion trade of the East India Companies, which grew steadily from the 1670s.[81] The evidence pointing to increased imports of silver in the eighteenth century must be balanced against the drop in British silver coming into the subcontinent in the closing decades of the century.[82] Nevertheless, if we project the seventeenth-century figure into the eighteenth, we arrive at a grand total of almost 28,000 tons of silver and gold, in silver equivalents, imported into India between 1600 and 1800, which represents a fifth of total global silver production in that period. This is likely to underestimate bullion flows into India in the eighteenth century. Nonetheless, it is revealing of India's place in the world economy of the seventeenth and eighteenth centuries and of its capacities as an exporter.

The precious metals – gold and silver – were not the only commodities used as money in India. There were also a number of lower-value monetary forms, which helped to fuel countless small transactions by peasants, weavers, artisans and laborers. The subcontinent imported vast quantities of copper and the trade in this metal from Japan to India generated sizable profits for the Dutch East India Company. The copper was minted in several regions of India into coins of small denomination. Cowries were also imported into eastern India and utilized as low-value coins, as were badams, a bitter and inedible almond, in western India.[83]

Claims that China absorbed the bulk of the silver that circulated in Asia are, therefore, incorrect. Until the nineteenth century, the Indian subcontinent continued to be a major importer of not only silver but also gold, copper, cowries and badams. The Indian subcontinent held this position in global trade – and was therefore able to claim large quantities of bullion – because of an insatiable appetite for Indian cotton textiles in markets across the world. As a consequence, the subcontinent was awash in money and a highly commercialized economic order emerged from the late sixteenth century.

Conclusion

By 1700 Indian cotton cloth was consumed in the four corners of the world. As it grew in popularity, efforts to imitate it sprang up around the world as well. In Safavid Iran, cloth manufacturers copied the printed and painted calicoes of Gujarat and sold some of them in Marseilles and elsewhere in Europe as *indiennes*. European buyers assumed that these cloths were of Indian provenance. In the Ottoman Empire, cotton cloth printing became a major manufacturing activity in Tokat and other towns and cities in Anatolia. These Ottoman products were also exported to Europe where they were widely demanded and consumed. The most fateful imitation of Indian cottons took place in Western Europe, where from the late seventeenth century calico printing workshops were established to print cotton as well as linen cloth in the Indian fashion. These led to attempts to manufacture the Indian cotton cloth itself and in Britain these efforts led to some of the most important technological breakthroughs of the eighteenth century. Before examining these responses to Indian cottons, the economic, political and social institutions of seventeenth- and eighteenth-century India merit more careful analysis, however. The vibrant export of textiles and the large-scale import of money are evidence of a sophisticated commercial and mercantile system. Yet both classic and contemporary commentators argue that the economic and political institutions of eighteenth-century India were inferior to those of Europe.

3 | *Political institutions and economic life*

Introduction

In the *Wealth of Nations* Adam Smith wrote that the nations of Europe were the most prosperous in the world while India and China were exemplars of past greatness, but present-day stagnation. Smith attributed the decline of these Asian regions to social and political institutions that constrained the operation of the market. In drawing this contrast between Europe and Asia, Smith was following a venerable tradition. We know that Smith had read the work of the seventeenth-century French physician François Bernier, whose "acrid account of the Orient exercised a deep influence on subsequent generations of thinkers."[1] Bernier drew an unflattering portrait of life in the Ottoman and Mughal Empires, where he argued that the inhabitants were oppressed by despotic rulers, denied access to the fruits of their labor, and took little economic initiative as they feared for the security of their property. His vivid descriptions influenced Montesquieu, who in several widely read works described Asia as unchanging ("the laws, customs and manners of the Orient – even the most trivial, such as mode of dress – remain the same today as they were a thousand years ago"), despotic ("power must always be despotic in Asia") and unfree ("in Asia there reigns a spirit of servitude . . . it is impossible to find a single trait that marks a free soul").[2]

These political and economic differences between Europe and Asia found their parallels in demographic regimes. Thomas Malthus argued that in Europe preventive checks, or rational procedures to limit family size, maintained the balance between land and people. In Asia, by contrast, preventive checks were absent, which meant that stocks of food and population were equilibrated through the unforgiving methods of nature, including famine, pestilence and epidemic disease. Asia, then, was home to spectacular disasters, both natural and man-made.

From these beginnings in Montesquieu, Smith, Malthus, as well as countless other lesser known figures, the belief in profound differences between Europe and Asia became a conventional wisdom in the nineteenth and twentieth centuries. The dramatic intellectual, political and economic transformation of nineteenth-century Western Europe, including industrialization, revolutions in government and the growth in scientific knowledge, at a time when Asia appeared unchanging, added further support to the argument for deep-seated contrasts. By the mid-nineteenth century, Marx could write with great authority, "Indian society has no history at all, at least no known history. What we call its history, is but the history of the successive intruders who founded their empires on the passive basis of that unresisting and unchanging society."[3]

In the twentieth century, Max Weber added rationality to the list of European differences, which he saw as reaching greater heights in Europe because of the theodicy of Protestantism. Marxists continued to see India and China as following aberrant paths because of their failure to develop capitalism, condemning them to an Asiatic Mode of Production. Neo-Malthusians argued for fundamentally different fertility behavior in Asia, which relegated it to backwardness. Neo-classical economists, most prominently Douglass North, saw the institutions of the market that emerged in Europe as more efficient than in Asia, leaving even the most advanced parts of India and China less dynamic.[4] Some combination of the above approaches informed Eric Jones' *European Miracle* and David Landes' *Wealth and Poverty of Nations*. And they continue to inform the debate on divergence to this day.[5]

This chapter examines these arguments for economic, political and demographic divides between the advanced regions of India and Europe. It finds that the Indian subcontinent was not dramatically different from Europe and that economically advanced regions such as Bengal, North and South India and Gujarat possessed sophisticated commercial systems which compared favorably with those in Britain, the most advanced region of eighteenth-century Europe. Although data are limited, demographic outcomes, as revealed by family and household size and fertility, were also not radically different in India. A competitive state system was also found in the Indian subcontinent, which led in the seventeenth and eighteenth centuries to political contestation and state support for economic improvement. The Indian subcontinent was also home to a culture of reason which was manifest in mercantile life and in the reorganization of state administrations.

All was not identical across the advanced regions of India and Europe, however. In some respects, it appears the economic institutions of Europe were more highly developed than those of India, including the integration of grain markets. In other respects, however, economic performance of the maritime regions in the subcontinent surpassed that of Europe, including the ability to export prodigious quantities of manufactured goods, which was explored in the previous chapter, alongside highly productive agrarian regimes, which enabled these same manufacturing regions also to export grain. Considering all the available evidence together, it appears that the advanced regions of India possessed a dynamic political and economic order which was not in its essentials inferior to what was found in Europe.

The state

Seventeenth- and eighteenth-century European thinkers took it for granted that states in Asia were despotic. The despotism of the "east" was an ancient idea, but its modern incarnation emerged in the sixteenth century. Living in the shadow of the expanding Ottoman Empire, Machiavelli wrote in *The Prince* that "the entire Turkish empire is ruled by one master, and all other men are his servants . . . they are all slaves, bounden to him."[6] Contrasts in political life between Europe and the Ottoman Empire were elaborated by Jean Bodin, Francis Bacon, James Harrington and others, and from the seventeenth century, these differences were extended further east and applied to Iran, India and China.[7]

Despotism had economic as well as political repercussions. According to François Bernier, agriculture in Mughal India was in a disordered state, which he attributed to the lack of private property in land. Since the emperor owned all the land in the realm, peasants had no incentive to invest and improve their holdings. Historians now understand that Bernier confused the right to collect revenue, which Mughal rulers allocated among their officials, with the ownership of the land itself. Bernier also argued that despotism restricted commercial life in Mughal India. Rather than investing in mercantile ventures, merchants concealed their fortunes to protect them from seizure by despotic rulers.

"They find no other remedy to secure their Wealth, than to hide and dig their Money deep under Ground," Bernier wrote.[8]

The unchecked power of despots also led to low standards of living for the bulk of the population. Peasants were crushed under the heavy weight of the land tax, which left them on the margins of subsistence. Irfan Habib has offered a classic description from Mughal India: "It was inevitable that the actual burden on the peasantry should become so heavy in some areas as to encroach upon their means of survival. The collection of revenue of this magnitude . . . could not be a refined process. When the 'arrayatos' (raiyat, peasants) could not pay the revenue, says [the European traveler] Manrique, they were 'beaten unmercifully and maltreated'."[9] Artisans and other laborers were also believed to be defenseless against the unchecked exploitation of state officials. We encountered in the previous chapter Francisco Pelsaert's early seventeenth-century criticism of Mughal officialdom – "the Governor, the nobles, the Diwan, the Kotwal, the Bakhshi, and other royal officers" – for their oppression of workers.[10]

The characterization of the state as despotic became a standard feature of histories of Mughal India and it is found in the influential writings of W. H. Moreland and Irfan Habib.[11] From these sources, despotism entered the debate on divergence and Eric Jones and David Landes saw it as central to the backwardness of India.[12] Since the late 1970s, however, historians of India have questioned this picture of Mughal authority and the despotic view has been much discredited. Political power in Mughal India is now seen as diffuse with many individuals sharing the mantle of authority. According to Christopher Bayly,

The Mughals claimed universal dominion . . . But for the majority of their Hindu subjects power and authority in India had always been more like a complicated hierarchy than a scheme of "administration" or "government". The Mughal emperor was *Shah-an-Shah*, "king of kings", rather than king of India . . . But many of the attributes of what we would call the state pertained not to the emperor or his lieutenants, but to the Hindu kings of the localities, the rajas or to the notables who controlled resources and authority in the villages. The emperor's power and wealth could be great, but only if he was skilled in extracting money, soldiers and devotion from other kings.[13]

In this revised vision of the Mughal state, power was not concentrated in the hands of the emperor but rather distributed among numerous centers of authority. The Mughal Emperor rested on top of these multiple holders of power and ruled with their consent. The power of the emperor was not absolute but limited, which explains the perplexed words of a seventeenth-century English East India Company servant who wrote that in the Mughal Empire "every man honours the king, but no man obeys him."[14]

A more limited conception of the state – as resting upon continuous negotiations and shifting alliances with other centers of power – has emerged in the Ottoman case as well. New writings on the Ottoman Empire argue that the power of the sultan was neither absolute nor despotic but itself constituted through competition with other political and military authorities. According to one description, the Ottoman state was a "bargainer, negotiating and embracing individuals, social classes, and especially groups such as bandits, in order to control them and to establish its centralized rule over a vast territory."[15] Similar arguments have been made for political power in eighteenth-century China. In the zones of Qing imperial expansion in the eighteenth century, Peter Perdue has described a political order which was centered on negotiation and contestation between Qing authorities and local power holders. These were frontier zones and profoundly different from provinces closer to the imperial center, but even in Qing China proper, the state was a paper tiger. "By the eighteenth century, it was evident that there existed a serious disparity between the ambitions and the capacities of the state . . . The inbuilt irony of this powerful, rationalized administrative system was that it was much more effective at the top than at the bottom. For all its administrative sophistication, it was only tenuously in control of subcounty government, and hence of its own fiscal base in local society," Philip Kuhn writes.[16]

The overturning of "Oriental despotism" challenges another purported difference between European and Asian state systems. The existence of a network of small states in Europe is thought to have created political competition, which contributed to economic and social dynamism. In Asia, by contrast, despotic imperial states prevented such contestation, which eliminated an important source of economic growth and change. Eric Jones has put it succinctly: "A large empire which monopolised the means of coercion and was not threatened by more advanced neighbours had little incentive to adopt new methods. The states of Europe on the other hand were surrounded by actual or potential competitors . . . The states system was an insurance against economic and technological stagnation."[17] Jones also argues that the European state system "spread power around, wrong-headed and incontrovertible systems-wide decisions could not be imposed by some central authority . . . Thus no negative centralist decision could thwart change."[18]

These claims for a European difference rest upon an inflated sense of the centralization and administrative and coercive capabilities of imperial states in Asia. In the case of Mughal India, the diffuse nature of political power translated into a decentralized administrative order in which there was great variety, fluidity and contestation. Despite a long tradition of viewing the Mughal state as a sophisticated bureaucratic entity with extensive political and economic control over its territories, Mughal administration is now seen as limited in extent and reach. As in other parts of the world, Mughal rulers and officials were attempting to develop the technical capabilities to govern more effectively and to exercise greater hegemony within their territories. They could not escape the fact, however, that the Mughal state was a loose imperial layer of authority that sat on top of the diverse forms of local power. Mughal imperial dictates were felt most keenly in the North Indian heartland of the empire, especially in the towns and cities. In much of the empire, however, the state derived its political power and collected its revenues through a process of complex bargaining and negotiation with pre-existing power holders.[19]

Since the Mughal state was unable to eliminate other centers of authority, the establishment of the empire did not mean the end of political competition in the Indian subcontinent. Even in the heyday of Mughal rule, there was contestation at all levels of the political system. Inferior kings rose up in rebellion against superior kings. Chieftains fought chieftains. Rajputs resisted Mughal demands. It was a world of intense political conflict. The early eighteenth-century decline of the Mughal Empire is now attributed in part to the growing power of local power holders or zamindars in northern India, who resisted the revenue demands of the imperial state. The "revolts" organized by zamindars severely weakened the political structure of the empire, making it vulnerable to further attacks from both within and without.[20]

Because of this political contestation, Indian forms of military fiscalism, in which rulers rationalized and expanded revenue systems with the goal of building up military power, propelled the development of states and economies in the seventeenth and eighteenth centuries. The pressure to amass greater military capacities, a prerequisite for political success in the competitive Indian world, gave rise to innovations in administration, including incipient state bureaucracies, fiscal rationalization, standardization of weights and measures, and military reorganizations. All of these required heavy state expenditures. To meet these new financial demands, states also promoted the economic development of their realms, including support for the expansion of agriculture, which will be examined shortly. Military fiscalism also led to technological innovation, especially in the domain of armaments manufacture, which will be explored in Chapter 7.[21]

Just as the political and administrative coherence of the Mughal Empire has been questioned and a greater appreciation developed for competition and contestation, so the centralized dominance of the Ottoman and Chinese states has also been re-examined. In the Ottoman case, the importance of provincial power and autonomy has come to be increasingly recognized as historians moved out of the central archives of Istanbul to those of the provinces. Similarly, in China, the self-image of the state as all-powerful and all-knowing was different from the reality on the ground. Research in these two regions, however, has not progressed to the same extent as that on the Indian subcontinent.[22]

Property, markets and commercial life

A second set of long-held differences between Asia and Europe lies in the realm of property rights and markets. A variety of theoretical approaches may be grouped under these headings, including those of classical political economists such as Adam Smith, neoclassical economists who work within the framework of the new institutional economics, and Marxian scholars who emphasize the centrality of capitalism as a mode of production. Despite the diversity of approaches, they are unified by a belief in the exceptionalism of the West.

For Adam Smith, the uniqueness of Europe lay in its highly developed commercial economy. In Asia, the market economy was prevented from reaching European levels because of constraints on trade, which impeded the operation of the market. "The Chinese have little respect for foreign trade," Smith wrote. "Your beggarly commerce! was the language in which the Mandarins of Pekin used to talk to Mr. De Lange, the Russian envoy, concerning it. Foreign trade, therefore, is, in China, every way confined within a much narrower circle than that to which it would naturally extend itself, if more freedom was allowed to it."[23]

China may have been relatively isolated from maritime trade for much of the Ming period, but the state ban on external trade, which was imposed in 1372, was lifted in 1567. Even during the so-called ban on external trade, there was substantial contact between China's coastal regions and parts of East and Southeast Asia, and goods were exchanged under the aegis of the tribute system. After the lifting of the Ming trade ban, substantial quantities of silver flowed into the kingdom, an indication of China's vibrant maritime trade.[24] By the eighteenth century, the Chinese economy became increasingly reliant upon external commerce, especially for the silver which fueled an expansion in the money supply and was vital for internal commerce.[25]

In India, Smith saw caste and insecure property rights as the major impediments to the market. The caste system compelled the Indian "to follow the occupation of his father," which introduced rigidities in the market for labor and prevented supply from equaling demand. As a consequence, "either the wages of labour or the profits of stock" could deviate for long periods from their natural rates, leading to less efficient economic outcomes. The insecurity of property in India exacerbated the inefficiencies of the market. "In most governments of Asia," Smith wrote, echoing Bernier, since men are "continually afraid of the violence of their superiors, they frequently bury and conceal a great part of their stock" in order to protect it from the depredations of their rulers.[26] The result was a less optimal investment of capital, according to Smith.

In a similar vein, neoclassical economic historians have pointed to property rights and more efficient markets as crucial for Europe's exceptional path. The classic study is *The Rise of the Western World* by Douglass North and Robert Paul Thomas which argued that "the development of an efficient economic organization in Western Europe accounts for the rise of the West."[27] While not all economic historians share North's approach to the study of institutions, many concur with his conclusions on the greater efficiency of markets and security of property in Europe, including Eric Jones who believed that the commercial system of Europe was superior and more dynamic.[28] The exceptionalism of Europe's economic institutions is even dated to medieval times and not seen as a recent feature of Eurasian economic life.[29] These claims for the superiority of European institutions and the insecurity and inefficiency that characterized economic life in India and China do not accord with the historical evidence, however.

Caste and commerce

Caste was certainly a feature of life in the India of the seventeenth and eighteenth centuries, but it was neither as rigid nor as prominent as it was to become after 1800. While there was some correspondence between caste and occupation, there was also a great deal of fluidity and mobility. In eighteenth-century South India, for example, some of the most highly skilled weavers belonged to untouchable communities while members of so-called weaving castes worked as agriculturalists, traders and soldiers. *Parayans*, the canonical landless laborers of nineteenth-century South India, were found in a range of urban occupations and their physical prowess drew the attention of military contractors in the late eighteenth century. In western India, in response to changing conditions of demand, a number of tailors shifted to dyeing in the eighteenth century. Similarly, in Gujarat, when cloth demand was high, "Kunbis [cultivators] learnt the art of weaving fine quality piece-goods from the Khatri weavers who employed them." Finally, Irfan Habib notes that Muslims, who represented about a third of the Indian population, possessed "some tendency towards hereditary occupations," but could respond more easily to "enhanced demand for a new craft." There is also evidence from many parts of the subcontinent for the existence of individuals following mixed occupations, which belies the assumption of caste-imposed specialization.[30]

Caste became a more rigid institution in the nineteenth century with the colonial transformation of Indian society. However, in the commercially and politically dynamic world of the eighteenth century individuals and groups moved not only between occupations but also up and down the economic and political hierarchy. Susan Bayly has noted that many rulers of the "new kingdoms and dynamic smaller lordships which came into being across most of India in the eighteenth century" were descendants of poor peasants or pastoralists, but they possessed remarkable martial and political abilities which propelled their rise to power. "Relatively few of the new lords and revenue magnates were superior 'caste Hindus' in the modern sense," she concludes.[31] Similarly, in late eighteenth-century Bengal, the historian Gholam Hossein Khan lamented the rise of low-born men of commerce to positions of political prominence, which is evidence of the social mobility that was available to men of talent or money.[32]

Finally, research has found that caste, rather than impeding economic activity, may have facilitated it. Caste connections helped the Nattukottai Chettiars, a major South Indian banking community, forge relations of trust which were indispensable for business transactions conducted over long distances. In the case of merchants in Benares in the late eighteenth and early nineteenth centuries, Christopher Bayly has argued that "extended linkages of kinship and marriage, perceived by contemporary Indians and later commentators as 'caste', played a significant role in reinforcing the community of trust and mercantile intelligence which was essential to long-distance trading." Mercantile activities were not shaped only by caste in Benares, however, and Bayly found that even tightly organized family firms placed deep faith in agents who were of different castes. The bulk of credit transactions were also conducted beyond the boundaries of kin and caste, which indicates that while caste facilitated some business activities, it was not, according to Bayly, "the prime parameter of mercantile organization."[33]

At a more fundamental level, the widespread assumption that commercial life was more advanced in Europe than in Asia is open to question. As shown in the previous chapter, from the late sixteenth century the Indian subcontinent absorbed enormous quantities of New World silver and as a consequence possessed highly monetized economies. This monetization penetrated to the bottom of the social order, as the import of copper, cowries and badams and other low-value money materials would suggest.[34] The contrast with England, economically the most advanced region of Europe, is striking. Even in the closing decades of the eighteenth century there were tremendous shortages of coins in many English commercial centers. Pat Hudson, for one, has described the hardships that workers in Yorkshire faced as they had to accept wage payments in tokens, store credits and other forms of truck. Manufacturers resorted to this form of payment in part because of the unavailability of sufficient supplies of coins.[35]

In the highly monetized world of eighteenth-century India, individuals were embedded in complex networks of exchange that linked local, regional and global economies, and most inhabitants of the advanced, commercial regions were reliant upon trade to meet their daily needs. There was little production purely for subsistence. To give one example, the large-scale export of cotton textiles, described in the previous chapter, depended upon a massive trading network that took cotton from the interior parts of the subcontinent, where soils and rainfall patterns were appropriate for the cultivation of the fiber, to weaving villages on the coast. In exchange, salt, indispensable for life in the tropical Indian climate, was taken from pans along the sea to the population centers of the interior. Similarly, there was a significant trade in rice along coastal waters in which the grain was taken from surplus to deficit areas. The very sizable trade in these three essential commodities – salt, grain and cotton – suggests that for many Indians subsistence was afforded through the market.

The commercial boom of the seventeenth and eighteenth centuries also produced Smithian growth, in which the expansion of the market led to an extension of the division of labor and gains in productivity from specialization, much as R. Bin Wong and Kenneth Pomeranz have identified for China.[36] In seventeenth-century Bengal, for instance, growing European demand for cotton textiles and raw silk led to a reallocation of labor and capital for the manufacture of these high-value goods. As a result, the productive capacity of the region was not only used more efficiently but also significantly expanded.[37] In a number of regions in India, a growing demand for the commercial products of agriculture in the seventeenth and eighteenth centuries, including high-value foodstuffs for urban consumption and crops such as cotton for an expanding manufacturing sector, sparked a shift to higher-yielding, capital-intensive techniques on more specialized and better quality soils. Irfan Habib has documented such changes in the rural economy of Mughal northern India from the late sixteenth century, where "towns had not only to be fed, but had also to be supplied with raw materials for their crafts."[38] In seventeenth- and eighteenth-century South India, a growing demand for cotton pushed cultivation onto more productive, heavy black soils that required larger inputs of capital for the purchase of special breeds of cattle and heavier plows.[39] Similar changes have been identified in Bengal, which "underwent an unprecedented degree of commercialization" in the eighteenth century, embedding the agrarian economy deeply in market relations, according to Rajat Datta.[40] By the early nineteenth century, the district of Tinnevelly, at the tip of the Indian subcontinent, was characterized by a complex commercial order with a "highly differentiated landscape of agrarian commodity production."[41]

Efforts to assess the efficiency of markets in Europe and India are in their infancy. Carol H. Shiue and Wolfgang Keller have compared grain markets in China and Europe and concluded that in the late eighteenth century there were no large differences in market integration between China and Western Europe. At the regional level, Shiue and Keller found that England, which had the most integrated grain markets in Europe, had a more unified market than the Yangzi delta, its counterpart in China.[42] Roman Studer has conducted a similar exercise for India and Europe in the eighteenth and nineteenth centuries, but on a more limited empirical foundation.

Studer found that grain markets in the Indian subcontinent were less integrated than in Europe and, on that basis, concluded that the market system in India was less efficient. The empirical basis for this conclusion is thin, especially for the period before the 1790s, for which he draws upon rice prices and wheat prices from three locations each.[43] His evidence becomes more abundant from the early nineteenth century, but that material is a poor guide to markets in the eighteenth century. Between 1820 and 1850 a number of Indian regions suffered a deep depression and de-commercialization in which markets became less integrated as the volume of trade contracted dramatically. (In some places, the downturn began even before 1820.)[44] It is also not clear if the greater correlation of grain prices that Studer finds across Europe was due to better market integration or to greater covariance in weather. It is well known that rainfall in the Indian subcontinent could vary quite widely even within short distances, which translated into large local divergences in grain harvests.[45] Even if Studer's findings are correct and there were differences in the functioning of grain markets between Europe and India, this does not mean that in the eighteenth century the economy of Europe was more advanced than that of India. For in other respects, Indian economic performance surpassed that of Europe. Most critically, the divergence between Europe and Asia from the late eighteenth century was not a matter of markets but of technology and, as will be shown shortly, British technical breakthroughs relied upon an explicit rejection of market outcomes.

It is also not appropriate to generalize from the workings of a single market to the operation of the market system as a whole, whether for

Europe or for India. In the Indian case, the trade in grain may not be the best guide to the integration and efficiency of markets. Cotton was likely to have been traded on a larger scale and was probably the largest bulk item in the internal trade of both North and South India in the eighteenth century.[46] Capital markets may have also been better integrated than grain markets in India. In the seventeenth and eighteenth centuries, sizable sums were moved around the subcontinent with an instrument known as a *hundi* or *hundwi*. Rather than risk transporting large amounts of cash, merchants and others deposited their money with a *sarraf* or banker and received an order, or a hundi, upon the banking firm for that amount in another place. Within the Mughal Empire in the seventeenth century the charges on such a transfer ranged from 0.7% to 2.5% and Irfan Habib has noted that "the English factors, even when writing to their masters in London, who would be familiar with the 'exchange' charges in Europe . . . never suggest that the rates . . . were high or exorbitant." By the mid-eighteenth century, the system of hundis eliminated the need for cash in a number of commercial transactions.[47]

The low costs of money transfer reflect the integration of capital markets in the Mughal Empire. Although the quantity of data is limited, it appears that there was a convergence of interest rates in the seventeenth century, precisely the period when the hundi was becoming a more widely used credit instrument. In the early decades of the seventeenth century, Agra had the lowest interest rates in the empire, according to the evidence compiled by Irfan Habib. Over the course of the century, rates in Surat and Ahmedabad fell and converged with those in Agra, which was more than 600 miles from the former and 550 miles from the latter. By the third quarter of the seventeenth century, rates in all three centers were in the 6 to 9% range per year. In the South, which was outside the Mughal Empire in this period, interest rates also fell dramatically over the course of the seventeenth century, but remained higher than rates in the major commercial centers of North and West India. The cost of transferring funds to the South from Mughal territories via hundis was also higher, which suggests a link between Mughal sovereignty and the integration of the capital market. While it is not clear why rates were higher in the South, it may have been due to a less developed banking system.[48]

The rates of interest in Mughal India were higher than those in seventeenth-century England, but capital could be obtained in whatever quantities desired, according to English East India Company servants. In 1675, the annual rates on loans to the Company at Surat were 6 to 9%. According to Habib, the interest that the Company paid was "a little higher than the market rates," which means market rates may have fallen in the 5 to 8% range. The corresponding rates in England, drawn from the annual interest on short-term deposits and long-term annuities and mortgages, were 4 to 6%. These figures show that rates in England were lower, but on some loans the interest that was demanded would have been approximately the same, falling between 5 and 6%. The proportion of loans that fell in this area of overlap is, of course, not known.[49]

Systematic data on interest rates in eighteenth-century India are not available. However, Christopher Bayly reports that in the closing years of the century, the English East India Company could borrow in northern India at 5, 7 and 12% per year, depending on how quickly the funds were needed. By the early nineteenth century, European merchants were able to raise substantial funds at 5% from local bankers.[50] While this North Indian rate was higher than that on the long-term debt of the British state in the late eighteenth century, it was approximately the same as British short-term rates, which stood at 4–5%.[51]

Alongside this credit market that catered to the East India Company and big Indian merchants, there existed a parallel credit system in which substantial sums of money were dispersed at zero or very low rates of interest. In Mughal India, such loans included *taqavi* (taccavi), which were advances from the state to peasant cultivators for the purchase of seed, cattle or investment in agricultural improvement. No interest appears to have been charged for these loans. Artisanal production in Mughal India also relied upon advances of money from merchants who did not charge interest, but demanded delivery of the product within a contracted period.[52] Both forms of credit, again at no interest, were widespread in the eighteenth century and they were found in North India, Bengal and the South.[53] While there are reports of very high interest rates for peasants from village moneylenders – one from eighteenth-century Bengal claimed 12.5% per month on loans for two to three months – the volume of these transactions is not known.[54] However, interest-free loans in the form of taccavi and advances to artisans were sizable in the seventeenth and eighteenth centuries and were essential to the workings of both agriculture and manufacturing.

The broad band of interest rates – from 0 to 12.5% per month – is evidence of a segmented market in which the cost of loans varied according to the economic standing and the creditworthiness of the borrower. In such a scenario, the existence of high interest rates would not reflect a shortage of capital but rather the risks associated with the loan.[55] In Surat, the "common" market rate in 1665 was 9% a year, but for "merchants of a cleare reputation" it was 6%. In Ahmedabad, the English East India Company borrowed money in 1628 at 12% a year, but a borrower who pledged gold for the loan obtained nearly the same sum at 6%, or half the price.[56]

Such differentiated markets were found in eighteenth-century Britain as well, which points to the importance of relations of trust and reputation in credit markets, whether in Europe or the Indian subcontinent. Credit is at its core a social relation and therefore carries multiple prices, which can vary by the individual and by the type of transaction.[57] In both Europe and India, when trust was high, interest rates were low. When trust was low, credit was only obtained at very high rates or not at all. While the range of interest rates in India may have been greater than that found in Britain – running from 0 to 150% per annum – large sums of credit fueled both trade and production. The existence of usurious rates in India, however, should not obscure the fact that in the seventeenth and eighteenth centuries credit in sizable quantities was available in Britain and India at rates of interest that were roughly similar.

On a final note, although only a few observations are available, the low rates of insurance for long-distance trade are another indication of the sophistication and security of the financial system and commercial life in India. In early and mid-seventeenth-century Gujarat, the insurance premiums for the movement of goods on land ranged from 0.5 to 2.5%. The transport of cash by land could be insured at the rate of 1%. The costs of insuring on water ranged from 2 to 2.75%, with the lower rate for coastal shipping in 1622 and the higher for trade between Surat and the Persian Gulf in 1649. Insuring the coastal shipment of cash was more expensive and came to 4.5% in 1665. Habib has speculated that these low rates derived from widespread use of insurance facilities, which reduced the risk attached to any individual transaction.[58]

The marine insurance rates of Surat do not appear to have been vastly different from those of London. Rates are not available for seventeenth-century London, but premiums in the early 1730s ranged from 1.25 to 1.8% for summer sailings within Europe, while winter rates could go as high as 2.4%, depending upon the destination. For sailings to and from North America, the rates were 2.4%. The Jamaica trade was the costliest to insure with a rate of 3% to the island and 4.8% on summer and 6% on winter returns.[59] In the seventeenth century London insurance costs were likely to have been higher. Jan de Vries and Ad van der Woude, for example, believe that this was the case in the Amsterdam insurance market.[60] And given that interest rates declined in North India between the seventeenth and eighteenth centuries, it is likely that insurance premiums also fell in that period, which would have put the Indian and British rates for the eighteenth century in close proximity. Although the evidence is admittedly sparse, the marine insurance markets in Gujarat and Britain appear to have operated on similar footings in the seventeenth and eighteenth centuries.

Property rights and agriculture

The sophisticated commercial and financial systems that were built in India are evidence that property rights were not as insecure as François Bernier, Adam Smith and other seventeenth- and eighteenth-century Europeans imagined. Wealth was not hoarded or hidden from political authorities. Rather, there was a sophisticated banking, and even insurance, system that operated across sizable territories, which facilitated commerce. In the case of India, funds were transferred with ease across most parts of the vast subcontinent with financial instruments such as the hundi and letters of credit. For the security of trade, there was a system of insurance, which merchants exploited to protect themselves from the risks involved in exchanges over long distances. In South Asia, then, it would appear that merchants were devoting their energies to protecting themselves not from their rulers, but from risks associated with ventures on sea and land.

The historical evidence is also beginning to suggest that Indian merchants, rather than seeking to shelter themselves from the depredations of the state, were increasingly exerting leverage against the holders of political power. Karen Leonard has argued that the late seventeenth-century decline of the Mughal Empire was due to a withdrawal of banker support for the state.[61] While Leonard's claims have been challenged in the Mughal case, the importance of commercial men for the exercise of political power has been widely documented for the eighteenth century. In most regions of the subcontinent, the wealth and financial acumen of mercantile men – whether bankers, tax farmers or traders – were becoming essential to the operation of states. According to Christopher Bayly, "The covert and subtly exercised power of merchant bodies imposed limitations on what eighteenth-century rulers could do, and allowed commerce to achieve a more privileged position in regard to the military aristocracy."[62]

In eighteenth-century China as well there are signs that merchants were increasingly important for the operations of the state. The merchants who oversaw the salt monopoly, for example, were a major economic force and an increasingly valuable source of revenues for the Chinese state. In 1682, the salt tax accounted for 8.87 percent of total revenues and this figure climbed to 11.83 percent in 1766. According to Antonia Finnane,

For extraordinary expenses involving military or hydraulic undertakings, the salt merchants were a ready resource and could be marshaled into "returning the imperial grace" by making large contributions to the imperial coffers. For their part, the merchants worked closely with the metropolitan government. The Imperial Household Department in Beijing . . . lent out sums of between a few thousand and a million taels of silver to the merchants, which they invested with profit both to themselves and to their creditors.[63]

The greater security for merchant property is not the only difference in property relations between Europe and Asia that historians have pointed to as decisive for divergence. An influential strand of Marxian historical writing, put forward most forcefully by Robert Brenner, argues that the configuration of property rights that arose in rural England is critical for explaining the industrialization of Britain. According to Brenner,

What distinguished the English industrial development of the early modern period was its continuous character, its ability to sustain itself and to provide its own self-perpetuating dynamic. Here, once again, the key was to be found in the capitalist structure of agriculture. Agricultural improvement not only made it possible for an ever greater proportion of the population to leave the land to enter industry; equally important, it provided, directly and indirectly, the growing home market which was an essential ingredient in England's continued industrial growth.[64]

Brenner drew this conclusion on the basis of a comparison of agrarian class relations in Europe, but he and Christopher Isett have come to essentially the same conclusion from a comparison of England and the Yangzi delta.[65]

Brenner's arguments are questionable from the perspective of both Europe and India. From the vantage point of Europe, while the productivity of land in England doubled between the late middle ages and the early eighteenth century, it is difficult to find evidence that agriculture made a profound contribution to industrial development in the eighteenth and early nineteenth centuries. First, the growth rate of agricultural output was much lower than that of population during the British industrial revolution. The men, women and children of Britain relied upon increasing quantities of imported grain or in many cases from the late eighteenth century depressed their consumption of food. Many in Britain went hungry, especially during the very difficult decades of the 1790s, 1830s and 1840s. "If one asks how British agriculture fed the expanding population during the industrial revolution, the answer is – badly," Robert Allen has concluded.[66] Second, there is little indication that agriculture was decisive as a home market for manufactured goods. Patrick O'Brien and Nicholas Crafts, in separate studies, estimated that consumption of manufactures by agriculturalists increased by 30 percent in the eighteenth century. In that period, manufacturing output increased threefold. After 1800 agriculture's consumption of manufactures became even less important and urban and export markets were more important. Clearly more than agricultural improvement was necessary to meet the demand for the products of British industry.[67]

The Brenner argument for the centrality of agriculture in European industrial development is doubtful from the vantage point of Asia as well. Brenner and Isett acknowledge that their claim for the exceptionalism of English agriculture may not hold if examined from the perspective of areas outside Europe, and they cite Japan in particular. This, of course, is a familiar argument, in which Japan is taken to be a Western European society in Asia in its social, political and economic institutions. But their argument is problematic from the standpoint of the Indian subcontinent as well. In the eighteenth century, the most economically advanced regions of the subcontinent were unique on the world stage in that they were major producers and exporters not only of manufactured goods, most critically cotton cloth, but also of foodgrain. South India, for instance, was famed in the seventeenth and eighteenth centuries for its painted, printed and patterned cottons from Masulipatnam, Pulicat, Madras and other centers. In the seventeenth century, South India also routinely sent large quantities of rice across the Bay of Bengal to Southeast Asian emporia such as Malacca, Macassar and Aceh, to Ceylon and around the tip of India to food-deficit areas on the west coast, and even further west to Mocha and Bandar Abbas. In the eighteenth century, rice exports from the south declined, but were still sent periodically to Ceylon and to Southeast Asia.[68] Bengal was famed throughout the world for its silk, fine muslins and other textiles, but was also well known in the Indian Ocean for its cheap rice, which was consumed in grain-deficit areas along both coasts of the subcontinent, Ceylon and Southeast Asia.[69] And Gujarat exported not only cloth to the Persian Gulf and Red Sea in the eighteenth century but also rice, wheat and *mung*.[70]

The surpluses that Indian agriculture generated suggest that agrarian institutions worked effectively. While the regime of property rights was not identical with that found in Europe, it extended sufficient security and stability for investment and sophisticated systems of production.[71] Political institutions also contributed to the creation and maintenance of this highly productive agrarian order by financing improvement and investment through the institution of taccavi, a process which will be examined in greater detail shortly. Indian agricultural surpluses were also achieved without "sweating" labor, which stands in stark contrast to the general intensification of work in other economically advanced centers of Europe and Asia in the eighteenth century. Li Bozhong and Kaoru Sugihara have shown the general expansion in industriousness in East Asia in the eighteenth and nineteenth centuries.[72] And eighteenth-century Britain is, of course, famous for the enormous quantities of work and effort that were elicited from laborers. The most striking evidence for the more minimalist approach to work in South Asian rice agriculture comes from the sowing of rice, which was discussed briefly in the previous chapter. The subcontinent, in contrast to many other regions of Asia, had developed alternatives to rice transplantation, which is notoriously labor-intensive. Francis Buchanan, who surveyed several districts of South India in the early nineteenth century, described some of these, including sowing seeds by broadcast and with seed drills. The rice seeds underwent elaborate preparation before they were sown (soaking in water, encasing in manure, etc.) in order to ensure higher germination rates and, therefore, more efficient use of seed, but still the savings in labor from these alternatives to transplantation were enormous. In Bengal as well, much rice was sown by broadcast well into the nineteenth century.[73]

Data on occupational distributions also point to the high agricultural productivity of the rice-growing regions in India. A 1775 survey of the area of Rangamati in Bengal reported that out of 256 households, only 101, or 39%, were cultivators. The remainder were scattered among a number of professions, the largest being officials (33 households), silkworm breeders (22), coolies (22), milkmen (17) and mendicants (13), but there were also cotton and silk weavers, smiths, oilpressers, shopkeepers and grocers, fishmongers, bamboo cutters and a barber. A 1791 census of the village of Sibpur, also in Bengal, revealed that out of 419 Hindu households, only 106 (25%) were pure agriculturalists while 15% were artisans, 22% were fishermen and 21% were upper-caste gentry.[74] While it is not known to what extent these local surveys are representative of Bengal as a whole, they do provide evidence of the diverse economic order and the substantial non-agricultural population in some areas in the eighteenth century.

While such detailed occupational surveys do not exist for the advanced parts of South India, it is possible to estimate the proportion of the labor force that worked in agriculture from scattered early nineteenth-century evidence. An 1804 census of Tanjore reported that 62% of the agricultural population consisted of landowners, who would not have done any of the work of cultivation, and 38% were laborers. While the fraction of the population that was agricultural is not given in this census, an 1850 source put it at 62%. Combining these figures, the proportion of laborers in agriculture in Tanjore is 24%. If another 5% is added for tenant-cultivators, which is probably on the high side, the agricultural proportion is 29%.[75] In other rice-growing districts the fraction of the population who were laborers in agriculture was about the same or lower. In Trichinipoly, an 1830 source gives it as 21%. In Tinnevelly, in 1823 it was reported to be 16%.[76] Therefore, the rice zones – where perhaps two-thirds to three-quarters of the population of South India was concentrated in the eighteenth century – had a small fraction of their population, somewhere in the range of 25 to 30%, devoting their energy to the work of agriculture. This is well within the realm of possibility when we consider the great productivity of South Indian rice cultivation – double cropping was common and triple cropping not unheard of – and that in England about 32% of the labor force was in agriculture around 1700.[77]

The economically advanced maritime regions of the Indian subcontinent, therefore, possessed highly productive agricultural regimes which fed a sizable non-agricultural population and at the same time generated grain surpluses which were exported to the trading world of the Indian Ocean. Yet, no significant industrial development emerged in South Asia. Therefore, the Brenner argument for the centrality of agricultural productivity, which he sees as an outcome of agrarian class structures and property relations, does not provide an explanation for the different paths of economic development across Eurasia. Britain's unique path of industrial development did not have its roots in agriculture.

Demography and ecology

A third area in which it is believed that Europe differed from Asia is in demographic regimes. This difference has its origins in the writings of Thomas Malthus, who argued that food production, which was set by the quantity of land, set a ceiling on population. Malthus argued that in Europe the equilibrium between population and food was maintained through preventive checks, which reduced fertility, the most important being late female marriage. In the absence of significant numbers of pre-marital pregnancies, with late marriage a woman's child-bearing years were shortened, which lowered fertility rates and population growth. This was a rational response to the need to limit population and was also spurred by the widespread desire in Europe to marry only after saving money to set up a household and family. In Asia, preventive checks were less in evidence so population grew, only to be reduced periodically by positive checks, such as famines, epidemics and social strife, which temporarily increased mortality. Malthus thought that the preventive response of late female marriage was not available to Chinese and Indians because of cultural attitudes that favored early and universal marriage for women, which were combined with a primordial desire for offspring, especially males.

These Malthusian contrasts became a demographic conventional wisdom in the twentieth century with the influential work of John

Hajnal, who argued that northwestern Europe was home to late marriage and small families, which were the outcomes of economic calculation, while in India and China, cultural values dictated earlier marriage and there were fewer pressures to reduce family size.[78] To arrive at this contrast, Hajnal compared twentieth-century demographic data from India and China with the historical evidence for eighteenth-century Europe. (With this procedure, Hajnal assumed that Asian marriage and household systems had remained unchanged for several centuries.) Alan Macfarlane made these differences in demographic behavior central to the explanation of economic divergence and argued that the lower rates of population growth in Western Europe led to higher rates of saving and therefore more investment and higher growth. In Asia, rapidly expanding numbers translated into more consumption and less saving, which produced lower growth rates.[79]

A growing body of research on the population history of India and China challenges a number of elements in the Malthusian view. In the case of China, this research shows that Malthus overestimated the extent and efficacy of the positive check. In the eighteenth century, Chinese famines, for instance, were less frequent and less lethal than long believed. New research on the demographic history of China has also found that levels of female fertility were much lower than Malthus believed, a conclusion which is supported by different kinds of evidence. For instance, mortality rates were comparable in Europe and China, which is a sign that the Chinese birth rate was not dramatically higher.[80] It also appears that female fertility rates in the eighteenth century were virtually identical in China and Europe due to a number of Chinese customs that limited childbearing. These included a long gap between marriage and the birth of the first child; an early suspension of sexual activity, which historians attribute to a "cultural tradition of carnal restraint"; and a late age for infant weaning, which lengthened the gap between pregnancies.[81] Finally, in eighteenth-century China infanticide, especially of females, was used to keep family sizes within the desired range, which acted as a check on population growth.[82]

These findings indicate that the Malthusian belief in a primordial Chinese desire for children and the less rational Chinese approach to fertility is not supported by the evidence. The evidence for the Indian subcontinent is more slender, but points to similar conclusions. The demographic history of the Indian subcontinent does not come into sharp focus until the late nineteenth century, when decennial censuses were established under British rule. Nevertheless, for several regions of the subcontinent local and regional demographic evidence from the early nineteenth century reveals a population and household pattern very different from that imagined by Malthus and his intellectual successors.

Let us begin with the structure of the family and household. John Hajnal argued that the nuclear family was unique to Northwest Europe, while from central Europe to Japan, with India and Southeast Asia included, the joint family prevailed. These different family structures had implications for fertility and population, according to Hajnal. In areas where joint families were the norm, it was easier for households to support married adults who were not fully employed, which led to higher fertility, higher birth rates and higher population growth rates. In northwestern Europe, the absence of joint households meant that underemployed adults could be supported only with difficulty. Therefore, young men and women delayed marriage, often by entering into service, and the later age of female marriage trans- lated into lower fertility, lower birth rates and lower population growth rates.[83]

Hajnal drew this conclusion from twentieth-century data on households in India and China. The historical evidence, however, shows that the joint family was less common in eighteenth- and early nineteenth-century India than is widely believed. Sumit Guha, in some of the most detailed historical inquiries to date, found highly individu- alist behavior among family members in eighteenth-century western India. Self-interested decisions about property produced fragmented – one could even venture to call them nuclear – family and household forms. Upon entering the early colonial period more detailed evidence on household form and structure is available for western India from small surveys and censuses. An 1820 survey of several districts found that the number of men per family ranged from 1.36 to 1.53. The figure was lower in rural areas, in some places coming very close to one male per family. The number of males per family was also low in families of unskilled laborers in towns, presumably because they were not tied to their natal family for the transmission of either property or skills, which enabled them to marry and leave the birth home at a lower age. Brahmins in the city of Pune had 2.13 adult males per family, the highest figure in the survey, which may reflect a later age of marriage for Brahmin men and a greater prevalence of joint family structures. Taking this data together, Guha concludes that the nuclear family was the norm in households in western India in the early nineteenth century.[84]

Family size was also fairly small in the early nineteenth century. Guha reports that a survey conducted in 1820 found 4.04 to 4.78 persons per family. The number of persons per house, which included unrelated servants and others, ranged from 4.43 to 5.40. Other surveys of the region over the next few decades yielded similar figures.[85] An 1822 survey of Bengal, Bihar and Orissa reported that there were 5.14 persons per house.[86] An 1821 survey of Cochin found 3.7 persons per house.[87] These figures for the Indian subcontinent are comparable with, or in some cases even less than, those for Europe. In England, between 1574 and 1821 the average number of persons per household was 4.8. In Denmark in 1787, the figure was 5.2 persons per house and in Norway in 1801 it was 5.7.[88]

Therefore, despite the early age of marriage for females in the subcontinent, the data on family and household size shows that in the late eighteenth and early nineteenth centuries the number of children per mother in India was comparable to the figures for Europe. This may have been due to high background mortality rates for infants and children, but data on this is not available till the latter part of the century, when economic and social conditions were very different. Small family size, however, was not only a function of mortality, but also fertility, for which data, again, is extremely scarce. Evidence from the late nineteenth century is striking, however, and shows that fertility in earlier periods may not have been inordinately high.

Some of this evidence comes from the central Indian province of Berar where the age distribution of the population in the late nineteenth century was not particularly young, which is "significant because, *ceteris paribus*, it implies . . . a population with only a 'moderate' – as opposed to a 'high' – level of fertility," according to the historical demographer Tim Dyson.[89] The low level of fertility may have been due to male out-migration which reduced the frequency of sexual intercourse and sometimes delayed cohabitation after marriage. The custom of breastfeeding also "played a major fertility-limiting role," Dyson writes, as a child was generally breastfed for a year and often two, three or more years.[90] Finally, widowhood served to depress female fertility. In the early decades of the twentieth century, 6 percent of women between the ages of 20 and 29 in Berar were widows. For women in their thirties and forties, the figures were 18 and 41 percent, respectively. Although widow remarriage was possible for many caste groups, it was not prevalent because of the difficulties it posed for inheritance of property and descent, according to Dyson. Widow remarriage rates may have also been influenced by economic conditions. In the prosperous first decade of the twentieth century, widows remarried at higher rates than in the more difficult decades that preceded and followed it.[91]

The rational approach that Indians brought to decisions about marriage and family has also been documented for the Punjab in the first half of the twentieth century where several strategies were followed to reduce family size and prevent the subdivision of land-holdings. These included forcing some sons to remain unmarried, which did not violate the cultural preference for universal female marriage, but reduced the number of heirs. Limits on male marriage were also combined with informal fraternal polyandry, a practice in which one brother married and the others shared conjugal rights in the wife. The brothers jointly raised any children, who inherited the property of all the brothers. These strategies could also be combined with female infanticide and the neglect of female babies.[92]

These examples are evidence that preventive checks did operate in the Indian subcontinent in the nineteenth and early twentieth centuries. While detailed evidence on preventive methods is not available for earlier time periods, female infanticide was practiced in the eighteenth century in some regions of the subcontinent.[93] Limits on widow remarriage, deriving from caste prohibitions as well as economic choice, would have also lowered population growth rates in the eighteenth century, especially for high-status Hindu groups. Therefore, it is not the case that the Indian subcontinent was only familiar with positive checks to population growth. In common with Europeans, Indians followed a number of strategies for limiting family size in accordance with economic, social and cultural goals and dictates.

These revisionist findings for India and China show that Malthusian arguments for significant demographic differences between East and West are not tenable. The contrasts in population dynamics were thought to be significant because the lower birth rates in Europe contributed to higher rates of saving and investment, and thus more accumulation of capital and eventually more rapid economic growth. It was not only a superior demographic regime that was thought to give Europeans an advantage in capital accumulation, however. Eric Jones has also pointed to fundamental differences between Europe and Asia in the frequency and severity of disasters. Cataclysmic events – whether earthquakes, famines, wars or epidemics – could quickly destroy a capital stock that had been pains-takingly assembled over generations. According to Jones, Europe was better insulated than Asia from such disasters and recovered from them more rapidly. These qualities contributed to Europe's exceptional path of development.[94]

For Jones, the most important climatic instability was fluctuations in rainfall. Europe was better protected from water-related disasters because of more stable rainfall patterns than Asia, where extremes such as drought and flooding were more common. European agricul-ture was also less prone to pests and plant diseases, especially insect threats which could destroy a crop very rapidly. As a consequence, in India and China shortfalls in food production, whether due to climate or biology, were more frequent, as were the famines that often accom-panied harvest failures. The result was a greater loss of life and property in Asia. Jones put it succinctly with reference to India, "There were insufficient carry-over stocks to provide against years when the monsoon failed over a wide region. Transport and communi-cations were too primitive to bring in food on a mass scale . . . A solution awaited not only better social organisation but the improvement of agricultural productivity and of communications."[95] And, "One harvest failure could cause serious mortality; two, closely spaced as they might be when exogenous changes in the weather were acting on agriculture, could bring catastrophe."[96] Conditions in China were much the same, save for the existence of cannibalism as a survival mechanism. "But certainly the European record nowhere approaches the Chinese for overall frequency of cannibalism," Jones writes.[97]

A close examination of the famine record in India in the seventeenth and eighteenth centuries reveals a different picture. The frequent food shortfalls Jones sees as characteristic of the Indian subcontinent as a whole were common only in areas that were reliant upon rainfed, as opposed to irrigated, agricultural systems. Late eighteenth-century evidence from one such dry locale in South India reveals that shortfalls of crops were not uncommon, but one should not generalize about South India, let alone the whole of the subcontinent, on the basis of these dry districts.[98] Dry areas were prone to crop fluctuations, but harvest shortfalls were generally localized, at times confined to a network of a few dozen villages. Although dry zones were crisscrossed by trade routes – they were the source of raw cotton, for instance – transport costs limited the scale and scope of the trade in grain. To deal with this limitation, the inhabitants were used to being geographically mobile and traveled to places where grain supplies were abundant. Relying upon extensive intelligence networks, it was typical for peasants to leave areas of grain shortage and migrate to where it was plentiful. This strategy was supported by the political institutions of eighteenth-century India, most critically a political system that did not limit the mobility of peasants, artisans and others. Therefore, peasants and craftsmen were not hindered in their search for grain. In fact, they received incentives to move in the form of revenue concessions and even loans for investment, or taccavi, which also helped to hasten recovery after disasters.[99]

The dry areas of the subcontinent were sparsely populated in the eighteenth century, exposing only a fraction of the Indian population to the most extreme vagaries of the monsoon. The bulk of the population was concentrated in river valleys and deltas where water supplies were more secure and a network of dams, waterways, wells and water storage systems meant that harvests were more reliable. Crop failures in these areas were extremely rare events. In the century before 1780, there was only one crisis of rice cultivation in the Tanjore delta, which was not only the rice bowl of the southern region, but also a source of rice for Ceylon, Southeast Asia and the west coast of India. In the late 1720s, Tanjore was struck by a series of harvest disasters whose origins remain obscure, but there is evidence that there were some poor monsoons. (One source has speculated that a political conflict led the rulers of Mysore to erect a dam on the Cauvery River, which reduced supplies of water to Tanjore. The subsequent shortages of water paralyzed rice growing in Tanjore, giving rise to a massive crisis in the late 1720s.) Aside from this brief interlude, however, Tanjore's rice regime was a model of stability.[100]

Such a record of security was characteristic of other parts of the subcontinent where there were also well-developed systems for water control, including Bengal and Gujarat. The famine of 1630 in the latter region has received much attention for devastating the most valuable province of the Mughal Empire. Yet, the region was famine-free for much of the rest of the seventeenth and eighteenth centuries. Similarly, the massive disaster of 1769–70 in Bengal has been used to illustrate the subcontinent's vulnerability to famine. Eric Jones points to the standard figure of 10 million dead from lack of food in those years and observes that the loss of life as a proportion of the continental population was ten times that of the devastating East Prussian famine of 1708–11.[101] The data to calculate mortality in the Bengal famine accurately are not available. However, Rajat Datta argues that this figure, while standard, is a gross exaggeration and he estimates that mortality was less than a tenth of that number. Datta also notes that the lack of epidemic disease in 1769–70 would point to lower mortality rates.[102]

Jones pays little attention to the long security and stability of Bengal's agriculture in the several decades before the late 1760s. Rather he assumes a "constant background of severe Asian famines."[103] Although droughts and food shortages were not unknown in Bengal, in the words of Rajat Datta, "nothing like 1769–70 had ever occurred in the province."[104] The crisis of those years was severe because of the unusually long drought that hit the western part of the region. From August 1769 to January 1770 not a drop of rain fell on the area and rice fields had so hardened that they were difficult to plow. The lack of water also destroyed crops that were essential for the work of Bengal's artisans, including cotton and mulberry.[105]

The Bengal famine of 1769–70 may be labeled the first great famine of the colonial period, however, and the English East India Company's response to the crisis deepened nature's impact. The Company had just consolidated its rule in the region and it stringently collected revenue. Its collections at the height of the crisis, in the fiscal years of 1769–70 and 1770–1, were higher than those in 1765–6. Writing after the event, Warren Hastings, the great eighteenth-century Company man and administrator, acknowledged that the drought of 1769–70 caused so much misery because revenue collection was "violently kept up to its former standard."[106] This was combined with minimal relief efforts by the Company state, in contrast to pre-British political practices as well as to those of Indian commercial and political leaders, who organized food distribution on a massive scale. In the city of Murshidabad, the Company devoted 100,000 rupees for poor relief, while four rich residents of the city contributed 47,250 rupees. In the city of Patna, one wealthy individual spent 30,000 rupees to purchase and transport rice from Benaras for the hungry and destitute, and "in this manner," according to a British account, "an immense multitude came to be rescued from the jaws of imminent death." Such relief efforts were feasible because supplies of rice were plentiful in the region as a whole. The drought was confined to several districts of western Bengal while the rest of the province had bumper harvests.[107]

Another failure of the Company state in Bengal was its reluctance to distribute taccavi, or advances of capital, to cultivators for the restoration of production systems after the drought and famine. "There was an insignificant amount of financial aid or taccavi provided to help the cultivators to begin production for the next agricultural season," Rajat Datta has written.[108] Support of this sort was a key obligation of pre-colonial states across the subcontinent and it was the duty of rulers to make extensive loans, typically at no interest as we have seen, for the maintenance and expansion of the agrarian order during good times and especially for the regeneration of that order after bad times. Agriculturalists used this money to obtain tools and equipment, restore irrigation systems, replenish cattle stocks and purchase seed. Therefore, in contrast to Europe, states in the Indian subcontinent were intimately involved with investment and improvement in agriculture. The Company state, however, failed to operate with these Indian principles, which slowed the recovery from the disaster.

In eighteenth-century India, because of institutions such as taccavi, agricultural production was restored rapidly after disruptions. One measure of the speed of recovery is rice prices, which even after major periods of grain shortfalls returned to their pre-crisis levels within a few years. In the case of South India in the late 1720s, rice prices peaked in 1729 and returned to their pre-crisis levels by the following year. Even after the Bengal famine of 1769–70, where taccavi was limited, rice prices returned to their pre-famine levels within two years.[109] Taccavi and other forms of state support for agriculture made possible quick recoveries not only from famines but also from warfare and other disasters. Christopher Bayly has shown that the economy of eighteenth-century North India weathered war and political change because of the "movement of resources – capital, labour and skills – across the landscape" and the "flexibility and adaptability of the contemporary political economy." Bayly argued that "the withdrawal of resources from some areas was often matched by their reinvestment elsewhere." Therefore, the fluid and flexible political and economic institutions of the eighteenth century made the advanced regions of the subcontinent enormously resilient.[110] The establishment of British rule destroyed many of these institutions, creating the brittle and crisis-prone system of the nineteenth century, which was not characteristic of the subcontinent in earlier eras.

Max Weber and individual and social rationality

The Malthusian distinction between preventive and positive checks rests on an opposition between reason and nature. The preventive checks of Europe were a calculated response to economic conditions, leading to superior strategies for survival. Asians, by contrast, were subject to their animal impulses and populations had to be kept in check through the relentless operation of the forces of nature, including dearth, disease and disaster. From the late nineteenth century, the writings of Max Weber gave greater prominence to differences in rationality between East and West. For Weber, the emergence of Protestantism in sixteenth-century Europe contributed to the development of a more systematic and instrumental approach to economic life, which produced an exceptional path of development.[111] Weber conceded that religious ideas in both India and China contained the seeds of rationalization, but these were blocked from their full development.

Capitalism for Weber was not simply the drive to make money or the greed for goods but a rational and methodical approach to economic activity, which made its appearance only in the West.[112] Although rational procedures of various kinds were developed outside Europe, they failed to have a revolutionary impact. "Calculation, even with decimals, and algebra have been carried on in India, where the decimal system was invented. But it was only made use of by developing capitalism in the West, while in India it led to no modern arithmetic or book-keeping."[113]

In his studies of Asia, however, Weber, in contrast to many other thinkers, acknowledged that India and China possessed highly developed and sophisticated forms of rationality, but these were impeded from entering "upon that path of rationalization which is peculiar to the Occident."[114] The "absence of all metaphysics and almost all residues of religious anchorage" made Confucianism, according to Weber, "rationalist to such a far-going extent that it stands at the extreme boundary of what one might possibly call a 'religious' ethic."[115] Despite this high degree of rationalism, an impersonal rationalization of the sort that Puritanism yielded did not develop in China because Confucianism "tended to tie the individual ever anew to his sib [kinship or clan] members." In other words, individual action was subordinated to the demands of the kin group, which posed an "obstacle to rationalizing the religious ethic."[116]

Weber's arguments on India are similar. He acknowledged the rationalism of the doctrine of karma, calling it one of the three most "rationally satisfactory answers to the questioning for the basis of the incongruity between destiny and merit."[117] Elsewhere, Weber called karma the "most consistent theodicy ever produced by history."[118] Therefore, Indians were capable of a high level of rational thinking and argumentation. Nevertheless, modern capitalism rooted in instrumental rationality did not emerge in the subcontinent because of the caste system, which was "completely traditionalistic and anti-rational in its effects."[119] Weber elaborated, "A ritual law in which every change of occupation, every change in work technique, may result in ritual degradation is certainly not capable of giving birth to economic and technical revolutions from within itself, or even of facilitating the first germination of capitalism in its midst."[120]

There is much that is problematic in Weber's comparative account. One may begin with its method, which is profoundly unhistorical, a fact that Weber himself acknowledged: "In order to make this attempt, the author must take the liberty of being 'unhistorical,' in the sense that the ethics of individual religions are presented systematically and essentially in greater unity than has ever been the case in the flux of their actual development . . . The author has always underscored those features in the total picture of a religion which have been decisive for the fashioning of the *practical* way of life, as well as those which distinguish one religion from another."[121] Faithful to these methodological dictates, in *The Religion of India*, Weber moves seamlessly from British census reports to writings from the classical age and quotations from the Vedas. These materials span some three millennia. Such a procedure serves to reinforce the notion of Indian changelessness. By contrast, in *The Protestant Ethic*, Weber's sources are chiefly from the seventeenth and eighteenth centuries, which is no doubt problematic, but the shorter time span that is covered makes it easier to portray Protestantism as a motor of change in world history.

Weber's procedure was to construct a series of essentialized civilizations – what he called ideal types – that are moored in space but not in time. There is no room for hybridities, dissonances and contradictions. This process of essentialization was aided by the focus on world religions. This approach to the various faiths of the world was itself a product of the late nineteenth century as exemplified by gatherings such as the World Congress of Religions in 1893. The defining of world religions had the effect of creating unity and coherence where there was none. Therefore, Weber in a variety of ways greatly simplified the complex task of discerning an economic ethic and rationalization potential in a set of beliefs about the meaning of the world and of life.

A sizable critique of Weberian understandings of Asia has accumulated over the years as historians and historically minded anthropologists have detailed the methodical and rational approach that individuals, especially in India and China, brought to their economic activities. In the Indian subcontinent, merchants engaged in careful calculations for their commercial transactions. Their methodical procedures were objectified in the form of sophisticated accounting techniques that even went beyond the recording of debits and credits in double-entry bookkeeping. According to Christopher Bayly, they "provided a map of the relationships between the family firm and the economy as a whole."[122] In the seventeenth and eighteenth centuries, manuals were written on the science of accountancy in northern India, which spread knowledge and practice of numeracy and calculation. These works, reflecting the syncretic culture of the region, drew upon the arithmetic and accounting systems of Hindu merchants and procedures from Iranian and Mughal sources and were composed in Persian.[123] There is evidence that the keeping of accounts was not restricted to merchants. Weavers in eighteenth-century South India, for example, were well known for keeping a record on cadjans (palm leaves) of their transactions – which could be extremely complex as they included advances of cash from several merchants, purchases of materials such as yarn, oil, tools and equipment, sale prices for cloth, and so on. This suggests that numerical thinking and economic calculation may have diffused quite widely among South Indians, but the evidence for this is very difficult to recover from the surviving sources. Frank Perlin also argues that the plentiful material on the profusion of small value moneys provides evidence that market transactions were common and thus a market mentality was widespread.[124]

In China as well economic practices in the seventeenth and eighteenth centuries were rationalized in a number of respects. In mid-eighteenth-century Hankou, for example, the family management of firms was giving way to professional managers. Over the next several decades a sizable number of business enterprises in the city were based on partnerships of merchants from a variety of regions and were organized on a joint-stock basis. By the mid-nineteenth century, a distinction between managing partners and investing partners, with the former having responsibility for the operation of the enterprise, had emerged. In order to keep track of the profits and losses that should accrue to each partner, sophisticated forms of capital accounting were utilized. Some of these techniques of accounting built upon classic forms that had been used in China for several centuries. Therefore, the use of accounts as a means for the methodical and rational pursuit of profit in China appears to have developed roughly in parallel with Europe.[125]

In both India and China, rationality and calculation not only informed the actions of individuals, but began to infuse the social order as a whole. In the subcontinent, this was most evident in changes in state practices in the seventeenth and eighteenth centuries in which a number of dimensions of revenue collection began to be rationalized. In seventeenth-century Rajasthan, state accounting documents began to be modeled upon the account books of merchants and took the merchant form of double entries that simultaneously kept track of inflows and outflows of funds. According to Christopher Bayly, this phenomenon was part of a larger interpenetration of commercial and state cultures in the Mughal period, which promoted rationalization at a social level. The Persian manuals on accounting, mentioned previously, emerged out of this syncretic culture of practical rationality. In turn, these works shaped the practices of commercial and political men as they both read and put into practice the knowledge the manuals contained.[126]

The rationalization of state revenue systems reached great heights in the seventeenth and eighteenth centuries in the Maratha territories of western India. In this region, Maratha rulers embarked upon a major project to standardize measurement systems, especially of land, in order more accurately to calculate the productive potential of their territories and, with this knowledge, to tax more efficiently.[127] The tasks of administration increasingly involved the use of paper for the storage and transmission of information, which gave rise to a proliferation of accounts and accountants. This in turn spawned an administrative cadre. Maratha rulers also compiled what Frank Perlin has labeled a "'library' of categories and techniques" which an expanding group of administrative experts possessed and transmitted to others and deployed in the interests of state power.[128] What we have here is the beginnings of a state bureaucracy that had wide resonances in the Indian subcontinent in the eighteenth century.[129]

Conclusion

A substantial body of research on early-modern India and China – in the case of the former much of it conducted from the 1970s – demands a radical revision of the belief in the superiority of the political and economic institutions of Europe. The advanced regions of India and China were dynamic commercial economies; engaged in substantial local, regional and long-distance trade; gave rise to economic specialization; and witnessed economic growth and high levels of prosperity. We no longer have a stagnant East that is contrasted to a commercially dynamic West. In demographic terms as well, the Malthusian differences between Europe and Asia are also largely without substance and Europe was not uniquely possessed of preventive checks while India and China had to resort to positive checks. On the political front, states in India were not despotic, which gave rise to sustained competition, propelling the development of administrative capacities, local and regional economies, and technological capabilities.

The rejection of these simplistic, classical dualisms makes the explanation of divergence more difficult. It cannot be attributed to the existence of Smithian growth in Europe and its absence in Asia. Nor can it be explained with reference to economic or political features which Europe possessed but Asia did not, such as more efficient markets, state competition, secure systems of property, uniquely productive agricultural systems, exceptional checks on population or instrumental rationality. To complicate matters further, while economic and property institutions are important, they can only partly account for differences in long-run economic growth. In one influential cross-national quantitative study, differences in these institutions explain only about a quarter of the variation in income, indicating that more than private property rights and restrained states are needed to explain the wealth and poverty of nations.[130]

S. R. Epstein observed that the modern industrial economy is at heart a product of modern technology. Institutional change – no matter how extensive or intensive – could not have produced an industrial order in the absence of profound technological breakthroughs. As Epstein put it:

Smithian growth was a necessary but not sufficient cause of the technological and organizational changes associated with modern industrialization . . . The reason why Smithian growth and industrial growth are not causally linked is that industrialization was first and foremost a technological revolution . . . The question of what caused the industrial revolution is therefore conceptually and empirically distinct from the question of what caused pre-modern, Smithian growth.[131]

The divergence between Europe and Asia was caused by differences in technological change. The next part, which consists of three chapters, examines the critical breakthroughs associated with cotton and coal in eighteenth-century Britain, but situates them in their global and ecological context, along with the political decisions and choices which promoted innovation in these areas. The final part returns to the subcontinent to examine the technological history of India and explores the economic and political context in which the technological frontier was expanded in the seventeenth and eighteenth centuries, only to contract in the nineteenth under British rule.

PART II

The divergence of Britain

4 | *The European response to Indian cottons*

Introduction

In the late seventeenth century consumers in Europe embraced the cotton textiles of India for their beauty, convenience and fashionability. European cloth manufacturers were less welcoming as they saw the Indian goods as a threat to their livelihoods and in many parts of Europe agitations were launched to block imports from the subcontinent, virtually all of which succeeded. Antipathy to Indian cottons was not the only response of European textile manufacturers, however. From the late seventeenth century, opposition to Indian goods was accompanied by efforts to imitate them. In Western, Southern and Central Europe, cloth printers set up shop with linen cloth from Europe or plain white calicoes from India and attempted to reproduce the chintzes that were so characteristic of the subcontinent. The growing demand for cotton fabrics led spinners and weavers to work with the unfamiliar fiber of the cotton plant to create the wide variety of plain, striped and checked cloths that were so desired in Europe, West Africa and the Americas. At times, the silk and wool opponents of Indian imports turned their fury upon local manufacturers who from the eighteenth century were slowly taking over markets with their new cotton goods.

The future was to be with cotton, however. From its home in the Indian subcontinent, the art of turning the cotton boll into cloth of extraordinary beauty, comfort and versatility migrated to Europe. Imitation in the seventeenth century led 150 years later to Western Europe becoming the center of the world's cotton manufacturing. The migration of this industry marked a great transformation in the global economy. The Indian subcontinent was displaced as the major supplier of cotton textiles to the world market and that honor fell to the leading manufacturers of Europe, especially of Britain. This shift is, therefore, of seminal importance for understanding the divergence in paths of economic development across Europe and Asia.

The movement of the cotton industry from India to Britain emerged from an arduous process of learning by doing in which British cotton manufacturers, as well as those in other European nations, worked to perfect their imitations of Indian cotton goods. These efforts to replicate Indian manufactures spanned plain white calicoes and muslins, printed cloths, and striped and checked textiles which were patterned in the loom with dyed yarns. It was not an easy process as European textile workers had to develop the skills and knowledge necessary to manufacture cotton cloth to Indian specifications and standards and to match Indian goods in price and quality. The key breakthroughs that made this possible were the inventions of spinning machinery in Britain in the 1760s and 1770s.

Stanley Chapman and Serge Chassagne have remarked that the problem that Europeans faced with cotton "was not to create demand, for that already existed in abundance, but to reach oriental standards."[1] With this perspective, a longstanding puzzle can now be answered: why did major technological breakthroughs in eighteenth-century British textile manufacturing take place in the relatively minor cotton industry, as opposed to the much larger and more established wool industry, and in the relatively new textile region of Lancashire, and not the historically important and longer established centers of wool? The successful innovator in cotton had a market of truly global proportions.[2]

Imitation of Indian cottons: calico printing

European attempts to imitate Indian goods began with calico printing and the first European cotton printing works were established in Marseilles in the 1640s. This port in southern France led the way because of its longstanding trade links with the eastern Mediterranean which gave the merchants and artisans of the city a long familiarity with the cottons of India, Iran, the Levant and Turkey. Within a few decades, cotton cloth printing had expanded to London, Amersfoort, Berlin, Frankfurt, Hamburg, Bremen and the Swiss cities of Neuchâtel, Lausanne and Geneva. In the eighteenth century, printing works diffused even more widely and reached Dublin, Antwerp, Stockholm, Copenhagen, Barcelona, Vienna, Munich, St. Petersburg, Moscow, Prague and Nuremberg. Printed cottons became one of the most important items of trade within Europe and, according to Chapman and Chassagne, by the 1770s they became "the most important fashion goods at the Leipzig fair," which was the commercial hub of Central Europe. The trade in these textiles gave rise to many fortunes, including those of the Rothschilds, who amassed the capital for their banking operations in the *"circuit de l'indienne."*[3]

Dyeing and printing cloth with designs had long been practiced in Europe. Since at least medieval times, linen had been printed with oil-based stains, but the colors were not fast and the coloring agents often gave off a disagreeable smell. These defects made such materials unsuitable for clothing or furnishings.[4] Much of the printing was also done with black patterns on a solid background, which was a far cry from the vibrant colors of the Indian goods. As one historian of chintz has put it: "There is no mistaking the Indian native work which was distinguished by the excellence of colouring – glorious rich tones of rose, from dark crimsons to delicate hues of pink, purples graduating to lovely lilacs, pastel shades of blues and other colourings printed into the designs."[5]

Imitating Indian goods then required expanding the repertoire of dyestuffs and discovering methods by which these colors could be made fast. It also required the application of these techniques to cotton, a material that Europeans had little experience with or knowledge of. Several early calico printers received technical assistance from knowledgeable dyers and printers from the eastern Mediterranean where the art of cotton cloth printing had been taken from its home in the Indian subcontinent. In Marseilles, two "master craftsman of chintzes" formed a partnership on 1 February 1672, and hired two Armenians "to paint fabrics in the style of the Levant and Persia." Similarly, the printing works in Amersfoort were founded in 1678 with the assistance of a printer from the Anatolian port of İzmir who provided expertise to local manufacturers.[6] The east to west migration of technical experts and of knowledge continued in the eighteenth century. The elusive secret of Turkey red, which had originated in India and spread to Turkey and Greece, was introduced into France in the late 1740s by an Armenian, Johann Althen, who was brought to Avignon under the auspices of the French Secretary of State, M. Bertin. A statue of Althen was erected in the city to honor his contribution to the Avignon cloth industry. In 1747, French manufacturers also engaged the services of Greek dyers.[7]

Technical details on dyeing and printing cotton cloth may have also been transmitted to Europeans by traders and travelers to the subcontinent who produced descriptions of Indian methods. Examples of these survive from the late seventeenth and eighteenth centuries. In 1678, an employee of the French Compagnie des Indes produced a report which included two chapters on the printing of chintz. In the eighteenth century, a number of French Jesuits amassed detailed descriptions of Indian methods and these became the basis for textbooks on cloth printing in France and Britain. These works were also consulted by Edward Bancroft for his monumental *Experimental Researches Concerning the Philosophy of Permanent Colours* (1794). In the closing decades of the eighteenth century, there was a veritable flood of works on the topic of printing on cotton, including Quarelles' *Traité sur les toiles peintes* (1760), Delormois' *L'art de faire l'indienne* (1770), D'Apligny's *L'art de la teinture des fils et étoffes de coton* (1776), *A Treatise on Calico Printing* (1792) and *L'art de peindre les toiles* (1800).[8] According to Edgard Depitre, in France "as much was written in the seventeenth and eighteenth centuries on the subject of 'toiles peintes' as on the subject of cereals so that it occupied the central authorities and inflamed the people; for three-quarters of a century it remained established as a burning problem and created lively discussions; it was the object of two edicts, and some eighty decrees in council."[9]

Wool and silk, being animal fibers, were not suitable for printing due to their "special affinity for tinctorial materials," as Paul Schwartz put it. Attempts to print on wool yielded only crude designs or fabrics that were not washable.[10] Printing on silk "was one of the most difficult processes to perform successfully" and "true whites could not be obtained."[11] Cloths woven from vegetable fibers were the only option for European printers who sought to imitate Indian goods, and they turned to cotton, linen and fabrics made from a mixture of the two materials for their work.

Of these, both manufacturers and consumers in Europe preferred cotton. Claudius Rey, a London weaver, wrote in 1719, "The first class [of women] are clothed with out-law'd India-Chints; those of the second with English and Dutch printed callicoes; those of the Third with ordinary Callicoes, and printed Linnen; and those of the last, with ordinary printed Linnen."[12] In 1732 a survey of cloth merchants in two Catalan towns found that three-quarters of the printed calicoes in their inventories were made from all-cotton cloth (*indianas* as they were called). Of the remaining quarter, the bulk was made from cloth that was a mixture of cotton and linen and only a small quantity from pure linen. Virtually all of the cotton cloth was of high-quality weave because the finer the cloth, the sharper and clearer the designs that could be imparted.[13] Later in the eighteenth century, Christoff-Philipp Oberkampf in France preferred to print on cottons, preferably Indian, whenever they were available. Similarly, in Switzerland printers opted for cotton over other materials.[14]

By the early decades of the eighteenth century, there was a clearly defined quality and status hierarchy in which Indian printed cloth was preferred over European cloth and cotton over linen. According to P. J. Thomas, Indian printing was deemed better than European because for the higher classes, "the calicoes printed in Holland and England were considered too vulgar."[15] Cotton cloth trumped linen because it took colors better. "Flax took color with greater difficulty than cotton," according to a leading expert on printing and dyeing.[16] But cotton's higher price restricted its consumption. This hierarchy of cloth preferences was disturbed, however, when states in Europe began to restrict the import of Indian cotton cloth.

In Britain, the import of Indian cotton cloth and the use and wear of printed cotton goods, with the exception of muslins and blue-dyed calicoes, were made illegal in 1721. The ban was designed to protect the sizable wool and silk industries from the encroachment of foreign goods and of the foreign fiber. British printers were permitted to import Indian white cloth to make chintzes for export, but for local consumers, although some Indian cloth was smuggled into the kingdom, European-made substitutes for the original cotton would have to suffice. In the 1720s, British printers worked with Irish and Scottish linen cloth, but these fabrics could not satisfy the demands of fine printing that had formerly been done on high-quality Indian calicoes. This higher-end market was satisfied at first with linen cloths from Germany, but these began to be replaced with a British-made mixture of linen and cotton that was marketed under the name of fustians.

Fustians had been manufactured in Britain for several decades and in Europe for several centuries and they were a heavy mixture of cotton and linen. The new cotton–linen fabrics that began to be manufactured in Britain from the 1720s were lighter than the traditional varieties and were a new type of cloth altogether, designed as a substitute for the light all-cotton cloths of India that had been highly prized in British printing works. Manufacturers of the traditional fustian, as well as silk and wool interests, opposed the introduction of the new lighter cotton–linen blend and argued that it should be subject to the 1721 ban on the use and wear of printed cotton cloth. After lengthy legal battles, in 1736 Parliament ruled that the new mixture should be classified as fustian and that it was permitted for use and wear in Britain. The weaving of the new cloth took off to meet the demands of the British printing industry.[17]

Although printing on the new lighter linen–cotton mixtures expanded for both local and export markets, the cloth proved to be an imperfect substitute for Indian all-cotton calicoes. According to one historian of British printing, "In 1720 the developing industry received a severe blow. At the instigation of the established wool and silk interests legislation was enacted prohibiting the use at home of all cottons printed in England . . . Thereafter, the London printers were limited to working for export, or to printing, for the home market, *on a less suitable fabric with a linen warp and cotton weft.*"[18] From the standpoint of the consumer, the linen–cotton cloth may have been less appealing than an all-cotton for several reasons, including comfort, convenience and color. The issue of color may have been important from the perspectives of both the manufacturer and the consumer as "some dyes took differently on cotton and linen, producing a speckled effect."[19] Dyes on the mixed cloth may have also been less permanent. In mid-eighteenth-century France, Michau de Montaran, *intendant* of commerce, reported that printed linen and cotton fabrics (*siamoises, toiles flambées* and *brochées*) "soon lose their colours, so the goods produced are not much use."[20] The poor colorfastness of linen may have been the reason why French weavers inserted dyed cotton yarns in the warp to form red, blue or brown stripes in cloth that was otherwise comprised of linen.[21] Similarly, across the channel, in the famous linen and cotton checks of Manchester, some of which survive in a sample book compiled by John Holker, Jr., in the mid-eighteenth century, "for the most part colored cotton threads form the checks," according to Florence Montgomery. The scarlet yarn in one piece was even made of wool.[22]

The calico printers of Britain faced two challenges in the eighteenth century. In addition to perfecting methods of dyeing and fixing the color, they had to find a suitable substitute for the all-cotton cloths of India. "The master calico printer's initial problem was to raise the quality of his unprinted fabrics to reach the standards of the oriental imports," Chapman and Chassagne concluded.[23] The problem of finding an appropriate cloth for printing was solved in the 1770s with Richard Arkwright's invention of the water frame, which could spin a cotton yarn that was strong enough to be stretched for the warp. This made the weaving of an all-cotton cloth possible in Britain. According to Chapman and Chassagne, "It was textile printing that provided the primary stimulus for Arkwright's enterprise."[24]

In 1774 Jedidiah Strutt, business partner to Arkwright, displayed in the House of Commons "a Piece of plain white, and a Piece of printed, Cotton stuffs (the warp being cotton, and spun by the said machine) manufactured from raw materials, near Blackburn, in Lancashire, which he said was better adapted for printing than any thing of the kind heretofore used for that purpose."[25] And consumers in Britain immediately took note of the new fabric. In 1776, a woman in Bedfordshire asked for "one of the *new* manufactory which are *Cotten* both ways . . . It is a great deal lighter than a Cotton, and the colours look more lively."[26]

The West African trade

European traders sold Indian cottons on the west coast of Africa from at least the sixteenth century. In the 1670s, factors of the Royal African Company found buyers for printed calicoes, chintzes, indigo-dyed calicoes and a variety of checked and striped cotton textiles which had been imported to England from the subcontinent and then re-exported.[27] As Chapter 2 showed, in the eighteenth century, Indian cottons were essential for European trade with West Africa. Between 1720 and 1740, Indian cotton cloth accounted for a third of British exports to the region. From the 1740s, Indian cloth represented a smaller proportion of British exports, but increased in terms of quantity because of the growth in the slave trade and the higher prices that slaves commanded on the coast of West Africa.

From the late seventeenth century European cotton manufacturers – inspired by the popularity of Indian textiles amongst Africans – set out to produce their own versions of the cloth. The striped and checked cottons that West Africans so highly prized became a focus of much of this activity and the Dutch may have taken the lead in imitating these varieties. As early as 1680, the records of English traders in West Africa report that Holland ginghams and Dutch vimbarees found buyers, as did annabasses which were made in Holland beginning in 1700.[28] British-made imitations of Indian goods are also mentioned from the early eighteenth century when Blackburn checks begin to appear in the accounts of slave traders. The sale of French imitations of Indian cottons commenced several decades later.[29]

For much of the eighteenth century, these European imitations found a limited market in Africa because they did not match the Indian goods in either quality or price. In 1751, for instance, Thomas Melvil wrote from the Cape Coast Castle that Manchester goods would sell better if they were less expensive.[30] This was to be a repeated complaint until the closing decades of the eighteenth century. It was not only price that limited the sale of European goods, however. In 1705, English imitations of East India goods were reported to be "not vendible" and "chints, not vendible being English." These remarks suggest deficiencies in manufacture. On occasion British goods did find buyers – in 1712 English-made chintz was sold in Whydah – but in general until the late eighteenth century, the British, Dutch and other European imitations of Indian goods were not of sufficiently high quality.[31]

The quality problems were few in number, but serious in scope. To manufacture checked and striped cloth, yarn was first dyed a variety of colors, ranging from blues to reds to greens and yellows. Europeans had a far easier time imitating varieties that contained only blue as they dyed in that color with some success. Reds were very difficult to achieve and for several decades Europeans searched for the secret of the red dyes that were used not only in the subcontinent but also in Turkey. The quest for Turkey red was a major preoccupation of the Society for the Encouragement of Arts, Manufactures and Commerce in London, for instance. In the case of some cloth varieties, Africans refused to purchase British imitations because they discovered that the colors bled upon washing, a criticism that was never leveled at Indian cloth. "In the indent for goods for 1753 I wrote for Manchester Bejutapauts and Negannepauts which were then in great Demand, but now the Negroes have found out that they will not wash," a letter from a factor in West Africa reported.[32]

Because of the lack of knowledge on dyeing cotton and linen, some British manufacturers resorted to making checked cloth for the African market with dyed worsted yarn, which was mixed with either cotton or linen. This was not a serious competitor to the authentic

Indian product. Another shortcoming of the European imitations was that very few of them were manufactured purely from cotton. The European versions of Indian checks and stripes relied upon linen yarns for the warp and confined cotton yarns to the weft. Naturally, this produced a cloth that was very different from the Indian originals in texture and color. Linen was stiffer and, as we have seen, took dyes differently from cotton. And in most cases, the addition of linen made the cloths less desirable to African buyers, which is why in the eighteenth century slave-trading merchants urged the manufacturers of Lancashire to make their cloth with as much cotton as possible.[33]

By the mid-eighteenth century British imitations found wider markets in West Africa because of shortages of Indian cloth. The quality of European goods had improved somewhat and there were even reports of Manchester imitations being preferred over the Indian originals, but in general, Indian goods continued to hold the upper hand. In 1765, the slave traders of Liverpool wrote:

The East India Company for many years past, have not had a sufficient quantity of sundry sorts of goods proper for the African trade, denominated prohibited piece goods etc. which has obliged your memorialists to send several ships to Holland for the same, the consequence of which is, a great sum of money is laid out there, in buying other goods for assortments, as also, in the equipment of the ships, which wou'd otherwise have centred amongst the manufacturers & others of this Kingdom. That the manufactures of this Kingdom exported to Africa are woolens, arms, and other iron-ware, hats, gunpowder, brass, and copper wares commonly battery, Pewter, lead etc. as *also checks and other goods made at Manchester in imitation of East India Goods, when the latter are at high prices, or not to be got, but some they cannot imitate and their imitation of many kinds is but indifferent.*[34]

Two decades later, in 1785, French merchants visiting Manchester were astonished at the high quality of the cotton cloth produced in the town. Samuel Taylor, a merchant and manufacturer, reported that "various French African merchants from Bourdeaux, Nantes, but particularly from Havre . . . examined the species of goods destined for Africa in several warehouses . . . and expressed their surprise at the quality and price of these goods."[35]

What happened in the twenty years between 1765 and 1785? One significant advance was in the art of dyeing. French experts, who had probably obtained their knowledge through Levantine connections, transferred the Turkish method of coloring red to Britain in the

1780s.[36] Far more significant than developments in dyeing, however, was the invention of machinery that could spin higher-quality cotton yarns at much lower prices. These machines literally transformed overnight the quality of Manchester goods. The first of these, James Hargreaves' spinning jenny, dramatically lowered the costs of spinning cotton yarn for the weft, which was a major achievement but not one that pushed forward the quest for an all-cotton fabric. This was achieved only after Arkwright's water frame, which created in Europe the capacity to produce cotton warp yarn on a large scale. Within a few years the jenny and water frame were supplemented by Samuel Crompton's hybrid machine, aptly named the mule, which spun yarns equal in quality to those that went into the fine muslins of the Indian subcontinent. Both cloth printing and the manufacture of cottons for overseas markets took off with the invention of these machines.

Innovation in British cotton spinning

Since the early nineteenth century explanations for British techno-logical breakthroughs in spinning have followed two distinct tracks. The first track is global in its scope and situates the activities of British cotton manufacturers in relation to Indian textiles. This line of argu-ment sees Indian cotton cloth as providing the inspiration for the British cotton industry. Technical change in spinning emerged from the need to compete with Indian goods, which meant the manufacture of higher-quality yarn, in particular yarn which could be used for the warp, at more competitive prices. Only in this way could Indian manufacturers be supplanted. The key problem for the British cotton industry for much of the eighteenth century, then, was the manufac-ture of higher-quality yarns.[37] The second track is narrower in its focus and centers on the supply and demand for yarn within Britain. In this explanation, little attention is given to the global context of cotton manufacturing or Indian competition. Rather, the problem that the British cotton industry faced was the quantity of yarn, which propelled innovation in spinning. The shortages of yarn became espe-cially acute after the diffusion of the flying shuttle which sped up weaving and led to greater demand for yarn. The forces of the market through supply and demand, then, induced innovation in spinning, which increased the quantity of yarn. This explanation has come to be known as the challenge and response model.[38]

The rest of this chapter traces the genealogies, so to speak, of these two radically different explanations for innovation from an examination of eighteenth-century sources and nineteenth- and twentieth-century writings on the British cotton industry. These genealogies reveal that the eighteenth-century participants in the British cotton industry had a global view and linked innovation in cotton spinning to competition with India. The challenge and response model arose in the early nineteenth century and its emergence was closely connected to the diffusion of Smithian political economy in northwestern England. Smithian ideas made accounts of the development of the British cotton industry more market-centered, putting the focus on supply and demand, and more Eurocentered, divorcing Britain from its Indian connections.

Histories of the British cotton industry

Edward Baines' *History of the Cotton Manufacture in Great Britain*, published in 1835, was the first major history of the British cotton industry. An outline of the work appeared several years earlier in the senior Edward Baines' *History of the County Palatine of Lancaster* and J. R. McCulloch and others encouraged the son to enlarge the work and publish it separately. The purpose of Baines' work was to "record the rise, progress, and present state of this great manufacture," which, as he noted in his preface, provided the economic support for a million and a half individuals in England and Scotland and accounted for nearly half of the exports of Great Britain.[39]

Baines began his sprawling work in India, which he described as "the birthplace of the Cotton Manufacture" and "where it probably flourished long before the date of authentic history." In describing the trade in cotton cloth, Baines wrote,

The commerce of the Indians in these fabrics has been extensive, from the Christian era to the end of the last century. For many hundred years, Persia, Arabia, Syria, Egypt, Abyssinia, and all the eastern parts of Africa, were supplied with a considerable portion of their cottons and muslins, and with all which they consumed of the finest qualities, from the marts of India ... Owing to the beauty and cheapness of Indian muslins, chintzes, and calicoes, there was a period when the manufacturers of all the countries of Europe were apprehensive of being ruined by their competition.[40]

From his starting point in India, Baines proceeded to describe England as "the second birth-place of the art" of cotton manufacturing. Baines was well aware, therefore, that the manufacture of cotton cloth moved from east to west and that technological change in the late eighteenth century produced a "wonderful commercial revolution . . . effected by the machinery of England." Or, as he elaborated, "The Indians have not lost their former skill; but a power has arisen in England, which has robbed them of their ancient ascendancy, turned back the tide of commerce, and made it run more rapidly against the Oriental."[41]

Baines lost sight of the Indian connection when he turned to the origins of innovation in spinning, however, which he attributed to problems of yarn supply.

None but the strong cottons, such as fustians and dimities, were as yet made in England, and for these the demand must always have been limited. Yet at present the demand exceeded the supply, and the modes of manufacture were such as greatly to impede the increase of production. The weaver was continually pressing upon the spinner. The processes of spinning and weaving were generally performed in the same cottage, but the weaver's own family could not supply him with a sufficient quantity of weft, and he had with much pains to collect it from neighbouring spinsters. Thus his time was wasted, and . . . the seller could put her own price . . . This difficulty was likely to be further aggravated by an invention [the flying shuttle] which facilitated the process of weaving.[42]

For Baines, the invention of spinning machinery was propelled by the forces of the market and the imbalance between supply and demand of yarn, which the flying shuttle made worse. These innovations in spinning were not connected in any way to Indian cotton textiles.

This dual approach to the early British cotton industry was reproduced in subsequent works. Paul Mantoux, for example, declared the British cotton industry to be "the child of the East Indian trade." Yet, the invention of machinery in spinning, according to Mantoux, emerged from the disequilibrium in the yarn market: "The widening gap between spinning and weaving was producing real uneasiness in the industry. There was much unemployment among weavers, and merchants were always wondering how they could manage to satisfy the ever-growing demand."[43]

Not all nineteenth-century writers followed Baines' lead and divorced innovation in spinning from Indian cottons, however. Thomas Ellison wrote, "The popularity of [Indian] goods suggested the obvious desirability of making a still further approach to the Indian article by producing a fabric composed entirely of cotton; but in the absence of a machine capable of turning out a yarn hard and strong enough to be used as warp (hitherto supplied by linen), this was found to be impossible; and it was to the production of such a machine that the efforts of the mechanics of the time were now directed." Nevertheless, when elaborating upon the course of invention, Ellison drew upon Baines, as well as Andrew Ure, and pointed to imbalances between spinning and weaving as playing the decisive role. Ellison wrote: "The necessity for some improvement in the method of spinning had become very imperative . . . the slow process of the primitive single-thread domestic wheel . . . was totally inadequate to meet the growing demands of the trade . . . especially after the invention of the fly-shuttle."[44] A similar analysis may be found in Wadsworth and Mann's classic study of the cotton industry. The authors were keenly aware of the importance of the Indian example, yet innovation was explained by supply and demand in yarn markets. With the introduction of the fly shuttle, "the cotton industry came to feel acutely the shortage of weft," they wrote.[45]

From the mid-twentieth century, however, the Indian connection came to be increasingly minimized or neglected altogether.[46] David Landes' authoritative study of European technology and industrialization, *The Unbound Prometheus*, makes only passing reference to Indian cottons. For Landes, far more critical for technological progress in spinning was "the difference in labour requirements for spinning and weaving: it took at least five wheels to supply one loom, a proportion ordinarily at variance with the composition of the population" and "given the state of technology, the price of yarn rose sharply from the late seventeenth to the mid-eighteenth century." Phyllis Deane, despite noting that the water frame enabled the "British producer for the first time to outclass the Indian producer in the quality of his cloth," attributed its emergence to yarn shortages: "It took three or four spinners to supply one weaver with material by the traditional methods, and where the fly-shuttle speeded up the weavers' operations the shortage of yarn became acute." And Eric Hobsbawm wrote, "As every schoolchild knows, the technical problem which determined the nature of mechanization in the cotton industry was the imbalance between the efficiency of spinning and weaving."[47]

With the publication of the classic studies of Landes, Deane and Hobsbawm, the challenge and response model had become a conventional wisdom. It is not surprising to find it reproduced in Martin Daunton's survey of British economic and social history ("improvements in hand looms and the mounting needs of weavers placed pressure on the supply of yarn . . . which stimulated the mechanization of spinning") and in Geoffrey Timmins' overview of technology in the Lancashire cotton industry.[48]

In the 1990s, a growing interest in global history brought the Indian dimension back into the picture, however. Patrick O'Brien, Trevor Griffiths and Philip Hunt, in an exploration of the "political components of the industrial revolution," recognized that English cottons were "born out of trade in Asian cloth." While they link in a general way the development of the cotton industry with that of the subcontinent, the primary focus of the essay is the contribution that state policies made to British industrialization, not the sources of technological change in textiles.[49] Elsewhere, however, Griffiths, Hunt and O'Brien take up the problem of spinning technology, and specifically the challenge and response model, on the basis of patent data from eighteenth-century Britain. They argue that if an imbalance between spinning and weaving propelled technical change, then innovations in spinning should be followed by an increase in patent applications for new methods of weaving, which would restore the balance between the two activities. And, of course, the opposite should happen in the case of innovations in weaving. Griffiths, Hunt and O'Brien find no such pattern.[50] They also note that the diffusion of the flying shuttle was "too circumscribed in its effects to be linked convincingly to the 'wave' of significant innovations and improvements in spinning."[51]

And what do other eighteenth-century sources, aside from patent records, reveal? Baines himself referred to only two sources in support of his argument. One source was from the nineteenth century and the other, while from the eighteenth, draws no link between the invention of spinning machinery and shortages of yarn. Baines' nineteenth-century source was Richard Guest, who published in 1823 a very short history of the cotton industry. Guest invoked the image of the weaver forced to walk "three or four miles in a morning, and call on five or six spinners, before he could collect weft to serve him for the remainder of the day; and when he wished to weave a piece in shorter time than usual, a new ribbon or gown, was necessary to quicken the exertions of the spinner." According to Guest, a solution was found when Thomas Highs, a reed maker in Lancashire, "being in the house of one of his neighbours, whose son, a weaver, had come home after a long, ineffectual search for weft, was, by the circumstances, roused to consider whether a machine could not be invented to produce a more plentiful supply of weft." Guest, however, does not offer any evidence from eighteenth-century sources in support of this assertion of shortages of yarn.[52]

Baines' eighteenth-century source was John Aikin's history of Manchester, published in 1795. Aikin wrote:

From the time that the original system in the fustian branch, of buying pieces in the grey from the weaver, was changed, by delivering them out work, the custom of giving them out weft in the cops, which obtained for a while, grew into disuse, as there was no detecting the knavery of spinners till a piece came in woven; so that the practice was altered, and wool given in warps, the weaver answering for the spinning. And the weavers in a scarcity of spinning have sometimes been paid less for the weft than they gave the spinner, but durst not complain, much less abate the spinner, lest their looms should be unemployed. But when spinning jennies were introduced, and children could work upon them, the case was reversed.[53]

Aikin does not appear to have obtained this information from his own investigations, but from James Ogden who wrote something virtually identical a dozen years earlier.[54] However, neither Ogden nor Aikin suggest that there was a chronic shortage of yarn. Nor do they suggest that it was shortages of yarn that gave rise to invention. What they say is that there were occasional shortages of yarn, that regulating the quality of yarn was difficult, and that invention made yarn more plentiful.

More eighteenth-century voices

Baines constructed his argument that chronic yarn shortages led to innovation in cotton spinning on the basis of very slender evidence. Nevertheless, his interpretation became the conventional wisdom on the matter and countless discussions of the cotton industry in Britain have appealed to Baines and his sources. Baines was unable to ground his argument more firmly because eighteenth-century sources do not support his interpretation of why there was a drive towards invention in cotton spinning.

A source that Baines did not pay much attention to, perhaps because he was located in Lancashire, was the Society for the Encouragement of Arts, Manufactures and Commerce in London. Mantoux cites a passage from the Society's proceedings announcing a premium, or reward, for a new spinning device that "will spin six threads of wool, flax, Cotton, or silk, at one time, and that will require but one person to work and attend it," which it offered, "having been informed that our manufacturers of woolen, linen and cotton find it exceedingly difficult, when the spinners are out at harvest work, to procure a sufficient number of hands to keep their weavers, &c. employed."[55] It is not clear how much stock should be placed in the judgment of the Society, however, since historians are in agreement that its ventures in spinning bore very few results.[56] Nevertheless, this statement does point to an imbalance in the yarn market, but it was a seasonal, not chronic, shortage. It was not only spinners who were in short supply at harvest season, however. In eighteenth-century Lancashire, evidence suggests that weavers also worked in the harvest, making it difficult to procure not only yarn but also cloth at that time.[57]

Seasonal shortages of labor and yarn were not the only reason for the Society's interest in spinning. According to Robert Dossie of the Society, "Nothing could be more beneficial to the public than the supplying means to promote the more general application of idle hands to spinning." Workhouses were ideal sites for spinning "because there," Dossie wrote, "the poor are for the most part, the public loss, maintained by the public in idleness."[58] These passages do not suggest a shortage of labor for spinning, but rather the opposite – an excess supply of laborers, who had to be supplied with work.

At the same time, there is evidence that the Society's interest in yarn stemmed from concerns about the poor quality of the locally made material and the dependence of the British cotton industry on imports. Dossie wrote that the Society sought "to introduce the spinning [of] those finer kinds of thread, or cotton yarn, which we are at present furnished with from foreign countries."[59] And in 1760, a premium was offered for "spinning not less than five hundred pounds weight of cotton yarn, nearest to the sort called *Surat* or *Turkey* cotton yarn."[60] These premiums may have emerged in response to a Mr. Moore who advised the Society to encourage cotton spinning in Britain because it fell "short of what is spun in foreign parts such as the East Indies, etc."[61]

That more than quantity of yarn was at issue is also borne out from the papers of Richard Arkwright and Samuel Crompton, towering figures in the history of cotton spinning. In 1774, Arkwright petitioned Parliament for a lowering of the excise on the printed all-cotton calicoes, which the water frame made possible, on the grounds that "Warp, made of Cotton which is manufactured in this Kingdom, will be introduced in the Room of the Warps before used, made of Linen Yarn in making *Lancashire* Cottons . . . Goods so made wholly of Cotton will be greatly superior in Quality to the present Species of Cotton Goods made with Linen Yarn Warps, and will bleach, print, wash and wear better, and by Means thereof, find further Employment for the Poor."[62] A petition to Parliament several years later, which recounted the origins of Arkwright's invention, said, "After some Experience, finding that the common Method of preparing the Materials for Spinning (which is essentially necessary to the Perfection of good Yarn) was very imperfect, tedious, and expensive, he turned his Thoughts towards the Construction of Engines for that Purpose."[63] Neither petition mentions quantity of yarn. Instead, they both point to the poor quality of the available material as the major factor in propelling the invention of the water frame.[64]

Samuel Crompton was taught to spin cotton as a boy and was later apprenticed for a year to a weaver, from whom he learned the art of cotton weaving. In 1802, Crompton, reflecting on his life, wrote, "About the year 1772 I began to endeavour to find out if possible a better method of making cotton yarn than was then in general use being grieved at the bad yarn I had to weave."[65] Several years later he elaborated upon this passage. "At that time all the obstacles which stood in the way of the most extensive and lucrative cotton trade ever known in this country was the want of good spining," he wrote. Crompton then went on: "A machine was introduced into the cotton trade for spining of cotton called a jenny which greatly increased the cotton trade by producing so far greater a quantity, so that we began to have warps of single spun yarn such as then could be produced, but it was of such a quality none but those who had to work it can tell for bad . . . if I could find one good thread of a yard long there was ten bad ones . . . and having full experience of all the process of preparing and spinning on the jenny – as well as on the single spindle – I became inflamed with a strong intense desire to rectifie the evils of our then process of preparing and spining of cotton."[66]

Elsewhere, Crompton wrote that his mule made possible both the production of goods based on fine yarn "which at that time the trade was much in want of" and "the extention of many sorts of cotton goods that were made in an inferior manner before."[67] By what standard were Crompton's judgments of inferiority and superiority made? And what were the fine goods that were so much in demand? The answer to both these questions is cotton cloth from India. Although Indian calicoes were not permitted to be imported for domestic use, they were imported on a large scale for the printing industry and then re-exported. And the importation of Indian muslins had never been limited, but the mule made it possible for British manufacturers such as Samuel Oldknow to replace the imported item with a locally made stuff. Crompton cited this as one of the great achievements of his invention:

That at the period when your Petitioner surrendered his invention to the Public, the East India Company supplied Great Britain and Ireland with fine muslins and calicoes, all preceding attempts to establish the muslin manufacture having failed, through the want of such yarn as the *Mule* afterwards supplied, which, rapidly superseding Bengal muslins, speedily became a leading article, not alone of home consumption, but of a most extensive and advantageous export trade of British-manufactured muslins and cottons.[68]

For Arkwright as well, Indian cloth was the standard of comparison, which is conveyed in his own early history of his invention. Stockings were the first items that were made from the yarn spun on his water frame, Arkwright recounted, but then he himself undertook the weaving of "calicoes," which were an imitation of the Indian namesake.[69] The demand for these goods was brisk and buyers purchased them for cloth-printing works and he could sell them as fast as he could make them.[70]

Other men connected to the cotton industry in the late eighteenth century concurred that the new spinning machines made it possible for the British to perfect their imitations of Indian cloth. In 1803, George Walker wrote that "to the vast improvements in our Cotton-Manufactories is to be attributed the great reduction in the prices of India Goods," which was obviously made possible by technological advances.[71] An anonymous pamphleteer wrote in 1800: "[Arkwright] was the first who made calicoes with cotton warps, and it is probably owing to him, that this branch of our trade is so extensive and in so flourishing a condition. Before that time, coarse calicoes were made with linen warps, procured from abroad, and those of a finer quality were purchased at the sales of the East India Company . . . Nankeens and ginghams are manufactures, which, without the improvements effected by the spinner, could not possibly have succeeded. These articles too were formerly brought from the east exclusively. But the most valuable manufacture, which has been created in consequence of the successful application of the spinner to perfect his machinery, is that of muslins." As a consequence of the advances in spinning, this author continued, Britain was able "to keep in the country millions of specie, which was heretofore sent to the East."[72]

Several years earlier, one T. Hawkes wrote that "the first step" of the cotton men of Manchester "was the imitating the manufactures of foreign nations; particularly those of India, in which they were particularly happy in the copying of them."[73] In 1780, "A Friend of the Poor" wrote, "When I look upon our machines . . . my heart glows . . . *Perhaps*, by new improvements, we may vie with the *East-India* goods in fineness and beauty."[74] Similarly, a manuscript entitled the "History of the Cotton Trade," which has no author and no date but appears to have been written in 1776, recognized the spur that Indian cottons provided for British manufacturers ("Great quantities of [striped and checked cottons] are exported to Africa, which was wholly supplied with India goods till within fifteen years past," for example), but made no mention of shortages of yarn as a problem for the industry.[75] Even in the mid-eighteenth century, the production at home of Indian goods was seen as a highly desirable end. In 1754, one Mr. Sedgwick, a wholesale trader in printed cloth, presented to the Princess of Wales a piece of English chintz printed on British cotton. According to the report, the Princess "was very glad we had arrived to so great a perfection in the art of printing, and that in her opinion, it was preferable to any India chints whatsoever."[76]

And the Indian connection was no less important for efforts to improve spinning before the great technical breakthroughs of the 1760s and 1770s. In the 1750s, Lawrence Earnshaw and James Taylor invented machines for the spinning of cotton yarn and both devices were intended to produce warp yarns, a clear indication that the goal was to manufacture an all-cotton cloth.[77] Lewis Paul, who pioneered the roller method of spinning in the 1730s, devoted his machine to the spinning of cotton and he received financial support from two prominent merchants, James Johnson and Samuel Touchet. "Of the three men engaged in the cotton trade who took up the machine, two – Johnson and Touchet – were intimately connected with the manufacture of checks for Africa, and their interests in cheap yarn of a quality comparable with that from India was evidently great enough to encourage them to take considerable risks in the hope of obtaining it," Wadsworth and Mann concluded.[78]

Competition with India inspired invention as early as the 1720s, when an entrepreneur by the name of Elias Barnes promoted a project for the manufacture of cotton goods in Britain and elsewhere in Europe. For several years, his chief object was the manufacture of muslins and he declared that if it succeeded, "the whole World will be our customers."[79] Barnes visited Hamburg, Berlin, Amsterdam and The Hague to advance the scheme. He offered to settle in France with two new machines, "one for spinning cotton, and the other for opening and mixing wool." French officials circulated the Barnes proposal among manufacturers and experts and accepted it, which "indicates the interest which the possibilities of the cotton manufacture had excited," according to Wadsworth and Mann. Barnes also claimed that "the British East India Company was opposed to him, presumably from the idea that he might be able to make a muslin thread which could be turned into a British-produced muslin cloth, and so harm their imports," J. R. Harris wrote.[80]

The link between Indian cottons and technological improvements in British cotton manufacturing was made even earlier. In 1691, one Mr. Barkstead reported to Parliament that he had invented a method "of making calicoes, muslins and other fine cloth of that sort out of the cotton wool of the growth and produce of the Plantations, and the West Indies to a great perfection as those which are brought over and imported from Calicut and other places in the East Indies."[81] In 1695 John Cary was of the opinion that "English workmen would exceed the East Indies for calicoes had they encouragement."[82] In 1701 an anonymous pamphleteer defended the trade with India on the grounds that "the *East-India* trade procures things with less and cheaper labour than would be necessary to make the like in England; it is therefore very likely to be the cause of the invention of Arts, and Mills, and Engines to save the labour of Hands."[83]

From the late seventeenth century, the desire to make a cotton cloth that came up to Indian standards propelled innovation in spinning. Competition with India better accords with the historical evidence than two competing explanations for invention in textiles in eighteenth-century Britain. Joseph Inikori has argued that the growing demand for cotton cloth in the Atlantic world, in which West Africa and the slave trade loomed large, propelled technological development. From mid-century, exports of cotton cloth to West Africa grew rapidly, which created an incentive to innovate to meet demand in that market, according to Inikori.[84] A shortcoming of this argument is that greater demand for cloth should have led to inventive activity in both weaving and spinning, but the bulk of innovation was concentrated in the latter. Therefore, the pressure for technological change appears to have been confined to spinning, which is consistent with the explanation given here.[85]

Robert Allen has argued that the high costs of labor and low prices for capital and energy explain the invention and diffusion of the spinning jenny in Britain, as opposed to France or India.[86] While the need to reduce labor costs made new machines for spinning profitable in Britain, such devices were not profitable elsewhere. Allen's argument also cannot explain the concentration of inventive activity in spinning as opposed to weaving, for high labor costs should have had an impact on both activities. In addition, Allen's explanation cannot account for why innovation in textiles in Britain took place in the relatively insignificant sector of cotton manufacturing, as opposed to the much larger and more economically important wool sector. The argument of this chapter has offered an answer to both of these puzzles. The attention given to spinning and the focus on cotton reflected the need to produce an all-cotton cloth that matched the quality of Indian textiles. For this, above all else, Europeans needed superior methods for the manufacture of warp yarn.

Smithian political economy and the British cotton industry

Arkwright, Crompton and many others connected to the cotton industry in eighteenth-century Britain themselves wrote that they were driven to innovate by the desire to produce cloth that equaled the fabrics of India. Despite this weight of evidence from the eighteenth century, breakthroughs in spinning have not been interpreted in this way. Rather, the invention of new methods is seen as a product of shortages in yarn and the workings of supply and demand. The problem was defined as one of quantity, not quality. By the 1820s, when Richard Guest, an important source for Edward Baines, produced his study of the cotton trade, a momentous intellectual shift from quality to quantity had taken place which radically transformed the understanding of innovation in the eighteenth-century textile industry.

On 3 November 1815, John Kennedy delivered a lecture entitled "Observations on the Rise and Progress of the Cotton Trade in Great Britain" to the Literary and Philosophical Society of Manchester.[87] Kennedy was a well-known figure in Manchester and its surrounding towns. He was a co-founder of the famous firm of "McConnel and Kennedy, Cotton Spinners," which was established in 1795 and in the nineteenth century became one of the largest spinning enterprises in Manchester. Kennedy was acquainted with many of the men connected to the cotton industry in its early days of growth and expansion after the great inventions of the 1760s and 1770s. He knew Samuel Crompton and he produced *A Brief Memoir of Samuel Crompton*, which he read before the Literary and Philosophical Society of Manchester in 1830.[88] He was also a close associate of Samuel Oldknow, the great pioneer muslin manufacturer. Edward Baines thanked John Kennedy for assisting him with his history of the cotton manufacture and Kennedy's writings are cited throughout Baines' great work. From all accounts, therefore, Kennedy was well acquainted with the heady, early days of the cotton industry in Lancashire and acknowledged to be an expert in its history.

Despite this long acquaintance with the cotton trade, Kennedy's "Observations on the Rise and Progress of the Cotton Trade" makes no mention of India or Indian cottons. Kennedy was not unaware of the role that Indian goods had played in the development of British cotton manufacturing. In his *Brief Memoir of Samuel Crompton*, he observed that Samuel Oldknow "took new ground by copying some of the fabrics imported from India, which at that time supplied this kingdom with all the finer fabrics, and which the mule-spun yarn alone could imitate."[89] Nevertheless fifteen years earlier, in his "Observations," Kennedy did not take up and develop the Indian link. Rather, he took a different tack to explain the rise and growth of cotton manufacturing in Britain.

Kennedy began by noting that "there were frequent fluctuations in the demand for cotton fabrics." "Under such circumstances," he argued, "when a stagnation took place it was natural that the manufacturer would, rather than be out of employment, endeavour to find a market for his goods in other countries . . . With their new connexions, the manufacturers soon found that they could not supply the increased demand for their new cloths." This set in motion an elaboration of the division of labor, beginning in the family and then extending to the neighborhood. Because of the greater subdivision of tasks, "the attention of each being thus directed to fewer objects, they proceeded, imperceptibly, to improvements in the carding and spinning, by first introducing simple improvements in the hand instruments with which they performed these operations, till at length they arrived at a machine, which, though rude and ill constructed, enabled them to produce more in their respective families." Eventually, "invention and ingenuity found their reward in the construction of machinery for carding and spinning."[90] In this passage one sees the deep influence of Adam Smith and his analysis of the extent of the market, the division of labor and innovation which is found in Book I of the *Wealth of Nations*. There Smith famously wrote, "The invention of all those machines by which labour is so much facilitated and abridged, seems to have been originally owing to the division of labour."[91]

By the second decade of the nineteenth century, an approach grounded in Smithian political economy had arisen to explain technological change in the cotton industry. Based on the self-equilibrating powers of the market, this approach appealed to the division of labor and the extent of the market as the major forces propelling invention, culminating with machinery. With this framework, and the central place it accords to the market, it is not surprising that the early nineteenth-century accounts of Richard Guest, published in 1823, and Edward Baines, which appeared in 1835, came to see quantity of yarn as the primary impediment to the growth of the cotton industry and the forces of supply and demand as signaling the need for technical change. These ideas were consistent with the Smithian political economy which came to dominate the economic thinking of the time. The problems of quality and competition with Indian goods, which cannot be expressed in the language of prices and markets or supply and demand, and which called for protection, not free trade, fit less comfortably with the Smithian paradigm.

The adoption of a Smithian framework to understand the rise of the cotton industry coincided with the growing acceptance in Lancashire of the free trade prescriptions of Smithian political economy. In the final quarter of the eighteenth century, the cotton men of Lancashire were unreceptive to the arguments for free trade and they favored protection from imports of Indian cloth. In the 1770s, for example, Richard Arkwright challenged an excise tax of 6d. on all-cotton cloth, which gave domestic manufactures of cotton–linen mixtures an advantage over Indian calicoes when it came to supplying printers in Britain. Arkwright did not demand the repeal of this tax, only that the all-cotton cloth he now manufactured be classified as fustian, which was subject to a lower excise of 3d. This gave tacit approval to the protection that British manufacturers received from Indian imports.[92]

Further evidence for the anti-free-trade stance of the cotton industry comes from a pamphleteer, who in 1785 defended the need for protection from Indian imports: "An alleviation of duties on India muslins and callicos, or giving encouragement to them by laying a heavier tax upon the cotton goods of this country, especially upon the infant manufacturer of muslins and fine calicos, must depress and discourage the industry."[93] In the late 1780s, the muslin manufacturers of Britain demanded protection from Indian muslins on the grounds that the recently established British industry was "in the greatest danger of being lost to the country" because of unfair Indian competition.[94]

From the final years of the eighteenth century, cotton manufacturers reversed course and became proponents of unrestricted trade in cotton yarn and cloth.[95] As cotton spinning grew rapidly in the 1780s and 1790s, manufacturers accumulated enormous inventories of yarn, which they began to export to markets in Europe. Representatives of weaving and knitting interests, fearing shortages of yarn, lobbied the British state for a prohibition on the exports or at a minimum heavy excises on yarn that was shipped out of the nation.[96] Spinning masters in Lancashire organized in defense of their right to export and appealed to the "wisdom of the Legislature not [to] sanction a proposal so directly hostile to the interests of the country, to the freedom of trade and the rights of private property."[97]

Free-trade interests grew even more vocal in 1812 during debates on the renewal of the East India Company's monopoly over trade with Asia. Lancashire cotton manufacturers opposed the Company monopoly on the grounds that access to the large and potentially very lucrative markets of India and China should be unrestricted. For George Lee, a leading cotton master in Manchester, "the general arguments against Monopoly" were "so obvious, and have been so perspicuously treated by various eminent theoretical writers," that the cotton men's demand for "unfettered Trade to India" was self-evident.[98]

When histories of the cotton manufacture began to be produced in the nineteenth century, beginning with John Kennedy's address to the Literary and Philosophical Society of Manchester in 1815, the cotton masters of Manchester and its environs were not only acquainted with the theoretical statements in defense of the freedom of trade but had become ardent defenders of the free market. They then began to interpret the rise and progress of the cotton industry in those terms, abandoning the mercantilist mentality of their eighteenth-century forebears.

Although younger than John Kennedy, Edward Baines was shaped by the same early nineteenth-century currents. In his career as writer, journalist and politician, Baines was committed to the cause of free trade and his entry into the world of politics was "on the occasion of an Anti-Corn Law meeting in 1825."[99] Five years later, in the *Leeds Mercury*, Baines defended "the clear and acknowledged right which every merchant has to the free exercise of his talents industry and capital in any way he may think best." According to Derek Fraser, he was "marked" as a doctrinaire and theoretical supporter of the free-market system.[100] For at least a decade before the publication of his history of the cotton manufacture, Baines advocated the freedom of trade and the efficiency of the market. It is not surprising that these ideas were incorporated into his history and shaped his account of the development of the cotton industry in eighteenth-century Britain.

Conclusion

Under the influence of Smithian political economy, early nineteenth-century historians produced accounts of the British cotton industry that were very much at odds with those found in eighteenth-century sources. Modern historians, with the exception of a few dissenters, neglected these voices from the eighteenth century and instead drew upon Edward Baines, Thomas Ellison and others from the nineteenth to argue that technological breakthroughs in cotton spinning were the product of a challenge and response and propelled by shortages of yarn. As a consequence, the Indian contribution to the mechanization of the cotton industry receded into the background or dropped out altogether in accounts of economic and technological change in eighteenth-century Britain.

The early nineteenth-century diffusion and popularization of Smithian political economy, therefore, led to a rewriting of the history of the British cotton industry in the image of its own theoretical pronouncements. Supply and demand and the logic of the market – rather than competition against the Indian subcontinent, mercantilism and state intervention and protection – became the categories with which eighteenth-century economic change was understood. Nineteenth-century understandings of the wellsprings of seventeenth- and eighteenth-century economic progress came to bear little resemblance to the actual sources of improvement in those centuries.

The adoption of a Smithian framework for interpreting innovation in the early British cotton industry also contributed in two ways to the production of Eurocentric histories. First, Europe was divorced from the global connections that for centuries had a profound impact on economic activity. From the sixteenth century, Europeans were embedded in a complex global system in which they were not always the dominant players. This was especially the case in relations with Asia, where the nations of Europe were no match for the productive power of India and China. This gave rise to a powerful drive to emulate Asian goods, most critically for long-run developments, the cotton textiles of the Indian subcontinent. A Smithian framework narrowed the focus to the national scale. It dispensed with the powerful pressures to emulate and imitate that Europeans felt and reduced economic and technological change to the forces of supply and demand.

Second, and better explored by historians of India and China, the Smithian economic framework was seen as inapplicable to areas outside Europe. For Smith, the commercial society he described and analyzed was uniquely European. Asia and Africa did not benefit from the commercial revolution, and therefore were stagnant and lagged behind the economies of Europe. Marx, an inheritor to this approach, substituted capitalism for commercial society, but remained faithful to the founder of political economy when he declared that capitalism was exceptional to Europe. Therefore, the introduction of Smithian ideas into the writing of history distorted that enterprise in two profound ways.

5 | State and market: Britain, France and the Ottoman Empire

Introduction

While Indian competition propelled British innovation in textiles in the eighteenth century, Britain was not the only nation in Europe – nor was Europe the only region in the world – to face the competitive challenge of India. And much as in Europe, cloth producers around the globe began to imitate Indian-made goods. This dynamic of competition and imitation reached great heights in several centers in the Ottoman Empire, where vast quantities of Indian cloth were consumed in the seventeenth and eighteenth centuries. The Ottoman centers, unlike Lancashire, failed to forge a revolutionary response to the Indian challenge, however. And Ottoman textile manufacturers, in contrast to those in Britain, did not reverse the longstanding east–west flow of cottons and establish a new global manufacturing order. The purpose of this chapter is to answer the question why Britain followed a different path in cotton textiles from the Ottoman Empire as well as its major competitor in Europe, the kingdom of France.

The divergent paths of Britain and Ottoman provinces cannot be attributed to technological stagnation in the Ottoman Empire. In military matters, Ottoman authorities kept up with technical improvements taking place in Europe and until the 1770s developed or imported from Europe cutting-edge knowledge and technologies for the production of gunpowder, the casting of cannon and the manufacture of small guns.[1] When it came to cotton textiles, however, the economic philosophy of the Ottoman state was different from that of states in Western Europe in the seventeenth and eighteenth centuries. While European state officials focused on production and protection for local enterprises and workers, Ottoman officialdom was concerned with consumption and the adequacy of supplies of goods at the right price without regard to their place of origin. Therefore, Ottoman and European attitudes towards the import of Indian cottons diverged, which shaped the potentials and possibilities for cotton manufacturing in these two regions.

While state thinking on the economy differed between Western Europe and the Ottoman Empire, in Europe itself mercantilist thinking was widespread, but the development of cotton manufacturing was uneven. French cotton manufacturing, for instance, lagged behind the British, although both polities followed mercantilist principles. The divergence between Britain and France was in part due to different applications of mercantilist ideas, which yielded very different policies on the ground. At the same time, Britain and France did not relate to the Atlantic economy in the same way, especially to the trade in slaves from West Africa. These varied orientations to the Atlantic Ocean, from which the Ottoman territories were completely cut off, meant that different forms of consumer demand shaped the cotton industries of Britain and France. Atlantic connections were favorable to the development of lighter cotton cloths of the sort made in India and these impulses from the sea were more powerful in Britain than in France. The paths of economic development in the eighteenth century were shaped not by the state or the market alone, but rather by a complex interaction between state policies and market opportunities.

Indian cottons in the Ottoman Empire

From its position straddling the Persian Gulf and the Mediterranean, Black and Red Seas the Ottoman Empire was open to a vast array of influences emanating from the Indian subcontinent, the Arabian peninsula, Iran, Central Asia, East and North Africa, Russia and Southern, Central and Western Europe. Despite the variety of connections, the history of trade in the Ottoman Empire has focused on exchange with Europe.[2] The abundance of European sources accounts in part for this historical bias. The customs accounts, merchant records and other materials in the archives of Marseilles and London provide a resource that no other trading partner of the empire can match. More important than even source materials, however, is the deeply embedded assumption that Europe was the center of economic activity and, as such, the preeminent shaper of the global economy in the seventeenth and eighteenth centuries. Because of this European bias, historians of the Ottoman Empire have turned from the East and directed their gaze westward. While several generations of historians have explored the impact of the West on the Ottoman economy and searched for the origins of western economic dominance in the eastern Mediterranean, very few have investigated the impact of the Indian Ocean trading system on Ottoman economic life. The author has not been able to find any books or monographs on the subject, while there have been dozens, if not hundreds, on Europe's impact on the Ottoman Empire.[3] A notable exception is found in monetary history where the Indian connection is difficult to avoid. The outflow of precious metals to the Indian subcontinent was an inescapable feature of Ottoman economic life in the seventeenth and eighteenth centuries and is one sign that the Indian Ocean trading world had a major impact on the Ottoman economy. This monetary history suggests that historians have paid a heavy price for neglecting the eastern connections of the empire.[4]

Indian cottons had been exported to the Middle East via sea and land since at least medieval times, but the explosion in global commerce in the seventeenth and eighteenth centuries – fueled by American silver – led to an enormous expansion in this trade. Cloth was carried overland along caravan routes that continued to operate well into the eighteenth century, bringing goods from northern, western and southern India to Iran and Iraq. The Ottoman Empire was also linked to the subcontinent via the sea and vast quantities of cloth and other goods flowed into ports in the Persian Gulf and the Red Sea from where they were transported by land and water to eager buyers in Egypt, Syria, Anatolia and southeastern Europe. Before the plague of 1772–3 in Iraq, according to one estimate, three-quarters of the merchandise on the caravan trade from Baghdad to Aleppo consisted of Indian textiles.[5]

Although the exact volume of trade from the Indian subcontinent to West Asia and the eastern Mediterranean will never be known, scattered estimates attest that it was sizable. In 1690, servants of the English East India Company reported that annual exports of cloth from western India to Iran and the Ottoman Empire were five times the size of cloth exports to Europe.[6] This was at the height of the "calico craze" when massive quantities of Indian cloth were pouring into London, Amsterdam, Paris and countless smaller cities and towns of Europe.

The Ottoman Empire continued to receive Indian cottons in the eighteenth century and it appears that much more cloth was imported into the empire from India than from Europe. From the 1730s, France became the major source of European cloth in the Ottoman territories, almost all of it woolens shipped from Marseilles. Reliable data on the size of this trade is available in French customs registers and these show that between 1750 and 1754 Marseilles exported annually 8.5 million livres of cloth to the Levant. Between 1786 and 1789, this figure fell to 6.6 million livres per year. Some of these goods were re-exported from the Ottoman Empire to Iran, but how much is not known.[7] As reported in Chapter 2, in 1785 a French merchant based in Istanbul estimated that 12.6 million livres of Indian cotton cloth were consumed every year in the Levant. In addition to these cotton textiles, 1.6 million livres of shawls and 1 million livres of cotton yarn were imported from India, for a total import figure of 15.2 million livres of cloth and yarn.[8] These are rough figures, but they show that in the 1780s French cloth exports to the Levant were less than half the value of the exports of India. Even the larger French export figures for the middle of the eighteenth century were substantially less than the Indian cloth exports of 1785.

According to Donald Quataert, there were "vast increases in the import of Indian textiles" into the Ottoman Empire in the eighteenth century, which led to concerns among the political class about the outflow of silver to India and the deleterious impact on local manufacturing.[9] In the final years of the century, Sultan Selim III, who reigned from 1789 to 1807 and sought to reform the state and build the economy, complained that he always wore "Istanbul-made and Ankara-made cloth. But my statesmen wear Indian-made and Iran-made cloth. If they would wear the cloths of our country, local goods would be in demand."[10] From this, Quataert has concluded that "the competitive assault [on Ottoman textile manufacturers] was not coming from European makers, but, rather, from the East."[11]

The strategies that British manufacturers used from the late eighteenth century to sell cotton cloth in Ottoman markets provide further evidence that Indian cottons had a longstanding and broad appeal. "Given the popularity of Indian cotton goods, beginning in the second half of the eighteenth century the European cotton exports to the Ottoman Empire consisted primarily of imitations of Indian products. As late as the mid nineteenth century the latter varieties constituted the bulk of European exports to the Levant," Halil İnalcık has reported. British manufacturers marketed their cloth in the Ottoman Empire with Indian names, evidence of an effort to lure customers away from the consumption of an Indian-made good.[12]

The boom in exports of raw cotton from the Ottoman Empire to Europe in the eighteenth century is another sign that Indian cloth was consumed in growing quantities in Ottoman markets. Over the course of the century, European demand for the fiber grew rapidly. Marseilles imported less than 5 million pounds of cotton and yarn a year from Ottoman territories between 1702 and 1704. By the late 1780s, this figure had grown to more than 24 million pounds. Therefore, the transformation of the Ottoman Empire into an exporter of raw materials – the classic colonial pattern of trade – began long before European goods manufactured with industrial methods invaded the market. The export of raw cotton was made possible by the import of low-priced cloth from the Indian subcontinent. It is likely that Indian goods satisfied demand for cotton cloth in the Ottoman territories, freeing up the raw material for export to overseas markets. The rise of the cotton trade, combined with Indian imports, therefore, appears to have had a profound impact on the eighteenth-century Ottoman economy. The next several pages will examine in greater detail the effects of cloth imports from India on Egypt and Anatolia, two populous and important regions of the empire.

Egypt

The rapid growth in European demand for raw cotton in the eighteenth century appears to have hit Egypt hard. Egypt was not a major exporter of the fiber, but it was a major consumer, importing raw cotton from growing areas in Syria. As Syrian cotton was diverted to European markets, the price of cotton in Cairo skyrocketed, more than quadrupling between 1718 and 1789. Much of this increase came after 1740, as can be seen in Table 5.1. Cotton was one of several fibers used in Egyptian textile manufacturing, the others being linen, wool and silk. The shares of these different fibers in textile output are not known, but cotton was by no means insignificant. A variety of pure cotton cloths as well as mixtures of cotton and other fibers were mainstays of production for local markets and for export. Consumers in France, for instance, prized the cotton dimities of Rosetta.[13]

Table 5.1 *Cotton prices in Cairo, 1687–1797 (paras per qantar,
in constant prices, 1687 = 100)*

	Price	Index
1687	278	100
1718	273	98
1729	426	153
1731	234	84
1732	300	108
1733	273	98
1734	266	96
1735	259	93
1736	238	86
1742	361	130
1747	558	201
1754	575	207
1782	817	294
1784	1021	367
1789	1200	432
1790	1200	432
1797	1320	475

Source: André Raymond, *Artisans et commerçants au Caire au xviii siècle*,
2 vols. (Damascus, 1973), vol. I, p. 65.

While there was an enormous run-up in the price of raw cotton,
cloth prices in Cairo increased much less over the century. A price
index assembled by André Raymond, and given in Table 5.2, shows
that there were short-term price fluctuations, but between 1700 and
1789 cloth prices increased by only about a third. Although Raymond's
index is based on prices for both linens and cottons, it is very surprising
that a fourfold increase in the price of raw cotton did not lead to a
more substantial increase in the price of these textiles.[14]

This lack of correspondence suggests that the prices of raw cotton
and cloth were determined in separate and unconnected markets,
even though cotton was a key input into Egyptian cloth manufacturing. The price of cotton was set by European demand, which was
increasing rapidly with the expansion of cotton manufacturing in
France, Switzerland and Germany. The price of cloth was set by
supplies of cotton cloth from the Indian subcontinent and these
abundant imports set a cap on prices. It is possible that French cloth

Table 5.2 *An index of cotton and linen cloth prices in Cairo, 1700–1789 (1700–1709 = 100)*

Years	Index
1700–09	100
1710–19	134
1720–24	174
1731–39	98
1740–49	115
1750–59	122
1776–81	109
1786–89	136

Source: Raymond, *Artisans et commerçants au Caire au xviii siècle*, vol. I, p. 65.

had the same effect as Indian goods (and this conclusion would be consistent with the European focus of Ottoman historiography), but the bulk of French exports to Egypt consisted of woolen cloth, which was not a direct competitor with lighter cottons and linens. France started exporting cotton cloth to Egypt only in the final quarter of the eighteenth century.[15]

Indian cottons would have competed directly with the cottons and linens of Egypt. Painted, printed and plain cotton cloth in a wide range of qualities – from coarse to superfine – had long been imported via the Red Sea into Egypt. André Raymond has concluded that in the eighteenth century "the total importation of 'Indiennes' is unknown, but it was certainly considerable."[16] The flood of imports from the subcontinent appears to have squeezed textile manufacturers in Cairo, especially in cotton, making it difficult for them to pass on their higher costs for raw material. They were caught in a price squeeze with rapidly rising costs for raw cotton but comparatively stable cloth prices. Higher raw cotton prices also reduced the competitiveness of Egyptian textiles, the export of which also declined in the eighteenth century. Other evidence points to distress among Cairo's textile workers in the period, including a decline in the assets of artisans, in whose ranks cloth workers were heavily represented. The size of the average artisan estate fell by 40 percent in the eighteenth century.[17]

Anatolia

In the final decades of the eighteenth century, Anatolia overtook Syria and became the major source of the Levant cotton exported to Europe. Much of this cotton was shipped from İzmir, which was transformed in the eighteenth century from an insignificant trading center to the major Anatolian port. In the early eighteenth century, İzmir accounted for about 10% of the cotton exports from the ports of the Levant to France. By the early 1750s, this figure was close to 45% and by the late 1780s had risen to 70%. Before 1750, the quantity of cotton exported annually was typically under a million pounds. By the 1780s, this figure was several millions.[18] The cotton from İzmir was grown in rich soils which lay within a 100-mile radius of the city and there is little evidence that the acreage devoted to cotton cultivation increased significantly in the eighteenth century.[19] As a consequence, the enormous growth in European demand for cotton pushed up the price, which tripled between 1700 and 1789. Much of this increase took place in the second half of the century when European demand for cotton grew rapidly.[20] The price increase in İzmir was almost as great as that in Egypt (where cotton prices rose almost fourfold) and it is likely that the impact on local textile manufacturers was much the same, given the extensive evidence for the widespread consumption of Indian cloth, which, as in Egypt, may have constrained the ability of local manufacturers to pass on higher cotton costs.

In 1812 Christophe Aubin, an agent for a Glasgow cotton manufacturer, traveled through Anatolia to collect information on the market for cloth. In İzmir, Aubin found that Indian muslins and some dozen varieties of calicoes and chintzes were enormously popular. He also noted that British imitations of Indian goods were making inroads in the market, which had led to a fall in prices for Indian goods. "India Muslins were five or six years ago of great consumption . . . The Turks were in those days very much prejudiced against all English Manufacture in imitation of India goods; but they have now changed their mind and buy what is cheapest. Thus the English goods have almost replaced the India Muslins which however may still be sold to a certain extent, but at lower rates than formerly," Aubin wrote.[21] The largest market for Indian cotton goods, not only in Anatolia but in the Ottoman Empire as a whole, was Istanbul, one of the largest cities in the world at the time. Aubin found that the city "draws a good many India Cotton Goods from Bagdat [Baghdad] but for some time fine India Goods have not been received from that Quarter and consequently they are now wanting. About 25 years ago considerable quantities of India Goods were received by way of Suez."[22]

Eighteenth-century sources, including materials found in the Ottoman state archives, confirm Aubin's observations. On the basis of Ottoman sources, Halil İnalcık found that an extraordinary variety of Indian cotton textiles were consumed within the empire, ranging from very fine muslins – used as turbans by prosperous men and veils by wealthy women – to inexpensive chintzes that were mass produced in Gujarat specifically for export to West Asia. It was much the same in the case of the Iranian market, where cloth was sent by the boatload as well as overland from Gujarat and Sind to the Persian Gulf.[23]

Ottoman imitations of Indian cloth

In much of Europe the import of Indian cottons introduced consumers to a wholly new fiber and new type of fabric. In the Ottoman Empire, however, the spinning and weaving of cotton had a long history and was central to economic life in a number of regions. In the case of seventeenth-century Anatolia, Halil İnalcık has concluded that "the cotton industry, in terms of dimensions of its production and trade, constituted the most important sector of the Turkish economy after grains."[24] There was also a sizable trade within the empire in cotton textiles, with production centers in Anatolia sending cloth north to the Black Sea, up the Danube River and even to markets outside the Ottoman territories. Ottoman imitations of Indian goods, then, took place in a very different context in which textile workers possessed extensive knowledge about cotton and its manipulation.

It is not clear when the Ottoman imitation of Indian cloth began, but by the seventeenth century imported goods were being copied in a number of regions of the empire, including the Balkans, Anatolia, Syria and even Cyprus. The imitation of Indian goods may have begun in Iran and from there transmitted to the Ottoman territories, which is a distinct possibility since many Ottoman buyers first learned of chintz from Iranian imitations of the Indian cloth. These Iranian copies were manufactured in Tabriz and Isfahan and reached some Ottoman markets before the real thing from India.[25] The Ottoman imitations of Indian goods spanned the spectrum of imports. Spinners and weavers copied the twills and light cottons of the subcontinent while dyers and printers created their versions of the colorful calicoes and chintzes from Gujarat and Masulipatnam. According to Gilles Veinstein, "There was hardly a single type of Indian fabric that did not have an equivalent in local production."[26]

By the eighteenth century, these imitations of Indian goods were even exported. In the late 1750s, M. de (Charles) Peyssonnel found that a "prodigious quantity of *indiennes* or painted cloth of Tocat and Kastambol" were consumed every year in the Crimea.[27] The main market in Europe for the Ottoman textiles was Marseilles, where both printed and plain goods were demanded in the eighteenth century. In the early part of the century, the French called this cloth "indiennes de Constantinople." Some of this cloth may indeed have been made in Istanbul but it would have been supplemented with the products of Bursa, Tokat and other cloth-printing centers in Anatolia. From the 1720s, substantial quantities of plain white cottons were exported to Marseilles to supply the "raw material" for the expanding printing works in the city. From the 1730s, the printers of Marseilles demanded dimities, primarily from Egypt but also from Cyprus, and from the 1750s quantities of plain white cloth from near Aleppo were added to the list.[28]

This export record suggests that Ottoman textile manufacturing achieved some success with its imitations of Indian cloth and found buyers both at home and abroad. Despite these achievements, Ottoman manufacturers encountered several hurdles. First, the Ottoman imitations were confined to lower-quality goods, which generated less income than finer cloth. Ottoman textile workers had enormous difficulties copying the superior varieties of calicoes and muslins.[29] Second, the rise of locally made substitutes for Indian cloth did not stem the growing tide of imports from the subcontinent. "Ottoman weavers successfully imitated Indian textiles; but, as customs registers indicate, this did not end or diminish their imports," İnalcık concluded.[30]

By the late seventeenth century the relentless import of Indian cloth plunged the Ottoman Empire into a monetary crisis. The Ottoman products demanded in the Indian subcontinent consisted of dates, coffee, horses and above all silver. For decades the precious metal had flowed out of the empire into the subcontinent to pay for cotton cloth, which led to shortages of money and instabilities in the monetary system. "Toward the end of the seventeenth century," İnalcık has written, "Ottoman demand for Indian shawls as well as fine Indian cotton fabrics (muslin and twill) and the unusual growth of imports signal the beginning of a crisis in the Ottoman economy."[31] The chronicler Naima, who died in 1716, was concerned that "so much cash treasury goes for Indian merchandise and the Indians buy nothing from the Ottoman realms nor even have need of anything . . . The world's wealth accumulates in India."[32] The Ottomans "could not prevent the outflow of specie to the east arising from the trade deficits in that direction," according to Şevket Pamuk, and as a consequence, "fluctuations in these commodity and specie flows brought increasing pressure on the Ottoman monetary system."[33]

From the seventeenth century, the large-scale import of Indian cottons sparked efforts to imitate these textiles in both the Ottoman Empire and Britain. By the late eighteenth century, Ottoman authorities were dealing with an economic crisis spawned in part by the unrelenting import of Indian cloth and a corresponding outflow of silver, while in Britain textile manufacturers were exporting ever-larger quantities of cotton yarn and cloth and even moving into the production of high-quality muslins. In markets in West Africa, Europe and the eastern Mediterranean, British cotton cloth was beginning to challenge the dominance of Indian cottons. And by the second decade of the nineteenth century, it was apparent that Britain had successfully responded to the Indian challenge and British cotton manufacturers were supplanting the subcontinent as the world's source for cotton cloth.

These divergent paths suggest that competition with the Indian subcontinent alone cannot account for British technological breakthroughs in cotton. The other crucial factor was the state and its policies. In Britain, Indian competition was managed and regulated with policies that created a more hospitable economic climate for cotton manufacturers to fashion their imitations of Indian goods. In the Ottoman Empire, by contrast, political authorities did little to assist cotton cloth production.

State policy and textile manufacturing: the British case

The policies of the British state played a critical role in the development of cotton manufacturing, the most important being protection for local manufacturers from Indian competition. This measure was adopted upon the urging of silk and wool interests, but the fledgling cotton works of Britain were the primary beneficiaries. It is a bedrock conviction of mainstream economics that restrictions on trade are harmful and reduce economic efficiency and social welfare.[34] This belief has led many economic historians to downplay the role of protection in the development of British cotton manufacturing. Robert Allen's *British Industrial Revolution in Global Perspective*, for instance, contains no discussion of restrictions on Indian cloth and Joel Mokyr's *Enlightened Economy* dismisses protection on the grounds that it was rent-seeking rather than value-creating.[35] The historical record, however, does not support these views, and the protectionist response to the Indian competitive challenge facilitated the development of skills, technology and markets, which were a precondition for the growth and expansion of the British cotton industry. As shown in the previous chapter, the focus on the market as the motor of economic change in cotton manufacturing is itself a product of the nineteenth century, supplanting the mercantilist framework that shaped both policy and history in the eighteenth.

In Britain, demands to restrict the import of Indian textiles were voiced from the mid-1670s, shortly after the "calico craze" commenced. For a decade, Parliament debated barriers on the import of Indian cottons and in 1685 a duty of 10% – on top of a pre-existing duty of 7.5% – was levied on Indian cloth. In 1690, the extraordinary duty was doubled to 20%. The cumulative effect of these measures, according to P. J. Thomas, was to discourage the use of Indian calicoes "to a certain extent," but they continued to be imported in sizable quantities because of the enormous demand for them.[36]

Because these taxes failed to reduce the import of Indian cloth – Thomas reports that "England was flooded with Indian calicoes and silks" – the clamor for protection reached even greater heights in the closing years of the seventeenth century. Wool and silk interests argued that tariffs were insufficient and demanded an outright ban on the importation of Indian cloth. A bill to this effect was introduced into Parliament in 1696, but it failed to gain sufficient support in the House of Lords, which was filled with friends of the East India Company, the importer of these goods. When news of the bill's defeat reached the streets of London, several hundred silk weavers "went in a body to Westminster" and petitioned Parliament for protection from Indian competition. The weavers also marched down Leadenhall Street to the offices of the East India Company and protested the

Company's imports of Indian cottons.[37] Again, in 1698, a bill to restrict Indian imports was defeated in the House of Lords, sparking massive weaver protests on the streets of London. Finally, in 1700, after intense lobbying and widespread weaver agitation, a bill prohibiting the import of Indian textiles passed in both houses of Parliament. Several varieties of cloth were exempted from the ban, however, most importantly white calicoes and muslins, which meant that the small British printing industry could continue to work with Indian material. And Indian cloth of all sorts could be imported as long as it was re-exported. A system of bonded warehouses was created to ensure that these textiles were not smuggled into the domestic market.[38]

The prohibition on Indian printed and painted cloth gave British printers a monopoly over the home market, which gave them a tremendous boost to production. Without Indian competition, British printing works rapidly enlarged their operations. For a few years they also benefited from the fact that the Parliamentary Act of 1700 sharply reduced the duties on Indian white cloth. (A 15 percent duty was restored in 1704.) Since it could no longer import printed and patterned cloths, the East India Company turned its efforts to procuring white cloths of all qualities and the cloth printers of Britain eagerly seized them for their works. The printing of calicoes had started in Britain in the 1680s, but it was on a small scale. After 1700, behind protectionist walls cloth printing in Britain took off.[39]

British printers soon fell victim to the envy and hostility of competing textile interests, however. In 1707, woolen manufacturers complained to Parliament that the competition of the British printing works was "more prejudicial to us than the importation of painted calicoes was before the passing of that act." The woolen workers lamented that formerly "the calicoes painted in India were most used by the richer sort of people whilst the poor continued to wear and use our woollen goods, the calicoes now painted in England are so very cheap and so much the fashion that persons of all qualities and degrees clothe themselves and furnish their houses in a great measure with them."[40]

Four year later, the printers of London confirmed that the ban on imports of Indian calicoes had enabled them to make great progress in the manufacture of handkerchiefs, a popular accessory. "Since the wearing *India Silks and Callicoes* Printed or Stained . . . has been restrained by an Act . . . The Article of Handkerchiefs has been greatly improv'd, and at length rendred so good and cheap, that great Quantities have been, and daily are exported to Her Majesty's Dominions Abroad," they wrote in 1711.[41] Fearing the further expansion of the industry, competing manufacturers turned their attention to the printed cloth made in Britain, almost all of which used cotton cloth from India.

In 1719, wool and silk manufacturers joined forces and mobilized for a complete ban on the importation of Indian cloth. In the summer of that year, the silk weavers of Spitalfields rioted in the streets of London, "tearing calicoes off the women's backs and throwing *aqua fortis* on their clothes."[42] The debate on the Indian trade moved quickly from the streets to the printing press and both critics and defenders of the trade voiced their positions in a series of pamphlets. From there, the debate shifted to the halls of Parliament and by the end of 1719 both the Lords and the Commons had been flooded with weaver testimonies from throughout Britain that blamed the imports of cheap Indian calicoes for the deterioration in their trade. Because of this pressure, in 1721 Parliament enacted a prohibition on the consumption of "all stuffs made of cotton or mixed therewith, which shall be printed and painted with any colour or colours, or chequered or striped." Once again, a few varieties of cloth were exempt from the Act, including muslins, neckcloths, fustians and calicoes dyed all blue.[43]

The exclusion of Indian goods gave a spur to their production in Britain itself. An anonymous "History of the Cotton Trade," which appears to have been penned in 1776, stated, "The prohibition of the wear of strip'd and check'd East India goods in the year 1722 gave further encouragement for Manchester to attempt the manufactures of various sorts of cotton stripes which have been so much improved of late years as to beat out the wear of Turkey strip'd goods in Britain and nearly of India strip'ed goods in America . . . and now great quantities are exported to the coast of Africa."[44]

The Act of 1721 also put an end to British printing on Indian cloth for the domestic market, but permitted it for export. This enabled British printers to use white cottons from India to supply chintzes to markets in Europe, Africa and the Americas, but the British cloth-printing industry had to find another way to meet the growing demand for calicoes within the British Isles. To satisfy this demand, British printers began to experiment with cloth from other materials, the chief alternative to cotton being linen, which had been used for printing even before the Prohibition Act of 1721. British cloth printers turned to the linen of Scotland, Ireland and central Europe as the material for their work. Chintzes made from linen, however, were considered inferior to those made from cotton. Recall the words of Claudius Rey from the previous chapter, who reported that in the early eighteenth century British consumers preferred printed cottons over printed linens, presumably because the former took and held colors better than the latter.

The British ban of 1721 on the import of plain, white Indian cottons fueled the search for a domestically manufactured cotton cloth that was suitable for printing. "It was protection which was almost entirely responsible for the use of English-made cottons by the printers. Had it not been for the artificial stimulus provided in 1721, it seems doubtful whether there would have been sufficient incentive to produce a satisfactory material in any quantity," Julia de Lacy Mann concluded.[45] The first breakthrough came in the 1730s with the weaving of a light cotton–linen mix. This cloth, which used linen as the warp and cotton as the weft, was not as heavy as the traditional cotton and linen mixtures that had been made in Europe for centuries and was close in weight and feel to the cotton calicoes of India. Still, it was not a perfect substitute for the Indian good, as we saw in the previous chapter, and it did not have the look, feel or color of a purely cotton chintz. Nevertheless, there was widespread opposition to this new cloth on the grounds that it violated the Act of 1721, which dictated that cotton could only be used in the manufacture of traditional fustians and other heavy linen–cotton mixtures, but the British state intervened again, this time in support of cotton. The cotton masters of Lancashire successfully lobbied Parliament and had their new fabric classified as fustian for legal and excise purposes.[46] Four decades later, an anonymous historian of the cotton trade wrote, "In the year 1736 when the wear of printed cottons was permitted the manufacture of cottons for printing was begun at Blackburn."[47]

This new, lighter fustian was only the first step in the tortuous path to an all-cotton calico. Behind protectionist walls, British cotton masters experimented with methods to make the cotton yarn that was essential for such cloth. It took another forty years and the crucial breakthrough was, of course, the invention of the water frame, which could spin yarn strong enough to withstand the tensile pressures of being stretched in the loom to form the warp. In these decades, British cotton producers were given a protected market in which they had great power to set prices, captive consumers for their goods, and room to learn and experiment with new techniques and methods. Since most varieties of Indian cloth were excluded from the market, British manufacturers also knew that the successful innovator would be able to supply the growing British market without fear of Indian competition. Over the course of the eighteenth century, British demand for cottons grew steadily, as has been documented by Beverly Lemire and John Styles and was described in Chapter 2. Indeed, these efforts to manufacture an all-cotton cloth may have been stimulated even earlier in the century with the passage of the Calico Act of 1700. According to Patrick O'Brien, Trevor Griffiths and Philip Hunt, that legislation alerted cotton manu-facturers to the growing protectionist sentiment in Parliament and signaled "that the home market might not remain open to Indian imports, even in plain form, and that the capacity to spin and weave cottons within the realm might be profitably expanded."[48]

The era of protection for cotton did not end with the great spinning inventions of the late 1760s and 1770s. In a final act of support for British cotton manufacturing, a sizable tariff was imposed on Indian muslins in 1787. After Crompton's invention of the mule, Lancashire began to spin very fine yarns, and a British muslin industry took off in the 1780s. Despite its early success, Indian cotton goods loomed large in the minds of British muslin manufacturers and continued to be perceived as a threat. The papers of Samuel Oldknow, the lone muslin manufacturer from the period whose records have survived, reveal a keen interest in the muslin imports of the English East India Company. His papers contain a Company auction catalog listing the varieties of Indian muslins that were imported and their selling prices. Oldknow also engaged in an extensive correspondence with his London agent on the Company's sales, the quantities of Indian muslin imports, and the market for them in the city.[49]

In the mid-1780s a depression in the muslin trade drove many manufacturers to the brink of bankruptcy. The muslin masters attrib-uted the downturn to "the interference of a foreign article, of the same fabric and quality, introduced by the East India Company into the British market" and they organized themselves into an association of "Cotton Spinners and Manufacturers of Callico and Muslin" to pres-sure Parliament for protection from the competition of Indian muslins.[50] In taking this action, they observed: "it has ever been the wisdom of the British Legislature to protect and nourish every home manufacture progressively, as it advanced to maturity – And that the cotton-trade, in particular, has already, on several occasions, experienced the fostering hand of the British Government."[51] Parliament responded with a duty of nearly 100 percent on imports of Indian muslins, which effectively shut them out of the British market. With this protection Lancashire muslin makers were given a monopoly of the market and higher prices for their goods, which allowed them to expand their works and perfect the process of manufacture.

From the late seventeenth century, British cotton manufacturing expanded in tandem with state policies of protection. The ban on imports of Indian painted and printed cloth in 1700 gave a great boost to a British cloth-printing industry, which was given the exclusive right to supply the home market. The ban on imports of Indian white calico in 1721 led British manufacturers to search for and develop a locally made substitute for what had formerly been imported from the subcontinent. This search was successful in the 1770s with the invention of Arkwright's water frame and then Crompton's mule. But the era of protection was not over. Tariffs on Indian muslin imports in the 1780s helped British muslin manufacturers to expand and improve their manufacturing capabilities. Trade policies were integral to the development of the British cotton industry.

Economic philosophy and state policy: the Ottoman Empire

In the Ottoman Empire, in contrast to Britain, the import of Indian textiles was never restricted. As a consequence, Ottoman textile manufacturers faced sustained and relentless competition from Indian goods. The lack of protection for manufacturing reflected an Ottoman economic philosophy that was radically different from that of seventeenth- and eighteenth-century Britain, and Europe more widely. Ottoman economic thinking centered upon provisioning the empire. The goal of the state was to ensure abundant supplies of essential commodities at reasonable prices with little concern for where the goods were produced. In this framework, high-quality cotton cloth from the subcontinent was viewed as a welcome addition to Ottoman markets. According to Mehmet Genç, "With respect to foreign trade, provisionism sought to keep the supply of goods and services to the internal market at an optimal level. Export was not encouraged, but rather curtailed by prohibitions, quotas, and taxes. Imports, by contrast, were fostered and facilitated." Genç adds that provisionism "did not require an import substitution policy as long as imports helped maintain the steady supply of goods and services." The state promoted local production to replace imports only in extraordinary circumstances, typically having to do with military supplies.[52]

Consistent with this economic and political philosophy, the Ottoman state supported only two major textile manufacturing efforts in the eighteenth century. The first was the manufacturing of woolen cloth to replace imports, which received state encouragement from 1703 to 1732. Fine woolen cloth was essential for military uniforms and the Ottoman state supported local production in order to reduce dependence on foreign suppliers. In the words of the Grand Vizier, the goal was to "make provisions to be self-sufficient of woolens from non-Muslim countries." State support consisted largely of financial assistance for a manufactory in Istanbul, but there was no attempt to restrain the competition of cheap European imports. "The survival of local woolen manufacturing under such market conditions required strong protectionist state policies," according to Mehmet Genç, but these were lacking and as a consequence the undertaking failed to yield cloth of the necessary price or quality.[53]

A second state-sponsored scheme produced sailcloth for the Ottoman navy. This enterprise was located in the Istanbul arsenal and began production in 1709. It was more successful than woolens manufacture and it continued to operate on a small scale into the nineteenth century. A number of factors contributed to its greater longevity, including superior technology of manufacturing and steady naval demand for sailcloth. The most important, however, was that in contrast to the woolens manufacture of the early eighteenth century it was given a monopoly over the local market, which meant that it faced little competition.[54]

The Ottoman economic philosophy of provisioning was a far cry from the mercantilism that dominated Europe at the time. In contrast to the Ottoman focus on plentiful goods for consumption, Europeans approached economic policy from the point of view of production. The aim of state actions was to expand productive capacity in order to broaden the economic base for taxation. The power of the state, therefore, was linked explicitly to the development and expansion of production. It was this thinking that led states in Europe to protect manufacturing from external competition. In the case of Indian cottons, with the exception of Holland, from the late seventeenth century protectionist measures were adopted across Western and Central Europe, even though they increased the prices of goods for consumers. As Sir Thomas Smith argued in 1549: "It were better for us to pay more to our own people for wares than less to strangers; for how little gains so ever go over, it is lost to us clear. But how much so ever the gains be, that go from one of us to another, it is all within the Realm."[55]

Restrictions on imports and encouragement for local production were found widely across Europe, but in Britain mercantile thinking was even more expansive. From the sixteenth century, British policy protected local economic activity, but it also sought to encourage the domestic production of imported goods. In perhaps the most revolutionary move, the British state supported the importation of raw materials that were not found at home so that they could be worked up to replace imported manufactures. This is why the import of raw cotton for the manufacture of cloth in imitation of Indian goods was neither novel nor unprecedented.[56]

The Atlantic market

State mercantilist policies were critical to the divergent paths that cotton manufacturing followed in Britain and the Ottoman Empire. Mercantilism alone, however, cannot explain why the British cotton industry diverged from those of other nations in Europe where protectionist measures against Indian cloth were also enacted, most importantly France, which had a sizable cotton industry in the eighteenth century. One difference between France and Britain was in the form of the protectionist policies, which Patrick O'Brien, Trevor Griffiths and Philip Hunt have noted.[57] France imposed an outright ban on cotton consumption, which hampered the development of the cotton industry for decades. (The consequences of this policy will be examined in more detail shortly.) A second difference between France and Britain has to do with the fact that British merchants participated in broader trading networks than their French counterparts – combined with state interest in these networks – which provided more lucrative commercial opportunities for British cotton manufacturers. The most important of these were found in the Atlantic world and included West Africa, North America and the Caribbean. To a greater extent than

French producers, British cotton masters were meeting the demands not only of local consumers, but also those at a far remove in the rapidly expanding trading world of the Atlantic Ocean. Britain also differed from the Ottoman Empire in this respect.

For much of the eighteenth century, the Atlantic was the most important overseas market for British cotton goods. Between 1752 and 1754, nearly 95% of British cotton exports found buyers in the Atlantic world. Twenty years later, between 1772 and 1774, this proportion had fallen, but still stood at 80%.[58] Until the mid-eighteenth century, West Africa was the most important of these Atlantic markets. Between 1752 and 1754, 60% of British cotton cloth exports were exchanged for slaves in West Africa. Even in the early 1770s, when the American market had grown in importance, West Africa absorbed nearly 45% of total British exports of cottons.[59]

The bulk of African demand was for checked and striped cloths, which were manufactured from cotton yarn that was dyed blue and red and then woven with plain white yarns to create intricate and colorful patterns. Some examples of British cloth for these markets are given in Figure 5.1, which shows two swatches of cloth woven in Blackburn and attached to a letter from the manufacturer to the Company of Merchants Trading to Africa as evidence of the high quality of the goods his weavers could make. A sizable fraction of these checks and stripes were destined for export and in 1759 almost half, and in 1769 almost three-quarters, of Lancashire's output of these textiles was shipped to West Africa.[60] Smaller quantities were also sold in the plantation economies of the West Indies, but the precise amount is not known.

In West Africa, British manufacturers competed directly with Indian goods and this competition propelled the development of the cotton industry. The previous chapter showed that African buyers preferred the all-cotton cloth made in India over the linen and cotton mixtures that Manchester had to offer, which compelled the cotton men of Blackburn and other centers in Lancashire to improve their wares. This fueled the search for improved methods of cotton spinning which culminated with the innovations of the 1760s and 1770s. In the markets of West Africa, British cotton manufacturers served their apprenticeship under Indian masters.

British cotton manufacturers, therefore, operated in a combination of protected and unprotected markets. They had protected markets at home and, as we shall see shortly, in their American colonies, where there was a

Figure 5.1 Swatches of Blackburn cloth woven for the West Africa market, 1751, National Archives of the United Kingdom: Public Record Office, T70/1517.

sizable demand for light printed cloth akin to the calicoes of India. At the same time, they competed directly against Indian goods in West African markets where cotton textiles were indispensable for the conduct of the slave trade. Therefore, it was a pairing of protection and competition – in a context of growing demand for cotton goods in both Europe and the Atlantic World – from which British cotton masters benefited.

From the late 1770s, West African markets absorbed larger quantities of British cottons, but they accounted for a smaller proportion of cotton exports, which may be seen from Figure 5.2. West African markets became more peripheral for two reasons. First, British cotton goods began to be exported to Europe where they had not

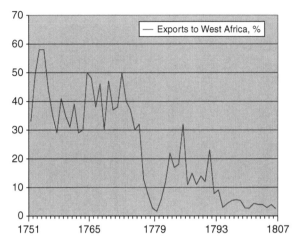

Figure 5.2 Exports of British cotton cloth to West Africa as a proportion of total cotton cloth exports, 1751–1807.
Sources: Exports to West Africa from Inikori, *Africans and the Industrial Revolution*, p. 444. Total exports from Schumpeter, *English Overseas Trade Statistics*, Tables X and XI.

traditionally been sold in large quantities. In the closing decades of the eighteenth century, European consumers had a voracious appetite for new varieties of velvets that came to be known as Manchester cottons, which become significant in the British customs records from 1775. And from the 1780s, the British breakthroughs in spinning produced a boom in cotton yarn and cloth exports to France, the Low Countries, and the Swiss and German territories. This further shrank West Africa's share of British cotton exports.

Second, West African markets became less important as North American demand took off. For much of the eighteenth century, North America had been the second market in the Atlantic for cotton goods, but it had tremendous potential for growth. The population of European settlers grew rapidly in the century; the settlers had high incomes, which they could devote to following consumer fashions; and their tastes closely tracked those of Europe. From New France to Philadelphia, the Carolinas and New Orleans there was a steadily growing demand for cotton goods in the eighteenth century, much as in Britain and elsewhere in Europe. North American merchant inventories indicate that by the 1760s and 1770s the appetite for cottons had reached sizable proportions.[61] The European settlers in North America also preferred printed stuff over other varieties of cotton cloth and in the late 1760s it was the largest overseas market for British printed cottons and linens.[62]

Since North America and the Caribbean were colonial markets, British cotton masters had a monopoly in them. With eager consumers in protected outlets British cotton manufacturers had an added incentive to experiment with perfecting the relatively new manufacture. Since the seventeenth century, with the aid of the Navigation Laws, a number of markets in the Atlantic were maintained as exclusive preserves for British manufacturers and shippers. Ralph Davis noted that the laws

were vitally important to England in the early decades of the colonial development; they excluded, as they were designed to exclude, the exercise of Dutch commercial, financial and maritime skills, which were well fitted to engross a large part of transatlantic trade. In time, changing conditions reduced the practical importance of the Navigation Laws, for they moulded the infant colonial trade so effectively that it developed the required character, and eventually matured in a form which was largely independent of the legal strait-jacket . . . Generation after generation the population of the colonies had become accustomed to take manufactures from British sources and sell through British factors.[63]

The research of David Ormrod has reinforced Ralph Davis' conclusions: "It was the mercantilist state which decisively shifted the balance of power and influence towards London, through the creation of a *national* entrepôt with an imperial trading network . . . Beneath the advantages conferred on England by geography and location lay the hand of a strong, centralized state, supporting and extending London's dominance with and beyond."[64] Therefore, British economic dominance of the Atlantic world did not emerge from the logic of the free market, but was supported by state action.

This discussion of the Atlantic shows that in the Ottoman case, unsupportive state policies included more than the lack of protection and encouragement for a nascent cotton industry. The Ottoman state did not use its political might to capture markets for its manufactures. As a consequence, the more limited outlets in which Ottoman producers could vend their imitations of Indian stuff also acted as a brake on the expansion of cotton. Most critically, Ottoman manufacturing was cut off from the Atlantic, which was booming in the eighteenth century. It was the "Golden Age of the Colonial Atlantic," in the words of one historian.[65] Vasco de Gama may not have sounded the death knell for the Ottoman, and more generally Mediterranean, economy in the sixteenth century, as was once believed. Nevertheless, by the eighteenth century, access to the Atlantic Ocean offered enormous possibilities for the development of manufacturing, from which the Ottoman Empire and, in fact, many parts of Europe were cut off.

French cottons: state policy and the Atlantic trade

The cotton manufacturers of France were less connected to markets in the Atlantic than their counterparts in Britain, which combined with state policies to limit the prospects of French cottons in the eighteenth century. Marseilles led the way in cotton printing in Europe, establishing printing workshops in 1648, three decades before those of London, Paris and Amsterdam. The goal of these early works was to produce at home imitations of the calicoes imported from Istanbul, Diyarbakir and Aleppo. Although these textiles came to France from the Ottoman Empire, they were most likely manufactured in Iran and the Indian subcontinent.[66] In the next twenty years another dozen printing works were set up in Marseilles and from there spread to other centers in France, including Avignon, Nîmes and Arles. Marseilles' easy access to technologies and skilled craftsmen from the eastern Mediterranean contributed to its early entry into the novel manufacturing process and the city served as a bridge between the Levant and Europe for the transmission of techniques in the printing and dyeing of cotton.[67]

Although France led Europe in the development of cotton printing, it was also the first state to restrict the consumption of cotton cloth. In 1686, a royal decree prohibited both the manufacture and the consumption of printed cottons throughout the kingdom. In 1689, the prohibition was expanded to include printing on wool and linen and, in 1691, the import of all white cottons and muslins was banned, except in Nantes, which supplied Indian cloth to French slave traders.[68] These prohibitions were enacted at the urging of wool and silk manufacturers who feared that they were losing markets to the new fiber. However, they had a devastating impact on the fledgling cotton manufactures. According to Olivier Raveux, the decrees "reduced to nil the developments which had taken place in Marseilles since 1648. Like all other French cities Marseilles had to cease production."[69] The printing industry was dismantled in France and reassembled in neighboring states. Masters and workers migrated to Avignon, which was under Papal control, Tuscany and other Italian regions, and Geneva and other Swiss cantons where they founded new enterprises and resumed the work of printing upon cotton cloth.[70]

In Britain the import and consumption of Indian calicoes was banned, but the domestic printing of cloth was never restricted. In France, however, not only the consumption but also the act of printing cloth was made illegal, which set back the development of the French cotton industry by several decades. While the manufacture of cottons was fairly easy to suppress, it was more difficult to eliminate the consumption of these goods. Edgard Depitre has observed that "all the severity of the regulations in the eighteenth century was concentrated on the manufacture: the diverse regulations of consumption were far more lax, far more imprecise in their enforcement."[71] Therefore, in the eighteenth century French consumption of cotton goods, both the lighter and heavier varieties, conformed to the north Atlantic pattern of steadily growing demand, but French manufacturers were not allowed to supply this expanding market. As already noted, between 1700 and 1789 cottons went from comprising 3 to 8 percent of the garments in Parisian wardrobes to between 20 and 40 percent, and the taste for cottons appears to have grown steadily over the century.[72] Painted and printed cottons from the Indian subcontinent continued to be smuggled into France and were widely available in the early eighteenth century, according to Serge Chassagne. These may have been supplemented with printed cloth from Holland and Britain.[73]

The ban on cloth printing was relaxed several times between 1686 and 1759, when it was finally repealed. These openings were not sufficient to allow the industry to grow significantly, however. As a consequence, cotton cloth manufacturing developed more slowly and fitfully in France than in Britain. In Marseilles, the longstanding freedom of the port was confirmed in 1692 and 1703 and the city was exempted from the act of 1686 and permitted to work with cotton. While this allowed a resumption of printing, it "did so slowly over two decades. Even if it was of short duration, the interruption left traces."[74] Between 1733 and 1750 cloth printing actually declined in Marseilles, going from 24 workshops with 280 workers to 14 workshops with 100 workers.[75] Only from the mid-eighteenth century did the industry pick up as it printed on white cloth imported from the Levant. Its final products were exported to Spain, the Italian states, the Guinea coast, the Antilles, Spanish America and New France.[76]

Despite the restriction on the manufacture and consumption of painted and printed cloth, cotton began to be used more widely in eighteenth-century France. In contrast to Britain, much of the cotton manufacturing was devoted to heavier varieties of cloth made from mixtures of cotton and other fibers, as is elaborated in the appendix to this chapter, rather than the imitation of the light cottons of India, which proved to be the revolutionary path of development. The cottons of India possessed a global market, while that for the heavy cottons of Europe was far more restricted. In 1788, Charles Taylor, himself a fustian manufacturer in Lancashire, admitted that calicoes and muslins were of "greater consequence to the commercial interests of this kingdom" than fustians and other heavy cotton cloth varieties.[77] The efforts to replicate Indian cloth also propelled efforts to substitute cotton for linen in the warp, which led to innovation in spinning. In the heavier varieties, linen yarn was adequate for the warp.

The limits on printing were the first reason why the imitation of Indian cloth was less extensive in France than in Britain. The small scale of the printing industry in Marseilles meant that there was little demand for cloth that resembled the all-cotton calicoes of India. And for much of the eighteenth century the printers of Marseilles found adequate supplies of white cloth in the Ottoman Empire.[78] The second reason was that the French had fewer outlets for their cloth than the British in the Atlantic world. In North America, the population of French colonies was much smaller than that of the British. From the early eighteenth century, the French commenced a thriving trade with San Domingue, but in general the market for cotton goods was smaller in the West Indies than in North America. French cotton cloth export data is not available, but it was unlikely to have been much different from that of the British who in the mid-1780s shipped only 7 percent of their cotton exports to the West Indies. By contrast, in the same period 29 percent of British cotton exports went to the United States and Canada.[79]

In the first three-quarters of the eighteenth century, West Africa was a major battleground for competition between Indian cloth and British imitations, but France trailed Britain in that trade. In the final years of the seventeenth century, slavers from France transported 1,000–2,000 Africans a year to the French West Indies and the figure rose to about 3,000 by 1713.[80] By contrast, between 1698 and 1709 the British carried nearly 14,000 slaves across the Atlantic each year.[81] The French trade grew after the Treaty of Utrecht in

1713, but still lagged behind the British, and for the eighteenth century as a whole, the French purchased 1.18 million African slaves, the British 2.53 million.[82] This, of course, meant that smaller quantities of French manufactured goods were exported to West Africa, including the cotton textiles which were in such high demand in that market.

For their indispensable cargoes of cotton cloth, French slave traders drew upon Indian imports, with a smattering of pieces from the Levant and Iran. A comprehensive inventory of France's exports to West Africa, such as that compiled by Marion Johnson for Britain, does not exist, but scattered evidence indicates that French slavers relied more upon Indian cottons. Three-quarters of the cargo of the *Prince du Conty*, which voyaged to West Africa in 1750, consisted of cotton textiles, and nearly 97 percent of these were of Indian manufacture. According to Gaston Martin, the ship carried "7,505 pieces of merchandise from India, except some tapsels counterfeit (*contrefaits*) or a net total of 7,263 pieces from India." The label *contrefaits* or counterfeit suggests a French or European imitation of an Indian good.[83] More revealingly, in the late 1760s and early 1770s, 600,000 livres (25,000 pounds sterling) worth of cotton goods from Rouen, the leading cotton manufacturing center in France, was exported every year to West Africa.[84] In those same years, British slave traders annually sold in West Africa 80,000 pounds sterling worth of British-made cotton goods, or more than three times the French total. And this was before the mechanization of spinning had penetrated very deeply into cotton production in Lancashire.

The importance of Indian cottons for France's trade with West Africa is reflected in the geography of French slave shipping. In the eighteenth century, almost half the slave-trading ships that departed from France set sail from the port of Nantes.[85] Nantes attained this position because it was also home to the French East India Company whose sales were conducted there for many decades. According to Pierre Boulle, "The great demand in Africa for Indian textiles was a factor in Nantes' decision to enter the slave trade."[86] The East India Company shifted its operations to Lorient in 1733, but the slave traders of Nantes were still well placed to purchase their cargoes of Indian calicoes, chintzes and checked and striped cloths. The merchants of Nantes also had easy access to the markets of Holland where the French Company's offerings of Indian goods could be supplemented with those of the Dutch East India Company.

From the 1720s cotton manufacturing arose in Nantes to make cloth for export to West Africa, thirty or forty years after the establishment of similar ventures in Lancashire. Slave trading interests organized and financed several of these schemes and the largest came to be known as *La Grande Manufacture* and contained as many as 100 looms at work weaving cotton cloth for export to West Africa. *La Grand Manufacture* remained in existence till 1786. Nevertheless, Boulle has concluded that "none of these new manufactures and industries made much of an inroad into the import–export ratio of the port of Nantes. If anything, the Atlantic city imported increasing amounts of goods for the slave trade from abroad as the century progressed."[87]

The prohibition on printing in France also hindered the production of cloth for West Africa and French slave traders relied upon the Indian subcontinent and Holland for their supplies of this variety. ("In the case of one type of textiles – printed cloth – Nantes' slave traders were thwarted for a long while from finding local alternatives to foreign and Indian imports by stiff regulations.")[88] These cloths were fairly easy to obtain during peacetime, but supplies were disrupted during wartime. In the 1740s, after the disruption caused by the War of Austrian Succession, the slave traders of Nantes successfully pressured the French state to repeal the prohibition on printing and in 1744 Marseilles was allowed to print cloth for export to West Africa.[89]

From the mid-eighteenth century, the political climate in France became friendlier to cotton and to the imitation of the Indian goods that were needed for the West African trade. French political authorities also realized that the restrictions on the manufacture of cotton had not stemmed demand for cotton goods but instead encouraged smuggling and illegal consumption. In 1759, the ban on printing was lifted, which led to the founding of a large number of printing works, including the famous workshop of Christoff-Philipp Oberkampf in Jouy. Even before the lifting of the ban, however, cotton manufactories began to spring up in Amiens and Angers, where a workshop "boldly produced imitation Indian textiles under the protection of local authorities."[90] But, by then, the cotton men of Lancashire had gained an insurmountable lead.[91]

Conclusion

As shown in this chapter, a broad constellation of state actions and inactions had a profound impact on economic fortunes in the seventeenth and eighteenth centuries. States used their power in a variety of ways to meet pressing economic needs and to achieve political and economic goals, whether it was to protect local manufacturing, as many rulers in Europe did, or to capture and retain markets, as the British did in the Atlantic. Neither type of state action was universal in the eighteenth century, as revealed by the Ottoman case. Ottoman political authorities approached the economy from a different perspective and with the different goal of provisioning, or satisfying the consumption needs of its people, as opposed to the European focus on the expansion of production. This difference had far-reaching economic consequences. Therefore, whatever one's theoretical position on the optimal or proper role of the state may be, on empirical grounds alone the state must be an integral part of the historical account, for political actions shaped economic life.

Longstanding explanations for why states intervene in the economy focus on the problems of market failure and the absence of critical factors for economic growth. State action is then seen as necessary to correct the failure or supply the factors. Market failures are a widely discussed theme in economic theory and economic history. State support for education, in particular, figures in the literature in economic history, and is taken up in the final chapter of this book. The problem of missing factors has also been a staple of writings in economic history. Alexander Gerschenkron provided a classic statement with reference to the scarcity of capital in nineteenth-century Russia where "the compulsory machinery of the government . . . through its taxation policies, succeeded in directing incomes from consumption to investment." "There is no doubt that the government . . . discharged its role in a far less than perfectly efficient manner . . . But when all is said and done, the great success of the policies . . . is undeniable," Gerschenkron concluded.[92]

The British and French state policies examined in this chapter do not fit either of the above frameworks and they were not responses to market failures or to missing factors. British seizure of markets in the Atlantic through violence and force had nothing to do with problems with the workings of the market. Nor did British and French bans on

Indian cloth imports correct any market shortcoming. These actions were taken to reshape market outcomes which were deemed to be unacceptable. They were self-conscious actions to protect and expand the national economy.[93]

In the case of Britain, Joan Thirsk, David Ormrod, Patrick O'Brien, Martin Daunton and others have described the variety of policies which were used from the sixteenth century to develop the British economy and transform the place of Britain in the European and then global economic order. We have already encountered the words of Thomas Smith who argued in 1549 that it was better to produce "within the Realm."[94] For nearly three centuries Smith's call to maximize production at home and minimize importation from abroad became the basis for a vision of economic progress. According to Joan Thirsk, Smith also "introduced new principles on which industries might be set up in England. They might use raw materials drawn from other countries."[95] This new approach expanded the possibilities for the growth of manufacturing, but their execution demanded vigorous state support, as Thirsk shows, including the resettling of foreign workers in England, the granting of monopoly privileges to manufacturers, and protection from foreign competition. By the early seventeenth century, these new projects were "yielding rewards to projectors, and giving work to large numbers of people in many different parts of the country." They illustrated the early benefits of a state that rejected the outcomes of the market.[96]

Although there were shifts in terminology (the language of projects and projectors became rarer over time), and policies did not have the coherence or reach of those that were to emerge in the nineteenth and twentieth centuries, the state continued to play a crucial role in the economic transformation of Britain before 1800. In a series of articles, Patrick O'Brien has argued that the navy and an exceptional fiscal system were critical to the growth of the early-modern British economy. The British navy captured and protected markets while the fiscal state created a political institution that was strong enough to promote economic improvement.[97] The making of economic policy became more sophisticated with time and by the early eighteenth century "variation of the tariff structure together with the redistribution of a large and growing customs revenue, via bounties, drawbacks and tax exemptions, provided the means to promote industrial interests, to encourage import saving, to stimulate the growth of re-exports vis-à-vis domestic consumption, and to modify the terms of trade between British exports and imports of foreign goods and raw materials."[98] This is the context in which the British state restricted the imports of Indian cloth. The purpose of these interventions into the economy was not to correct market failures or to supply missing factors, but to interfere in the operation of the market in order to preserve British employment and manufacturing and to transform Britain's place in the global trading order. And behind these protected walls, British cotton masters experimented with an imported raw material and sought to imitate and surpass Indian goods. State intervention of this sort was to be a staple of British policy making well into the nineteenth century and Martin Daunton has labeled it "the visible hand."[99]

The centrality of the state for economic life in both Europe and Asia suggests a deeper point about the relationship between the state and the market. Differences in the efficiency of markets across the advanced regions of Europe and Asia do not explain divergent paths of development. Of course, with all other things being equal, well-functioning markets are preferable, but the purpose of state policy in Europe was not to exploit market outcomes – even if they were efficient – but to reshape the impact of the market in order to promote economic change and growth. Rather than the efficiency of markets, the effectiveness of states and their political and economic philosophies were more important for economic development.

The approach of this work is to ask not if states should intervene in the economy but how state actions shaped economic paths. That is, it begins with the empirical fact that state policies, whether to constrain the operation of markets or to maintain a regime of free trade, had profound economic consequences. A non-interventionist state was not always superior, as the Ottoman case shows, where the unconstrained import of Indian cotton cloth led to monetary and manufacturing problems. For eighteenth-century actors, it was clear that state policies had a great impact on economic life, which is why many individuals in Britain and France devoted time and energy to shaping these policies. And these actors understood that protection could promote the development of manufacturing and industry. In the late 1780s, the muslin manufacturers of Britain, for instance, were unequivocal on the contribution that protection made to the development of British cottons.

It was not only state policies on trade that varied between Britain, France and the Ottoman Empire. These states also differed sharply in their relationships to labor. The regimentation and intensification of work, the massive increase in working hours, and the rise of new forms of work organization such as the factory were crucial for growth and industrialization in eighteenth- and nineteenth-century Britain. These changes increased the efficiency of labor and cheapened the costs of production, which made it possible for British manufacturers to compete more effectively. Writing of Samuel Oldknow, George Unwin said, "The effect of the competition of India combined with that of Lancashire and Scotland was to give Oldknow a stronger impetus towards the adoption of the factory system."[100] This remaking of the lives of laborers to meet the needs of manufacturers was dependent upon state policies and regulations, including measures such as the combination acts, limits on the mobility of workers, and the regulation of labor contracts.[101] Such state policies had a long history in Britain, but they received further justification from mercantilist thinking, which was deeply concerned with the efficient deployment of labor for national wealth and competitiveness.[102]

The relationship between state and labor that was found in eighteenth-century Britain had no counterpart in much of Asia. In the Indian subcontinent, the use of state power to discipline labor became a staple of policy only with the establishment of British colonial rule.[103] Until then, laboring groups had greater power in the political and economic order than their counterparts in Britain. Laborers in the subcontinent were in a stronger position in dealings with their superiors. They possessed more secure contracts, whether in weaving, agriculture or other services. And, perhaps most importantly, there was little state regulation of the labor market in support of those who utilized labor.[104] Such exercise of state power was foreign as well to the Ottoman Empire where guilds continued to flourish in the eighteenth century. Artisans, therefore, enjoyed monopoly privileges and power in the marketplace for longer than in Britain. In France as well, laboring groups were in a stronger position than in Britain. "Despite a distinct preference for a harsh brand of discipline on the part of most master artisans, entrepreneurs, and local officials, the laboring classes were not cowed and not without influence. Labor legislation under Louis XVI demonstrates that, for many influential government decision makers, both in theory and in practice, the laboring classes had to retain significant autonomy of action on the shop floor," a study of French industrialization between 1750 and 1850 concluded.[105] Therefore, the political institutions governing labor in Britain were not necessarily the norm even within Europe and they too contributed to Britain's eighteenth-century economic divergence.

APPENDIX

The French path of heavy cottons

Before the restriction on cotton printing was lifted in 1759, French manufacturers in Rouen – and in several other centers where Rouen goods began to be copied – focused their energies on making the heavier mixtures of cotton and linen rather than on imitating the lighter cloths of the Indian subcontinent. The focus on heavy cotton varieties may have begun with the *arrêt* of 1709 by the Parlement of Rouen, which permitted the use of cotton wefts, and these began to be used with silk warps to weave *siamoises*, an imitation of the robes that ambassadors from Siam had worn for an audience with Louis XIV in 1684 and 1686.[106] Linen warps soon replaced the silk in order to produce a lower-priced cloth. Other mixed textiles were also woven with cotton and linen in Rouen, including fustians and even some lighter cloths such as handkerchiefs, which the growing popularity of snuff made an essential accessory.[107]

The expanding use of cotton in Rouen was not free of tensions and troubles, however. After a decade of rapid growth, city officials became concerned that cotton spinning in the surrounding countryside was creating shortages of workers for agriculture. For about ten years, there were heated debates between the supporters and opponents of restrictions on the cotton industry, but the Parlement of Rouen opted to give fairly free room for its development. From the 1730s, according to Serge Chassagne, "nothing more hindered the victorious expansion of cotton," but the French cotton manufacturers were already several decades behind those of Britain.[108]

A survey conducted in 1727, the findings of which are contained in Table 5.3, reveals that 59 percent of the cotton workers in Rouen, the major cotton manufacturing center in France, produced siamoise. In the eighteenth century, the term siamoise encompassed a large variety of linen, silk and cotton mixtures, but until at least mid-century these cloths were heavier than the cottons of India. A source from 1722 reports that the cotton goods made in Rouen replaced "little cloths

Table 5.3 *Distribution of cotton workers in Rouen, 1727*

Type of cloth	Number of workers	Percent of total
Siamoises	14,988	59
Striped toiles, linen and cotton	2,664	11
All cotton toiles	3,160	13
Fustians	400	2
Linen and cotton handkerchiefs	344	1
All cotton handkerchiefs	3,704	15

Source: Depitre, *Toile peinte*, pp. 147–8.

made of wool."[109] According to the eminent textile historian Florence Montgomery, "Their similarity to English worsteds, especially to striped camlets, is unmistakable, and doubtless these less expensive fabrics were made in the hope of capturing from England the bulk of the trade with Spain, including the more important West Indies and South American colonies. . . Striped siamoises made of linen and cotton were used for inexpensive coverings, summer slipcovers, bed covers, and hangings from 1737."[110]

Later in the eighteenth century the term "siamoise" was extended to lighter textiles. In 1762, the French *Manuel historique* listed thinner cotton and silk dress goods under the category of siamoise, but no samples of these cloths survive. By the 1770s, siamoise also designated a plain white cloth made from cotton or cotton and linen and twenty-seven such swatches are contained in the John Holker, Jr., papers, dated 1779. The absence of thinner siamoise swatches from earlier in the century, however, suggests that they were not manufactured before the 1750s or 1760s.[111] For much of the eighteenth century siamoises were cloths that were heavier than the average Indian calico and most definitely thicker and more substantial than muslin.

The activities of John Holker, Jr., who from the 1750s played a key role in the transfer of British cotton know-how to Rouen, also indicates the prominent place that heavier cottons held in the city. French officials saw Holker as useful "because he was familiar with the manufacture of fustians in Lancashire, and this implied a knowledge of cotton velvets."[112] In his first visit to England to recruit workers for Rouen, Holker financed an apprenticeship for one Peter

Morris to be trained in the cutting and shearing of fustians. Morris arrived in Rouen in 1755. In his first batch of a dozen English workers, Holker brought over at least three men who were expert in fustian manufacture. The other workers possessed knowledge of calendering and of loom and equipment manufacturing. Calendering was of special interest to the French because they believed that their velvets were inferior to those made in Britain because of poor finishing. Experts in fustians and velvets also loomed large in later contingents of migrants from Lancashire to Rouen. It is striking that not a single worker that Holker recruited is identified as an expert in any of the vast array of cloths that Lancashire manufactured in imitation of Indian goods.[113]

6 | *From cotton to coal*

Introduction

The breakthroughs in cotton spinning, which were complemented by advances in weaving technology from the early nineteenth century, reversed the longstanding trading relationship between Europe and Asia. The new order was first apparent in overseas markets for Indian cloth, where British goods began to displace Indian. By the early nineteenth century, British cotton masters began to market their imitations of Indian goods, often giving them Indian names, in the Americas, West Africa and the eastern Mediterranean and began to supplant Indian products. From the 1820s, British machine-spun yarn began to be exported to the subcontinent itself, commencing the deindustrialization of nineteenth-century India. And from mid-century, the cotton cloth of Lancashire began to be exported in enormous quantities to the Indian subcontinent – the birthplace of cotton.

The rapid growth of the cotton industry between 1770 and 1830 is impressive and there is little doubt that by the second quarter of the nineteenth century, Lancashire lay at the center of a new global textile manufacturing order. Despite the remarkable changes in the British economy in these decades, the rise of cotton alone would have produced a shallow economic transformation in Britain as well as elsewhere in Europe. The truly revolutionary industrial development of nineteenth-century Europe would not have been possible without coal and the new energy economy to which it gave rise.

As E. A. Wrigley has established so eloquently, the adoption of coal made possible unimagined levels of energy use in Britain.[1] The growing exploitation of coal also led to a number of major technological advances. The substitution of coal for charcoal in the smelting of iron made available enormous supplies of ferrous metal at lower prices. The demands of mining coal and the need to pump water from great depths contributed to the development of the steam engine. From the 1820s, in a further revolutionary development, the coal–iron and coal–steam complexes were combined in the railway.

Why did this new energy economy emerge in Europe and not Asia? From a comparison of Britain and the Yangzi delta, Kenneth Pomeranz has argued that Britain's coal complex was the fortuitous outcome of location and easy access. While the major commercial and manufacturing centers of Britain were found near rich deposits of coal, the Lower Yangzi delta, which was the most prosperous and economically advanced region of China, was situated at a great distance from the major coalfields of the north.[2] Although resource endowment explanations for economic development have long been popular, even a cursory reading of works such as Michael Flinn's *History of the British Coal Industry* makes it evident that vast human energy and ingenuity were required to make coal a viable item of trade and consumption in Britain. British coal was not simply disgorged from mines to hearths. Its consumption required innumerable innovations in transport and these were made possible by a steady and stable market, which in turn depended upon extensive state protection and regulation in the seventeenth and eighteenth centuries. Therefore, endowment and location are far from the full story of the rise of coal in the British Isles. By contrast, in China such vital state support and encouragement for coal were absent.

The cotton revolution

The application of machinery to the manufacture of cotton textiles had global repercussions. From the 1770s, cheap machine-spun cotton yarn was exported to a number of markets in Europe. British cotton weavers mounted spirited opposition to this trade because it increased the price of their materials and reduced demand for their cloths, but spinning interests triumphed and no limits were placed on exports. From the 1790s, British cloth was exported to the Ottoman Empire where it began to displace local production as well as imports from the Indian subcontinent. From around 1810, according to Christophe Aubin, a representative of a Glasgow cotton firm dispatched to gather information on the Ottoman market, British cloth succeeded in undercutting Indian goods. This led to a steady expansion, especially after 1825, in demand for the textiles of

Lancashire. At the same time, British cloth made rapid inroads at the expense of Indian in the markets of West Africa and North America.[3]

Textile manufacturers in the subcontinent suffered grievously with the rise of Lancashire and the rapid growth in exports of British cotton yarn and cloth. By 1820, the English East India Company had terminated its cloth trade and closed down the network of factories that had been purchasing Indian cottons for nearly two centuries. Indian merchants also felt the pressure of British competition in export markets and the decline in their business. All of this, of course, happened long before substantial quantities of British yarn and cloth began to be consumed in the subcontinent itself. By the 1820s, therefore, a new global economic order was clearly in place.[4]

The repercussions of British cotton's meteoric rise were felt at home as well as abroad. According to estimates by Nicholas Crafts and Knick Harley, in 1831 the cotton industry accounted for 17 percent of value added in British manufacturing, or almost a fifth of the income generated in industry.[5] The Lancashire cotton mills represented an unprecedented concentration of productive capacity. In the late 1830s, more than 400 million pounds of raw cotton were being processed and spun every year in the region.[6] (By contrast, in the eighteenth century, South India's consumption of cotton was measured in the tens of millions of pounds.)[7] With this extraordinary scale of manufacturing, the cotton industry spurred the development of the entire northwest region.

Cotton's contributions included the development of the machinery industry in Britain, the rise of engineering as a specialized branch of technical knowledge, and a great expansion in the ranks of the mechanically adept. John Aikin, the late eighteenth-century historian of Manchester, noted these changes:

The prodigious extension of the several branches of the Manchester [cotton] manufactures had likewise increased the business of several trades and manufactures connected with or dependent upon them . . . To the ironmongers shops, which are greatly increased of late, are generally annexed smithies, where many articles are made, even to nails . . . The tin-plate works have found additional employment in furnishing many articles for spinning machines; as have also the braziers in casting wheels for the motion-work of the rollers used in them; and the clock-makers in cutting them. Harness-makers have been much employed in making bands for carding engines, and large wheels for the first operation of drawing out the cardings, whereby the consumption of strong curried leather has been much increased.[8]

A. E. Musson and Eric Robinson, from an examination of the *Index to Wills of Lancashire and Cheshire Record Society*, concluded, "Mill-wrights and iron-founders rarely appear before the eighteenth century, but become increasingly numerous with the mechanization of the cotton industry. We also discover more specialized manufacturers of textile machinery, such as hand-loom, shuttle, and reed makers."[9] John Kennedy, an early cotton spinner, observed that the growth of the cotton trade "created a new demand for artificers in various branches . . . [who] became very useful in the construction of machinery."[10]

Kennedy also noted that several of the early innovators in cotton manufacturing were not mechanics, most notably Samuel Crompton, and that their early machines were rudimentary, made largely of wood with simple tools. While the first mules were not complex, the machine became more intricate, incorporating metal rollers, clock-work and iron. The growing complexity of machines increased the demand for experienced and knowledgeable mechanics, and many craftsmen, including smiths, joiners and shoemakers, came into the cotton industry from other trades because of the offer of higher wages. Therefore, while highly skilled workers of various sorts were found in Lancashire before the mechanization of cotton spinning – and those associated with mechanical arts such as clock making were critical to British technical breakthroughs – the increasing demand for more sophisticated machinery gave rise to a larger pool of men with such specialized forms of knowledge.[11]

The cotton revolution and energy

By 1830 the rise of Lancashire had reversed the longstanding flow of textiles from Asia to Europe and reshaped the world economy. This was achieved without a profound transformation in sources of energy for the process of production, however. The innovations that revolutionized the cotton industry – the jenny, the water frame and the mule – were designed to be powered by hand, animal or water. These machines were adapted to steam power in the late eighteenth century, but the adoption of steam as the motor force was a long and uneven process. Certainly by the late nineteenth century, the cotton industry was the largest user of steam power in Britain. An industrial census of 1870 reported that 280,602 horsepower in the cotton mills came from steam. By comparison, steam engines contributed 164,511 horsepower to blast furnaces for ironmaking and 92,000 horsepower for woolen and worsted manufacturing. Even so, until the 1870s mules continued to be powered by hand for the spinning of finer counts.[12]

G. N. von Tunzelmann's social saving calculation – that in 1800 steam engines accounted for only 0.2 percent of the national income of Britain – is well known. Less famous is his careful and painstaking reconstruction of the growth of steam power in the cotton industry. Von Tunzelmann estimates that in 1800 steam engines accounted for only 1500 to 2000 horsepower in the cotton mills, which he sees as evidence that they "had a belated effect on the spectacular expansion of the cotton industry in the last quarter of the eighteenth century."[13] In the nineteenth century, the choice between steam and water was based on the relative prices of the two sources of power. Between the 1790s and the mid-1830s, the price of water power remained stable and there was little incentive to make the switch to steam.

In the depression of the late 1830s and early 1840s there was a decline in profitability in cotton manufacturing. In an effort to restore profits, mill owners began to operate their machinery at higher speeds, thus intensifying the pace of work. The decline in profitability was even more marked in the late 1840s, and according to von Tunzelmann, this produced another push towards running machinery faster. The Factory Act of 1847, which reduced the length of the working day to ten hours, further contributed to an intensification of work and a speeding up of machinery. It was in this context that a large-scale shift was made from water to steam. Only with steam power could machines be run at the higher speeds that owners demanded, and from the late 1830s, the steam engine displaced the water wheel on an expanding scale.[14] The switch to steam was by no means automatic, but shaped by the conditions of profitability and by relations between mill owners and their workers. For several decades, water, an old and longstanding source of energy, was adequate for the needs of cotton production, which was also the case in the United States where a sizable machine-based cotton industry was built on the basis of water power.[15]

The slow diffusion of steam power in Lancashire suggests a more general point. The nineteenth-century British economy relied on non-revolutionary sources of power for a very long time. Animate sources of energy dominated in agriculture and made huge contributions to industry. The remarks of Raphael Samuel on this subject are worth quoting at length:

In mid-Victorian England there were few parts of the economy which steam power and machinery had left untouched, but fewer still where it ruled unchallenged. At both top and bottom a mainly hand technology prevailed, at top because of the irreplaceability of human skills, at bottom because of the plentiful supply of drudges. High technology industry – what some Marxists call "machinofacture" – was for the most part confined to the factories, but even here mechanization was very far from complete. One might refer to the pot-makers at a steel-works, the rag-sorters at a paper-mill or to the bottle hands whom Dodd describes at Day and Martin's, Holborn, meting out blacking from vats. In the Lancashire mills the "self-acting mule" depended on the nimble fingers of the piecers, while power-loom weavers kept their machines at work by "shuttle-kissing", threading the weft with their lips. In ironmaking the whole scale of enterprise was transformed by technical innovation, but labour remained absolutely primary at the point of production itself. As the *Morning Chronicle* Commissioner wrote in 1850, after investigating the Monmouthshire iron works: "Although capital is the motive power, it is upon the rude virtues of the workman that the entire system of manufacture . . . rests".[16]

Samuel's description of early nineteenth-century iron work captures the prodigious quantities of labor that went into building British economic might, and therefore economic divergence:

Cort's puddling furnace, which revolutionized the work, was chemical rather than mechanical in its action. It cheapened the production process and made possible an enormous increase in output, but it made labour itself a great deal more severe. The puddler, who had the key role in the new process, was given a task that was simultaneously highly skilled and exhausting, turning a viscous mass of liquid into metal. He worked in conditions of tremendous heat, violently agitating the metal as it boiled, rabbling it from side to side in the furnace . . . The men had to relieve each other every few minutes, so great was the exertion and so intense the heat, but even so it was said that every ounce of excess fat was drained from them.[17]

Nevertheless, in the final decades of the eighteenth century, and roughly paralleling the growth of cotton, an economy of iron and steam – centered around the exploitation of coal – was beginning to take shape in Britain. Although its impact on British economic growth may have been slower than many older accounts recognized, it did eventually reshape transport, construction and communications in Britain, and around the world. This coal, iron and steam complex did not have a counterpart in the economically advanced regions of China or India. To explain this other economic divergence in Eurasia, we turn to the domain of ecology, more specifically to forests and woods.

Ecological change in Eurasia

In *The Unending Frontier*, John Richards describes an early-modern world in which human settlement and activity expanded across the globe, at the expense of "forests, woodlands, wetlands, and savannas," leading to dwindling supplies of resources that had been obtained for millennia from the natural world.[18] Perhaps the most crucial of these was wood, which met a variety of needs. Wood was the most important fuel for cooking, heating of homes and manufacturing. Wood was a major building material. Wood was the chief ingredient in countless tools, agricultural implements and machines. However, by the eighteenth century a number of regions in the world were experiencing acute shortages of this essential material.

In the British Isles, the scarcity of wood may have been impinging on economic activity from as early as the sixteenth century. In the seventeenth century in the Netherlands, which had limited woodlands to begin with, the lack of wood for fuel had led to the large-scale burning of peat. In the eighteenth century, the forests of Central Europe were feeling the pressure of more intensive exploitation. One observer wrote in 1720,

It is known even without my remembrance, how much all Germany, and especially worthy Saxony, has increased in great quantities of all things good due to a long enjoyed peace . . . Yet, despite this fortune, there is a small inconvenience because through cleaning and clearing the arable and meadows almost everywhere a scarcity of wood will arise, so that to supply it, a great deficiency is felt in these middling countries.[19]

This was not a lone voice. "Felling of wood has increased to such an extent for some time that almost everywhere bare mountains and clear cut forests reveal to everyone their poverty of wood," wrote another commentator.[20] Although a crisis of wood was mounting in several parts of Europe, there were some zones of abundance. Parts of France were generally better provisioned than her neighbors. And of course Scandinavia and Russia were well forested in 1800 and later.

The story in China is one of growing shortages of timber. Although some forests remained in the frontier areas of the empire, core zones of population and economic activity were largely denuded of trees by 1800. Evidence for this environmental state of affairs is abundant for a number of regions. Peter Perdue and Robert Marks have documented growing deforestation in the major provinces of Hunan and Guangdong. The Lower Yangzi was becoming increasingly treeless in the eighteenth century. It was much the same in Tokugawa Japan where dwindling forests were leading to growing environmental problems.[21]

This crisis of wood spawned a number of responses in Eurasia. The first were conservation measures which sought to control and limit access to forests and their timber. Conservation was also achieved through innovations that raised the efficiency of energy use. A second was the rise of silviculture and plantation forestry, which attempted to regenerate forestlands. A third was the development of substitutes to wood for a wide variety of tasks. The most revolutionary response to wood shortages emerged in this third area and came from the substitution of coal for wood, which in Wrigley's famous words replaced an organic source of energy with an inorganic one.

The growing adoption of coal in place of wood took place in both Asia and Europe. North China may have led the way with its greater use of coal from the eleventh century. According to Robert Hartwell, the exploitation of coal in this period was propelled by deforestation and the resulting shortage of wood in the northern parts of the empire.[22] Jumping ahead to the early-modern period, Sung Ying-hsing's great seventeenth-century manual on Chinese technology reported: "Coal is obtainable everywhere, and is used for the smelting and calcination of metals and stones. South of the Yangtse River, coal is found in mountains that are bare of trees. We need not discuss the situation in North China." The translators of this work have interpreted the last sentence – that there is no need to "discuss the situation in North China" – as implying that coal use was widespread in the north because of extensive deforestation. The seventeenth-century manual also noted that coal was used in the Middle and Lower Yangzi in places named as Wu and Ch'u: "Of the bituminous coal, which is mostly produced in Wu and Ch'u, there are two types: the high volatile type is known as 'rice coal' and is used in cooking, while the low volatile is called 'iron coal' and is used in smelting and forging metals."[23]

Substantial quantities of coal continued to be consumed in China in the eighteenth and nineteenth centuries. Peter Golas has hazarded a guess that in the nineteenth century China probably produced several million tons of coal a year and that some of the pits were as large as those found in Europe in the eighteenth or nineteenth centuries.[24] Coal was consumed on a large scale for household and manufacturing uses in Beijing, which was situated a short distance from sizable deposits. Supplies of coal were transported to the city on camels and state authorities took a keen interest in this trade. Coal continued to be mined and utilized for the smelting of iron in the Shanxi area of North China, which is not surprising given that this had for several centuries been the center of Chinese coal mining and the region contained large and easily accessible deposits.[25]

The consumption of coal was not confined to North China in the eighteenth century. Golas reports that coal use spread to South China during the Ming period and in some areas became widespread.[26] There is evidence from the nineteenth century that substantial deposits of coal – although not rivaling those of the north or the west – were exploited in central and southern Hunan. By the mid-nineteenth century, there was a sizable trade in coal from Hunan to Hankou and from that city down the Yangzi to Nanjing and Shanghai, and Golas estimates that 150,000 tons were shipped every year on this route.[27] We have a description of the first leg of this trade from Baron Richthofen who visited Hankou in 1870: "The amount of Lui-Yang extracted coal is already large. It is used in all the places down the Siang river. Most of it is carried to Hankau, where some, considered a trifling amount by the Siang-tan coal dealers, is sold to the foreign steamers. Some is carried as far as Kiukiang and Nanking."[28] That little coal went to steamships indicates that this trade had not arisen to meet the fuel needs of this new mode of transport on the Yangzi. Steamships were introduced on the river in 1860, but in the previous year Lord Elgin visited Hankou and was astonished by the scale of the coal trade in the city. William Rowe has drawn upon Chinese sources and also concluded that there was a sizable trade in coal before westerners arrived in Hankou.[29] In 1870, von Richthofen predicted a great future for the coal deposits of Hunan if a market could be found for the "excellent anthracite." "The establishment of deep mining, the abolition of transit and other dues on coal, and the provision for cheap freight on the Yang-tse, may co-operate to allow the coal to find its way to Shanghai as a permanent article of export," he wrote.[30]

From the late seventeenth century, coal was also used as an energy source in Japan when supplies of wood were exhausted, especially in the area of Kyushu which was close to coal deposits. In the eighteenth century, growing industrial demand for fuel led to further experimentation with coal. According to Conrad Totman, salt and sugar makers and potters from the Nobi Plain westward, in particular, replaced wood with coal. At the same time, Totman has reported that the increased exploitation of coal produced a backlash because of the "noxious fumes and sticky, destructive fallout." Both the mining and burning of coal "caused water pollution that led to conflict, litigation, instances of compensation, and efforts at regulation." In some places, the pollution from coal sparked a return to wood as the primary fuel.[31]

In Europe, coal had been used for domestic purposes since at least the Roman era. In medieval times, there is evidence that the use of coal continued or revived in parts of the British Isles, in the vicinity of Liège, in a variety of centers in central and southern France, and in Aachen and the Ruhr district. In the seventeenth and eighteenth centuries, coal production and consumption expanded in response to growing shortages of wood. The mines of Liège and France increased production to meet the growing demand for energy and coal began to replace wood in salt making, lime burning and metal forging. Coal also began to be exploited on an expanding scale in the German-speaking areas of Central Europe. In 1697, the government of Saxony issued an "Item of Resolutions in Wood and Forest Matters," which instructed that "to remedy the wood scarcity as soon as possible, subjects, in particular black and lock smiths, who can obtain mineral coals, must use them for their needs or at least no longer give them wood or charcoal." Similar orders were issued a few decades later when forest officials were told "to find peat and mineral coals, to accustom the inhabitants as much as possible that they use it for their homes and crafts instead of firewood."[32] For guidance on how coal could be used, the Germans turned to the British, and from the late seventeenth century a number of English writings on coal were translated into German. The turn to Britain for knowledge of coal is not surprising given that that from an early date it was the leading producer of coal in Europe. According to Paolo Malanima, by 1800 Britain accounted for 85 percent of European coal consumption.[33]

Between 1550 and 1700 English coal production may have grown more than tenfold.[34] Expanding demand for fuel in the vast London market and the relative ease of water transport from the major coal mines of northern England to the southeast were significant in this expansion. In the early eighteenth century, London was the destination for more than 70 percent of the coal shipped along the east coast and much of this coal went to the homes and hearths of the city.[35] John Hatcher estimates that before 1700 domestic uses accounted for about half of the total coal consumption in England, and Michael Flinn reports a similar proportion for the early eighteenth century.[36] While demand for domestic use was vital, coal displaced wood and charcoal in industrial processes over the course of the seventeenth century, especially in lime burning, brewing, glassmaking and salt manufacturing.

In the eighteenth century, the trend towards the greater industrial use of coal continued, especially after mid-century when iron manufacturing began to utilize it for more processes. In 1750, the iron industry consumed 0.4% of English coal. By 1775, this had grown to 2.3% and by 1800 to 12.0%. In 1830, iron production consumed nearly a fifth of British coal. In these decades, the demand for domestic consumption did not flag. Between 1775 and 1830, domestic demand declined from 42.5% of total output to 37.9%, but in terms of quantity, it more than tripled. The seemingly insatiable appetite for coal and the invention of new uses for it propelled the rise of a new energy economy in Britain.[37]

The steam engine and the use of coal in manufacturing were the two key elements in this new energy complex. While coal was exploited in a growing number of manufacturing processes, the most revolutionary was in iron smelting, where the substitution of coal for charcoal dramatically lowered the price of iron and increased its supply. Iron began to be used on a larger scale, replacing wood and other organic materials in construction, machinery and transport. The steam engine was a new prime mover which took advantage of the growth in energy supplies that coal made possible. The improvement and diffusion of the steam engine itself, as is well known, was intimately connected with the pumping of water from coal mines.

Why Britain?

Why did this new energy complex take off in Britain, but not in China where coal had been consumed for several centuries? For Kenneth Pomeranz, the answer to this question lay in the location of coal. In Britain, coal deposits were widespread and easily conveyed to water, the cheapest form of transport for low-value, bulky commodities. In China, the major deposits of coal lay in the north, far from the major population centers of the south, especially the Lower Yangzi delta, China's most advanced region. Coal in northern China was also not within easy proximity of water transport. As a consequence, Pomeranz argues that the Lower Yangzi was unable to expand its ecological possibilities in the eighteenth and nineteenth centuries. In his words, "It was hardly likely that coal in particular would have attracted much attention from the Lower Yangzi's artisans and entrepreneurs; there was little coal either in the region itself or in places easily accessible to its traders."[38]

One problem with the Pomeranz argument is that there is quite a bit of evidence for the use of coal in the Lower Yangzi. The previous section gave several examples of coal consumption along the Yangzi in the nineteenth century. While they mostly pertain to the vicinity of Hankou, which lies in the Middle Yangzi, there are also indications that coal was carried further down the river into its lower reaches at Nanjing and Shanghai. Its use in the Lower Yangzi is also revealed by Lord Elgin, who reported in 1858 that coal was used in kilns to manufacture lime in a town that lay on the Yangzi River between Hankou and Shanghai.[39] There is also evidence from the eighteenth century for the mining and use of coal in the Lower Yangzi and its periphery.[40] Coal was also mined further south in China, which is evident from Figure 6.1, which is a painting from the 1790s of a coal mine in Guangdong. The painting depicts a minehead next to a waterway and coal being brought to the surface and loaded upon a boat, which indicates that coal deposits were scattered around China and they were exploited in the eighteenth century.

A second problem with the Pomeranz argument is that it ignores the fact that not all coal in Britain was brought to the surface and easily

Figure 6.1 Detail of a view of the coal depot at Ying-tih-heen, in Shaouchow foo (Guangdong), late eighteenth century, British Museum, London, Landsdowne MS.1243. (vol.ii.33). © The Trustees of the British Museum.

carried to boats or ships. From most mineheads coal had to be transported some distance on land, which meant that access had to be obtained through the property of others and economical methods of carriage had to be devised. From at least the seventeenth century, British mine operators and coal transporters worked to improve and cheapen the costs of land transport. "One of the most significant developments in the later seventeenth century," according to John Hatcher, "was the spectacular growth in the output of collieries located some distance from the south bank of the Tyne, which was made possible by the provision of wooden waggonways along which coal could be cheaply transported."[41]

Therefore, the location of coal alone cannot explain the different patterns of coal use in Britain and China and the emergence of a new energy complex in the former. More critically, a comparison of the histories of coal in China and Britain shows a striking difference in the policies of the state. The British state took a more active interest in coal, both directly and indirectly, than did the state in China.

John Nef has described in great detail the contribution made by the seventeenth-century English state to the development of coal and he devoted the final part of his classic two-volume study to "Coal and Public Policy." There Nef wrote, "The expansion of the coal industry created numerous problems which could not be ignored by the central government. An examination of the Privy Council Register, the Calendar of State Papers, the proceedings of the Treasury, and the records of debates in the Commons and the Lords, yields convincing evidence that the regulation of the coal trade was not left entirely to the judiciary and to the municipal authorities, but was a subject of continual concern to the national government."[42] A history of the British coal trade, published in 1835, recounts one dramatic episode of state intervention in the seventeenth century. During the struggle between Charles I and Parliament, the trade in coal from Newcastle was severely disrupted and the "inhabitants of London, especially the poor, were perishing for want of fuel." The House of Commons took the "management of the coal trade into their own hands; and a great quantity of coals were subsequently sent up to London, where they had previously risen to the enormous price of four pounds per chaldron. . . [and] the collieries were set to work with redoubled vigour."[43]

As this passage makes apparent, the coal trade was of great import-ance because it was essential for the survival of Londoners. As Nef put it, "Obstructions placed in the way of the traffic in coal along the east coast threatened the very existence of a large part of the population now gathered together in the capital. For coal had become, as seventeenth-century writers continually pointed out, no less essential to the lives of the citizens during the winter months than bread itself."[44] This continued to be the case in the eighteenth century when the most important factor in the well-being of eighteenth-century Londoners may have been the price of coal. It was not only residents of London who were dependent upon the coastal trade in coal, how-ever. Over the course of the seventeenth and eighteenth centuries, coal became an indispensable source of energy in a number of provincial centers. And because coal was used in the manufacture of military equipment, including guns, saltpeter and gunpowder, the defense of the trade was aligned with the defense of the realm.[45]

The coal trade was also of great importance for state authorities as it became a reliable and easy source of revenue. Coal was an ideal commodity for taxation. Its bulk made it difficult to smuggle. A sizable fraction of the British supply came from two small districts in the Tyne and Wear valleys and reached the sea through two narrow rivers, which made the collection of taxes inexpensive. Finally, the size of the trade was growing, which promised steadily expanding revenues. From the late sixteenth century, the English and later British state took a keen interest in protecting and regulating the coal trade to ensure supplies of coal for London and other urban centers and to guarantee a stream of revenue.

One set of state policies revolved around the export of coal. In the late sixteenth century, there were wide-ranging debates on the wisdom of permitting the unimpeded export from both England and Scotland. While consumers in the British Isles called for an export ban, producers fought any restriction on their trade. A compromise was reached in 1590 and a duty of 5s. per Newcastle chaldron (approximately two tons) was levied on exports from all English and Welsh ports.[46] The duty not only satisfied the domestic consumers of coal, but also created a new source of revenue for the state. In the seventeenth century, this export duty was periodically increased and in the early eighteenth century eliminated for a short time, but then restored and raised to even higher levels.[47]

The duties, by discouraging the export of coal, kept the price lower for users in Britain. Their impact on prices must be balanced against excise taxes that were placed on coal that was transported by sea and consumed domestically. These excises were imposed in the seventeenth century and by 1700 had reached 3s. 6d. per ton. The taxes had their greatest impact on London, which was heavily reliant upon coastal shipping for its coal supplies. Coal sold in London was further encumbered by additional levies that raised funds for a variety of uses in the city. William J. Hausman has estimated that in the eighteenth century these taxes accounted for a third of the selling price of coal in the city. (The price to the consumer was 30s. per chaldron. The taxes came to 10s.)[48] There was vociferous

opposition in both Newcastle and London to the levies, but their value
to the crown – in 1789 they stood at more than half a million pounds
or 3 percent of total revenues – and their ease of collection – the cost of
collecting the tax was about 15,000 pounds a year – meant that it took
decades to abolish them. The coal excises were not fully eliminated till
1831 and export duties remained in effect till 1845.[49]

Both John Nef and Michael Flinn argued that the taxes on coastal
shipping impeded the economic development of Britain. In the words
of Flinn, "There can be no doubt at all that . . . the fiscal policies of the
eighteenth- and early nineteenth-century governments exercised a
most powerful brake on the development of the industry." Nef echoes
this assessment of the taxes, but in even more expansive terms: "They
undoubtedly handicapped the general growth of British industry and
foreign trade during the eighteenth century, and were probably a
factor in retarding the remarkable economic development which is
called the Industrial Revolution."[50] Such bleak assessments must be
tempered, however. The London market, which most felt the weight of
the taxes on the coastal coal trade, has received a disproportionate
share of attention from historians because of the abundant source
material, but London's consumption, while sizable, represented only
a part of total British demand. And London's share declined in the
eighteenth and early nineteenth centuries. In 1700, the city accounted
for about 15% of British coal consumption. By 1750, this figure had
fallen to 13%; in 1800 it stood at 8% and slipped further to 7% in
1830.[51] The small weight of London, and therefore, the small fraction
of coal that came under heavy excises, is why Flinn himself acknowledges that the growth of the British coal industry in the eighteenth
century was steady and continuous. Between 1700 and 1830 coal
production increased more than "tenfold" and "growth accelerated
steadily up to 1815."[52]

Even if the excise on coal reduced consumption in London and
production in Newcastle, it likely contributed to the expansion of coal
mining in other regions of Britain, including the Midlands, Lancashire
and Yorkshire, where the tax did not apply. The tax was also an
incentive to expand manufacturing outside London, especially in the
Midlands and in northwestern England. Therefore, the overall effect
on British economic development is in need of more careful analysis.

Even while taxing the coal of Londoners, the British state took
action to protect the residents of the city from extraordinarily high

prices and in the eighteenth century intervened "with unfailing regularity" in the London market.[53] Municipal officials accumulated stocks of coal to supply the poor in times of shortage or high prices. At times the London government also instituted price maximums and checked the excessive profits of London coal dealers, including punishment for engrossing the commodity or collusion among sellers to raise prices.[54] London officials also regulated the quality of coal marketed in the city and ensured that the measurement systems used by coal sellers were accurate.

Collusion among coal dealers was not confined to London, but was also found among the mine owners of the northeast. The British state acted to restrict these as well and from the seventeenth century to the early nineteenth century a number of Parliamentary Acts were implemented to break up combinations in Newcastle. These measures helped to increase the supply and lower the price of coal and in this way benefited the consumer. T. S. Ashton and Joseph Sykes remarked that after the passage of an anti-combination act in 1730 the price of Newcastle coal fell from 15s. to 9s. 6d. a chaldron. When the act expired in 1739, the price rose to 13s., only to decline again in 1744 to 11s. when another measure was passed to limit collusion among the coal dealers of Newcastle.[55]

Another important state policy was protection for the coastal trade in coal, which was designed both to protect the revenues obtained from coal and to provision London with essential supplies of fuel. In 1750, about 55 percent of the coal produced in the northeast, or more than 20 percent of the total coal production of Britain, was transported by sea to the south.[56] Piracy was an almost constant threat to these ships and in the seventeenth century Dunkirkers harassed and took coal ships ransom. Privateering remained a problem into the eighteenth century and in 1704, "the Lords gave their assent to an Act for the increase of seamen, and security of the coal trade."[57] Michael Flinn writes, "In wartime – and in the seventy-six years between 1739 and 1815 there were forty-five years of war – there were the twin hazards of enemy privateers and the press-gang . . . In May 1779, for example, French privateers got among the collier fleet soon after it had left the Tyne and several of the ships were attacked, captured, and immediately ransomed, and in September the American privateer, *Paul Jones*, interfered with the trade . . . 'Privateers so much invest the coast,' wrote Delaval's agent from Hartley in 1779."[58]

The wartime disruption in the coastal trade dated back to the mid-seventeenth century when, during a confict with the Dutch, north–south shipping ground to a halt and the price of coal skyrocketed in London. Trade was restored only after the intercession of English battleships that convoyed the coal ships along the coast. According to Nef, "The lesson was plain. Now that London had become dependent upon the north of England for her fuel . . . the nation must have a navy strong enough to keep the enemy from blocking the passage along the east coast." As a consequence, after the conclusion of the Dutch War, "the trade was never left altogether without protection from pirate vessels or enemy battleships, and before the end of the seventeenth century the convoy system was greatly improved."[59] The Royal Navy continued to protect the shipping of coal in the eighteenth century and naval vessels accompanied coal convoys along the coast.[60]

Britain was endowed with bountiful deposits of coal, but human ingenuity and state policies shaped its exploitation. The state protected the coastal trade in coal in order to provision London and to collect its coal revenues. With this protection, for which the Royal Navy was essential, and with the regulation of the sale of coal, the state helped to maintain stable demand for the mines of the northeast. The coastal trade also benefited both the navy and merchant shippers as it was a training ground for sailors. In the eighteenth century, the coastal shipping fleet from Newcastle to London was known as the nursery for British seamen.[61]

The British state and iron

The British state supported the consumption of coal directly, as just described, as well as indirectly. The most important indirect support was a series of policies that encouraged iron production within the kingdom. These began in the mid-sixteenth century during the reign of Henry VIII when word reached the Privy Council that the Dutch were to institute a ban on the export of iron to England. Fearing shortages of the essential metal, Henry VIII brought to England a French gun-founder and a Dutch gunsmith and these two men helped to advance the smelting of iron and the manufacture of iron guns, mortar pieces and shot. In the second half of the sixteenth century, three to four dozen French ironworkers were working in the Weald of Sussex and they assisted in the production of armaments for a war with France. According to Joan Thirsk, the district had a monopoly on the casting of iron guns for the next two centuries, but also developed iron goods for domestic use, in the seventeenth century supplying places like Barbados with iron pots in which slaves cooked their food.[62]

Despite the expansion of iron production from the mid-sixteenth century, England continued to be dependent on imports. Some observers feared that this endangered the defense of the realm since the army and navy were reliant upon foreigners for an indispensable material. While contemporary observers greatly exaggerated the quantity of imported iron in the sixteenth century – in the 1580s it stood at 1,200 to 1,300 tons per year, about 13 percent of domestic production – foreign iron became more important over time. By the end of the seventeenth century, imports accounted for half of ferrous metal consumption in Britain.[63] By 1750, imports satisfied nearly 60 percent of British demand and the nation was to be dependent on foreign sources of iron until the nineteenth century.[64]

According to Michael Flinn, English producers were prevented from meeting a larger proportion of demand because of higher costs of production, which stemmed from high charcoal prices, low-quality ore, high overhead costs due to shortages of water, and most importantly high costs of labor. "Nevertheless," Flinn writes, "a fairly substantial tariff kept up prices sufficiently to make iron production in this country profitable until the new techniques of the later eighteenth century gave England the advantage."[65] Tariffs on iron increased almost fivefold in the first half of the eighteenth century – going from 10s. a ton in 1688 to 48s. 6d. in 1759 – and they made iron smelting economically viable and gave iron producers the space in which they could experiment and innovate, especially with the use of coal in place of charcoal in the smelting and refining processes.[66]

The successful substitution of coal for charcoal turned Britain from a high- to a low-cost producer of iron. Although by 1709 Abraham Darby had solved many of the technical difficulties of smelting iron with coal, the change in technique did not take place till the second half of the century when the price of charcoal began to rise rapidly. And as noted, throughout the eighteenth century, the price of iron had been artificially inflated with steep import duties, which gave British ironmasters a cushion to innovate and develop new techniques. From the 1790s, armed with new technologies of production, British ironmasters drove foreign competitors out of the domestic market. In these years, British iron received support from even higher tariffs on imports, which were raised from 2.81 pounds per ton between 1782 and 1795 to 6.49 pounds per ton by 1813. The increased duties had the effect of sharply reducing "foreign sales of bar iron in Britain."[67]

British measures to restrict iron imports emerged in part from strategic considerations. There were longstanding fears of dependence on outside sources for a commodity that was so essential to the British economy and military. This was compounded in the eighteenth century by diplomatic and political tensions between Britain and Sweden, which erupted into open hostilities on two occasions. Tariffs on Swedish iron, by reducing imports, were one way in which dependence could be tempered. Another was to encourage the production of iron in the British colonies of North America, but because of staunch opposition from British iron producers this project never bore much fruit.[68] The same British ironmasters, however, innovated and adopted coal to bring down the costs of production, which eliminated the need for imported iron.

While the cost reductions were achieved with the utilization of coal in the smelting and refining processes, high tariffs provided an economic context that made this innovation possible. In a world of free trade, the structures of prices and costs in eighteenth-century Britain would have been less hospitable to experimentation and risk taking. And as Charles Hyde has argued, the adoption of coal after 1750 was very much a rational response to the changes in the relative price of charcoal.[69] Prices, which were reshaped by heavy tariffs, had an impact on the choices of British ironmasters.

The state and coal in China

While the British state adopted a number of policies that promoted the use of coal, the Chinese state did much less. In 1740, Chinese authorities issued a decree encouraging the private mining of coal throughout the empire, a sign that imperial officials were aware that coal production needed to be expanded to meet the energy needs of the empire. The overture to private mining operations was also a realization that the benefits of greater coal production outweighed the possible political and social instability created by growing numbers of miners. Since a major miner revolt of the mid-fifteenth century, Chinese authorities had sought to restrict private mining for fear that when the mines ran out the workers would turn to banditry.[70] Although the impact of the decree of 1740 was probably minimal, the extraction of a variety of minerals did grow rapidly in the eighteenth century, which gave rise to what has come to be known as the mid-Qing mining boom.[71] Aside from the decree of 1740, there is no other evidence for central state interest in coal. Nor is there much evidence of Chinese state interest in iron, despite its economic and ecological importance.

Although the central state did not engage with coal, there were instances of local official intervention. One example comes from a report penned by a county magistrate, Lu Chen-fei, in 1629:

I would observe that south of Ching-yang lies the Ching River, providing direct access to the Wei, on which there is a continuous flow of merchant shipping. Ching-yang, however, relies on the damming of waterways and loads are not carried by boat, the people being unaware of the advantages conferred on them by nature. Leaving aside the question of whether grain might be transported or timber floated in the form of rafts, this is even true of coal. Ching-yang is densely populated and has nothing to burn as firewood. The people depend on carriers and carts to supply them with fuel for cooking; and the effort used up in transport is a source of distress. A picul of coal never costs less than 0.4 of an ounce of silver, and may rise above 0.5 or 0.7 of an ounce. It is not always a lack of food-grains which prevents people from lighting a fire in wet or snowy weather. After having become aware of this, every time I went to the banks of the Ching River I would stand overlooking the current and gauge the depth. When I asked the boatmen about it they said: "The Ching River is quick-rushing, with numerous rocks, and is of varying depth. Merchant ships do not dare to travel on it." I sent my officials to inspect it, on foot along the riverside together with some boatmen. They reported that even in the shallowest places, if the water were only a foot or so deeper, it would take even a war-junk. I was delighted and declared it suitable for shipping. Even so, the people were apprehensive that accidental difficulties might arise. They grudged a small outlay, and so barred the way to subsequent profit. I therefore had a long, narrow boat constructed, and told sailors to pilot it to Ming-chiao-k'ou in Lin-t'ung county and fetch coal from there. They made the trip [of perhaps 50 miles] and had the coal unloaded in a mere three days. The transport cost was only seventy percent of that needed for carriers and carts.[72]

There is also little evidence of state intervention in iron production in China, even of the indirect sort that has been described for Britain, which was due to the more secure position of iron production, as compared to Britain, and the fact that it was in little need of state support or encouragement. In the seventeenth and eighteenth centuries, there were several major centers of iron smelting in China. In the north, the region of Shanxi had been the site of iron works for many centuries. The area also pioneered the use of coke as a substitute for charcoal in the eleventh and twelfth centuries. Baron von Richthofen visited Shanxi in 1870 and described the smelting process, "Crucibles of refractory clay . . . are filled with a mixture of small pieces of anthracite and crushed iron ore. All the spaces between crucibles are carefully filled out with anthracite, and a layer of the fuel is spread on top."[73] Shanxi was not the only iron center that used coal for fuel. In the early 1870s, von Richthofen reported that large and small blast furnaces in Hunan used coal in smelting iron ore.[74] Von Richthofen also reported that in Hunan iron ore was carried to places on the Yangzi "where it is smelted with coke from Siang-hiang."[75] Despite these examples, much of the iron smelting outside North China was done with charcoal as the fuel.

In western China, iron had been manufactured in Sichuan province since the Han period. Smelting was carried out in large blast furnaces that used water power with charcoal fuel. Although the production capacity was large, most of the output met demand for ferrous metal in the region itself and little iron was exported. Transport facilities within the region were excellent, but those that connected Sichuan to other parts of China were more limited, which may have been why little iron left the province.[76] Another charcoal-fueled iron center was in the southern province of Guangdong where there is extensive evidence for large-scale blast furnaces in the eighteenth century. These furnaces were located in the mountains of the province, near supplies of wood for charcoal. Wood may have been growing scarcer, however. A seventeenth-century writer warned that "if the mountain is bare, even if there is a great deal of iron it will be of no use. This is why 'iron mountains' are not easy to find."[77] Much of the pig iron was transported from the mountains by river to the city of Foshan where it was fabricated into a variety of products that were sold in other parts of China and in Southeast Asia. The ironworkers of Foshan were celebrated for their refined foundry work and accomplished craftsmanship. They were especially famous for the "thinness and smoothness" of their woks.[78] Iron from Guangdong was also demanded widely in Southeast Asia. Siam was a major market, especially in the closing decades of the eighteenth century when iron was needed for the manufacture of armaments during a war with Burma. Sizable quantities of iron from southern China were also exported to Java in the late seventeenth century.[79]

Unlike Britain, therefore, China did not face competition from less expensive iron from abroad. Nor does it appear to have faced shortages of the metal. For these reasons, the Chinese state did not implement measures to encourage the manufacture of iron, which could have led to greater coal consumption. Notwithstanding the lack of such state policies, iron smelters in several parts of the empire were utilizing coal and coke in their operations.

The Chinese state's lack of interest in coal and iron did not derive from a hands-off approach to the economy. The early Qing state was heavily involved in a few areas of economic life which were consistent with Chinese ideals of statecraft and the capacities of the state. In the eighteenth century, the most important arena of state activity was a vast granary system that stockpiled grain and moved it from surplus to deficit regions. The state obtained much of the grain from tribute in kind, which was supplemented with state-financed purchases. In some cases, rather than storing foodstuffs, granaries held money which was used to buy grain as needed. By the early eighteenth century, sizable reserves of food had been amassed in much of the empire and at mid-century grain stocks in several provinces exceeded 1 million bushels, reaching 3 million bushels in a few places. By the 1790s, there may have been more than 15 million bushels stored in the system, to be released at times of high prices and scarcity.[80] R. Bin Wong, Pierre-Étienne Will and others have concluded that sizable numbers in the empire relied upon state granaries and that they were critical for provisioning the population and averting famine in the eighteenth century.[81]

For the emperor and imperial officials, the granary system was of the highest political importance as it defused social tensions and political conflicts. In 1742, for instance, severe flooding destroyed crops in Jiangxi and state officials distributed food to the poor at prices below those in local markets. "Without the distribution of granary reserves," according to Wong, "it is likely that the number of riots that took place in the spring of 1743 would have been far greater than the 160 that actually occurred."[82] As this passage indicates, the granary system did not eliminate rural unrest – Wong has written also that "during the Qing dynasty, spontaneous uprisings in reaction to chronic shortages of food and high prices were a persistent phenomenon" – but it reduced the threat to the state.[83]

The Chinese state did not operate the granary system only for its political utility. In the eighteenth century, the granary system entered what was to be the final phase of a long history of grain storage and distribution in China, which had their origins in Neo-Confucian ideals of the proper duties of a ruler towards the ruled. For the Manchu emperors of the Qing Empire, a well-functioning granary system contributed to the legitimacy of their rule.[84]

The granary system absorbed vast state resources, both financial and human, and its operation precluded the possibility of similar intervention in other goods or in other areas, which points to limits on the power of the early Qing state. Eighteenth-century China was lightly taxed, which was a key element of the Qing political compact. "Since a prosperous people were expected to be a contented and peaceful people, light taxes had their own self-serving political logic for officials. A burdensome government that levied heavy taxes was more likely to provoke rebellion, possibly raising a serious challenge to social order," R. Bin Wong has written.[85] Since the resources of the state were limited, its capacities were circumscribed. Aside from the granary system, the Qing state was incapable of executing far-reaching economic policy on a routine basis.[86]

With the granary system the Chinese state sought to guarantee the welfare of its population. However, with the distribution of food the state was only able to address a symptom of agrarian distress, but not resolve its root causes. A growing source of much agrarian difficulty in several regions of eighteenth-century China, including along the Yangzi River, was increasing ecological problems, including flooding and erosion, which were propelled by the filling in of bodies of water and the cutting down of trees. The clearing of wooded lands was certainly due in part to the energy needs of the region, but it also resulted from the growing demand for agricultural land. Especially devastating was the clearing of the hills by landless "shack people," which unleashed flooding in heavily settled river valleys and low-lying lands. The granary system could not stem the expansion of the arable into the hills or arrest the resulting ecological difficulties in areas such as the Lower and Middle Yangzi. An expanded use of coal would also not have been a solution to these problems, as they did not have their origins in shortages of energy.

In some cases, the exploitation of coal deposits actually made the ecological situation worse. In the Lower Yangzi delta, China's most prosperous region,

Coal mining, which might have ameliorated the fuel shortage and thereby promoted economic growth, also contributed to limits on such growth. It led to deforestation and erosion, directly for mining operations and indirectly through encouraging reclamation of slopelands for grain production to feed the workers. Strip-mining of shallow seams of coal also might spread pollution from mine tailings to irrigation water and agricultural land. Both erosion and water pollution increased the risks to agriculture downstream.[87]

In places such as the Lower Yangzi coal was not the answer to the problems of flooding and erosion caused by widening deforestation. By the late eighteenth century, a more radical solution than coal – and it appears the mineral was used on a not insignificant scale along the Yangzi – was needed to stabilize the social and ecological order. Precisely such a solution was found in eighteenth-century Japan and through rigorous state policies, forests stabilized and ecological decline was stemmed.

The state and forests in the Yangzi and Japan

"By the beginning of the nineteenth century the long-term environmental costs of deforestation were clear," Anne Osborne has written in her study of land reclamation in the Lower Yangzi highlands.[88] Local elites, local officers and state officials in Beijing were aware that the denuding of the hills along the Yangzi River for cultivation by shack people was leading to serious ecological problems in the rich farmland of the lowlands. In the vicinity of Huizhou, in the year 1788, "heavy rains caused flooding and disastrous mudslides; fields were covered, houses buried or swept away, people and livestock killed."[89]

The identification of the problem was far easier than the formulation of a solution, however. While bringing the highlands under the plow reduced the fortunes of local elites whose lands were situated downstream and destroyed by flooding and silting, those who owned the hillsides profited from the high rents that the shack people paid for land. Even if local elites were undivided and were unanimous in their desires to limit the cutting of trees on the hills, local officials did not always side with them and instead defended the rights of the poor shack people to cultivate the land. Local officials were often not powerful enough to take on the shack people, who were famous for their ferocity. The short two- or three-year tenures of local officialdom were a disincentive to taking strong action against a potentially violent foe and prevented the sustained formulation and implementation of measures to protect the forest lands.[90]

In this context, a coherent and forceful imperial state policy could have protected and empowered local officials. The Chinese state did take up the problem of the shack people from the mid-eighteenth century, at first out of a concern for the threat to social control that the shack people posed. From the 1780s, however, the destabilization of lowland agriculture was becoming apparent and the shack people were expelled from the hills of southern Anhui. In the early nineteenth century, this policy was extended to the whole Yangzi region and restrictions were placed on the reclamation of land by outsiders. Shack people who had resided in the area for some years were permitted to remain, however. The cultivation of maize, which was seen as the crop that was most destructive to the highlands ecology, was also banned. The planting of tree crops and perennials were also encouraged to hold the hillside soils. Not much came of these policies, however, and the expansion of settlement into the hillsides of the Yangzi region continued into the nineteenth century with ecologically disastrous consequences.[91]

The failure of the Chinese state has been traced to its weak powers of enforcement. As Osborne puts it, "The physical size of districts, and the difficulty of communications in the highland zones, the small size of the magistrate's staff and the corruption and unreliability of his underlings, probably made a policy requiring a case-by-case monitoring of contracts and repatriation schedules unenforceable by the state."[92] As a result, the Chinese state in the eighteenth and nineteenth centuries was reliant upon the cooperation of local elites, who, as we have seen, were divided on the issue of land reclamation in the highlands and the cutting of forests. At a deeper level, Osborne notes that the termination of highland reclamation would have intensified pressures on land somewhere else in the empire and this larger problem of land shortages defied any easy solution.[93]

In contrast to the Yangzi delta, Japan, which also experienced deepening problems due to the cutting down of trees, succeeded in using state power to stabilize and restore its ecology. From the mid-seventeenth century, Japan faced acute difficulties as a result of widespread deforestation. Although the picture remains far from complete, a construction boom, growing demand for fuel, fodder and fertilizer, and the expansion of cultivation into forested hillsides gave rise to erosion and flooding in many parts of the archipelago. In turn, the growing scarcity of forests, and the resources they yielded, led to competition and conflict over the woodlands that remained. Villagers and villages fought each other and rulers fought the ruled for the dwindling supplies of forest products.[94]

From the mid-seventeenth century, these deteriorating environmental and economic conditions led the rulers of Japan to intervene in the use and management of woodlands and to introduce a series of measures to regulate the production, distribution and consumption of timber and other forest products. The earliest of these sought to protect and preserve woodlands that "sheltered homesteads, villages, fields, roads, streams, or shores from damage by flood, wind or other natural forces."[95] In the closing decades of the seventeenth century the regulations were extended to the forests that produced timber, fuel and other products. At the core of these orders were rules that dictated who had access to the resources in particular tracts of wooded land and in what quantities. Because of the great variety in types of forests and the different demands on them, there was enormous local variation.

Such rules would have served little purpose without an effective means of enforcement, however, and this was the second dimension of forest policy in late seventeenth- and eighteenth-century Japan. The centrality of enforcement is captured in an order issued by the *bakufu* or Shogunate in 1684:

In the hills above streams that empty into the Yodo and Yamato rivers, open fields and swidden are forbidden. All are henceforth to be reforested. In your own lands, as well as in adjoining areas under *bakufu* or other jurisdiction, you are to send vassals to investigate two or three times a year and establish forests with all due care. Inquire of finance officers about those officials handling forest duties.[96]

The creation of this regulatory apparatus required the development of state administrative capacities. Japan had to be surveyed and forest tracts identified and recorded. Forest use had to be monitored and managed and disputes over the rights to woodlands and their products mediated and resolved. All of this required a cadre of officials who operated on the ground. While the shogunate played a key role in the implementation and enforcement of these regulations, it only controlled about a quarter of the territory in Japan. The remaining three-quarters were in the hands of local lords (*daimyo*) who also shared a concern for the preservation and regeneration of forests and therefore regulated the woodlands under their control. The shogunate's policies served as a model for the roughly 250 local lords who replicated them, taking into account local conditions within their territories. While there were small tracts of forest under the command of individuals or village communities, by the late seventeenth century the greater part of the wooded area of the archipelago had been brought under the control of shogun and lords. Therefore, the bulk of the forested lands in Japan came to be regulated. The overseeing of forests was expensive, but was seen as essential to resolving the growing fiscal crisis of both shogun and daimyo.[97]

The above regulations stabilized Japan's forests, but they failed to restore earlier levels of output of wood and other forest products. As a result, demand continued to exceed supply and Japan "labored under continual stress produced by competition for timber, fuel, fertilizer material, and fodder."[98] The solution to the crisis of wood supplies was to physically expand the stock of trees through planting, silviculture and forest plantations. Recommendations to plant trees appeared from the mid-seventeenth century ("plant a thousand seedlings for every tree") and there was a "vast outpouring of commentary and advice" on the whys and hows of increasing the forested area of Japan.[99]

The planting of trees and the creation of plantations required substantial resources. They were labor intensive, had low seedling success rates and required continual monitoring and inputs of labor and capital for up to several decades for the replenishment of seedlings, the elimination of competing plants and thinning to allow maximal growth. Seedling areas also needed to be patrolled for fire, theft and damage. The costs of tree cultivation could be borne most easily in areas that were situated near large markets for lumber and wood. Despite these costs, by the eighteenth century Japan began to enter the age of regenerative forestry. The pressures to find a solution to the forests also mounted because of a growing gap between supply and demand for wood and trees.

Afforestation took off from the middle of the eighteenth century as a result of institutional innovations, in particular various kinds of leases on state land for tree planting, which made reforestation easier. Shogun and lord also spearheaded the planting of trees by political authorities, which became widespread from the 1760s. Private tree planting also grew and silviculture entrepreneurs entered the business of afforestation, sometimes on land leased from shogun and lords. "By the early nineteenth century Japan had moved well into the era of plantation forestry," Conrad Totman writes. Although the data is fragmentary, "the adoption of plantation culture was translating into increases in timber production, if not gross forest output."[100]

Japan did not break through from an organic to an inorganic economy in the eighteenth century. Nevertheless, from an East Asian perspective, Japan had undergone a revolution and it entered the nineteenth century with a radically different economy and ecology than the advanced regions of China, most importantly the Lower and Middle Yangzi where deforestation and the attendant problems of erosion and flooding reached critical proportions. These ecological problems may have contributed to the Taiping Rebellion, and the effects of the rebellion worsened ecological destruction along the Yangzi. According to Anne Osborne, "The Qing state did not succeed in protecting the forests which sheltered the watershed of the Lower Yangzi region, and reaped the tragic harvest of that failure in the mounting crisis of water-control and subsistence in the region in the later nineteenth century."[101] "By the end of the imperial period (in round numbers, 1900)," Mark Elvin writes, "most of China Proper had been stripped of the forest cover."[102] Japan, by contrast, was by 1800 well on her way to stabilizing her forests and the ecological and economic benefits of this political success bore abundant fruit in later years.

According to Conrad Totman, the "changes that Japan underwent during its era of later-Tokugawa stasis enhanced their capacity to utilize [in the nineteenth century] the rudimentary industrial practices then developing in Europe."[103] Forest policy must rank high on this list of Tokugawa achievements. With the stabilization of forests, Japanese agriculture was put on a more secure footing and grew steadily after 1800 when it was positioned to profit from new opportunities and new technologies. From the 1860s to the 1890s, Japan even exported food.[104] Economic growth in the countryside, both in agriculture and in manufacturing, was essential to Japanese economic success in the nineteenth century, but this growth would not have been possible without the ecological policies of the seventeenth and eighteenth centuries.[105]

The Japanese case shows that there was more than one solution to the problem of deforestation in the early-modern world and therefore more than one path to the nineteenth century. While the British exploitation of coal was to prove to be the more revolutionary, the alternative was not a descent into chaos. The rulers of Tokugawa Japan demonstrated that forests could be restored with strict and innovative political action. But it should not be forgotten that even the British path of coal benefited from state support of various kinds.

Whither India?

And what of the Indian subcontinent, which has been absent from the discussion of this chapter? Looking at the world as a whole, between 1500 and 1800 there was a steady expansion of human settlement and activity, but the process of deforestation and ecological decline unfolded at very different rates in different regions of the world. By the eighteenth century, large parts of western and central Europe were increasingly treeless, as were Japan and major regions of China, but the Indian subcontinent did not experience equivalent levels of deforestation until the nineteenth and even twentieth centuries. This unevenness in the pattern of ecological change is essential for understanding the divergent energy path of the Indian subcontinent.

In the seventeenth and eighteenth centuries, forests were felled and the reach of settled agriculture expanded in the subcontinent. The frontier was pushed back most notably in Bengal where a fertile and well-watered delta that yielded enormous quantities of rice repaid the arduous effort of clearing the jungle. There was also a notable and steady pushing out of the arable in west Punjab and the Deccan plateau. Nonetheless, by the end of the eighteenth century, many of the long-settled and densely populated regions of South Asia continued to possess substantial forests. Take the Ganges–Yamuna Doab, which lies in the heartland of northern India and has been home to "thousands of years of agricultural activity." In 1800 the Doab was a highly productive agricultural region; Michael Mann describes it as "amongst the most intensively worked land in north India." Despite this status as a major center of agrarian activity in the subcontinent, "the Doab's most notable natural feature was its forests," according to Mann, and they covered 20 percent of the land in the area.[106]

Even in the long-settled eastern Gangetic plain, in the seventeenth century advancing Mughal troops were accompanied by woodcutters, who cleared forests, and plowmen, who worked to bring the land under cultivation.[107] In Bengal, where land was rapidly brought under the plow in the seventeenth and eighteenth centuries, forests and wetlands abounded, especially in the hills where iron was smelted and in the virgin territories of the eastern section of the province.[108] And it was much the same in most parts of southern and western India. James Paterson, who traveled through South India in the 1770s, reported abundant forested and *jungli* areas. And Francis Buchanan traveled through the hills of the south where slash and burn agriculture, shifting cultivation and iron smelting were still conducted on a large scale in the early nineteenth century, indicating the abundance of forested area. Hugh Cleghorn wrote in the mid-nineteenth century, "In the beginning of this century, an immense almost unbroken forest covered the Western Ghats, from near the watershed to the most elevated ridges, – left to nature, thinly peopled, abounding in wild animals, and all the higher portions, without exception, covered in timber."[109]

The abundant woodlands of the subcontinent provided both valuable resources and ecological security, but this changed after 1800. In the Ganges–Yamuna Doab, the nineteenth-century clearing of the forests, which had "guaranteed the climatic stability of the entire region," led to a rapid rise in average temperatures and irregular rainfall. In the mid-nineteenth century, pankas were introduced into British barracks for the first time. And hot winds, particularly the sand- and dust-filled wind from the desert of Rajasthan, became more intense as the forest barrier was removed. The greater heat and wind combined to loosen the soil, which left it unprotected and vulnerable to erosion from the heavy rains of the monsoon.[110] In South India, unregulated cutting led to cycles of drought and flooding, which affected irrigation and therefore food production and the security of the agrarian population.[111]

In the eighteenth century the forests of the subcontinent also provided a number of valuable resources. They were a major source of green manure for agriculture. Their abundant supplies of forage and water and their cool temperatures made them ideal centers for animal breeding. Forests also provided valuable commodities, including minerals, honey, wax, medicinal plants and game birds. Most importantly of all, they yielded wood in great abundance. The ample supplies of timber, particularly the teak of the west coast, attracted Europeans who turned to Indian shipyards for construction of oceangoing vessels. These forests were also the source of the rich supplies of charcoal that fired the iron-smelting furnaces of the subcontinent, which dotted the hilly regions of the interior from North to South India. The iron that was produced was of extremely high quality and not only met demand for ferrous metal within the subcontinent, but was even exported to Southeast Asia and the Middle East.[112]

Because of ample supplies of wood in the eighteenth century, the advanced regions of India did not come under the ecological pressures that were pressing so hard upon western and central Europe and large sections of China and Japan. In the absence of these pressures, there was no urgent need to experiment with the coal and lignite that was found in eastern and southern India, either for domestic or industrial heat or for the smelting of iron. When the abundance of wood is recognized, it is not surprising that no Indian language possesses a word for coal.

PART III

The Indian path

7 | *Science and technology in India, 1600–1800*

Introduction

In the two chapters that form the third and final part of this work, the focus is once again on India and the Indian path of economic development. This chapter explores the growing Indian interest in scientific and technical knowledge from the late sixteenth to the late eighteenth century. The next chapter turns to the early nineteenth century when the sophisticated Indian knowledge order continued to offer enormous possibilities, but the constraints of British rule narrowed the economic options. Within a few decades of the rise of British power, the reservoir of technical know-how that had been amassed over the previous 200 years began to be dissipated. Colonial India was, therefore, a very different place than the India of the early-modern period.

The examination of science and technology in this chapter serves two purposes. The first is to fill out the picture of Europe and Asia before divergence that was given in Part I of this book. The opening chapters described a dynamic and commercialized India, which was a major center in the global economy between 1600 and 1800 and witnessed significant economic growth and political change. The advanced regions of the Indian subcontinent experienced an extraordinary commercial boom with huge inflows of silver, gold, copper and money forms. A sophisticated mercantile order organized the manufacture and export of cotton textiles and moved large quantities of goods around India and across the Indian Ocean. Merchant power grew and became entwined with state power, especially from the late seventeenth century. In the same period, political competition intensified and gave rise to military fiscalism which required merchant support and a far-reaching reorganization of states and armies.

Running parallel to these economic and political developments were changes in the realm of knowledge. As this chapter shows, states and elites were interested in scientific and technical knowledge for its political and military utility. Craftsmen, artisans and workers in the subcontinent absorbed skills from Europeans and other outsiders in the seventeenth and eighteenth centuries and generated technological change in a number of areas, including shipbuilding, armaments production and agriculture. Finally, at the highest levels of Sanskrit intellectual life, from the sixteenth century scholars aimed to reject tradition and construct new forms of knowledge. The Indian path of the seventeenth and eighteenth centuries was composed of complex changes in commerce, politics and knowledge.

The second purpose of this chapter is to examine an influential argument that attributes Europe's divergence to an exceptional scientific culture. For Margaret Jacob and Joel Mokyr, Europe's scientific rationality and quest for useful knowledge were essential for the momentous technological breakthroughs of the eighteenth century. "Industrial development occurred first in Britain for reasons that had to do with science and culture, not simply or exclusively with raw materials, capital development, cheap labor, or technological innovation," according to Jacob.[1] Mokyr concurs, "To create a world in which 'useful' knowledge was indeed *used* with an aggressiveness and single-mindedness that no other society had experienced before was the unique Western way that created the modern material world. It is this useful knowledge that first unlocked the doors of prosperity and threw them wide open."[2] Research in the areas of science and technology in seventeenth- and eighteenth-century India is still very much in its infancy. Nevertheless, the material presented in this chapter indicates that the scientific exceptionalism of Europe is in need of rethinking.

This chapter does not dispute the importance of knowledge for technological change, but questions several elements of the Jacob and Mokyr understanding of science and technology. On the question of science, it supports a broadening of the concept in both intellectual and geographical terms, which is precisely the direction in which much scholarship on early-modern science is now moving. On the question of the relationship between science and technology, it finds the concept of the mindful hand, which challenges the distinction between pure knowledge associated with the mind and applied knowledge exercised by the hand, to be more appropriate. On the question of the uniqueness of the European regime of knowledge, it differs from Jacob and Mokyr and identifies a number of examples of precisely such a quest in the Indian subcontinent.

From the seventeenth century, growing state competition in India led states and elites to seek out scientific knowledge and technical experts for their political usefulness and the contribution they could make to economic and military improvement. Indian rulers, as did their European counterparts, took a keen interest in attracting skilled and knowledgeable workers to their territories, exploiting foreign sources of knowledge, whether embodied in individuals or texts, and codifying information for study and dissemination. The picture of useful knowledge in India that emerges in this chapter is centered on the state, but this may be an artifact of the surviving source materials. While there is evidence that private individuals participated in the quest for knowledge, their activity has left fewer details in the archival record.

Although there is more material on the activities of states, it is by no means abundant, and our information on scientific and technical activity is limited in several respects. A number of observers report that medical practitioners, shipbuilders, surveyors, architects and many others worked with manuals and texts, but very few of these works survive today. The demand for the information contained in such writings declined in the nineteenth century when a number of economic activities shrank or even disappeared under colonial rule. As a consequence, there was little motivation to preserve and transmit the knowledge they contained for the use of future generations. There is also very little information on the social backgrounds of individuals who possessed scientific and technical knowledge or the conditions under which they worked. Next to nothing is known about their education or the networks in which they operated and exchanged information. Finally, there are no descriptions of sites of production such as shipyards or armament works. Little is available on how they were organized, how they exploited technical knowledge, the relationship between elites and knowledgeable workers at such sites, and the technologies of production.

Because of these limitations, a great deal must be deduced about the state of knowledge and skill from descriptions of the objects that were manufactured at these sites of production, many penned by European observers. The ships, guns, cannons and other commodities that were made in India suggest a sophisticated and dynamic culture of technical knowledge. The design and construction of these objects were technically advanced and highly complex. The descriptions of these objects also provide evidence of changes in technique in order to meet new needs and conditions. There are also reports that until the nineteenth century Europeans learned from the knowledge possessed by Indian workers and scholars. Therefore, while Europeans forged a different and revolutionary path of economic and technological change, neither an interest in useful knowledge nor a dynamic of technical change were unique to Europe in the seventeenth and eighteenth centuries.

From European to global science

Margaret Jacob and Joel Mokyr argue that the rise of science was crucial for the industrial development of Europe. For both authors, the essence of European science was the application of rationality in new ways, including experimentation, which methodically isolated a phenomenon for study, and the description of nature using the language of mathematics. Experimentation and mathematics came together in the work of Isaac Newton, who represented the pinnacle of early-modern European scientific achievement. The connection between Newtonian mechanics and industrialization is elusive, however, and numerous innovators had no rigorous scientific training, which Jacob recognizes. "If we go to the lead mines of Derbyshire, to the industrial center of economic development in the late eighteenth century, there too we find evidence of mechanical knowledge applied by mine owners who possessed no known formal or academic scientific education," she writes.[3] This is why Jacob appeals to a culture of science that informed the work of manufacturers and innovators and was vital for industrial development in Britain.

Mokyr attempts to make this scientific culture more precise and argues that eighteenth-century Europe experienced an Industrial Enlightenment which contributed to economic development in two ways. This Industrial Enlightenment, first, "sought to reduce access costs by surveying and cataloging artisanal practices . . . to determine which techniques were superior and to propagate them." It then "sought to understand why techniques worked by generalizing them."[4] To generate these useful forms of knowledge, the Industrial Enlightenment relied upon experimentation and a scientific mentality, which "imbued engineers and inventors with a faith in the orderliness, rationality, and predictability of natural phenomena."[5]

While Jacob does not transport her arguments beyond Europe, Mokyr argues that the useful knowledge generated by the Industrial Enlightenment explains the divergence between East and West. "The effective deployment of that knowledge, scientific or otherwise, in the service of production is the primary – if not the only – cause for the rapid growth of Western economies in past centuries," Mokyr writes.[6] "Nothing of the sort," according to Mokyr, "can be detected at this time in the Ottoman Empire, Japan, India, Africa, or China."[7] This view of Europe as exceptional is consistent with Mokyr's earlier work on the history of technology, where he concluded that "by 1750, Europe had consolidated its technological superiority over the rest of the world. From the Bosporus to Tokyo Bay, the Oriental empires were falling behind by isolating themselves from the West and experiencing a slowdown in their own technological progress."[8]

Mokyr makes these claims about the uniqueness of Europe, but on the basis of very little engagement with the history of science and technology for any region of Asia in the seventeenth and eighteenth centuries. The conventional wisdom among economic historians of Europe is that these areas of the world had little to offer by way of scientific or technical knowledge. David Landes is typical. On India, he writes, "Indian society did not know technological change."[9] On China, "Along with indifference to technology went resistance to European science." And, "China itself had long slipped into technological and scientific torpor, coasting along on previous gains and losing speed as talent yielded to gentility."[10] From here Landes asks why China did not produce its own scientific revolution.

This question – why did no part of Asia forge a scientific revolution? – has loomed large in generations of scholarship. It informed Joseph Needham's massive investigations of science and civilization in China and one finds the question in studies of Indian, Arab and Ottoman science. The efforts to provide an answer have led to wide-ranging speculation on what went wrong or what blocked the emergence of revolutionary scientific methods in India, the Islamic world and China. (This is much the same approach that is taken to the problem of divergence and which this book rejects.) As a consequence, the scientific work that was actually being conducted in various regions of Asia in the seventeenth and eighteenth centuries has been obscured and received little attention. Nathan Sivin calls the focus on the scientific revolution problem, as he labels it, "disastrous" because it has led historians to devalue and not comprehend "scientific quests other than the one from which modern science most directly sprang."[11]

And from what did modern science spring? For Jacob and Mokyr, the answer is the scientific revolution, which gave rise to a method of experimentation and precision and a mentality that saw the natural world as intelligible.[12] Historians of science, however, have revised their accounts of the scientific revolution and now portray it as a less revolutionary break in the pursuit of knowledge. "Many historians," according to Steven Shapin, "are now no longer satisfied that there was any singular and discrete event, localized in time and space, that can be pointed to as 'the' Scientific Revolution."[13] The term itself was coined in the 1940s and its inventors conceived of it "as the seventeenth-century transformation of human thought into a form close to that of 'scientific knowledge' as defined by twentieth-century philosophers of science. Its defining events were taken to be those in which knowledge approximating to the ideal of general mathematical causal laws seemed to be achieved."[14] Much writing on the scientific revolution is therefore a projection of mid-twentieth-century constructions of science into the early-modern world, according to Andrew Cunningham and Perry Williams.

Historians have also begun to appreciate the variety of activities that came under the label of science in the seventeenth and eighteenth centuries. As Shapin puts it,

Historians now reject even the notion that there was any single coherent cultural entity called "science" in the seventeenth century to undergo revolutionary change. There was, rather, a diverse array of cultural practices aimed at understanding, explaining, and controlling the natural world, each with different characteristics and each experiencing different modes of change. We are now much more dubious of claims that there is anything like "a scientific method" – a coherent, universal, and efficacious set of procedures for making scientific knowledge.[15]

Therefore, early-modern science was more than a project of deductive reasoning, experimentation and the elucidation of mathematical laws, as Jacob and Mokyr would have it. Much scientific activity rested upon careful observation of natural phenomena and many contributors to early-modern science both in Europe and elsewhere did not conceive of themselves as scientific men, but engaged in the study of the natural world out of interest as merchants, soldiers and healers. Similarly, much early-modern science did not rest upon mathematics or a mathematical interpretation of nature.[16]

When seventeenth- and eighteenth-century science is viewed in these broader terms, many knowledge-producing activities in the Indian subcontinent paralleled those found in Europe. The experimental method may not have been widely practiced, but there was a sustained engagement with the natural world in an effort to understand its workings. And as we will see, Indians drew connections between greater knowledge of natural phenomena and human and economic improvement, much as Europeans did in the seventeenth and eighteenth centuries. Indians also endeavored to compile and codify knowledge for useful purposes.

Historians are also moving away from seeing early-modern science in national or regional terms and emphasizing the larger networks, some of them global, that were essential for the generation of new knowledge. Individuals in the Indian subcontinent were very much a part of these networks and therefore contributors to a global scientific enterprise. This cosmopolitan approach to the creation of early-modern science reinforces the argument advanced in this chapter that the European quest for knowledge of the natural world was neither unique nor exceptional in the seventeenth and eighteenth centuries. European scientific men communicated with their counterparts in India and elsewhere. Similarly, the knowledge of Asians was critical for the development of what later came to be seen as "European science."

A growing number of historians are reinterpreting early-modern science along these lines. Harold Cook, for example, calls Hendrik Adriaan van Reede tot Drakenstein's *Hortus Malabaricus* – in Cook's opinion, "one of the great botanical works of the [seventeenth] century" – a joint Indian and European production. "The information in the *Hortus* about the medicinal uses of the flora of Malabar was almost entirely due to van Reede's consultation with local experts," Cook writes.[17] The list of Indians who contributed to the *Hortus* included not only botanists and physicians, especially a renowned medical man by the name of Itty Achuden, but also the Raja of Cochin, Vira Kerala Varma, who sponsored some of van Reede's work. Richard Grove has gone even further than Cook and argued that van Reede and other Europeans adopted the taxonomical schemes found in Malabar. Rather than being "inherently European works," Grove argues that van Reede's *Hortus Malabaricus* and Garcia d'Orta's *Colloquios dos simples e drogas a cousas medicinas da India* "are actually compilations of Middle Eastern and Asian ethnobotany, organised largely according to non-European precepts."[18]

There are a number of other examples of collaboration between Asians and Europeans in the creation of what was later taken to be European scientific knowledge. Harold Cook himself gives several in addition to that of van Reede's *Hortus Malabaricus* in his *Matters of Exchange* and Kapil Raj gives others in his *Relocating Modern Science*. Raj calls the *Jardin de Lorixa*, a fourteen-volume French text on the plant life of eastern India, a "hybrid work containing a number of disparate elements reconfigured into a new homogeneity." The *Jardin* emerged from a collaboration between European and Indian experts and is a particularly striking example of "a substantial corpus of such works that had been produced in Asia," according to Raj.[19] The work was compiled in the early eighteenth century by Nicolas L'Empereur who drew upon Indian writings on medicine as well as the knowledge of Indian healers, botanists, gardeners and merchants. At the same time, the final product was not a simple translation and differed from Indian texts in that it was elaborately illustrated, in contrast to the palm-leaf *materia medica* that circulated in the subcontinent.[20]

Kapil Raj also argues that modern mapping emerged out of an interaction between British and Indian surveyors and was therefore a hybrid and global form of knowledge. "Large-scale terrestrial survey operations in South Asia . . . built on pre-existing indigenous surveying institutions and their workforces . . . The British depended crucially on their indigenous intermediaries and the role of South Asians, and local technical culture was not negligible in this history," Raj writes. Only later did it come to be seen as a European or colonial enterprise and the Indian dimensions lost or excised.[21]

The work of Harold Cook, Kapil Raj, Richard Grove and others reveals that there was a vibrant scientific community in the Indian subcontinent in the seventeenth and eighteenth centuries. These findings form part of a revisionist trend that argues that claims for the stagnation and backwardness of knowledge in South Asia in this period have been overdrawn. The chapter now turns to this work, but with the proviso that much of this research is in its early stages and that there is much to be done before it can approach the depth and density of the scholarship on science in early-modern Europe.

Science in India

In the seventeenth and eighteenth centuries Indian science made important advances in several areas, including astronomy, a field in which Indians had a long record of sophisticated mathematical and observational achievements, as well as mathematics and natural history. There was also great interest in European scientific knowledge in a number of Indian regions. These scientific efforts were part of a flowering of intellectual and philosophical life in both Sanskrit and Persian, the great cosmopolitan languages of the Indian subcontinent. In Persian, knowledge was codified and disseminated in the form of dictionaries, encyclopedias and manuals and textbooks which provided instruction on topics such as personal deportment, the writing of letters and documents, the mechanical arts, agriculture, accounting and revenue collection. There was also a burgeoning interest in travel writing, which satisfied a growing demand for information on the lands that lay outside the subcontinent. Some of this Persian material will be discussed in greater detail shortly as it was important for political and commercial life in the period.

From the mid-sixteenth century, the world of Sanskrit learning was transformed in India, and according to a growing body of scholarship, a new mode of inquiry which self-consciously strove to break with older forms and to generate novel approaches to knowledge is in evidence. In sixteenth- and seventeenth-century writings on *mimamsa* (hermeneutics), for instance, "Authority is routinely called into question, and, for some at least . . . attacking, rather than upholding, what have heretofore been regarded as the truths of the system – becomes the primary business," according to Lawrence McCrea, with the outcome that "nothing could be taken for granted, and all established positions in the system were potentially open to criticism."[22] Sheldon Pollock concludes that "Sanskrit intellectual history, especially of the early modern period, is as much about changes in modes of argument, new genres and styles of writing, and crossing disciplines, as it is about foundational doctrines and system boundaries . . . What exactly constituted 'the tradition' became a central object of study – and sometimes breaking with tradition became a central goal."[23]

There are also signs that the search for the "new" among intellectuals working in Sanskrit furthered scientific inquiry. In the early eighteenth century, the ruler of the South Indian state of Tanjore composed two medical texts which posed profound questions on the purpose of scientific knowledge. The texts queried "the very basis of medicine," according to Dominik Wujastyk, and asked "whether it is worth engaging in a science and practice which appears entirely this-worldly." The Tanjore king concluded that advancing medical knowledge was valuable because it helped man attain a healthy body, which was necessary to achieve the four aims of Righteousness, Wealth, Love and Liberation.[24] Wujastyk also adds that the king's writings on medicine reached into the Sanskrit intellectual tradition to develop arguments that strike "one as very modern." We may go further and note that these ideas resonate with Enlightenment notions of improvement.[25]

The connection between these new intellectual developments and the study of the natural world remains to be elaborated, however. Scholarship in the histories of both ideas and science in early-modern India is very much in its infancy. "The greater part of the intellectual history of India from the sixteenth to eighteenth century, at least the part embodied in Sanskrit texts, remains to be written, since these texts have yet to be accessed, read, and analyzed," Sheldon Pollock writes.[26] Historians also have little access to the lifeworld of these authors and thinkers and, as Pollock notes, "It is almost impossible, even for so late a period, to get a sense of how Sanskrit intellectuals actually lived."[27] Nevertheless, while "no Indian Enlightenment lies hidden from view," Sheldon Pollock has concluded that "new activity evinces a new valuation of both the origins of the disciplines and the traditions of their transmission."[28]

Much the same can be said of the history of science in early-modern India. Historians of science and mathematics in India have devoted the bulk of their energies to the ancient and colonial periods. As a consequence, the study of science from the late sixteenth century to the late eighteenth century has been overshadowed in favor of the achievements of antiquity and the new modern context created by colonialism. Both these perspectives, that Indian science declined from ancient greatness and that colonialism was the harbinger of the modern, are now questioned and early-modern scientific life is beginning to be the object of growing interest and study. Although much is still unclear in this period, these centuries are emerging as a time of dynamic and new scientific, as well as technological, activity.[29]

Scientific activity in India

Indian efforts to understand the natural world in the seventeenth and eighteenth centuries spanned a number of areas of inquiry, including medicine, botany, mathematics, astronomy and chemistry. States and rulers financed some of these efforts and such political patronage appears to have been widespread across the subcontinent. State support went to fields such as astronomy and mathematics, which were longstanding fields of study, but also extended to the acquisition of European scientific knowledge. The Raja of Cochin's patronage of van Reede's *Hortus Malabaricus* has been mentioned, but in the seventeenth and eighteenth centuries a number of states drew Europeans to their realms, organized the translation of European scientific works into Indian languages, or dispatched Indians to Europe for study. With these undertakings rulers sought to create centers of scientific inquiry, which received further support from libraries that dotted the Indian political landscape and which were assembled with the patronage of states and rulers.

Mathematics and astronomy had long been major areas of inquiry in the Indian subcontinent. An understanding of the movement of heavenly bodies was essential for the creation of accurate calendars and the position of the planets determined auspicious times for rituals and for celebrations of life-cycle events such as marriages. Astronomical observations, in particular the movement of planets in astrological terms, were also used to determine the passage of the seasons and the coming of the monsoon, information which was needed for the timing of agricultural operations. The work of astronomers led to advances in mathematics and developed skills of observation. It also contributed to the mapping of the subcontinent. Given the importance of this knowledge, astronomers and observatories received the patronage of Mughal rulers in the seventeenth century and the many successors to Mughal authority continued this tradition in the eighteenth.

The making of instruments, including astrolabes and celestial globes, was essential for observation and measurement of the skies. The metallurgical, mathematical and manufacturing skills that were developed in instrument-making were also applied to other problems and fields. An especially talented instrument-making family resided in the city of Lahore and from that base "seven members of this family, belonging to four generations, signed their names on about 87 astrolabes and 21 celestial globes" in the sixteenth and seventeenth centuries.[30] The manufacturers of these complex instruments possessed sophisticated mathematical learning and in the early seventeenth century their knowledge of trigonometry and geometry was called upon in the design and construction of major Mughal buildings. This was the zenith of Mughal building and these skilled mathematicians contributed to the construction of the Taj Mahal and the Agra Fort. According to Iqbal Ghani Khan, "The architectural masterpieces . . . would not have been possible had Jahangir not encouraged this family of geometers to develop their trigonometric skills into architecture."[31]

In the eighteenth century, Raja Jai Singh, who ruled the Rajput kingdom of Amber from 1722 to 1739, was the leading patron of astronomy in the Indian subcontinent. With Jai Singh's financial support five massive observatories, housing instruments made of lime and stone, were built in the North Indian cities of Delhi, Ujjain, Jaipur, Benares and Mathura. Jai Singh chose to build his instruments from masonry after discovering defects in those made from wood and metal. Those of wood were unwieldy and those of metal were large and heavy as well as unreliable in the extreme temperatures of North India, where they expanded in the hot summers and contracted in the cool winters, yielding incorrect observations. Many of Jai Singh's instruments were conventional measuring devices, including astrolabes, mural quadrants, meridian circles and azimuth circles. However, he and his team of astronomers invented several new ones for the measurement of solar time, solar altitude and the positions of celestial objects. A number of these devices yield highly precise observations and required very precise manufacture, some of them requiring tolerance at the level of millimeters.[32]

Despite the shortcomings of wood and metal instruments, such devices may have also been used at Jai Singh's observatories. These include astrolabes and yantras, which were devices for measuring time from the position of the sun during the day and stars at night.[33] Jai Singh's astronomers also conducted some observational work with telescopes, which were manufactured in the kingdom, and one astronomer wrote, "With the telescope we have noted certain facts in contradiction to the well known texts. For instance, we have seen with our own eyes that Mercury and Venus get their light from the sun the way the moon does . . . The planet Saturn appears oval in shape. Around Jupiter are seen four bright stars circling the planet. On the face of the sun there are spots."[34]

The primary purpose of Jai Singh's astronomical labors, however, was to accurately chart the movement of stars and planets for the formulation of calendars and possibly for astrological uses. Jai Singh was particularly interested in improving the accuracy of the solar calendar, especially for the timing of life-cycle rituals and for the prediction of eclipses.[35] The astronomical tables that were compiled under his patronage were used widely in northern and eastern India in the eighteenth century. These tables also came to see the orbits of the planets around the sun as following an ellipse as the massive data collected by Jai Singh's astronomers did not fit a circular orbit. Jai Singh himself is reported to have written: "The predecessors of astronomy, namely Hipparchus and Ptolemy and others, gave the principles of the movements of planets and description of the orbits of their movement but their description is far from the truth . . . Above all, it should be mentioned that the orbits have elliptical shape in one of the centres of which lies the sun."[36]

The team of astronomers that Jai Singh assembled consisted of Indians and Europeans, the latter comprised mainly of Jesuits from the Portuguese settlement of Goa. Jai Singh also corresponded with a French Jesuit, who was resident in Chandernagore in eastern India. To learn more about European learning and methods, Jai Singh sent a team of his astronomers to Portugal where they obtained instruments, books and astronomical tables. With Jai Singh's patronage, a fine library of astronomical literature was established and Indian astronomers and mathematicians translated and discussed the findings of European scientists.[37] In the late eighteenth century, William Hunter reported that a Brahmin scholar had shown him Sanskrit translations of "several European works, executed under the orders of *Jayasinha* [Jai Singh], particularly Euclid's *Elements* with the treatises of plain and *spherical trigonometry*, and on the construction and use of logarithms, which are annexed to Cunn's or Commandine's edition . . . Besides these, the *Pandit* [the Brahmin] had a table of logarithms and of logarithmic sines and tangents to seven places of figures; and a treatise on conic sections."[38] Jai Singh's interest in European knowledge was not restricted to astronomy. He also commissioned the translation of a European book on perspective drawing, which was designed to aid the work of builders, engineers, technicians, artists and draftsmen. To make the knowledge accessible to practitioners, the translation was made into Hindustani, specifically the dialect used in the vicinity of Delhi and Agra, rather than into Sanskrit or Persian, the languages of high culture and the literati.[39]

Jai Singh's observatories and interest in European astronomy are famous. Less well known is that his sponsorship of translations from European languages was squarely in the tradition of Mughal rulers of the seventeenth century. Under Aurangzeb, François Bernier was appointed court physician and the texts that he possessed were translated into Indian languages. This commenced a long dialogue between Bernier and North Indians on philosophy and medicine in which Bernier communicated Cartesianism, atomism and other developments in seventeenth-century European thought as well as recent additions to medical knowledge, including the circulatory system and other advances in anatomy.[40] In the eighteenth century, patronage for translation was found in both North and South India, which indicates both the broadness of Indian interest in European scientific thinking and the vitality of Indian intellectual and scientific life. This interest in European advances is reflected in several major libraries that were assembled in the eighteenth century, whose existence runs counter to the assumption of Indian scientific indifference.

Starting in the south, the state of Mysore contained an extensive collection of scientific works. The library was assembled in the closing decades of the eighteenth century by Tipu Sultan and located in his palace in the capital of Seringapatnam. The library was dismantled after the British defeat of Mysore in 1799, but we are fortunate to possess what appears to be a partial inventory of its holdings, which was compiled in the early nineteenth century by Charles Stewart.[41] According to this catalog, the library possessed a large number of manuscripts in the sciences. Tipu Sultan had purchased some of them, including the *Jami al Ulum*, a treatise on universal science by the Sufi, Mohammed Ghos of Gwalior. This work included chapters on astronomy, geography, physics, music, theology, war, agriculture and horticulture, omens, talismans, chemistry and the magnet. There was also a Deccani text, entitled *The Complete Equestrian*, which contained instructions on how to purchase and breed horses, manage the stud and cure the "several disorders to which they are liable." In addition, there was a natural history of animals in Arabic, which had been dedicated to Shah Abbas the second and which Stewart described as "very excellent." Mughal works were also found in the collection, including a compilation of knowledge on the manufacture of artificial gems, fireworks, and colors and paints of all kinds, to which was appended a work on the art of dyeing cloths, silks, etc. The author of this text, Zein al Aabidin, had collected these materials during the reign of Aurangzeb.

The library also contained several scientific works that Tipu Sultan had commissioned, including a treatise on cloth dyeing and perfume manufacture. This work suggests that the ruler was seeking to develop cotton manufacturing within his kingdom, which lay outside the major textile-exporting centers of South India. Tipu Sultan had also financed the translation of French and English works on natural history and botany. These appear to have been part of a larger project in which "forty-five books on different sciences were either compiled, or translated from different languages, under his immediate inspection or auspices," Stewart writes. Unfortunately, further details are not given on these translations. Also in the library were treatises on arithmetic and mathematics in Persian and Arabic that covered a wide range of mathematical systems. There was a work on arithmetic, the author of which was unknown, but which was described in the catalog as laying out the Hindu system. There was also an "excellent treatise" on mathematics and geometry written in 1681 by Lutif Allah, an engineer in Delhi, as well as a work on Euclidian geometry, which had been translated from the Greek. And not surprisingly, there were large numbers of works in Persian and Arabic on astronomy and medicine, some translated from other languages. On the latter topic, there were translations of the complete London dispensatory and of an English work on electrical and medical experiments.

The library and its collections reveal the Mysore state's broad interest in scientific and technical subjects. It also shows that the Mysore state had a keen interest in obtaining knowledge from outside the subcontinent and making it available for local scholars through projects of translation. Finally, the knowledge thus obtained was applied to improve production in a number of areas, ranging from animal breeding to textile manufacturing. Tipu Sultan's own interest in scientific matters is conveyed in a description of a meeting with him by William Smith:

I exhibited the following experiments, viz. head and wig, dancing images, electric stool, cotton fired, small receiver and stand, hemispheres, Archimedes's screw, siphon, Tantalus's cup, water-pump, condensing engine, &c. Captain Doveton was present, and explained, as I went on, to the Sultaun, who was giving an instance of his being acquainted with some of these experiments. He has shewn us a condensing engine made by himself, which spouted water higher than ours.[42]

Another major South Indian library was found in the city of Tanjore and came to be known as the Sarasvati Mahal Library. It was founded in the sixteenth century as the Royal Palace Library and was expanded in the eighteenth century under the patronage of the Maratha rulers of the kingdom, especially in the closing decades of the century by King Serfoji II. Serfoji had mastered several European languages, including English, German and French, and was believed also to possess a smattering of Latin and Greek. The king purchased substantial numbers of European books on scientific subjects, including works on chemistry, electricity, mathematics, medicine and veterinary science. He also patronized local scholars in their scientific studies. A horticulturalist named Pallikondan Maistry from Madras, for example, was employed to propagate fruit and cultivate flowers and to write a book in Marathi on grafting, manuring and other techniques for plant cultivation. Serfoji also financed translations of European works. For example, the English works on anatomy in his possession were translated into Marathi and Tamil to make these texts more widely accessible.[43]

The library also contained "an air-pump, an electrifying machine, an Ivory skeleton, astronomical works," which are further indications of the scientific interests of its patron.[44] Serfoji purchased a barometer and surgical instruments as well as a printing press. After meeting the king, one European visitor remarked, "he passes his life in a course of rational amusement and study."[45] Another reported that Serfoji "quotes Fourcroy, Lavoisier, Linnaeus, and Buffon fluently."[46] With these efforts, Serfoji "created a configuration of institutions to facilitate the production and dissemination of new knowledge." And the library became a center of study not only for local scholars and intellectuals but also for Europeans who lived in the region.[47]

Shifting our gaze, the greatest library in eighteenth-century North India was located in Lucknow, the capital of the kingdom of Awadh. This library was assembled under royal patronage and in the late eighteenth century it was reputed to contain some 300,000 volumes. According to one chronicler, only 700 of these volumes had been inherited from the libraries of the Mughal kings. Although few details are available on the contents of this library, others in North India in the same period assembled by "up-start Afghans" contained works on geography, travelogs, poetry, medicine, hunting and hawking and encyclopedias on natural history, agriculture, veterinary sciences and alchemy.[48]

The library in Lucknow may have quenched the intellectual thirsts of huge numbers of scholars who flocked to Awadh because of its status as a center of the Islamic rational sciences in northern India. While the Firangi Mahal is the best known of the educational institutions which arose in the kingdom in the eighteenth century, there were others that maintained the technical interest and technological activities initiated by the Mughals. Perhaps the clearest sign of technological vitality in eighteenth-century Awadh is the ease with which learned individuals absorbed the knowledge of the French who became an increasingly prominent presence in the kingdom in the late eighteenth century. The most impressive of these Frenchmen was the polymath Claude Martin, whose interests ranged from the manufacture of weapons to astronomy, electricity, surgery and indigo.[49] More details are available on the scientific activities of Khaliluddin Khan, who became the ruler of the kingdom, in the early nineteenth century. Around 1820 he ordered a large telescope from Britain and established an observatory in Lucknow. The Nawab also pursued the study of philosophy, chemistry and mechanics. His interest in mechanics led him to steamships and the design of a new screw-type propeller is attributed to him.[50]

The British conquest of India put an end to state patronage for intellectual pursuits and also erased this history of scientific inquiry in the eighteenth century. The destruction of the libraries of the subcontinent in the early years of British rule symbolizes both these historical shifts. Many repositories of books and manuscripts, including those in Mysore and Lucknow, were ransacked during the turmoil and warfare that came with the rise of British power and their collections destroyed or dispersed. It is important to remember that the "Persian manuscript collections in London, Paris, Oxford, Cambridge, Dublin, Glasgow, Berlin and even in Aberystwyth were once busy libraries in India," Iqbal Ghani Khan has reminded us.[51] The destruction of these libraries and the fragmentation of the communities of scholars who worked in them have led to a forgetting of the vibrant intellectual life which existed in eighteenth-century India. The backward conditions of the nineteenth century have then been taken to represent what existed in earlier periods.

The scattered information that is available on the contents of these libraries suggests a broad range of scientific interests in the eighteenth century. Astronomy and mathematics loomed large, but another major area of scientific interest in the seventeenth and eighteenth centuries was natural history. A number of treatises and manuals were produced in these centuries compiling information on soils, plants and other material of relevance to agricultural and horticultural operations. It is likely that these works reached a large audience, which is supported by the fact that a number of works were produced in the vernaculars, which had a broader readership than Persian and Sanskrit. The Indian subcontinent had a thriving scribal culture, which would have made these texts widely available. The Indira Gandhi National Centre for the Arts estimates that some 30 million manuscripts in Indic languages survive in repositories around the world today, which Sheldon Pollock writes "represent the merest fraction of what once must have been produced."[52]

Intellectuals, practitioners and even skilled workers possessed texts. Kapil Raj reports that medical healers in South India traveled with palm-leaf works and European physicians and botanists were eager to gain access to them and the knowledge they contained.[53] A South Indian manual on shipbuilding survives from the seventeenth century and it has been described as "an excellent guide-book in Tamil for shipbuilders and sailors."[54] Surveyors and astronomers relied upon a number of texts and in the late eighteenth and early nineteenth centuries many Europeans had these works translated in order to gain knowledge of Indian "surveying techniques and methods for determining latitude."[55] In the climate of the subcontinent, such written material must either be preserved carefully or recopied periodically. However, the information many of these texts contained lost its relevance in the nineteenth century as a consequence of the colonial transformation of economic life, which eliminated many occupations and made irrelevant many domains of skill and knowledge. As a result, manuscripts were neither preserved nor recopied for future generations and many such texts were lost. What survives is the tip of the iceberg of these materials, so to speak.

Finally, major libraries and educational centers were magnets that attracted scholars from around the subcontinent. In the early-modern period, Benares, for instance, drew Sanskrit intellectuals from across India for both religious and scientific studies.[56] The circulation of scholars, as well as skilled workers, diffused ideas and techniques. All of this suggests that early-modern South Asia was not caught in an unscientific vacuum. There was a great deal of locally generated interest in science and mathematics as well as a desire to import scientific knowledge from outside the subcontinent. In the area of technology also, the picture is far from the conventional wisdom of disinterest in change or improvement.

Technological change in the Indian subcontinent

Since at least Mughal times, rulers, elites and state officials were concerned with issues of technology and methods of production. The late sixteenth-century Mughal Emperor Akbar was famous for his keen interest in manufactures and he himself turned his hand to a number of crafts, including carpentry, blacksmithing, stone quarrying, ribbon making and textile manufacturing. European visitors to the Mughal Emperor's court were struck by what one Jesuit described as a delight in the "mechanical arts." Akbar is credited with several inventions, including a method for the construction of prefabricated, multistory buildings from iron and wood. The frames for the buildings were made of iron tubes, which could be easily assembled, disassembled and transported to set up camp during military and hunting expeditions. The tubes were connected much as scaffolding is today, containing male and female ends which were inserted into each other. Akbar may have used a similar technique in the manufacture of cannon barrels that could be disassembled for ease of transport. The pieces may have been fitted into each other and the joints reinforced with rings to withstand the pressure of firing.[57]

Techniques for cooling air and water have also been attributed to Akbar. The cooling of air was achieved by means of the *khas* root which was stuffed into frames made of bamboo. When water was thrown on the *khas*, according to Abu'l Fazl, "winter seems to arrive in the midst of summer." Cool water was obtained by dissolving saltpeter in water. A flask submerged in this mixture was chilled in a matter of minutes.[58] Akbar also took an interest in shipbuilding, which he established on the banks of the Ravi in the city of Lahore, close to supplies of timber in the foothills of the Himalayas. Because of their size, ocean-going ships faced difficulties sailing in the shallow stretches of the river. This problem was solved by building ships on barges, which were sailed down the Ravi to the Arabian Sea. According to Irfan Habib, this system anticipated the "camel," a barge that could be submerged to take on a ship and then raised to transport it over shallow waters, which was invented in the Dutch dockyards in 1688.[59]

Akbar was also a patron of the technologically inclined and he and his courtiers designed and built a broad range of machines. They devised animal-powered geared devices to lift water to great heights at Fatehpur Sikri, which for a time served as Akbar's residence. Mir Fathu'llah Shirazi, a renowned Iranian scholar, theologian and physician, spent several years at Akbar's court and he is credited with helping to invent a grain mill which was placed on a cart and powered by the turning of the vehicle's wheels. (Carts that milled while they moved, Habib reports, date from the seventeenth century in Europe.) A similar geared machine, powered by animals, was devised to bore gun barrels. Although no examples of the machine survive, based on drawings Irfan Habib has concluded that the "technical completeness of the diagram strongly reinforces the supposition that here an actual, not an imaginary, machine is being described."[60] Akbar also played a role in the diffusion of techniques for pattern weaving of cloth from Iran, China and Europe, for which he brought skilled artisans from Iran to North India.[61]

Mughal technical interest extended into cartography as well. Very few maps from the Mughal period exist, but other sources point to a sophisticated cartographic tradition. For instance, the globe in the famous painting *Jahangir Embracing Shah Abbas* reveals a familiarity with European maps of the early seventeenth century which was combined with Mughal geographical knowledge. The latter is revealed by the accurate depiction of the river systems of the subcontinent. The Mughal maps that the painter Abu'l Hasan drew upon for this work do not exist, which means there were "Mughal cartographic sources of which we have no surviving example."[62] An important set of mid-seventeenth century Mughal maps – Irfan Habib describes them as "breath-taking in their coverage and arrangement" – survives in the form of a not entirely careful later redrawing. Nevertheless, these indicate an accurate knowledge of distances within the empire, the location of important physical features and the coastline of the sub-continent.[63] Mughal attention to matters of geography is captured in an account by the Jesuit António Monserrate, who accompanied Akbar on an expedition to Kabul in 1581: "The distance of each day's march is measured with a ten-foot rod by special officers . . . These measurements are afterwards found very useful in computing the area of provinces and the distances of places apart, for purposes of sending envoys and royal edicts, and in emergencies."[64]

Mughal interest in matters of technology and production was not confined to the court of the emperor. Iqbal Ghani Khan has found a number of manuals of administration from the seventeenth century, which were designed to instruct elites on how to manage large households and estates. The manuals contained sections on accounting, inventory-keeping, area calculation, agriculture, crop-yield estimation and crop-sharing techniques – knowledge that would have been essential for the estimation and collection of revenue. A subset of these manuals was devoted to horticulture, which supported the voracious Mughal elite appetite for the cultivation of exotic plants and trees, especially those transplanted from Central Asia. These works contained information on soils, planting, grafting, the ripening of fruit and irrigation, and included discussions of Persian wheels, stone channels, siphons, sluices and regulators. In addition, elites maintained diaries detailing their agricultural and horticultural experiments and significant numbers of them have survived from the seventeenth and eighteenth centuries. The culmination of Mughal efforts to compile knowledge was the Imperial Book of Regulations, which was assembled towards the end of the reign of Aurangzeb with the aim of putting together useful knowledge on diverse topics. The book contained extensive information on the honorable crafts, ranging from iron, gold and other metal working to sewing, weaving, cotton carding, pottery, dyeing, cooking and alchemy.[65] Ghani Khan concludes that "the details in the technical manuals written for the Mughal elite suggest a much wider role for the written technical word than has so far been assumed."[66]

Administrative and agricultural manuals continued to be produced in eighteenth-century North India, but they became more specialized, according to Ghani Khan. In contrast to their Mughal predecessors, the eighteenth-century guides were written with specific locales or regions in mind, which allowed them to be tailored to climatic and ecological conditions. Eighteenth-century works on cotton cultivation, for instance, contain more technical details than their seventeenth-century predecessors. They also use more indigenous terms and convey more detailed information on yields, soil types, and the irrigation and labor needs of different varieties of cotton. This information could be coupled with closer supervision of cultivators to increase yields. Other texts that date from the eighteenth century in North India include translations into Persian and Urdu of English handbooks on cannons and guns. Local works on handguns were also produced in this period, including the *Nushka-i Dilkusha*, a late eighteenth-century work from Bareilly. There was also a burgeoning travel literature, which reported on journeys to Central Asia, Iran and other parts of the Indian subcontinent. Dictionaries of revenue terms were also compiled in the eighteenth century and these included technical details and information on agricultural operations as well.[67]

Textual activity that sought to codify and make available technical knowledge represents only one part of elite interest in problems of production and technology in the eighteenth century. There were also a number of state-sponsored schemes for technological improvements which emerged in response to the fiscal and military pressures of the period. Growing military demands, including the rise of standing armies and more expensive weaponry, led several states and rulers to improve systems of production in order to increase the wealth, and therefore the taxable base, of their territories. The Rajput state of Kota, for example, embarked upon experiments to improve seed strains and grafting, to breed superior varieties of oxen, and to develop new plow designs appropriate for the different soil types found in the kingdom, including a new double-yoked plow, the Konkani, which was better suited for heavy soils than the traditional Rajasthani plow. The heavier plow led to the expansion of cultivation into areas that had been previously too difficult to work and the name suggests that it may have been an adaptation of one found in the Konkan region of western India. The Kota state disseminated this new agricultural knowledge throughout the kingdom with a series of state-sponsored fairs. We know of these efforts in Kota from a passing discussion of them in the writings of James Tod. It is likely that such state promotion of technical change was found more widely, but it has left little trace in the archival record.[68]

Some of the greatest detail on such state support for technological progress comes from the South Indian state of Mysore in the late eighteenth century. Under Haider Ali and Tipu Sultan the Mysore state embarked upon an ambitious program of economic development with the aim of increasing the wealth and revenue of the realm. There is extensive evidence for a push towards agricultural improvement, with policies designed to expand irrigation, bring fertile land under cultivation and promote the adoption of valuable cash crops, including sandalwood, sugar and black pepper. A sophisticated system of revenue incentives was designed to meet these aims. In addition, under Tipu Sultan, efforts were made to improve the breeding of cattle, which were critical not only for agricultural operations, but also for the transport of goods and military supplies.[69]

The push for improvement in Mysore also extended to manufacturing. The European-style military that Mysore sought to create required the expansion of metal-working facilities, especially iron. In the 1780s, orders were issued for the construction of twenty new iron-smelting furnaces within the kingdom. Mysore also developed a major armaments industry, which cast cannon in both brass and iron, and manufactured enormous numbers of high-quality firearms. According to French observers, the quality of these guns was equal to the best of Europe. In 1787, for instance, Tipu Sultan returned a shipment of 500 French guns because they did not match the quality of his own manufactures. From all reports, these workshops used sophisticated technologies of both local and imported design, including a machine to bore cannon which had been installed with the assistance of a French artisan or technician. The machine was designed to be operated with a waterwheel, but had been adapted to be run on bullock power.[70] Irfan Habib notes that making this conversion would have required the manufacture of gearing from iron to transmit the necessary power, which "must surely have required a creditable level of craftsmanship."[71]

The Mysore state's keen interest in improving the technology of manufacturing was not confined to the production of armaments, but extended to clocks, paper and glass, as well as a number of other goods. Francis Buchanan, who surveyed the region in the early nineteenth century, called Tipu Sultan a "wonderful projector," and reported that Mysore had succeeded in manufacturing "broad-cloth, paper formed on wires like the European kind, watches, and cutlery."[72] In the 1780s, a diplomatic delegation from Mysore to the Ottoman Empire, France and Britain was also assigned the task of collecting information on manufacturing and techniques of production in the countries they visited. "Industries and rarities of each city and territory . . . should be written down in front of each of you . . . Requests should be made in the proper and necessary manner to the Sultan of Turkey and the King of France, for obtaining artisans expert in the manufacture of muskets, guns, clocks, glass, mirrors, chinaware, and cannon-balls, and for such other craftsmen as may be there . . . obtaining from them bonds of agreement to come to this Court," the delegation was instructed. The diplomats were also directed to find "good carpenters and ironsmiths, for construction of ships, and other craftsmen that are not available in this country, should be brought from the country of Turkey and of the French King. Similarly, a skilful astronomer, geomancer and physician should also be brought." Tipu Sultan was also eager for his emissaries to send home samples of coal (for which he combined the Persian words for stone and charcoal) and dispatch to the kingdom the "services of four expert persons as are skilled in recognizing the presence of (ores of) stone-coal." (Tipu Sultan's condensing engine, which Andrew Bell remarked upon, may have sparked his interest in coal.) He also ordered that foreign workers expert in gun manufacturing were to be recruited to Mysore, even though he observed that "there are numerous artisans capable of making muskets and guns under this government," which is evidence that the ruler saw that foreign knowledge could be useful even in areas where there was substantial local expertise.[73]

The push for technological experimentation and innovation was not restricted to the courts of rulers, but also found at points of production, for which the most abundant information comes from the shipyards of India. The entry of European ships into the Indian Ocean brought dramatically different techniques of shipbuilding. Europeans used caulking, iron nails, pumps, sheathing and iron anchors, all of which were alien to the Indian subcontinent. Indian builders selectively adapted European knowledge and from the sixteenth century produced a new hybrid tradition.

While European ships were made watertight with caulking between the planks, Indian ships were sealed through rabbeting and other techniques. Indian shipbuilders failed to adopt caulking, but this was not due to inadequate knowledge of the method or a lack of materials. Indian shipping men were familiar with oakum, for instance, which was imported for other uses. The Indian disinterest in caulking appears to have stemmed from the fact that it was not technically superior to local methods and it dramatically increased the costs of ship construction. On the technical front, in the early sixteenth century a European wrote that with Indian methods, the builders "join the planks so well that they keep out the water most excellently."[74] And on the issue of cost, Europeans were attracted to Indian shipyards because of the lower prices that were achieved when caulking was eliminated. As one writer declared, Indian methods dispensed with "all caulking worke, ocum, pitch, and tarr, with the expence of a many carpenters and caulkers."[75]

Although Indians displayed little interest in caulking, they quickly and enthusiastically adopted iron nails for joining together planks. Before the early sixteenth century, Indian shipbuilders joined planks with rope and stitching. The great merit of this technique was that it made the hull more flexible and thus the ship safer at sea. "The pressure of water and any sudden stress worked on all the lashings. If the stitching rope broke at one point, the load immediately spread to the neighbouring cords," K. N. Chaudhuri writes.[76] Stitching also made it easier to repair ships and replace damaged planks. Stitched ships were vulnerable to Portuguese naval attacks, however, and within a decade of Vasco de Gama's arrival in India, ships began to be built with iron nails in the Portuguese style. Iron nails were most quickly adopted in the construction of ships for long-distance sailing and for ships that were armed, but stitching continued to be used in ships built for the coastal trade in which the sailing distances were much shorter. Several other innovations inspired by European example were also taken up by Indian shipbuilders and ship captains. Locally made iron anchors began to replace large stones; pitch began to be applied to cables and cordage; pumps for the bailing of water began to be found onboard Indian-made ships; sheathing began to be increasingly common by the seventeenth century; and telescopes appear to have been used for shipboard observation.[77]

By the late seventeenth century, the quality of Indian ships was so high ("the shipbuilders of the Coromandel coast around Masulipatnam had thoroughly mastered the technique of European naval construction," K. N. Chaudhuri writes) that English private traders began to have their ships made in the subcontinent.[78] In the mid-eighteenth century, a European traveling in the Indian Ocean wrote that "there would be no exaggeration in averring that they build incomparably the best ships in the world for duration, and that of any size, even to a thousand tons and upwards. The reign of their ships is much larger than that of the European-built ships. It is not uncommon for one of them to last a century owing mostly to their workmanship and the nature of the wood they employ."[79] Charles Carter, who had thirty-five years of experience building and repairing both British and Indian ships, testified to Parliament in 1814 that the pumps, blocks and carriages on the Indian-made ships were equal to, if not better than, the best of Britain. "The pumps," Carter reported, "are made of such durable materials, and put together in such a manner, that they will last as long as any material in this country, except copper."[80]

The flow of technology in shipbuilding did not only go from Europe to India. In the early nineteenth century, F. Balthazar Solvyns, a Flemish artist and author of a work on boats in Bengal, declared that "the present-day Hindus can still offer models to Europe. The English have borrowed from the Hindus many improvements which they have adapted with success to their own shipping."[81] Although Solvyns does not elaborate, one Indian improvement that had its admirers, but had not yet been transferred to Europe, was the use of *gulgul*, which a British shipowner described as a "kind of hard lime, a cement that is laid at the bottom, and it hardens like stone; and in case the copper was to get off, it would not be penetrated by the worm."[82] Indian innovations such as gulgul indicate that the knowledge and technological capabilities of Indian shipbuilders were in some respects superior to those of Europe.

A storm off the coast of Madras in 1811 bore testimony to the high quality of Indian shipbuilding. Two vessels, one made in India and the other in France, were caught in a severe gale and driven ashore. The French-made ship immediately broke into pieces, while the Indian "laid for several months, in the surf at Madras, which is supposed to be the most violent surf in the world, perfectly entire," according to a British witness. Carpenters had to be employed "at great expense" to break up the ship and in the end it was blown up with gunpowder.[83] The superior quality of Indian ships cannot be attributed only to the superior properties of teak, as opposed to oak, which was the timber of choice for shipbuilding in Europe. In the early nineteenth century, vessels built in Rangoon, where good teak was abundant, were reputed to be of much lower quality than those built in Bombay or Calcutta, which is evidence that the skill and technical knowledge of Indian shipwrights and workers contributed to the excellence of Indian ships.[84]

From the 1730s, the English East India Company began to have ships made in India, initially for its trade within Asia but then for passages to Europe as well. By the late eighteenth century, warships for the British admiralty also started to be built in Indian shipyards. The technical ability of the Indian shipwrights was very high. Plans were sent from Britain and executed under the authority of an Indian master builder. Shipping interests in Britain, from owners of fleets to builders, widely opposed the construction of ships in India and in 1796 complained to Henry Dundas, an influential Member of Parliament, that "the families of all the shipwrights in England are certain to be reduced to starvation" as long as Indian shipyards were allowed to compete with those of Britain. Parliament responded to these pressures and in 1815 passed the Registry Act, which imposed a 15 percent duty "on goods imported in India-built ships: that only British ships should import goods from south and east of the Cape of Good Hope." Additional clauses restricted the use of Indian sailors and mariners. This act delivered a blow to the future of Indian shipbuilding and it will be examined again in the next chapter.[85]

It was not only shipbuilding that posed a threat to British producers. From the mid-seventeenth century, as we have seen, British textile manufacturers faced the competitive pressures of Indian cotton cloth, which were also resolved through protection. In the late seventeenth century, the fan makers of England complained about Indian imports.[86] In the eighteenth century, cabinetmakers opposed the import of furniture from India.[87] And shipyards were not the only sites of innovation and technical change in the eighteenth century. Another major location of technological dynamism were the arsenals of India where the military demands of the eighteenth century set in train innovations in the casting, boring and design of cannons, improvements in the manufacture of small guns, and even advances in rocketry.

European reports on Indian armaments technology in the seventeenth and eighteenth centuries were uniformly positive. Jean-Baptiste Tavernier, who visited the subcontinent in the seventeenth century, reported from Golconda that "the barrels of their muskets are stronger than ours, and the iron is better and purer; this makes them not liable to burst."[88] In the eighteenth century similar assessments were made of guns from Awadh in North India, the Maratha states in western India and Mysore in the south. According to Randolf Cooper, "British military men in South Asia historically had a healthy respect for South Asian matchlocks, which were often judged to have superior range and velocity over European muskets."[89] The military historian H. A. Young has written that

Muskets and swords were being made in many parts of India [in the eighteenth century]; Travancore was making them at Udaygiri about 1757; Mir Cossim was manufacturing firelocks at Monghyr in 1763, and these latter ones were said to be better than the best Tower-proof muskets sent to India by the Company, especially in the metal of the barrels and in the flints, which were made of agates found in the Rajmahal Hills. Shuja-ud-Dowlah was said to have made amazing improvements in the manufacture of small arms in 1768. The French made serviceable muskets at Chadarghat, a suburb of Hyderabad, while Seringapatnam had eleven armouries for making, finishing, and repairing small arms.[90]

Indian manufacturers made impressive advances in other areas of armaments production as well and a study of the Anglo-Maratha campaigns has concluded that in the early nineteenth century Maratha military technology was superior in a number of respects to that of the British. The Maratha forces carried higher-quality small guns, which since the early eighteenth century were better suited to the Indian climate and Indian gunpowder.[91] The Marathas possessed a striking advantage in big guns as well and their metallurgists manufactured a new type of cannon that contained an interior iron-bore cylinder with a brass sleeve cast over it. The iron liner extended the life of the guns and the surrounding barrel in brass lowered their weight, which made them easier to transport and maneuver in battle, reducing the number of draught animals, fodder and men that were needed for the artillery corps. According to Randolf Cooper, "The brass sleeve also proved sufficiently 'elastic' to minimize the potential threat posed by barrel brittleness, hairline casting flaws and crystalline-like fractures associated with manufacturing iron cannon barrels."[92]

British military men were great admirers of the Maratha method of combining iron and brass. One Charles Stuart marveled at the perfection of the casting which was "done so well that there is not the smallest separation between the two metals." Stuart also reported that the larger cannons were equipped with a sophisticated elevating screw, which was made in such a way that it could be "used with a certain amount of interchangeability." Europeans did not develop this technology till the nineteenth century.[93] Another British military figure, George Constable, who was one of Britain's "leading experts on general purpose field artillery," was present in India during a Maratha campaign and wrote that the guns were "far superior to anything Britain possessed" and "obtained permission . . . to forge and cast ordnance on the same principle" in London. After testing Constable's guns, British military observers urged the adoption of the Maratha designs.[94]

Rocketry was another Indian military innovation that left a deep imprint on the minds of many British. The Mughals in the seventeenth century and the Marathas in the eighteenth century used rockets, chiefly to frighten enemy forces because the range and accuracy of their rockets were not great. In late eighteenth-century Mysore, rockets were used to great effect against the British, however, which suggests some technical improvements, and reports of the effectiveness of the weapons circulated in Britain. The Mysore rockets were more advanced than any found in Europe. They had a range of 1 to 2 kilometers and they were manufactured from iron tubes, rather than wood or paper, which made possible higher bursting pressures in the combustion chamber and therefore increased the thrust. The success of these South Indian rockets inspired William Congreve to experiment with the Mysorean designs in the Woolwich Arsenal in London. This led to the manufacture of rockets with iron tubes for British forces, which were used in North America in the War of 1812 and inspired Francis Scott Key's "Star Spangled Banner," with its reference to the "rockets' red glare."[95]

Regimes of useful knowledge

For Joel Mokyr the regime of useful knowledge that emerged in eighteenth-century Europe holds the key to the dramatic technological breakthroughs in textiles, iron, steam power and a growing list of other areas from the nineteenth century. Europe's Industrial Enlightenment and commitment to useful knowledge were unique and had no counterpart in Asia, according to Mokyr, and they were, in the final analysis, about cultural attitudes. Mokyr writes, "It has once again become 'kosher' if not quite de rigueur to speak of 'cultural beliefs' . . . My interest is about the beliefs people held about their physical milieu."[96] Europeans possessed different attitudes than Asians on the possibilities of understanding the natural world and on using that knowledge for practical ends.

The material presented in this chapter shows that a drive to understand nature and to use that knowledge in new ways was not confined to Europe. The content of this knowledge of the natural world differed in Europe and India, but what was unmistakably present in both regions of the world were attitudes that valued such intellectual inquiry. Similarly, in the Indian subcontinent the fruits of these inquiries were used for practical purposes. Therefore, a belief in the importance of understanding and compiling knowledge of the natural world, of different processes of production, and of attempting to meld knowledge and skill into new products and new ways of making things was a part of the cultural mix of early-modern India.

Useful knowledge, even if it is a cultural phenomenon, must be transmitted, diffused and acted upon to lead to economic change. Mokyr sees this process as reducing access costs or "the marginal cost involved in acquiring knowledge possessed by someone else in society."[97] It is possible that both Europe and India possessed a cultural milieu of useful knowledge, but that the mechanisms to communicate and exploit such information were superior in Europe. An examination of the possible paths of transmission, however, suggests that there were no profound differences or advantages for Europeans.

Knowledge could be transmitted in two ways. The first was through the written word, which played a role in both the Indian subcontinent and in Europe. Knowledgeable men in both places had access to texts, some they owned personally and others they consulted in repositories such as libraries. But when it came to the written word, Europe may be thought to have possessed an advantage with its invention of print technology, which lowered the cost of texts.[98] Mokyr, however, concludes that "in and of itself printing was not decisive, or else the Industrial Revolution might have occurred in the sixteenth century" and "as far as skills and workmanship were concerned, it is possible to exaggerate the importance of books and periodicals as means through which technical knowledge was accessed."[99]

Mokyr's skepticism about the contribution of print to the diffusion of useful knowledge is shared by others. Adrian Johns, for instance, has argued that print did not become a reliable source of truth and information till the nineteenth century. There is a difference between "the distribution of books and that of knowledge," as Johns puts it.[100] Aside from the reliability of the truth claims that appeared in print, the utility of the written word for technical matters is doubtful. As Simon Schaffer notes, "Several historians perceptively stress the difficulty of describing, let alone managing and changing, craft skills with encyclopaedic means."[101] In the important area of coal, little of the knowledge that the British possessed was written down or codified, which is a striking illustration of the limits of the text for transmitting techniques.[102] And this was coupled with the problem that few workers, whether in India or Europe, had access to texts, which was noted in late eighteenth-century France: "Workers read very little but observe narrowly and imitate readily."[103]

The second mode of knowledge transmission was face to face and took place in schools, universities, lecture halls, associations and workshops or other sites of production. Much more is known about these modes of communication in Europe than in the Indian subcontinent. As was already noted, it is very difficult to recover from existing sources the nature of intellectual and associational life in the Indian subcontinent in the seventeenth and eighteenth centuries, which leaves a serious gap for the historian. It is evident that there was some remarkable assimilation of information, such as the case of Bundla Ramaswamy Naidu, an obscure author of an 1820 tract on the British revenue system in South India, who refers in his work to Montesquieu's *Spirit of the Laws*.[104] How and why Ramaswamy Naidu had access to Montesquieu is not known, but this example is evidence that the Indian subcontinent was not devoid of associational life in the eighteenth century and that these associations attracted ordinary men such as Ramaswamy Naidu. Christopher Bayly's *Empire and Information* also provides an important corrective to views that Europe was exceptional in this respect and portrays a social order in India that was rich in debate and the exchange of knowledge and information.[105]

The European university system is again often seen as unique and thought to have had no counterpart in India. Mokyr is hesitant to accord the university great weight in the diffusion of useful knowledge. "Oddly enough, the role of formal educational institutions in the reduction of access costs was quite modest in the first century of the Industrial Revolution," he observes.[106] A final way in which thinkers and scholars were brought together in both Europe and India was through the auspices of the state. As shown in this chapter, the patronage of states in India was critical for intellectual exchange and for the diffusion of knowledge through translations and libraries. Such state support was also found in eighteenth-century Europe, and appears to have been especially important outside Britain.[107] At the same time, states in Europe could erect barriers to the access of knowledge, the most important example being the patent system, which may have helped to generate new technical thinking. Increasingly historians of Europe do not see the patent system as crucial in either the generation of new technologies or in impeding their spread in the eighteenth century, however.[108] It is difficult, then, to point to a path of face-to-face knowledge transmission which was unique to Europe and essential for technological change.

One face-to-face path not yet mentioned, but which was found in both Europe and India, is the transmission of technique and technical knowledge by artisans and skilled workers. The worker possessed of skill figures in Mokyr's account of useful knowledge. "Much of the knowledge that counted was not written down or depicted in the (increasingly detailed and sophisticated) technical drawings of the age, but embodied in implicit forms we would call 'skills,' 'dexterity,' and other synonyms for what is known as tacit knowledge," Mokyr writes.[109] Other historians of science and technology in Europe give the skilled worker even greater prominence in both the transmission and the generation of useful knowledge. Liliane Hilaire-Perez, for instance, argues that in Europe "artisans were key actors in technical innovation and in the diffusion of new knowledge." They possessed an "increasingly complex" technical culture and they operated in an open world in which knowledge was diffused and shared. When artisans interacted, knowledge was generated and transferred. When they moved, knowledge moved with them. Finally, artisans operated in a commercial world and thus knowledge attained economic value and was disseminated through the marketplace.[110]

It is likely that artisans and other skilled workers played similar roles in seventeenth- and eighteenth-century India in both the invention and the transmission of new techniques and methods. The importance of these actors for technological progress can also explain the many efforts of eighteenth-century rulers to attract skilled workers to their realms, several of which have been related in this chapter. It is extremely difficult to gain access to the worlds of workers in early-modern India, but the limited evidence that is available suggests that the astute and knowledgeable worker was indispensable in developing, absorbing and transmitting skills and ideas. One revealing report comes from Thomas Bowrey, who wrote in the late seventeenth century that the "very expert Master builders" he met on the Coromandel Coast "learnt theire art and trade from some of the [English], by diligently Observeinge the ingenuitie of Some that built Ships and Sloops here for the English East India Company and theire Agents, Soe that they build very well and give good reasons for what they doe."[111] (Bowrey also noted that "the best Iron upon the Coast is . . . Vended here . . . with the Workmanship alsoe."[112] This suggests cooperation between different types of workers, in this case carpenters and other experts in wood, blacksmiths and most likely the makers of tools.)

Indian workers also possessed a high degree of skill and knowledge and a number of European writers admired their vast storehouse of sophisticated and practical scientific understanding.[113] William Roxburgh, for instance, a British naturalist who spent decades in South India and produced a monumental study of plants on the Coromandel Coast, wrote that "the native knowledge in practical chemistry is more extensive than we have generally conceived it to be," which he supported with descriptions of several processes that he witnessed in South India. The first was "practiced by almost every artificer that works in brass" and was a technique to recover the valuable zinc from "the small bits, turnings and filings," which would otherwise be lost. The process consisted of heating the scraps with sulfur and water. The copper fused with the sulfur, while the zinc did not, which allowed the latter to be isolated for future use. According to Roxburgh, this process was of "recent discovery at home." A second procedure which was also of recent origin in Britain, but practiced in India for some 100 years, was "a method of preparing red, yellow and white pigments for painting from calyx of lead by means of common salt." The British state had recently granted a patent for the production of these colors by a similar process, Roxburgh noted. He further added that Indians were "very conversant" in the method of smelting the different metals that are produced in Britain and remarked that the Indian process of refining silver yielded a product that was superior to the English standard. Finally, as were countless other Europeans, Roxburgh was impressed with the abilities of Indians to dye cloth and fix colors by methods that Europe did not possess.[114]

Other Europeans in the late eighteenth and early nineteenth centuries were also impressed by the technical achievements of Indian artisans and workers. The techniques and knowledge of iron smelting, in particular, received widespread admiration because of the high quality of Indian iron. James Franklin, who toured the iron works of central India in the early nineteenth century as the Superintendent of Iron Mines, wrote: "Their smelting furnaces, though rude in appearance, are nevertheless very exact in their interior proportions, and it has often surprised me to see men who are unquestionably ignorant of their principle, construct them with precision in so simple a manner."[115]

Indian workers were also not lacking in mechanical skills. There is limited evidence of clock making in seventeenth- and eighteenth-century India, but as we have seen in this chapter, metallurgical skills were highly advanced and the application of these to the manufacture of astrolabes, muskets and flintlocks would have required a high level of precision skill. Further evidence for such abilities comes from a description of a "magic machine" in Lahore in the late sixteenth century, which delighted Akbar. When a rupee was thrown into it, the coin fell to the bottom, and "upon this a parrot . . . began to turn around and, then, two birds began to chirp at one another. Then a small window opened, and a panther put forward its head . . . and a shell came out of its mouth to fall on a dish which was placed on the head of a tiger, and the shell came out of the tiger's mouth." Although Irfan Habib notes that the device was probably built with levers, balances and possibly pulleys, as opposed to gears, it does point to a high level of mechanical ability.[116]

While the skills fostered in clock making were important for some technological breakthroughs in eighteenth-century Britain, they were not necessary for all, and the number of men with these mechanical skills expanded in the wake of industrialization. Clock makers were needed for Arkwright's water frame, but not for the spinning jenny, Crompton's mule or the steam engine. As we shall see in the next chapter, manufacturing developed at a very slow pace in early nineteenth-century India, which meant that there was little development of essential mechanical skills, and the skill gap between Europe and India widened into an almost unbridgeable chasm.

To conclude, in terms of knowledge and technique, in the eighteenth century Indian workers were by no means inferior to those found in Britain or elsewhere in Europe. While in some areas British workers had developed more specialized skills, such as clock making, the obverse was the case in other domains of production, especially in agriculture, textiles and some forms of metal working. And skilled workers were critical in both Europe and India for the generation as well as the transmission of useful knowledge. Giving central place to skilled workers raises questions on the relationship between those individuals and other possessors of technical know-how, whether elites, scientists or scholars, and how we are to understand the sources of technological dynamism. Does this mean a return to the old debate on whether the scientist or the worker was more important for technological change? And what of the social, economic and political context, which has loomed so large in the previous chapters? Do they have no place in this discussion? To answer these questions without falling into the trap of European exceptionalism, this chapter concludes with a discussion of the mindful hand.

Conclusion: the mindful hand

In the 1950s Charles Gillispie wrote that the proposition that "theoretical science exerted a fructifying and even a causative influence in industrialization" is appealing, but it is "extraordinarily difficult to trace the course of any significant theoretical concept from abstract formulation to actual use in industrial operations." "Consider the more significant achievements in basic science," Gillispie continued, "and range these accomplishments side by side in the mind's eye with the crucial points of technological advance in the industrial revolution . . . and it is immediately evident that no apparent relationship existed between these two sets of achievements except the vague and uninteresting one that both occurred in a technical nexus."[117]

Historians of science and economic historians continue to debate the relative contributions of scientists and workers to the development of modern technology. On one pole are those who see science as making a minimal contribution to the great technological break-throughs of industrialization, at times reversing the arrow and arguing that scientific knowledge expanded as a consequence of advances in technique. D. S. L. Cardwell writes,

The development of machines like the steam-engine in the eighteenth century almost forced man to recognise the enormous power, the *puissance*, of heat, the grand moving-agent of the universe. The sight of a primitive steam-engine tirelessly pumping ton after ton of water out of a mine, or a crude early locomotive hauling a train of trucks along a rough, uneven railway-track, did more for science than all the speculations of the philosophers about the nature of heat since the world began.[118]

From this perspective, the key players in the progress of technology were skilled workers whose knowledge, tacit and other, led to improvements in the process of production.

On the other pole, in opposition to arguments that give pride of place to the skilled worker, are others who counter that scientific knowledge was the major force behind the inventive activity of the seventeenth and eighteenth centuries. Perhaps most prominently, in the late 1960s A. E. Musson and Eric Robinson wrote,

Contrary to long-accepted ideas, the [industrial revolution] was not simply a product of illiterate practical craftsmen, devoid of scientific training. In the development of steam power, in the growth of the chemical industry, in bleaching, dyeing and calico-printing, in pottery, soap, and glass manufacture, and in various other industries, scientists made important contributions and industrialists with scientifically trained minds also utilized applied science in their manufactures.[119]

Margaret Jacob and Joel Mokyr are, in many respects, heirs to this Musson–Robinson tradition.

This chapter has declined to choose between these opposing camps. Historians of science and technology are beginning to reject this choice as well. As Lissa Roberts and Simon Schaffer put it, "Articulations between knowledge, know-how and technique were intimate and complex. Distinguishing between high-status sciences and lowly labour obscures much more than it reveals and is extremely anachronistic." Instead of separating these two activities, they argue that scientific knowledge and technical skill were generated together. They have labeled this simultaneous creation of knowledge and skill the mindful hand, with which they refer to the "hybrid activities involved in the intimately related processes of material and knowledge production."[120] Therefore, there was no simple line of causality running from knowledge to technique, or vice versa, but rather joint processes that simultaneously generated both.

In addition to rethinking the division between science and technology, with the mindful hand, Roberts and Schaffer seek to "overcome and to depart from a potent distinction between celestial knowledge and temporal power."[121] Knowledge, they argue, was not autonomous or independent of the political and economic order, to be drawn upon as needed. Instead it was created in interaction with the economic and political environment. Therefore, much as this book has argued, the mindful hand sees the production of knowledge as closely linked to social, political and economic context. This was certainly the case in the Indian subcontinent, where a number of knowledge activities described in this chapter were sponsored by rulers who viewed them as essential for the exercise and expansion of political power in the seventeenth and eighteenth centuries. While the activities of states may have best survived in the documentary record, interest in skill and knowledge was also a private activity, as most strikingly reflected in the shipyards of the subcontinent, where private individuals saw the potentials for profit and amassed knowledge and put it to work in new activities. Therefore, the Indian subcontinent in the seventeenth and eighteenth centuries was home to complex articulations and interactions between knowledge and skill, or mind and hand, and the economic and political order.

This was no less true of Europe, where the development of mental and manual knowledge took place in a vastly different political and economic context, which explains why the path of technological change in the eighteenth century proved to be different. In Western Europe, and particularly in Britain, the mindful hand operated in an environment of global competitive pressures and growing ecological scarcity. For without innovation in textile manufacturing, British textile masters, most importantly in cotton, were shut out of the huge textile marts of the eastern Mediterranean, West Africa, the Americas and the Indian Ocean. And without an energy revolution, which led to growing experimentation with coal and a number of major technical breakthroughs connected with that mineral, not only manufacturing enterprises but also households faced a more dim future. Strikingly, neither of these pressures operated in the Indian subcontinent, whether in more advanced or less advanced regions. While not all regions in the Indian subcontinent benefited equally from the cotton textile export boom of the seventeenth and eighteenth centuries, even the most backward areas did not face the outflow of specie and competitive pressures that Western Europe confronted, for they possessed their own cotton industries. Nor did they face the constraints of energy that several parts of Europe increasingly weathered.

It is thus striking that the most revolutionary technological breakthroughs of eighteenth-century Europe were in two areas, textiles and energy, which worried Indians little. It is also striking, as explored in the next chapter, that a number of innovations in these two areas were transferred rather seamlessly to the Indian subcontinent in the early nineteenth century, which suggests that levels of skill and knowledge, or the mindful hand, were not dramatically different between Europe and India. These points suggest that the secret to Europe's scientific and technological verve must be found in the specific challenges that Europeans faced, not in any purported cultural, economic or social exceptionalism.

8 | Modern industry in early nineteenth-century India

The early nineteenth-century governments of continental Europe shared a tradition of direct participation in industrial and technological development. Their institutions and their official outlook both meant that it was logical for them to play an active role at a time of genuinely modern industrialization.[1]

Introduction

The industrialization of Britain transformed the economic landscape of the world. From the late eighteenth century, British economic success was emulated, initially in Europe, but then around the globe. While historians no longer consider industrialization as a straightforward transplantation of British technology and now view it as a complex amalgamation of foreign and indigenous knowledge, techniques and institutions, there is little doubt that in many parts of the nineteenth-century world there were numerous attempts to introduce British machines and methods. The literature on early French industrialization, for example, is replete with stories of espionage, recruitment of British skilled workers, transfer of British know-how and the importation of British inventions.[2]

Modern industry, as exemplified by British manufacturing, came to be desired because it was seen as essential for the exercise and consolidation of state power. The new techniques for iron working, for instance, were critical for the production of modern armaments. And industrial methods of manufacturing vastly expanded output and therefore the revenue potential of emerging nation-states. As Friedrich List wrote in 1841, "At a time when technical and mechanical science exercise such immense influence on the methods of warfare, when all warlike operations depend so much on the condition of the national revenue . . . at such a time, more than ever before, must the value of manufactures be estimated from a political point of view."[3]

Because of its link to political power, modern industry came to be highly sought after in the nineteenth century. Although industrialization in Europe and Asia was not a simple replication of a British model – there were many paths to a modern industrial economy – it is undeniable that the push to produce more and at lower prices on the basis of new technologies was widespread. The question that this chapter asks is why the advanced regions of India and China – which were in the eighteenth century major global economic centers – were unable to follow France, Belgium and Germany and emulate British successes. For the divergence between Europe and Asia is not only about the rise of Europe, but also about the failure of much of Asia to keep pace.

Chapter 6 presented the beginnings of an answer to this question for the Yangzi delta, which was unable to stabilize its ecology, in contrast to Japan. With its more effective state policies, Japan entered the nineteenth century with a more secure agrarian economy and was better poised to exploit new opportunities in the new global order. Because of growing ecological problems, rebellion and economic conflict racked the Yangzi, and may have contributed to the disaster of the Taiping.[4] The focus of this chapter is not China or Japan but India. The last chapter showed that the Indian subcontinent possessed a vast reservoir of skilled labor in the eighteenth century and earlier chapters gave evidence of a sophisticated mercantile order, an abundant stock of capital, if interest rates are a reliable guide, and activist rulers who embarked upon ambitious projects of economic improvement and military modernization. Despite these economic capacities, nineteenth-century India descended into levels of poverty that were unprecedented, the most striking evidence for which is the estimated 12 to 29 million Indians who died in famines in the quarter-century between 1876 and 1902.[5]

The debate on the nineteenth-century Indian economy

For more than a hundred years the reasons for the limited industrial development of nineteenth-century India have been debated. Externalists place primary responsibility upon British colonialism in the subcontinent. In the words of Romesh Dutt, the famous late nineteenth-century critic of British rule:

All the old industries, for which India had been noted from ancient times, had declined under the jealous commercial policy of the East India Company; and when Queen Victoria ascended the throne in 1837, agriculture was left the only national industry of the people. Little was done to foster new industries after the Crown assumed the administration of India in 1858; and the last decades of the century still found the Indian manufacturer and artisan in a state of poverty and decline.[6]

Internalists give primacy to social, cultural or economic conditions within India. In this vein, Vera Anstey wrote,

India is suffering from arrested economic development, and is still, in many respects, mediaeval . . . We have seen that certain religious ideas and conventions, and the rigid social stratification and conservatism based upon those ideas and conventions, still pervade every sphere of life, and limit economic development at every step. The resulting weakness of the "economic motive," and lack of economic enterprise, have prevented full advantage from being taken of existing knowledge, and have prevented adequate use from being made of India's great natural resources.[7]

For much of the twentieth century the externalists dominated the debate, especially during the heyday of nationalism in the Indian subcontinent, but the internalist position has become increasingly influential. Tirthankar Roy, for one, has criticized the emphasis on British colonialism and argued that resource endowments were the crucial constraint on economic development in modern India: "A first step toward a useful alternative approach would be to replace imperialism with economic structure – that is, the constraints and opportunities that took shape under resource endowment patterns that took time to change . . . Indeed, economic change in colonial India can be seen as a process wherein resource constraints were temporarily overcome by reallocation and increasingly industrious labor."[8] Niall Ferguson has taken the re-evaluation of colonialism even further and writes that "Victorian India was booming. Immense sums of British capital were being invested in a range of new industries: cotton and jute spinning, coal mining and steel production."[9]

Despite these shifts in prevailing wisdom, the colonial state had a powerful impact on the Indian economy. Colonial trade policies checked industrial activity and channeled it into less fruitful lines. The state's failure to invest in public goods such as education and institutions to promote and expand technical knowledge – staples of

European economic policy at the time – hampered the development of industry for decades. The highly skilled and knowledgeable workers of the eighteenth century, and the possibilities they held out for economic change in the nineteenth, were dissipated and not capitalized upon.

New industrial techniques in the Indian subcontinent

Writings on Indian industrialization in the nineteenth century focus primarily on the period after 1850. Morris D. Morris's very substantial contribution to the *Cambridge Economic History of India*, "The Growth of Large-Scale Industry," devoted only four pages to what he called "The Prelude: 1800–1850." Classic works on Indian industrialization, from D. R. Gadgil's *Industrial Evolution of India in Recent Times* to Amiya Bagchi's *Private Investment in India* and Rajnarayan Chandavarkar's *Origins of Industrial Capitalism in India* focus on the period after the mid-nineteenth century.[10] The disproportionate attention given to the cotton mills of Bombay and Ahmedabad and the jute mills of Calcutta, all of which were only established from the 1850s, reinforced the neglect of the early nineteenth century.

The decades between 1800 and 1850 were a pivotal period in the industrial development of the Indian subcontinent, however. In those years, the booming early-modern textile-exporting regions – Gujarat, Bengal and South India – made the painful adjustment to lower overseas demand for their wares. At the same time, the establishment of British power eliminated numerous Indian kings both large and small, and the closing down of royal courts and political centers with their elaborate rituals of consumption – along with sizable military forces – meant a sharp fall in demand for manufactures of all kinds.[11] Finally, from the 1820s British-made cotton yarn, cloth and iron produced with new industrial techniques began to invade Indian markets themselves.[12]

While the quantitative estimates on the extent of deindustrialization continue to be debated, there is little disagreement that the first half of the nineteenth century was a very difficult time for artisans and manufacturers. Weavers, for instance, were in the early ranks of indentured migrants from South India, which reflects the crisis of the textile industry.[13] Longstanding export markets for Indian cotton cloth were lost to British manufacturers and trade statistics suggest that

British cotton goods were making inroads in the Indian market itself. High levels of British revenue demand further deepened the economic disruption. From the 1820s to the 1840s, a severe economic depression gripped the areas under British control and led to steep falls in agricultural prices. This added to the weight of the British revenue demand, which was fixed in money terms. The first several decades of British rule were a period of profound economic dislocation and decline.[14]

Despite this turmoil, a number of new technologies and new methods of manufacturing from Europe were introduced into the Indian subcontinent in the early years of the nineteenth century. Steam engines, rolling mills and spinning machines were put to work in a variety of centers, including South India, Bengal and Bombay. These efforts predate, sometimes by several decades, the modern cotton industry of Bombay, which is typically taken to be the starting point of Indian industrialization. These enterprises were technical successes – Indian workers learned quickly to operate, maintain and even build machinery – but they were not economically viable. Without political support, the markets for these undertakings were limited. This suggests that the early nineteenth century represented a missed opportunity. The conditions for modern industry became less propitious later and the cost and complexity of machinery and the capital and skills required to put it to work outstripped the capacities of the Indian economy.

Cotton spinning

Cotton-spinning machinery from Europe was imported into the subcontinent from the second decade of the nineteenth century. Around 1817 or 1818, modern spinning machines powered by steam were erected by Europeans in Calcutta, but little is known about their fate. In the 1830s, a spinning and weaving factory was in operation in Fort Gloucester, about fifteen miles from Calcutta. In 1840, there were five steam engines at work in the mill and the annual output was 700,000 pounds of cotton twist. The enterprise formerly had 100 power looms, but by 1840 these were no longer in use and all the power generated by the steam engines was shifted to spinning, which was more profitable. According to one of the owners, the mill spun yarn that ranged from 20 to 50 count. The lower counts were cheaper than British imports and the higher counts were comparable in price. In 1840, the mill had one European superintendent "for the machinery generally; but with that exception it is all worked by natives." And the natives were deemed "very expert" in their duties. The steam engines were fueled by coal from Burdwan.[15]

More details are available for cotton-spinning works in the French possession of Pondicherry where production *à l'européenne* began in 1831. A modern mill was established by several Frenchmen with substantial support from the French state, which subsidized the cost of shipping the machinery from Europe, extended low-cost loans for the project, and offered production subsidies. The machinery itself was French-made for the most part, except for the steam engines which were British. During the 1830s the factory employed 150 workers and produced 700 pounds of yarn per day. The quality of the yarn was very high and in 1834 it received an honorable mention at an exposition in Paris. The factory was expanded in 1839 with the addition of new machinery and output increased to 1,200 pounds of yarn per day and employment grew to 280 workers. In 1838, a second, smaller cotton-spinning factory – with a daily production of about 230 pounds of yarn – was added.[16]

The French state had two reasons for supporting these manufacturing ventures. First, it wanted to reverse the early nineteenth-century decline of the Pondicherry economy. A Pondicherry official noted in 1825 that "blue cloth is at the moment the only article of export which is advantageous to the colony and which feeds our commercial relations with the metropole."[17] Second, the yarn was needed for the weaving of cloth – which was then dyed blue with indigo – for export to Senegal, where it was exchanged for gum Arabic, an essential ingredient for the French cloth-printing industry. West Africans refused to buy French imitations of the South Indian cloth because they were not of the proper texture, color or even smell. Before introducing spinning machinery, the French brought a master weaver from Rouen, one Thomas Geodefroy, who was reputed to be one of the best weavers in that city, to transmit recent innovations in looms to local artisans. And Michael Gonfreville, a chemist, was given the task of improving indigo-dyeing techniques.[18]

The spinning mills employed large numbers of South Indian men, women and children. Mechanics from France were responsible for the installation of the spinning machinery and the steam engines which powered them. They were also responsible for the initial period of maintenance. In 1829, the men behind the project requested state support for the passage of a mechanic and two assistants to Pondicherry, along with a metalsmith, a turner in wood and metal, and a fitter who knew how to make combs and shuttles for weaving. These workers were to "reside in India for six years" and "instruct Indian workers and found a model workshop for the country."[19] By 1832, a number of Indian workers had been trained in mechanics and machine maintenance and the spinning works dispensed with many of its European experts.[20] With a limited staff of Europeans, and large numbers of unskilled and skilled Indians, the spinning works continued to operate successfully for a number of years.[21] In the opinions of the French owners of the enterprise, the Indian workers were as intelligent and capable as those in France.[22]

Steam engines

An exhaustive inventory of the steam engines in operation in early nineteenth-century India is not available. Nevertheless, steam engines were in wide use by the 1830s in Calcutta, Bombay, Pondicherry and perhaps Madras. The Boulton and Watt records reveal that between 1775 and 1825 the firm received a total of 110 overseas orders for steam engines. Fifteen of these were from India, which was, after the Netherlands, the second largest export market for Boulton and Watt. Steam engines by other manufacturers, including Maudeslays, Butterley, the Eagle Foundry and Fawcett and Littledale, were also sent to India, but information on what quantities is not available.[23]

The export of Boulton and Watt engines to India was first raised in 1792 when a flourmill project in Calcutta and a steam-powered fountain in Awadh were under consideration. The first steam engine in Bombay was used to pump water at the dockyard in 1809.[24] Later engines were found in iron working, minting, mining and shipping. The mints in Calcutta and Bombay, which had five and three engines respectively, represented the biggest concentrations of steam power in the early nineteenth century. Matthew Boulton himself designed national mints for Russia, Denmark and Brazil and "the Indian mints seem to have represented the most advanced technological thinking in mint design anywhere in the world at the time and embodied complete flow production systems in which the bullion flowed in at one end and the coinage out at the other."[25]

Contemporaries attributed the appeal of steam power in India to the labor savings it made possible. "The greatly augmented demand for labourers in Calcutta has rendered the procurement of Coolies more difficult and precarious than I can well describe," the Calcutta mint master wrote. At the mint, steam engines replaced the work of 1,500 men. In just the operation of the capstans, steam power replaced 243 workers and slashed costs by two-thirds. In the Bombay docks as well, the "manual labour requisite to free [the docks] from water" was given as the chief factor behind the adoption of steam power.[26] These remarks indicate that the labor shortages that characterized the late pre-colonial economy continued to operate in the early-colonial.

As was their practice, Boulton and Watt sent an experienced mechanic with each engine for assistance with the setting up of the machine and the initial maintenance. These mechanics suffered from high mortality rates. Of the ten men sent to Calcutta in 1823, four died by the end of 1825 and a fifth suffered from "continuous intoxication." Because of high death rates, it is likely that local men had to take over much of the work of steam engine maintenance, but the sources have little to say on this matter.[27]

The number of engines imported into the subcontinent before the 1820s was not large, but concentrated in the advanced regions of Bengal and the South and the rising economic center of Bombay. Despite the small number, according to Jennifer Tann and John Aitken, India was home to "some remarkable steam-powered industrial proto-types, many years before the onset of industrialisation."[28] Jennifer Tann and M. M. Breckin conclude that by 1825 India was at the second of their three stages of steam engine diffusion and development. In stage two, "a more widespread interest is shown in the engine, a greater number are purchased, and the spread of information can be observed along the routes of kinship, religious, social, and related trade connexions." Canada, Denmark and the Netherlands were the other countries in stage two at this time. Only France, Belgium, Germany and the United States had reached stage three, which was marked by the establishment of local steam engine manufacturing.[29]

Tann and Breckin conclude their study in 1825, but several steam engines were manufactured in Calcutta later in the decade under

European supervision, including a high-pressure engine for a soda-water factory, two condensing engines for a foundry, a four-horsepower boat engine in 1828 and a six-horsepower engine in 1829.[30] By 1840, according to the Parliamentary testimony of C. E. Trevelyan, facilities for engine and machinery repair were located in the Calcutta Mint, the Cossipore Iron Foundry and in the shipyards of Mr. Jessop.[31] And by 1845 some 150 steam engines were in use in the Bengal Presidency.[32]

Coal mining

In the 1790s, as we saw in the previous chapter, Tipu Sultan in Mysore wanted to learn more about coal and asked his emissaries who were traveling to the Ottoman Empire and Europe to return with samples. Coal had not been exploited before the colonial period, but the introduction of steam engines into the subcontinent fueled a search for the mineral, which was further stimulated with the rise of steam shipping. From the early years of the nineteenth century, the English East India Company financed geological surveys in its territories and these revealed substantial coal deposits in several parts of its possessions, most importantly in eastern India. The largest was the Raniganj coalfield in the Burdwan district of Bengal. The coal was of fairly high quality and the mines were also located near waterways which allowed for cheap transport.

As the crow flies, Burdwan is 130 miles from Calcutta. Coal was discovered in the area in 1774 and serious mining commenced in 1815. Coal was transported on water from Burdwan to Calcutta during the rainy season and in the late 1820s some 300–400 boats made three or four trips every year. Production picked up from 1824 and reached 15,000 tons in 1832. In 1836, Dwarkanath Tangore purchased the major mine in the area and became the largest supplier of coal in eastern India for both steam engines and steam transport. The Burdwan coal was of high quality and the best of it was rated at 90 percent of good English coal and, according to a source from 1830, it could be had in the markets of Calcutta for only a half to two-thirds the price. The coal from Burdwan was also exported to Singapore where it fueled steam engines. In 1830, some 2,000–3,000 people were employed at the mines, with a single European in charge. The mines were relatively shallow, with shafts extending to about ninety feet from the surface. A steam engine was used to pump out rainwater. In Calcutta, the coal was used by the Cossipore Foundry, the Sherrif and Company brickworks, the Cossipore and Fort Gloucester Mills and the Assam Company's sawmill and steamers. Burdwan coal was also sent to upcountry users, including indigo, silk, sugar and rice mills.[33]

Shipbuilding

In the eighteenth and early nineteenth centuries, Indian and European merchants, including the English East India Company, the Royal Navy, and Danish, Dutch and Portuguese private traders, had large numbers of vessels built in Indian shipyards. The appeal of Indian ships did not appear to lie in their lower price. While information is limited, in the early nineteenth century the costs of shipbuilding in India and Britain appear to have been comparable. In 1814, a British expert testified to Parliament that he knew of only one instance in which an Indian-built ship was more costly than British-built vessels. Another expert estimated that the costs of shipbuilding were about 5 pounds per ton less in India than in Britain. In 1816, however, the British Navy Board reported that Indian ships cost 34 pounds per ton and British a little under 33.[34]

The real cost advantage of Indian ships derived from their greater durability. According to British shipping men, Indian vessels lasted from two to four times as long as British.[35] Even if these figures are an exaggeration, an additional ten, twenty or forty years in the life of a ship represented a significantly higher return on an investment. British observers also concurred that the costs of repairs were lower for Indian ships, which reduced not only the operating costs but also the time when a ship, and the valuable capital it represented, was out of circulation. According to figures submitted to Parliament in 1814, the cost of repairs after five voyages for a Thames-built ship was 11,572 pounds. Those for an Indian vessel came to 5,693 pounds. Another set of figures reported that the cost of repairs after four voyages for two Indian ships came to an average of 12,572 pounds each (these were also reported to be old ships), while for four ships built on the Thames, the figure was 20,792 pounds each. Repairs represented a significant ongoing cost and over the lifetime of a ship could add up to more than the initial purchase price.[36]

The first vessel was built in the shipyards of Calcutta in 1769 and production peaked in 1821. In those five decades, 272 ships were built in the city. The industry went into decline after 1821 because of the entry of cheaper British-made competitors. Between 1827 and 1839 only five ships were built in Calcutta. Nevertheless, two major dock-yards for the repair of ships and the outfitting of paddle wheels were in operation in the 1830s. The shipbuilders of Calcutta pioneered the construction of steam-driven vessels in the subcontinent. In 1823, two sixteen-horsepower engines that had been purchased in Canton were attached to a vessel built under the direction of James Kyd.[37] Calcutta shipyards also designed and constructed the engines for steamships. One of the first was the *Snake*, which served as a towboat in the Hooghly as well as on military expeditions in Burma and the Persian Gulf. W. H. Carey reported that the *Snake*'s engines "were designed and built by a Parsee," and he believed that they "were the first ever manufactured in India."[38]

Shipbuilding had an even longer history in Bombay than in Calcutta. The European East India Companies and European private traders had been commissioning ships on the west coast since the seventeenth century. In 1735, the English East Company established a shipyard in Bombay and Lowji Nusserwanji Wadia of Surat was appointed as master builder. Over the next half century the Wadias built over sixty vessels. The Bombay ships were held in high regard and in the eighteenth century the Wadia shipyard was considered one of the finest in the world. The city's reputation continued into the nineteenth when Reginald Heber opined that "the ships built by native artists at Bombay are notoriously as good as any which sail from London to Liverpool."[39]

In the 1820s the Wadias embarked upon the construction of ships suitable for steam power and they launched the first Bombay steam vessel in 1829, driven by two eighty-horsepower engines. The Wadias were keen to expand their technical knowledge, particularly for the building of steamships, and in 1838 Jamsetji Bomanji dispatched his son and nephew to Britain to study naval architecture. The pair spent three years studying under the master shipwright of the Royal Dock-yard at Chatham. They reportedly visited dockyards in other parts of Europe as well.[40]

Despite the excellent quality and reputation of ships built in Bombay and Calcutta, both centers went into decline from the

1820s. One reason was the rise of iron ships in Britain against which Indian builders were unable to compete. According to Daniel Headrick, "What destroyed Indian shipbuilding was British iron."[41] Satpal Sangwan has objected to what he sees as the technological determinism of this statement and argued that "alongside British 'iron,' we must take note of British 'policy'" which discouraged the use of Indian-made ships.[42] Sangwan gives great weight to the Registry Act of 1815, which has already been discussed in the previous chapter. By imposing a "15 percent duty... on goods imported in India-build ships; that only British ships should import goods from south and east of the Cape of Good Hope," the act effectively eliminated the use of Indian-made ships in the trade with Britain.[43] In 1840, R. Montgomery Martin testified in Parliament that the Registry Act was "a direct impediment thrown in the way of India-built, owned, and manned shipping, in its intercourse with other countries beyond the limits of the Cape of Good Hope." Martin also referred to the act as "navigation laws," which suggests that he saw it in the tradition of seventeenth-century laws that protected and advanced British shipping and commercial interests.[44]

The political element explains two other factors in the decline of Indian shipbuilding. The first is the timing. Iron ships plied both Atlantic and Indian waters from the 1820s, but it took three decades for them to triumph over their wooden competitors. The British Post Office and Lloyd's of London, for instance, did not accept that iron ships were the equal of wood till the mid-1850s.[45] The decline of the Indian industry dates from the early 1820s, however, close on the heels of the Registry Act of 1815, long before the commercial victory of iron. Second, British iron ships threatened shipbuilding as well as shipping throughout the world, but as Headrick himself notes, these activities survived in a number of places, including France, Italy and Japan, where states intervened to protect domestic industries and carriers. Policies to protect Indian shipbuilding were not possible in the colonial economy of nineteenth-century India, however.[46]

Iron working

In the late eighteenth and early nineteenth centuries iron was produced in dozens of centers in the subcontinent and both English East India Company officials and European experts had nothing but praise for the quality of the metal as well as the knowledge and skill of Indian workers. The smelting was done with charcoal in small and medium furnaces. Yields were middling, but the metal possessed superb properties. From the late eighteenth century, the quality of Indian iron received wide acclaim in Europe and descriptions of the irons and steels produced in the subcontinent appeared in the *Philosophical Transactions*, the *Journal of the Royal Asiatic Society*, the *Proceedings of the Royal Society*, the *Quarterly Journal of Science, Literature, and the Arts* as well as in several travelers' accounts. Even Michael Faraday conducted experiments on wootz, an Indian steel.[47]

In the early nineteenth century, the superior properties of Indian iron generated interest in the production of the metal along European lines for the Indian market. In Bengal, several Europeans floated proposals for the building of large-scale iron works and the Bagpore Iron Foundry was established in 1812. The leading figure in Bagpore was Andrew Duncan, an iron man from Carion, Scotland, who had also spent fifteen years in Russia setting up iron works.[48] Details about the Bagpore iron works are limited, but it appears to have failed fairly quickly. An 1814 letter from the Import Warehouse Keeper at Fort William, Calcutta, gives some insight into why the venture failed: "Amongst all the various descriptions of metals which are applicable for the provision of dead-weight for ships connected with trade to the Eastward of the Cape of Good Hope, iron is the one which can originally be procured under the most advantageous rates and the description which holds out to importers the most reasonable prospects of final indemnification."[49] As long as British iron was in demand as dead weight cargo for ships sailing to India, and therefore its costs of transport subsidized, Indian iron making had bleak prospects. As a consequence, the Calcutta government concluded that "not much advantage will be derived from an iron foundry in this country."[50]

Far more successful was a large-scale iron works established in South India. In this case, however, the goal was not to supply the Indian market but rather to export the iron to Britain itself, which was more appealing to English East India Company authorities. In 1825, the Madras Council received a proposal from a J. M. Heath to develop an iron-smelting works in the presidency along European principles. Before embarking on the project, he requested an exclusive privilege to produce iron by those methods for the duration of the

Company's charter.[51] Heath repeated the request in 1829 and reiterated his demand for "provision which should defend me from competition for a reasonable period." He supported this request with examples from England, where "such protection was given in the reign of King James, I think, to the persons who first attempted to make iron with pit coal," and Russia, where "such protection was afforded to the first persons who established iron works." Heath's exclusive privilege was granted after the second request, but progress on the construction of the works was not made till the 1830s.[52]

The Madras Council, when considering Heath's petition in 1825, noted that "the policy, as well as justice, of affording temporary protection from competition to the authors of any new inventions, or to those who encounter the difficulty, expense, and risk of endeavouring to establish any new manufacture, or to open any new channel of commerce, is, we believe, generally admitted" and that "without an example set by him it will not be engaged in by any other person within the period for which this privilege is proposed to be granted."[53] Heath, however, did not receive his exclusive privilege for the above reasons and the decision was connected neither to the justice of the practice nor to the fact that such protection was "generally admitted." He was granted the privilege because the iron he was to produce would not compete against British iron, whether in India or Britain, and it would be exported to Europe where it would pose a powerful competitive challenge to the high-quality iron of Sweden.[54]

Soon after, Heath erected his iron works in the town of Porto Novo, on the coast of the Tamil country, about 125 miles south of Madras. Iron ore was brought from the interior, in the vicinity of Salem, and was sailed down the Cauvery River, which held sufficient water for this purpose six months of the year. The ore was of very high quality and its supply was "inexhaustible." Heath proceeded to build two new furnaces, which were larger than those customarily used in South India. The yield of each was estimated to be 20 tons of pig iron per week. He also built two cupola or blast furnaces and two reverberatory furnaces. The machinery for the works consisted of a four-horsepower steam engine, a blower, which was driven by bullocks, and a rolling mill. Utilizing wood and charcoal fuel, Heath designed a smelting works to produce wrought iron using the puddling and rolling method.[55]

A Company inspection of the facility in late December 1837 reported that the works consisted of four smelting furnaces with two steam engines of twelve and sixteen horsepower and blowing apparatus attached to each engine. There was also a casting house with a powerful crane and other equipment and a forge with two heavy hammers and a tilt worked by a twenty-five-horsepower steam engine. There were five puddling furnaces and eight refineries for converting the pig iron to wrought, along with blowing apparatus. Most of the machinery for a rolling mill was in place, including a thirty-five-horsepower steam engine, and a building had been erected to house it, but the rolling mill had not yet been put into operation. In addition, there were several smaller furnaces, godowns for storage of charcoal and blacksmith shops. The value of the buildings and machinery, etc. was estimated to be over 260,000 rupees.[56]

From the mid-1830s, the works exported substantial quantities of iron to Britain and it received very favorable reviews from British experts, who declared it to be of the "highest quality" and the equal of the best Swedish iron.[57] In 1839, it was reported that Porto Novo iron had replaced imports from Sweden in the Royal Arsenal of Woolwich.[58] The South Indian metal was also used in the construction of the Britannia Tubular Bridge over the Menai Strait.[59] Along with its high quality, the Porto Novo iron was extraordinarily cheap. Including the cost of transport, the wrought iron sold for 20 pounds per ton in Britain. The best grades of Swedish iron sold for 40 pounds per ton and the best British-made charcoal sheet iron for 35.[60]

In establishing his manufacturing enterprise, Heath had great success with Indian workers. Heath brought two expert workmen from Britain to set up and operate the works. After only a year Heath wrote,

When we commenced the manufacture of malleable iron we had no hope that we should be able to dispense with European labourers in several branches of the business; during the year which has since elapsed, the natives have made such progress in all departments of the manufacture that we think it probable that when the current engagements with our European workmen shall have expired, we shall not find it necessary to procure any new men from England.[61]

The Indians, therefore, were quick learners and adept at puddling iron and maintaining the machinery and works.

Technical problems appear to have been the least of the problems
that Heath and the Porto Novo Iron Works faced. Throughout the
1830s, Heath complained that the enterprise was undercapitalized
because the demands for both fixed and working capital were very
high in the establishment and operation of the works. A substantial
manufacturing center had been built from nothing with a huge investment of funds in machinery and buildings. The machinery had
been transported to India, a six-month voyage, and set to work, which
took many months. There was a long stretch of time, therefore, before
the investment began to reap a return.[62] Much working capital was
also sunk into the final wrought iron, which did not yield a profit
until it had been transported to Britain and sold. In the early years of
the enterprise, markets for the Indian iron had to be developed in
Britain, which further lengthened the time before the realization of the
investment.[63]

Heath was able to raise some capital from Europeans living in
Madras and he also worked tirelessly to obtain additional funds in
Britain. His financial savior, however, came in the form of the East
India Company, which extended substantial quantities of credit to
him, eventually even canceling interest payments. For the Company
to make sizable loans to a private manufacturing enterprise was
extraordinary, to say the least, and it is the only instance of such loans
that this author has found in early nineteenth-century South India. It
was some unusual circumstances that led to Company support for the
iron works, however.[64]

From the mid-1820s, South India descended into a great depression
which was to last till the 1840s. From the early 1830s, Company
officials began to worry about the bleak commercial conditions in
Madras. The export of cotton textiles from the region had virtually
disappeared, save for a small trade in blue goods to the Guinea coast.
This was the trade for which modern spinning mills were set up by the
French in Pondicherry. Exports of raw cotton to China had also
plummeted and there was only a minor trade in that item to Europe.
Finally, indigo exports had also dwindled to insignificant proportions.
As a consequence, there was a steady export of specie to Europe to
pay for imports from Britain.[65] If an export trade in iron could be
established – according to some knowledgeable men in Britain, Indian
iron could be sold anywhere in the world – Madras would have a
lucrative commodity that could be exchanged for goods from abroad.

Indian iron was especially attractive to Company officials because it did not compete with a British manufacture.[66] When exported to Britain, it displaced an import from Sweden, not a locally made good. In the 1830s, British manufacturers continued to rely upon Sweden for the high-quality iron that was needed for the production of steel. The possibility of substituting Indian iron for Swedish was raised as early as 1814 by the naturalist Benjamin Heyne, who wrote that "a quantity sufficient to substitute for that which is derived from Sweden might be allowed to be introduced from India without detriment to any but the foreign manufacturer of the article and the merchant engaged in the Swedish trade."[67]

This condition – that the South Indian iron was not to compete with British – gained Company support for the undertaking, but it severely limited the market for its products. And since these markets were outside the subcontinent, mainly in Britain, the working capital requirements for the venture were much greater. The Porto Novo Iron Works found it difficult to sell their good locally because by the 1830s, substantial quantities of British pig iron were flowing into India. Even though the iron was of inferior quality, the British product sold for about half the price of the Porto Novo iron and was adequate for many local uses.[68] Enlarging the Indian market for Porto Novo by taxing imported iron was ruled out as the Company would not implement a policy that would reduce the market for British manufacturers. At this time, Swedish iron paid a tariff of over 6 pounds per ton when imported into Britain, but the Indian market was kept completely free for imports of British iron. The Porto Novo Iron Works operated within these constraints for a few decades until it quietly closed down in the 1860s, despite solving the problems of transferring British technology and know-how to an Indian context.

Industrialization in early nineteenth-century India

The preceding survey of manufacturing in early nineteenth-century India, in combination with material given in previous chapters, leads to several observations about the potential for modern industry in the early colonial period. First, Indian entrepreneurial ability was not in short supply. The knowledge and skill of Indian merchants was most evident in the Indian Ocean trading system, in the western part of which, according to Pedro Machado, Gujarati cloth merchants out-competed Portuguese and British traders because of their superior information and better connections to the sources of cloth. Gujarati merchants were able to communicate annual or seasonal shifts in tastes in southeastern Africa to production centers in western India more efficiently and with these superior networks they dominated these markets against their European rivals.[69]

The servants of the English East India Company were well aware of the ability and talent of Indian traders. In the early nineteenth century, a Company official in Calcutta observed, "The formerly timid Hindoo now lends money at respondentia on distant voyages, engages in speculations to various parts of the world, and as an underwriter, in the different insurance offices, erects indigo works in various parts of Bengal, and is just as well acquainted with the principles of British laws, respecting commerce, as the generality of European merchants, and enjoys moreover two very great advantages over the latter: the first, in trading on his own instead of a borrowed capital; and, secondly, of living and conducting his business at probably 1/10th of the expense of the European."[70] Asiya Siddiqi concludes from a study of the complex business world of Jamsetjee Jejeebhoy that in early nineteenth-century western India "neither financial resources for business enterprises, nor entrepreneurial initiative and skill were wanting."[71]

Indian entrepreneurs also had an interest in new techniques of production and introduced new technologies and methods. Nevertheless, Europeans, from the English East India Company to private individuals, were the primary conduits for the transmission of novel machines and methods to the subcontinent. By no means was this unusual in the nineteenth century, however. Foreign investment and the foreign transfer of know-how were crucial for the dramatic industrial development of Belgium, France and Germany. While in Belgium and France much of this came from Britain, a number of French and Belgian artisans, engineers and entrepreneurs transmitted new techniques to the areas that became Germany.[72]

Although the English East India Company, as well as the French in Pondicherry, supplied private individuals with capital for their enterprises, there does not appear to have been a shortage of capital in the first half of the nineteenth century. Any problems in raising sufficient funds stemmed from the difficulties of linking those holding capital with those demanding it. Research on capital markets in Britain in this period reveals that British firms confronted many of the same problems.[73] Some years ago Radhe Shyam Rungta concluded that

capital scarcity does not seem to have been a major factor impeding industrial growth in this era [before 1850]. No doubt the promoters of some manufacturing enterprises did not find it easy to raise the necessary capital; yet it would be hard to find any instance where a scheme had to be shelved or an enterprise discontinued for want of capital alone. There is also no evidence to suggest that the Company servants, the free merchants or the agency houses had to import any capital from abroad although in one or two cases it was thought better to raise funds in London.[74]

Rungta supports his conclusion that capital was abundant with evidence on the enormous demand in Calcutta and Bombay for bank shares and government debt issues. According to Rungta, "Banking shares commanded almost an immediate premium of 60 to 70%." And "the Bank of Bombay was obliged to increase its share capital from Rs. 3,000,000 to Rs. 5,225,000 to meet the wishes of its numerous applicants."[75] Although Rungta does not give any interest rates, we know from Chapter 3 that in the early nineteenth century the English East India Company was able to borrow in North India at 5 percent. Other sources report that in the early 1820s, money was plentiful in Bengal and the government borrowed as much as it needed at 4 percent, which increased to 5 percent in 1825 with the onset of the Burmese war and the greater government demand for funds.[76] The impediment to industrial enterprise in this environment does not appear to have been the supply of capital but rather the limited demand for investment in new manufacturing firms.

There was also no lack of skilled and knowledgeable workers and mechanics. Although we do not have direct access to sites of production, the available evidence indicates that virtually all the new industrial undertakings in the first half of the nineteenth century were able to find skilled workers and then train them to operate imported machinery. These new enterprises were also able to educate Indian mechanics who took over from Europeans and maintained and repaired steam engines, spinning machines, rolling mills, steamships and other new and imported technologies. Complaints about the inadequate supplies of skilled workers were voiced in only one case, that of the Bengal spinning mills which were established in 1817. In the other enterprises for which information is available, proprietors report that skilled labor to operate and maintain machinery was not a problem.

While detailed evidence on the mechanical abilities of Indian workers is not available for the undertakings just described, such information can be extracted from the instrument workshops of the survey of India. From the late eighteenth century, the devices – chronometers, perambulators, theodolites, etc. – that were needed for the survey were imported from Britain. The British perambulators, however, were not rugged enough for the rough Indian terrain and climate and new ones designed by British members of the survey began to be manufactured in India itself, and came to be known as the Madras perambulators. These were based on the "principle of endless [perpetual] screw and differential plates," and although no information is available on how they were made, Indian workmen were likely to have contributed to their manufacture. The making of these devices also required cooperation between carpenters and metal workers, likely in both brass and iron, and the best ones were made in Madras.[77]

Over time, Indian workers were also trained to repair a variety of the instruments. At first the skilled workers for these tasks were drawn from arsenals in different regions of British India.[78] In the 1830s George Everest helped to establish a workshop in Calcutta for the survey department, which both expanded the capacity for repairs in India and gave rise to more specialized and more highly trained workers. A Mr. Barrow, who was introduced to Everest by William Richardson of the Royal Observatory, was put in charge of the workshop, for which he purchased machines and trained staff.[79] Barrow proved to be an unreliable workman and Everest, who was a talented mechanic and instrument maker, recommended that he be replaced by an Indian, Said Mohsin Husain. According to Everest, "There is nothing whatever, save [the division of astronomical circles], in which . . . Said Mohsin is not [Barrow's] equal, and . . . [in] many points . . . his superior, being in far better practice as a workman."[80] Everest later expanded on Said Mohsin's skill and pointed to his work on

Heliotropes, lamps, barometer pumps, theodolites . . . everything in short which constitutes the duty of a mathematical instrument maker to repair, exceeding by far which Mr. Barrow did in the same period . . . the two astronomical circles – . . . if it had not been for Said Mohsin, there would have been no prospect whatever of bringing that delicate . . . job to termination . . . If Mr. Barrow had ever dreamed that it would be practicable for the Seid to make . . . and use the cutting tool with expertness, he would have thought twice before he broke out into open disobedience. [Said Mohsin] has been present at the measurement of 3 bases . . . Whenever any portion of the complicated base-line apparatus was deranged he put it to rights. When the large theodolite by Troughton was found at first trial unfit for work, he rectified its defects. When the reverbatory lamps . . . were still useless . . . he rendered them eminently efficient. When the cranes . . . were unavailable for . . . raising the large theodolites to the summits of the observing towers, he constructed others.[81]

Said Mohsin was given the title of "Mathematical Instrument Maker," and he assembled a "valuable team" of workmen that included carpenters, turners, filemen, firemen and hammermen, who formed a field workshop. At that site, equipped with a specially built lathe and tools from Britain, the group manufactured a number of instruments for the survey, including heliotropes, lamps and several barometer pumps of Everest's design. Everest described the brass articles which the team produced as having "the English finish about them, and [they] are not to be distinguished from the productions of the most celebrated artists of Europe."[82] Said Mohsin also taught himself how to divide astronomical circles, which he did successfully for Everest. For the circles, he also designed and constructed a stop, which Everest called "an exquisite contrivance, . . . as remarkable for its neatness and simplicity as for its efficiency; furnished with a graduated micrometer head, of which one revolution is equivalent to the difference between the graduating lines of the whole degree and the five-minute spaces."[83]

Said Mohsin was clearly an exceptionally talented mechanic, but there were a number of other men of skill and ability in Calcutta and elsewhere in India who have barely left an imprint in the archival record. Everest, in his efforts to recruit workmen for his field workshops in North India, received a number of offers of talented men from the ordnance works in Kanpur, Fatehgarh, Agra and elsewhere.[84] The survey department's Calcutta workshop trained a number of individuals who drifted away to other places of employment in the city where they were "eagerly sought for by those who work on their own account – Mr. Augier, Mr. Jessop, Mr. Gray, etc."[85] Some of these Indians most likely contributed to the successful efforts in the city to build steam engines and steamships and to maintain these and other new machines that began to be used in the workshops of the city, and which have been described in this chapter.

The ease with which Indian workers were trained in instrument making for the survey of India, which required fine, precision labor, as well as other undertakings, ranging from iron smelting to spinning works and steam engine maintenance and building, suggests that the gap in knowledge between Europe and the Indian subcontinent was far narrower in the early nineteenth century than is conventionally believed and that the high levels of skill and technical ability of the eighteenth century continued into the early British period. Many of the constraints that have long been believed to have held back Indian industrialization in the nineteenth century – lack of entrepreneurship and shortages of skilled labor and capital – are, therefore, difficult to sustain for the period before 1850. Nevertheless, there were significant limits on the growth and development of new manufacturing enterprises, the most critical being the policies of the English East India Company state, which ruled India until 1858. These policies were varied and dealt with matters such as trade, investment in education, patronage for learned activities, and the development of technological capability.

Of these, trade policies have received the most attention and, since the nineteenth century, the British colonial state has been criticized for its failure to protect Indian manufacturing. Romesh Dutt, for example, quoted Montgomery Martin approvingly in his classic economic history of India: "Under the pretence of Free Trade, England has compelled the Hindus to receive the products of the steam-looms of Lancashire, Yorkshire, Glasgow, &c., at mere nominal duties; while the hand-wrought manufactures of Bengal and Behar, beautiful in fabric and durable in wear, have had heavy and almost prohibitive duties imposed on their importation to England."[86] The case of the Porto Novo Iron Works well illustrates the difficulties that new Indian enterprises faced without tariff protection, which is why J. M. Heath pressured Company authorities to raise the tax on imports of British iron. The Company state failed to do much else as well. The range of possible state activities, and the full extent of what the British had no interest in undertaking in India, is evident from what states in Europe were doing in these decades.

State and economy in nineteenth-century Europe

The absence of state support for industrial development in India stands in stark contrast to the policies found in Europe in the eighteenth and nineteenth centuries. European authorities did not hesitate to use the levers of the state to advance manufacturing, which they did in a variety of ways – from the creation of state enterprises to trade policy and the patronage of education. These examples from Europe suggest a broad range of political and economic possibilities that were not exploited and therefore not capitalized upon in British India.

The state and trade policy

In contrast to manufacturers in nineteenth-century India, industry in Europe received the benefits of protection, and barriers to imports, including tariffs as well as outright prohibitions, were erected in Europe from at least the seventeenth century. Protectionism was of great importance for the textile trades and, as we have seen, in the eighteenth century cloth manufacturers in Britain, France, Spain and several other places were insulated from the competition of Indian cottons. In Britain, protection was extended to several other major commodities, most importantly iron for which tariffs on imports from Sweden and Russia rose steadily in the eighteenth century, even increasing more than threefold between 1781 and 1813.[87]

In the nineteenth century, many parts of Europe protected local manufacturing from the competition of lower-priced British goods. In the early years of the century, France had the most extensive system of protection in Europe – under the aegis of the continental system – and the absence of British competition gave French manufacturing the opportunity to grow rapidly. The number of large-scale cotton mills in France increased from 6 in 1789 to 272 by 1814, for instance. According to Jeff Horn, the French used the protection that the self-blockade offered to mechanize, adopt new methods of manufacturing and develop technologies, leading to "impressive" gains in the cotton, silk and chemical industries.[88] Even with the dismantling of the continental system after the defeat of Napoleon, high tariffs continued to be the norm in France for several decades. Horn concludes that these limits on imports stimulated metal working and machine building as they preserved the market for French manufacturers.[89]

High tariffs were critical for the development of a French iron industry based on new technologies. In the eighteenth century, tariffs on iron were designed to exclude imports from Sweden, which led Europe in both price and quality. In 1814, tariff rates were revised based on the prevailing prices for Swedish iron and were set at a level that shielded French iron works from imports. When setting the rate, however, French authorities had not foreseen a flood of cheap coal-based iron from Britain and the tariff was set too low to deal with this new competition. To counter the new threat, in 1822 the tariff was raised from 50 percent to 120 percent, which increased the price of British iron and sharply reduced its import. The rate was kept high till the 1850s and while the French industry did not simply reproduce British techniques and methods, behind high tariff walls it adopted selectively from the new menu of technologies and blended them with pre-existing techniques to build a modern iron manufacturing sector. According to Rainer Fremdling, "The tariff policy indeed succeeded in shielding the new products from France, but the process innovations still made their way into the country."[90]

Iron production in Belgium and Prussia also benefited from tariffs on imports. "Transportation costs and moderate protective duties screened Wallonia from the British competition while an ambitious government programme for industrial development was established on the British model," according to Fremdling.[91] In the German states, British pig iron found it difficult to compete against the higher-quality charcoal-smelted local iron and tariffs on imported iron were moderate in the first decades of the nineteenth century. In the 1840s, British prices fell and duties were then raised to protect local producers.[92] Tariff protection was also found in textiles. In 1840, the Prussian Commercial Union levied duties on cottons that ranged from 30 to 120 percent and on woolens from 20 to 50 percent.[93]

Tariffs raised prices for imports, thereby making it profitable for European entrepreneurs to invest in new technologies and new methods of production. Protection was, therefore, critical for the transfer and development of novel techniques, which has been widely recognized. The role of protective tariffs in transcending resource constraints has been less appreciated, however. According to Fremdling, "Protection allowed the emergence of iron industries based on mineral fuel even where the natural resource endowment was less favourable than in Britain." In many parts of Europe the quality and location of coal, along with facilities for transport, were less optimal than in Britain. Nevertheless, in the early nineteenth century, protection made it possible for a number of areas to overcome these shortcomings and begin to develop coke-fueled iron industries. With this foundation, iron output expanded quickly when demand grew rapidly with the dawn of railways. This was precisely the path taken to a modern iron industry in nineteenth-century Germany, for example. Even resource endowments, a supposedly immutable and natural phenomenon, cannot be taken as determinative for economic development. They too may be reshaped by political action.[94]

State support for technological capability

European state support for industrial development did not only take the form of protection from the competition of imports. In Britain, from at least the reign of Henry VIII, political authorities used the power of the state to expand the technological capabilities of the realm. Henry VIII brought gun makers and iron workers from France and Holland to England to set up iron works in the Weald of Sussex, primarily to develop high-quality iron smelting for the making of armaments. Other skilled workers came to Britain in the sixteenth and seventeenth centuries from France, Flanders and elsewhere, including "German miners and metal workers, French and Italian glass makers, Dutch and Flemish cloth makers."[95] In the sixteenth century, central European miners may have brought to England the technique of running small wagons on wooden rails, the progenitor of the modern railway.[96] Such "importation" of skilled labor was widespread in Europe in the eighteenth and nineteenth centuries.

French rulers and policy men engaged in a massive system of industrial espionage in the eighteenth century in order to obtain skilled workers and the technological secrets of the British, and the French government was successful in recruiting many dozens, if not hundreds, of British artisans and mechanics and resettling them across the English Channel. These men brought with them a vast reservoir of knowledge and expertise as well as many varieties of machines and tools. Alarmed by the threat to their economic and technological edge, the British state legislated fines and other penalties on anyone "who enticed or tried to persuade any skilled worker in wool, iron, steel, brass or metal, or any clockmaker or watchmaker 'or any other artificer or manufacturer of Great Britain' to go abroad."[97] The first such British legislation was passed in 1719, but it could not stem the tide of John Holkers, John Wilkinsons and their brethren from leaving Britain, most often to go to France, but also to the Low Countries, Central Europe and Russia.

French and other efforts to recruit knowledgeable British men continued in the nineteenth century. In 1814, for example, "an Englishman named James Jackson with broad entrepreneurial experience and different sorts of metallurgical skills" was induced to settle with his family in France.[98] Such examples may easily be multiplied. In 1840, according to one observer, "We find in France that the principal foremen at Rouen and in the cotton factories are from Lancashire; you find it in Belgium, in Holland and in the neighbourhood of Liège," and in the cotton mills of Vienna, "the directors and foremen [are] chiefly Englishmen or Scotsmen, from the . . . manufactories of Glasgow and Manchester."[99] The reliance upon British experts, therefore, was not only a French phenomenon, but was found more widely in Europe. And Britain was not the only source of technical expertise in the nineteenth century. In Prussia, for instance, both Belgian and British men with knowledge of coke-iron techniques helped to transfer that technology.[100] There is little doubt that these mobile men contributed to the diffusion of new techniques and methods, and both states and private enterprises spent large sums to attract and learn from them.

Education was another area in which states contributed to the building up of technical capacity. Through high-end institutions such as the École Polytechnique in France, the Hauptbergwerks-Institut in Prussia, the Technical Universities in a number of German states, and low-end schools for mechanical training, states in nineteenth-century Europe played a pivotal role in the creation and diffusion of new industrial knowledge. States also financed the travels of technical experts who went abroad to learn about new technologies and methods. In the case of Prussia, the state technical institute "supported study trips to Britain (on which German officials sometimes stole plans and smuggled machinery out of the country), trained students in the new techniques, and made grants to promising industrialists."[101] In Belgium, "the government instructed and financed G. M. Roentgen to visit British iron-works. He returned as an enthusiastic propagandist for the 'English method' [and] conceived of measures the government should take in order to modernize the Walloon iron industry."[102]

David Landes, otherwise a severe critic of state intervention in the market, acknowledges that these efforts bore valuable fruit:

Here the state made the major contribution ... Only the government could afford to send officials on costly tours of inspection as far away as the United States; provide the necessary buildings and equipment; feed, clothe, house, and in some cases pay students for a period of years. Moreover, these pedagogical institutions were only part – though the most important part – of a larger educational system designed to introduce the new techniques and diffuse them throughout the economy.[103]

State enterprises

State-owned enterprises were found in Europe from at least the seventeenth century. In old-regime France, Colbertian state firms, *manufactures royals*, as well as state-granted monopolies, *manufactures privilégiées*, operated through the eighteenth century in armaments, metallurgy and luxury industries. In Central and Eastern Europe, there were also a number of state manufacturing enterprises, especially in industries that were necessary for armaments production.[104]

This longstanding tradition continued into the early nineteenth century. In Belgium, there was substantial state investment in shipbuilding and other undertakings. The Prussian state established coalmines and iron works in Silesia in the late eighteenth century and these made major contributions to the Prussian economy for several decades. The Prussian Mining Corps, a state body, spearheaded the restoration of mines and the introduction of new techniques in the Saar and the Siegerland. According to Eric Brose, there are "scores of examples of private operators following the state's lead by introducing steel cables, steam-powered wagons, and mine railroads."[105] By the mid-nineteenth century, 20 percent of Prussian coal production came from state mines.[106]

State-owned iron works made significant contributions to the metal industry in Prussia and were the first in continental Europe to "continuously use coke for smelting pig iron."[107] The state enterprises aided the advance of technology in private iron-smelting works as well, and Brose writes, "There can be no doubt that the owners of [private] operations benefited from the [Prussian Mining] Corps' early experiments in the Rhineland at Geislautern and Sayn, and Upper Silesia at Rybnick. Indeed, in the case of the Laurahütte, state engineers drew up the initial plans and were hired as the first furnace managers."[108] Prussian state support was also found in textiles. As late as 1842, the first worsted weaving mill with power looms in Prussia was established by the state.[109]

Nevertheless, direct economic activity of this sort was not the most significant state contribution to European industrialization in the nineteenth century. Two others loomed larger. The first was railways, which in Belgium, France and the German territories were built with heavy state support. In Belgium, from the 1830s the state itself designed and built a railway system. As a consequence, "In some ways Belgium led Europe in railway building. She was ahead of all the continent in ordered construction and ahead of England in that she had a railway policy," in the words of John Clapham.[110] In 1850, Dionysus Lardner wrote, "The extraordinary expedition with which the Belgian rail roads were completed has been mainly caused by the circumstance of their having been executed by the state."[111] In France, there was a public–private partnership and the state built some components (land, track, bridges, tunnels) of the railway network, subsidized others, and played a role in the management of the system. In the German lands of Central Europe, state railways co-existed with private lines. In 1875, nearly half of the railway network in Germany was state-owned, however.[112]

The Belgian state had a keen appreciation of the economic benefits of the railway. The rates were kept low, despite a growing budget deficit, to encourage economic development and to capture trade between the ports of the North Sea and Central Europe. With its railway network, Belgium built up industrial production, particularly in coal and iron.[113] Since they were state undertakings it was easier for the authorities to give "the additional demand for iron on to Belgian ironmasters, although they charged higher rail prices than the British."[114] In France, "railway demand made modern iron works in the French coalmining areas economically viable for the first time" and Germany took a roughly similar path as well.[115] In Prussia the building of the railway system pushed forward the development of an iron industry based on coke from the 1840s. For iron rails, the lower quality of the coke-smelted iron was not an issue, which allowed the enormous expansion of iron works that used coal technology in a relatively short span of time. By the 1860s, "many iron processing plants were established applying modern British technology and existing capacity was enlarged, which enabled indigenous producers to meet railway demand for rails and other finished iron products."[116]

The other great state economic enterprise was the military. Armaments production had stimulated economic activity across Europe and Asia in the seventeenth and eighteenth centuries and had been pivotal for technological progress as well as the expansion of manufacturing. This was no less the case for Europe in the first half of the nineteenth century. As early as 1824, despite the peace that prevailed in Europe after the defeat of Napoleon, Prussian military experts requested the appointment of special military attachés in its European embassies in order to keep abreast of foreign military advances.[117] Within a few years the diplomatic situation had deteriorated and the Prussian state stepped up the attempts to improve military technologies. A young engineer at the War School declared that it was "the mission of the current generation to examine the real value of inventions" and to adopt those with "practical value in war."[118] The Prussian army undertook extensive research and experimentation in machinery for manufacturing, standardization of parts, metallurgy for cannons, and rockets and rocketry. In 1828, a Commission on Science and Technology was established to investigate any area that had potential military applications and its members reported to the highest levels of the Prussian state. The extent to which military advances percolated into the civilian economy remains to be investigated, but the Prussian army certainly contributed to the expansion of the technological frontier.[119]

State and economy in nineteenth-century India

The state made crucial contributions to the advance of technology and the creation of new industrial enterprises in Belgium, France and Germany in the early nineteenth century. Rulers and policymakers did not do the same things in all places and there was no single package of policies. France, for example, relied more heavily upon protection than did the German states between 1800 and 1850. And Prussia utilized state enterprises to a greater extent than France. Nevertheless, protection of local manufacturing, the establishment of institutions for technical education, the recruitment of skilled workers from foreign territories, the deployment of technical missions abroad to learn of technological advances and the formation of state enterprises were used in various combinations to propel the development of industry and manufacturing.

Some of these policies had eighteenth-century antecedents in both Europe and the Indian subcontinent. The British economy relied upon significant state actions in support of economic and technological advance. Naturally, what the British state did in the eighteenth century was very different from what other European states undertook in the nineteenth, in the aftermath of British technological breakthroughs. Despite these differences, political backing for industrialization may be identified in all cases of "success" in the eighteenth and nineteenth centuries.

In British India, however, such state policies were conspicuously absent. Nineteenth-century political neglect was a marked departure from the eighteenth-century pattern in the Indian subcontinent in which new regional states, driven by military and revenue needs, increasingly promoted manufacturing and pushed forward the advance of technology. The patronage of Indian rulers maintained the high pitch of agricultural production and supported institutions for the generation and transmission of knowledge. The English East India Company state, however, was compelled to do none of them and therefore it did nothing. The Company made no attempt to protect the new industries that were being formed in the early nineteenth century, despite appeals from many British and Indians for such protection. As we have seen, J. M. Heath pressed the English East India Company to erect tariffs so that Indian iron manufacturers could meet local demand. Similar demands for protection, or at least equalization of tariffs between Britain and India, were voiced by other manufacturers in the subcontinent as well as the East India Company itself, which feared economic stagnation and even decline in its Indian possessions in the second quarter of the nineteenth century.

Rather than protecting local manufacturing, the structure of taxes in the early nineteenth century gave an advantage to imported goods. From 1813, locally made cloth in Bengal paid an internal transit duty of 15% when carried to Calcutta, Dacca or other towns and cities in the province. British cloth was exempted from these internal tolls and paid a nominal import tax of 2.5%. Charles Trevelyan noted the inequity of the system and criticized "the anomaly of foreign goods enjoying a preference in the home market over the produce of native industry."[120] British and Indian exports were treated differently in other parts of the empire as well. In Australia, Indian goods paid a duty of 5% while British goods were imported duty-free. In Ceylon, Indian goods paid 10%, British 4%, while in the Cape of Good Hope the duties were 10% and 3%, respectively.[121]

The Company state also took little interest in expanding the technological capabilities of Indians. There was little state effort to bring individuals with knowledge or skills to the subcontinent in order to transmit this information to Indian manufacturers or workers. This was a marked contrast to the eighteenth century when kings brought every passing European to their courts and interrogated him for his technical expertise. Under British rule there was also little patronage extended to learning or education, which again is a marked contrast to pre-colonial practices.

In 1812 Lord Minto, the Governor-General of India, noted the British disinterest in building libraries or schools and the deleterious impact of this policy on scientific and technical knowledge:

It is a common remark, that science and literature are in a progressive state of decay among the natives of India. From every inquiry which I have been enabled to make on this interesting subject, that remark appears to me but too well founded. The number of the learned is not only diminished, but the circle of learning, even among those who still devote themselves to it, appears to be considerably contracted. The abstract sciences are abandoned, polite literature neglected, and no branch of learning cultivated but what is connected with the peculiar religious doctrines of the people. The immediate consequence of this state of things is, the disuse, and even actual loss, of many valuable books.[122]

Minto linked this crisis of knowledge to British policy:

The principal cause of the present neglected state of literature in India is to be traced to the want of that encouragement which was formerly afforded to it by princes, chieftains and opulent individuals under the native governments ... the justness of these observations might be illustrated by a detailed consideration of the former and present state of science and literature at the three principal seats of Hindoo learning, viz. Benares, Tirhoot and Nuddea. Such a review would bring before us the liberal patronage which was formerly bestowed, not only by princes and others in power and authority, but also by the zemindars, on persons who had distinguished themselves by the successful cultivation of letters at those places. It would equally bring to our view the present neglected state of learning at those once celebrated places.

Minto warned that "unless Government interpose with a fostering hand, the revival of letters may shortly become hopeless, from a want of books, or of persons capable of explaining them."[123]

Twenty years later little had changed. In 1832, a member of the Madras civil service wrote, "It is only of late years that the government have taken any steps for promoting the Education of Natives." These recent efforts were on a small scale, however. In the South Indian region of Coimbatore, which had a population of about 800,000, the British were spending 400 rupees per year on two schools. Revenue collections in the district ranged from 2 to 3 million rupees per year, which translates to 0.013 to 0.02 percent of revenues dedicated to education.[124] In Bombay, a former Member of Council revealed that there were 1,705 schools in the British possessions in the region, for a population of nearly 4.7 million. Only 25 of these schools were set up by the British, the remainder were village schools. As a consequence, the fraction of the population in schools was 1 in 133 while in Britain it was 1 in 16.[125]

The British disinterest in investing in materials for developing technical capabilities extended to their own facilities. In 1853, after the Government of India ordered that young artillery officers should be instructed "in the scientific operations of the foundry," the head of the foundry, a Mr. Broome, requested scientific books and periodicals to help him with this task. The majority of the military board thought that this was a "quite unnecessary expense and presumed that Superintendents usually bought those they desired at their own expense. The Governor-General also did not consider it necessary 'at present' to subscribe for any professional periodicals, but directed that any scientific works available in other offices might be supplied." H. A. Young writes, "The cost of the publications asked for was probably less than the value of the time of the many high officials who wrote lengthy minutes on the subject, but doubtless a dangerous precedent was avoided!"[126]

The British destruction of Indian political centers, therefore, had profound consequences for the technological capacity of the subcontinent. The full ramifications – social, cultural, economic, technical, scientific – of the dismantling of Indian states and the loss of their powers of patronage have yet to be fully explored. Christopher Bayly ventured into this territory with his recognition that courts were major sources of demand for vast quantities of manufactured goods, both luxury and ordinary.[127] But courts were also the source of money for a variety of social purposes and public goods, including investment in agriculture, institutions for the production and dissemination of knowledge, and efforts to gather together scholars as well as skilled workers.[128] With the dismantling of this political order, the institutions of knowledge and learning were destroyed and, under British rule, there was little rebuilding of them in the nineteenth century. The colonial state of knowledge, as with many other things, is then taken to be characteristic of India rather than a product of British rule.

Finally, unlike the states of nineteenth-century Europe the East India Company state made no attempt to stimulate Indian industry with its own enterprises or through preferential purchasing of Indian manufactures. If anything, state purchasing was designed to create demand for the industrial products of Britain. In the case of the military, some weapons were made in the subcontinent under Company rule, but the bulk was imported from Britain. Therefore, a large part of the industrial benefits of the Indian army, which was one of the largest in the world at the time, went to Britain.

The Company manufactured some big guns in foundries in Bengal, but in the opinion of one commentator, "it is curious that the Company took no steps to make guns themselves till late in the eighteenth century and no adequate steps till well on in the nineteenth."[129] The casting of big guns began in Bengal in 1770, initially at Fort William and later in Cossipore. Within a few decades, the guns manufactured there were reported to be better and cheaper than those imported from Britain. In 1818, several pieces of Indian-made ordnance were examined by artillery experts at Woolwich and the workmanship and finish were pronounced "superior to those of the Royal Arsenal."[130] Over the next few decades the Cossipore foundry concentrated on the casting of brass guns; iron guns were all imported. The neglect of iron left the operation unprepared for the manufacture of steel guns from the mid-nineteenth century. As a consequence, the making of big guns in India was more or less at a standstill from the Rebellion of 1857 to the early twentieth century.[131]

The situation when it came to small guns was even bleaker for Indian manufacturers. The East India Company had muskets that were captured in battle repaired and refurbished locally. It never manufactured muskets in India, and all new ones were imported from Britain.[132] This policy did not stem from any shortcomings in Indian guns. As one military expert has noted, despite the excellent gun-making tradition in eighteenth-century India, the British "only established a small-arms factory in 1905, when a rifle factory was erected on a part of the site of the old gunpowder factory at Ishapore, and its first rifle was completed in 1907."[133]

Because of these armaments-purchasing policies, the British failed to stimulate the whole gamut of activities connected to metal working, including the development of iron smelting with coal, the use of newly developed machinery for the making of metal components, and the standardization of parts manufacture. The British policy on armaments in India very much parallels its approach to the railways in the second half of the nineteenth century in which there was little attempt to purchase material locally. As a consequence, almost all the metal for the vast railway system that was built in India was imported from Britain, providing a valuable stimulus to British industry. "Rails, points, fishplates, machinery, locomotives, even sleepers, were almost all built outside India . . . Interested not in India's financial and industrial development but in Britain's, the colonial government and the railway companies followed policies from which British industry and financial institutions were the primary beneficiaries. Indeed, the Government of India urged companies to 'buy British.'"[134]

There were a number of reasons for British disinterest in developing Indian industry or expanding Indian technological capability. The reluctance to support education and learning was due in part to a desire to govern India with minimal expenditure. The English East India Company ruled India on a profit–loss basis. Investment in education, agriculture, the economy – anything at all, in fact – was viewed as a deduction from its earnings. As Christopher Bayly has observed, in the 1820s and 1830s major pronouncements were made on the improvements that British rule would bring to India (Macaulay's "Minute on Education" was the most famous of these). Little improvement was actually carried out, however, because of the expense that it would entail.[135]

The reluctance to expand the technological capabilities of Indians was also rooted in a British desire to monopolize knowledge. British control of information was considered crucial for colonial power and prestige. H. A. Young has written in the case of artillery, "The East India Company did what they could to discourage the spread of knowledge of this subject and in 1770 informed Bombay 'that the natives must be kept as ignorant as possible both of the theory and practice of artillery'." In 1813 the Court of Directors considered closing the Company's gun foundry in Bengal for fear of "disseminating a knowledge of casting ordnance among the natives."[136] Similar misgivings about the transfer of technical knowledge to Indians were found in the surveying department. "Early as 1768 the Paymaster General had expressed disapproval of any person who was not 'in the Company's Civil or Military service' being employed on survey," R. H. Phillimore has recounted. "This prejudice persisted forty years and longer, and eventually led to a definite prohibition against the instruction of any 'native' in the art of survey, or the employment of any local man, however efficient, even as a draughtsman."[137]

Finally, the English East India Company undertook little industrial development in the first half of the nineteenth century because the Indian economy was subordinated to the needs of an industrializing Britain. In the minds of many British, the subcontinent was to serve as a market for manufactured goods from Britain and in return was to supply raw materials. These hopes were expressed as early as the 1780s when muslin manufacturers in England and Scotland recommended that the East India Company import Indian raw materials such as cotton and dyestuffs instead of manufactures such as cotton textiles so that "a mutual interest be form'd betwixt [the Indians] and our manufacturers." "Such a system would enable both Countrys to foster and to support each other. The interest of India would by this means become the interest of Great Britain and while the former flourished by a substitution of more productive articles of commerce, the latter would become rich in the immediate support . . . for nursing her rising manufactures," the British cotton manufacturers declared.[138] Similar sentiments were expressed over thirty years later in testimony before a Select Committee of the House of Lords: "It is obvious that it will be far better for the Indian to raise cotton than to spin and weave it, when he can procure the manufactured article he wants cheaper than he can make it, by exchanging it for the raw material."[139] These sentiments were even found among private British in India. In 1825, George Jessop, an engineer in Calcutta, for instance, opposed the encouragement of iron production in India because it was "inimical to the interests of Great Britain."[140]

For India to serve as an auxiliary to British industry, the Indian market had to remain free to receive exports from Britain, which ruled out tariff protection for Indian manufacturing. And in the nineteenth century the Indian market remained among the freest and the most open in the world. In the first half of the nineteenth century, therefore, Britain was protected from Indian manufactured exports (ships, cotton textiles, etc.), while India was subjected to a regime of free trade. This led manufacturers and dealers in cotton and silk piece-goods in Calcutta to petition the Privy Council for Trade in Britain:

The fabrics of Great Britain are consumed in Bengal without any duties being levied thereon to protect the native fabrics. That the fabrics of Bengal are charged with the following duties when they are used in Great Britain: on manufactured cottons, 10 percent. On manufactured silks, 24 percent . . . They, therefore, pray to be admitted to the privilege of British subjects, and humbly entreat your Lordships to allow the cotton and silk fabrics of Bengal to be used in Great Britain "free of duty," or at the same rate which may be charged on British fabrics consumed in Bengal.

The above petition, which was signed by 117 Indians of "high respectability," indicates that Indian merchants and manufacturers were aware that British trade policy discriminated against manufacturing in the subcontinent.[141]

Requests for a more equitable distribution of taxes also came from "London merchants connected with the East India trade." In 1832 eleven of these merchant houses petitioned the Court of Directors of the East India Company to request a drawback on the 2½% inland duty that Bengal piece-goods paid when carried to Calcutta for export to the United Kingdom. These merchants declared that it was "not only reasonable and fair, but a measure of wise policy towards the natives of India, to reduce, as much as may be practicable, so great an inequality in duties, which give so marked a preference in favour of British goods."[142]

Conclusion

State support was not sufficient for the creation of an industrial economy in the nineteenth century. There are numerous examples of state-sponsored failure from around the globe. Nevertheless, it was also the case that without state assistance of some kind – and the form that this took varied widely from place to place – industrialization was impossible. This was the situation in nineteenth-century India where the British colonial state had little desire or interest in promoting industrial development.

To point to the centrality of the state is not to deny an important role to private actors. The choice between the market and the state is a false one, for both state support and a well-functioning market are necessary for the development of a modern economy. The historical record yields abundant evidence for this conclusion. Cases extend from Britain in the eighteenth century to France, Belgium and Germany in the early nineteenth, to Japan in the late nineteenth and to Korea in the late twentieth. In the early nineteenth century, the Indian subcontinent possessed some of the most economically and commercially advanced regions in the world. Merchant and entrepreneurial abilities and artisanal and craft skills were highly developed and continued to be so for several decades. Without state support and encouragement, however, commercial and technical acumen could not be translated into an industrial economy.

The first half of the nineteenth century represented a missed opportunity for economic life in the subcontinent. In these early days of colonial rule, the skill and knowledge possessed by Indian artisans and mechanics were far closer to those of their counterparts in Europe than was to be the case later in the century. In these decades, the transfer of European techniques and machines was, therefore, much easier than it was later. By 1900, the knowledge gap had widened and Indian technical skills had fallen far behind the standards of Europe. Much worker knowledge was also lost within one or two generations of the establishment of British rule, as the variety and scale of manufacturing activities in India was sharply reduced. Without shipbuilding, iron smelting, gun making, cloth dyeing and so on, skills disappeared, and without the rise of new manufacturing enterprises, they were not translated into new forms of production.

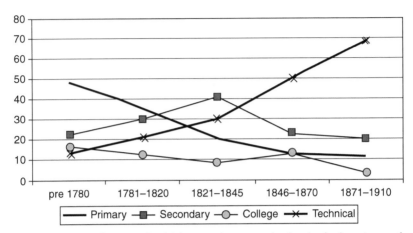

Figure 8.1 Distribution of British great inventors by level of education and birth cohort.
Source: B. Zorina Khan and Kenneth L. Sokoloff, "A Tale of Two Countries: Innovation and Incentive among Great Inventors in Britain and the United States, 1750–1930," in Roger E. A. Farmer (ed.), *Macroeconomics in the Small and the Large: Essays on Microfoundations, Macroeconomic Applications and Economic History in Honor of Axel Leijonhufvud* (Cheltenham, 2008), p. 148.

At the same time, the technical know-how necessary for the operation of new industrial techniques and methods grew by leaps and bounds. This scaling up of knowledge is captured in Zorina Khan and Kenneth Sokoloff's work on the great inventors of Britain, which shows that in the early nineteenth century a primary education was sufficient to make seminal technical contributions. Within a few decades, however, the educational background of inventors ratcheted up, which may be seen in Figure 8.1.

The supply of capital was also more plentiful in the early part of the nineteenth century than in later decades. In real terms as well, capital was more abundant because the price of machinery and other equipment rose steeply over the course of the century as the scale of operations grew and became more complex. David Landes has noted that the size of a typical factory steam engine in Britain increased six- or sevenfold between the 1780s and the 1820s, going from six to eight horsepower to fifty horsepower and more.[143] The increase in the scale of industrial activity from the 1820s to the late nineteenth century was even greater.

Given the importance of the state for economic change and development, explanations for poor economic performance in colonial India that focus on culture or resource endowments are misconceived. Economic decline in nineteenth-century India was intimately connected to colonialism and state policies which discriminated against the economic well-being of Indians.

Since the late eighteenth century Smithian and later neoclassical economic thinking has opposed state activism and intervention. For Adam Smith, state actions interfered with the operation of the market and thereby reduced the efficiency of the commercial order. The critique of state action has also been expressed in terms of the opportunities for rent-seeking that are created and the economic distortions that are introduced as a consequence. These objections to state intervention in the economy are both normative and prescriptive and they yield policy recommendations for free trade and the unfettered operation of the market.

For the past, they imply that economic performance would have been superior if state action, save the minimal enforcement of the rules of the market and property rights, had been absent. Joel Mokyr, for instance, writes that the mercantilist state was "a mutually beneficial alliance of the fiscal needs of the state and special interests . . . These interests deployed state power to secure benefits . . . in exchange for revenues needed by the government . . . Monopoly profits were easier to tax, and thus both sides gained, but *at the expense of the economy at large.*"[144] When framed this way, it is a counterfactual proposition that cannot be tested. But what is striking is that in the cases of economic success in the eighteenth and nineteenth centuries, whether Britain, France, Japan or Germany, state actions of many kinds were critical to the process of growth and change. In those places where such state activism was absent or state capacities less developed, in the case of this book the Ottoman Empire, British India and China, economic outcomes were inferior.

Since Adam Smith, it has been customary to see economic life as a reflection of man's true nature. "Man's propensity is to truck, barter and exchange," Smith famously wrote. Since the economy is rooted in nature, and not in the institutions of man, it functions best when it is left free to its own devices. It must, therefore, remain independent of man-made institutions to the greatest extent possible, including the state and the sphere of politics. This is why some of Smith's most scathing criticisms were directed towards the mercantilist states of Europe, which were frustrating the natural workings of a market system. The fact that the major targets of Smith's pen were states is in itself revealing and suggests that the relationship between economic and political life is more complex and that these spheres of activity are imbricated in ways that Smith did not consider.[145]

State actions and policies themselves constitute the economy in profound ways. Even the market economy, which Smith took to be natural, is constituted by political power, as S. R. Epstein has shown in the case of medieval and early-modern Europe. Epstein writes, "Pre-modern markets, like modern capitalist markets, were the artifacts of political and legal systems that were in turn the outcome of political negotiation and contestation." He then concludes that "pre-modern Smithian growth, which was a function of market integration, therefore depended ultimately on the progress of state sovereignty."[146] In this framework, the development of the market economy was not a matter of the state once and for all setting the rules of the game, as the new institutionalist economic historians such as Douglass North would have it, but of the steady growth and constant exercise of state power.

Economic growth and technological transformation in the eighteenth and nineteenth centuries likewise benefited from state activities, and economic progress in these centuries was intimately connected to the rise and consolidation of the modern state. The debate between economists on the necessity of state intervention, then, misses the more important point that rulers and state authorities were driven to develop the economy and put it on a modern footing to serve their own interests of greater power. To achieve this goal, states remade economic life in the eighteenth and nineteenth centuries. In a number of respects, the modern economy is an effect of the development of the modern state.

9 | Conclusion

The industrialization of Britain was a slow and protracted process, but by the early decades of the nineteenth century it was evident that the path of economic development in Western Europe had diverged from that of the Indian subcontinent. With the rise of the British cotton industry the major textile-exporting centers in the world migrated from India to Europe. The growing use of coal and steam revolutionized sources of power as well as transport and dramatically expanded the scale of production and output in the British Isles. Britain had given birth to a new industrial economy.

Why did these changes emerge in Europe and not the advanced regions of Asia? This work has given a new answer to this very old question. In a nutshell, it has argued that historians must move away from the search for what made Europe economically, socially or culturally different and instead focus on the social needs, economic pressures and political responses that produced different paths of change in the eighteenth century. The British path was a coming together of global competitive pressures, ecological shortfalls and a mercantile state. No other advanced region faced these pressures and combined them with a state that had such capacities to forge a revolutionary response. While the highly commercialized regions of the Indian subcontinent had their own sources of political and economic dynamism, and there was undoubtedly significant technological change taking place, the pressures were not such that radical transformations were needed or risky paths had to be pursued.

The novelty of this answer to the puzzle of European divergence rests in part on new empirical material. The uniqueness of Europe's science and technology has been widely accepted but little examined. The empirical material on India brought together here presents a very different picture for the seventeenth and eighteenth centuries. Similarly, the many cases of successful technology transfer from Western Europe to India in the early nineteenth century are evidence of greater comparability in skill and knowledge between these two regions than has been previously appreciated. And a re-examination of data on silver flows and minting in the Mughal Empire complements voluminous research on the export of cotton textiles from Gujarat, Bengal and southeastern India and provides information on the commodity that balanced this outflow of cloth. Finally, with respect to eighteenth-century Britain, the papers of the early cotton masters, as well as other writings connected to the cotton manufacture, suggest that the drive to supplant Indian goods loomed large in the minds and activities of British textile men. These same materials point to the importance of the protection of trade for British economic life.

The argument given here also rests on a rethinking of the categories which have been used to study the problem of divergence. In the last quarter century, historians have engaged in a profound interrogation of the frameworks and concepts with which they comprehend and write about the past. Basic categories themselves have been historicized, and therefore denaturalized, and made the subject of historical investigation. In part, this is a product of the cultural turn in which historians inspired by Michel Foucault and others have studied the discourses and practices that establish regimes of truth. Such questioning of historical categories happened on a broader front, however, and was not inspired only by the cultural turn but emerged in the writing of social history as well. Works such as Eric Hobsbawm and Terence Ranger's *Invention of Tradition* simultaneously historicized the idea of tradition, showing it to be often a nineteenth-century product, and inverted the longstanding arrow of historical change from tradition to modernity.

In this work, three elements that appear in much writing on economic divergence between Europe and Asia have been systematically criticized and rejected. These are Orientalist constructions of Asia, in particular India, a focus on the market as the driver of economic change, and historical anachronisms in the framing of the question. While Orientalist thinking on the East has earlier antecedents, it, along with the market and anachronistic ways of thinking about divergence, became entrenched in the nineteenth century and continues to shape the contours of the discussion on divergence to this day.

As we have seen, Orientalist writings saw the society and economy of India as backward and inferior to that of Europe. François Bernier's vision of the East as the land of despots was an early and influential strand. A second conceived of economic and commercial life, along with reason and science, as underdeveloped in India. Much of this was captured in a vision of India as lacking in history and therefore unchanging for centuries, if not millennia. James Mill, for instance, wrote in *The History of British India*, "From the scattered hints contained in the writings of the Greeks, the conclusion has been drawn, that the Hindus, at the time of Alexander's invasion, were in a state of manners, society, and knowledge, exactly the same with that in which they were discovered by the nations of modern Europe."[1]

The assumption that India had no history led to the projection of the colonial Indian society of the nineteenth century into earlier periods. Most famously, Marx elevated the self-sufficient village, which emerged in the 1820s and 1830s, into a timeless feature of the Indian countryside. The agglomeration "in small centres by the domestic union of agricultural and manufacturing pursuits . . . had brought about, since the remotest times, a social system of particular features – the so-called *village system*, which gave to each of these small unions their independent organisation and distinct life," Marx wrote.[2] He supported his understanding of India with reference to an early nineteenth-century report of the British House of Commons, but in Marx's mind, the Indian present stood for the Indian past. Marx is not alone in projecting the static and stagnant economy of colonial India into earlier historical epochs and many have done this both consciously and unconsciously.

For many, the backward and abysmal economic conditions of the nineteenth century may make it difficult to imagine a different kind of India in the not so distant past. As shown in this work, however, the period between 1600 and 1800 was a time of great economic and political dynamism in the advanced regions of the Indian subcontinent. Vibrant production of cotton textiles for export led to sizable inflows of silver, gold, copper and cowries which fueled a commercial revolution. Political competition led to state centralization and advances in science and technology, especially in areas that could be of benefit to the state such as armaments production.

From the second decade of the nineteenth century there was a sustained economic regression in Bengal, South India, Gujarat and other regions of seventeenth- and eighteenth-century dynamism. An early sign of decline was the falling demand for Indian cotton cloth in markets around the world as Indian manufacturers were displaced by Lancashire. From the 1820s, British machine-spun yarn began to be found in the markets of Bengal, Bombay and Madras and local hand spinners started to be undercut. The fall in Indian cloth exports led to a fall in imports of silver into the subcontinent, which since the sixteenth century had turned the wheels of commerce. The contraction in international trade, in turn, led to a decline in the internal trade of the advanced regions of the subcontinent and culminated in a dramatic de-commercialization from the 1820s, and perhaps even slightly earlier.

Trade was not all that declined, however. The dismantling of the Indian state system led to a loss of demand for a variety of goods, particularly armaments, which had been a source of technical and manufacturing dynamism in the eighteenth century. The rise of the British colonial order also translated into a loss of patronage for institutions that produced and diffused knowledge. Education suffered. Libraries were looted, burned in battle or dismantled. Scientific and technical inquiries were not supported. As a consequence, there was a profound loss of knowledge and skills in the first several decades of the nineteenth century and an enormous technical gap opened between the subcontinent and Western Europe. The Indian society and economy that emerged in the nineteenth century was, therefore, radically different from what had preceded it and should not be projected into the seventeenth and eighteenth centuries.

Similarly, the critique of state intervention in the economy, which became an increasingly important principle of economic thinking from the late eighteenth century and entered into the heart of British economic life in the nineteenth, should not inform interpretations of economic change in earlier periods. As shown in this book, the ascendance of Smithian political economy in early nineteenth-century Britain led to a profound reinterpretation of economic change in the eighteenth century. The understanding of innovation in the British cotton industry shifted from competition with India and state protection to the forces of the market and supply and demand. When the first authoritative histories of the British cotton industry were written in the early decades of the nineteenth century, they were influenced by the market ideas of the day. In the seventeenth and eighteenth centuries, however, there was little debate that the state could promote economically desirable outcomes. And there is little doubt that states from Western Europe to Japan were intimately involved in shaping paths of economic development. The image of the optimal and efficient, self-regulating market economy had little purchase before the publication and diffusion of the *Wealth of Nations*.

From the late seventeenth century the British state restricted imports of Indian cotton cloth, which gave an impetus to local cloth printing and then to local cotton cloth manufacturing, which were given a monopoly over the British market. Over the course of the eighteenth century the British state steadily increased tariffs on iron imports from Sweden and Russia, which gave local ironmasters a guarantee of high prices for their goods as they experimented with coal and new techniques of smelting. And British state protection for trade, whether through the Navigation Acts which helped to create British dominance in the Atlantic or through the protection of coastal convoys of coal, aided British economic growth and expansion. The British state was not alone in its activism. From the mid-seventeenth century, the Japanese state crafted policies to preserve and revive forested areas, which stabilized and restored the forest ecology. In China, the Qing granary system was critical for the redistribution of food from surplus to deficit areas of the empire. In the Indian subcontinent, rulers patronized institutions for the development of scientific and technical knowledge and kept agricultural production at a high pitch with advances to cultivators or taccavi.

State interventionist policies continued in the nineteenth century. In Britain itself, protectionism would remain in force till the repeal of the Corn Laws in 1846. In France, Belgium and Germany, a broad range of policies were instituted to promote manufacturing. The deleterious impact of laissez-faire, in which such state support is not extended to the development of the economy, is evident from British India where technology transfer was impeded, the establishment of new industrial methods of manufacturing was aborted, and technical skills and knowledge atrophied or disappeared. In the Indian case, British officials justified their hands-off approach with an appeal to the authority of Adam Smith, but the needs of British manufacturing loomed large in the making of such policies. Therefore, an intellectual agenda came to be set in the nineteenth century which favored a free operation of the market, and gave shape to much historical interpretation, even though many practical men continued to favor an activist state.

Finally, the nineteenth century bequeathed an anachronistic framework to the study of divergence. Efforts to identify what Europe had
and Asia did not, whether capitalism, reason or coal, reduced economic
change in the eighteenth century to either industrialization or its failure.
It projected modern industry, which became the universally desired goal
of economic development from the nineteenth century, into earlier
periods. As argued in this book, an industrial economy was not
premeditated but emerged from a configuration of political, economic
and ecological forces and pressures in seventeenth- and eighteenth-
century Britain. The British response to these forces and pressures,
both technological and institutional, forged the nineteenth-century
industrial order. The advanced areas of Asia were themselves undergoing profound economic and technological change in these centuries.
The paths they followed were radically different, however, because of
the radically different political, economic and social contexts.

The argument of this book rests on an analysis of the systematic
differences in economic and political structures across the advanced
regions of Europe and Asia. While some structural elements analyzed
here have figured in the debate on divergence, most importantly the
ecological, others have been less discussed, such as the ways in which
the global trade in textiles and the relation between the state and
economy created varied contexts and possibilities for change. Many
structural differences considered critical in previous works, including
the efficiency of markets, scientific and technological dynamism,
demographic patterns, state systems and so forth, have been given little
weight because, as this book argues, the empirical evidence suggests that
in these areas the advanced regions of Europe and India were far more
similar than previously thought.

The argument of this work does not rest only on an analysis of
structure, however, for it is not structures that shape history but the
actions of individuals. While structures differed across the advanced
regions of Europe and Asia and provided both different pressures and
different possibilities, it was the preferences, choices and actions of
individuals operating within these structures that gave rise to different
paths of historical development. These actions included inventing new
techniques of production, state officials defining and implementing
policy, and associations of individuals agitating for political support.

The attention given to agency has two important implications,
the first for our understanding of economic life and the second for

the study of divergence. With respect to divergence, the attention to agency leads to the comparison of historical processes or paths of change. The objects of comparison are dynamic entities. If only structures are compared, the result is exercises in comparative statics as it is presumed that a particular structure will lead to given outcomes. And an exceptional structure will give way to exceptional outcomes. Sufficient consideration is not paid to the process by which that outcome is reached. It leads to history writing in which there is a beginning and an end, but no middle. What this book has sought to do is to see divergence as the outcome of processes of historical change and to supply the missing middle.

The attention given to agency makes the economy a human creation. A focus on structures constructs the economy as lying beyond human intervention and subject to its own imperatives and iron laws, whose inevitability and inviolability are reinforced by the naturalism of economics, whether derived from Adam Smith's grounding of economic life in man's propensities or from neoclassical assumptions about human behavior. The framework of this book sees the paths of economic development in the eighteenth and nineteenth centuries as very much the product of human creativity and choice, not the product of timeless laws.

Notes to the text

1 Introduction

1 Joseph E. Stiglitz, "The Contributions of the Economics of Information to Twentieth Century Economics," *Quarterly Journal of Economics*, 115 (2000), p. 1459.

2 For a powerful statement see Amos Tversky and Daniel Kahneman, "Loss Aversion in Riskless Choice: A Reference-Dependent Model," *Quarterly Journal of Economics*, 106 (1991), pp. 1039–61.

3 The classic statements are Adam Smith, *An Inquiry into the Nature and Causes of the Wealth of Nations*, 2 vols. (Oxford, 1976); Douglass C. North and Robert Paul Thomas, *The Rise of the Western World: A New Economic History* (Cambridge, 1973). Also see Eric Jones, *The European Miracle: Environments, Economies and Geopolitics in the History of Europe and Asia* (3rd edn., Cambridge, 2003), pp. 162–6; Jan Luiten van Zanden, *The Long Road to the Industrial Revolution: The European Economy in Global Perspective, 1000–1800* (Leiden, 2009), chap. 1.

4 Robert Brenner, "Agrarian Class Structure and Economic Development in Pre-Industrial Europe," in T. H. Aston and C. H. E. Philpin (eds.), *The Brenner Debate: Agrarian Class Structure and Economic Development in Pre-Industrial Europe* (Cambridge, 1985), pp. 10–63; Robert Brenner and Christopher Isett, "England's Divergence from China's Yangzi Delta: Property Relations, Microeconomics, and Patterns of Development," *JAS*, 61 (2002), pp. 609–62.

5 John Hajnal, "Two Kinds of Preindustrial Household Formation System," *Population and Development Review*, 8 (1982), pp. 449–94; Alan Macfarlane, *The Savage Wars of Peace: England, Japan and the Malthusian Trap* (Oxford, 1997), chap. 1; Jones, *European Miracle*, chap. 2.

6 See David S. Landes, *The Wealth and Poverty of Nations: Why Some Are So Rich and Some So Poor* (New York, 1998), pp. 174–9 and Margaret C. Jacob and Matthew Kadane, "Missing, Now Found in the Eighteenth Century: Weber's Protestant Capitalist," *American Historical Review*, 108 (2003), pp. 20–49. The ghost of Weber also looms over Gregory Clark, *A Farewell to Alms: A Brief Economic History of the World* (Princeton, 2007), although Clark's explanatory framework is very different.

7 Margaret C. Jacob, *Scientific Culture and the Making of the Industrial West* (Oxford, 1997); Joel Mokyr, *The Gifts of Athena: Historical Origins of the Knowledge Economy* (Princeton, 2002). Also see Jack A. Goldstone, "Efflorescences and Economic Growth in World History: Rethinking the 'Rise of the West' and the Industrial Revolution," *Journal of World History*, 13 (2002), pp. 323–89.

8 For an excellent overview, see Jack Goody, *The East in the West* (Cambridge, 1996), chaps. 3–4. For interest rates, see Chapter 3 of this book.

9 S. Arasaratnam, "The Rice Trade in Eastern India 1650–1740," *MAS*, 22 (1988), pp. 533–42; Sanjay Subrahmanyam, "The Portuguese, the Port of Basrur and the Rice Trade, 1600–50," *IESHR*, 21 (1984), pp. 433–62; Prasannan Parthasarathi, "Rethinking Wages and Competitiveness in the Eighteenth Century: Britain and South India," *P&P*, 158 (1998), pp. 79–109; Prasannan Parthasarathi, "Agriculture, Labour, and the Standard of Living in Eighteenth-Century India," in Robert C. Allen, Tommy Bengtsson and Martin Dribe (eds.), *Living Standards in the Past: New Perspectives on Well-Being in Asia and Europe* (Oxford, 2005), pp. 99–109; Sashi Sivramkrishna, "Ascertaining Living Standards in Erstwhile Mysore, Southern India, from Francis Buchanan's *Journey* of 1800–01: An Empirical Contribution to the Great Divergence Debate," *Journal of the Economic and Social History of the Orient*, 52 (2009), pp. 695–733.

10 R. Bin Wong, *China Transformed: Historical Change and the Limits of European Experience* (Ithaca, N.Y., 1997) and Kenneth Pomeranz, *The Great Divergence: China, Europe and the Making of the Modern World Economy* (Princeton, 2000).

11 William Lavely and R. Bin Wong, "Revising the Malthusian Narrative: The Comparative Study of Population Dynamics in Late Imperial China," *JAS*, 57 (1998), pp. 714–48; James Z. Lee and Wang Feng, *One Quarter of Humanity: Malthusian Mythology and Chinese Realities, 1700–2000* (Cambridge, Mass., 1999), pp. 88–92; Sumit Guha, *Health and Population in South Asia: From Earliest Times to the Present* (New Delhi, 2001), chap. 3.

12 C. A. Bayly, "Pre-Colonial Indian Merchants and Rationality," in Mushirul Hasan and Narayani Gupta (eds.), *India's Colonial Encounter: Essays in Memory of Eric Stokes* (New Delhi, 1993), p. 18; William Rowe, *Hankow: Commerce and Society in a Chinese City, 1796–1889* (Stanford, 1984), pp. 73–6; Goody, *East in the West*, chap. 2.

13 Edward Said, *Orientalism* (New York, 1978).

14 The writings of Christopher Bayly, Frank Perlin and David Washbrook were pivotal. See C. A. Bayly, *Rulers, Townsmen and Bazaars: North Indian Society in the Age of British Expansion, 1770–1870* (Cambridge,

1983); Frank Perlin, "Proto-Industrialization and Pre-Colonial South Asia," *P&P*, 98 (1983), pp. 30–95; D. A. Washbrook, "Progress and Problems: South Asian Economic and Social History *c*.1720–1860," *MAS*, 22 (1988), pp. 57–96.

15 Karl Marx, "The British Rule in India," in Robert C. Tucker (ed.), *The Marx-Engels Reader* (2nd edn., New York, 1978), p. 656.

16 Lucien Febvre, *The Problem of Unbelief in the Sixteenth Century: The Religion of Rabelais*, trans. Beatrice Gottlieb (Cambridge, Mass., 1982), p. 5.

17 Raymond Williams, *Keywords: A Vocabulary of Culture and Society* (London, 1976), p. 137.

18 The method followed in this book rejects approaches that identify economic growth and change as the product of preconditions. In this it has been inspired by H. J. Habakkuk, who observed in 1965, "There is scarcely one of these pre-conditions which cannot be shown to have been absent in the case of some acknowledged case of growth. Indeed, it is not difficult to cite cases where the absence of what is commonly regarded as a pre-condition proved to be a positive stimulus to growth." See H. J. Habakkuk, "The Historical Experience of Economic Development," in E. A. G. Robinson (ed.), *Problems in Economic Development: Proceedings of a Conference held by the International Economic Association* (London, 1965), pp. 118–19.

19 Pomeranz, *Great Divergence*, p. 8.

20 This approach is inspired by Rajnarayan Chandavarkar, who writes, "There is no reason to assume that the outcome of economic development was predetermined . . . Rather, at every step, it was the interaction of a whole constellation of social forces . . . that determined the sometimes wayward direction of change." See his "Industrialization in India before 1947: Conventional Approaches and Alternative Perspectives," *MAS*, 19 (1985), p. 637.

21 See Maxine Berg, "In Pursuit of Luxury: Global Origins of British Consumer Goods in the Eighteenth Century," *P&P*, 182 (2004), pp. 85–142 and *Luxury and Pleasure in Eighteenth-Century Britain* (Oxford, 2005).

22 C. Knick Harley, "Reassessing the Industrial Revolution: A Macro View," in Joel Mokyr (ed.), *The British Industrial Revolution: An Economic Perspective* (2nd edn., Boulder, Colo., 1999), p. 205.

23 N. F. R. Crafts and C. K. Harley, "Output Growth and the British Industrial Revolution: A Restatement of the Crafts–Harley View," *Economic History Review*, n.s. 45 (1992), p. 709; Harley, "Reassessing the Industrial Revolution," p. 171.

24 Karl Marx, *The Eighteenth Brumaire of Louis Bonaparte* (New York, 1963), p. 15.

25 For a good overview of some of these developments, see Samuel Bowles and Herbert Gintis, "Walrasian Economics in Retrospect," *Quarterly Journal of Economics*, 115 (2000), pp. 1411–39.

26 Tversky and Kahneman, "Loss Aversion in Riskless Choice."

27 My approach may be contrasted with that of Robert Allen, who argues that the spinning jenny was invented in Britain, and not India, because of differences in the structure of prices. He does not consider that the global trade in textiles may have created different imperatives in the two places, which meant that individuals faced different economic situations and problems. Indians were not seeking to break into the global textile trade, while the British were, for instance. See Robert C. Allen, "The Industrial Revolution in Miniature: The Spinning Jenny in Britain, France, and India," *JEH*, 69 (2009), pp. 901–27.

28 It focuses on comparisons with India because there is a sizable literature on China, including Wong's *China Transformed* and Pomeranz's *Great Divergence*.

2 India and the global economy, 1600–1800

1 Immanuel Wallerstein, *The Modern World System II: Mercantilism and the Consolidation of the European World-Economy, 1600–1750* (New York, 1980), pp. 7–8.

2 There is now a voluminous literature on the Indian Ocean, but see K. N. Chaudhuri, *Trade and Civilisation in the Indian Ocean: An Economic History from the Rise of Islam to 1750* (Cambridge, 1985); K. N. Chaudhuri, *Asia Before Europe: Economy and Civilisation of the Indian Ocean from the Rise of Islam to 1750* (Cambridge, 1990); Ashin Das Gupta and M. N. Pearson (eds.), *India and the Indian Ocean 1500–1800* (Calcutta, 1987); Sanjay Subrahmanyam, *The Political Economy of Commerce: Southern India, 1500–1650* (Cambridge, 1990); Rajat Kanta Ray, "Asian Capital in the Age of European Domination: The Rise of the Bazaar, 1800–1914," *MAS*, 29 (1995), pp. 449–554.

3 The classic statement is C. A. Bayly, *Rulers, Townsmen and Bazaars: North Indian Society in the Age of British Expansion, 1770–1870* (Cambridge, 1983), chap. 6.

4 For a good overview see Andre Gunder Frank, *ReOrient: Global Economy in the Asian Age* (Berkeley, 1998), pp. 92–117.

5 Ibid., p. 127.

6 Giorgio Riello and Tirthankar Roy (eds.), *How India Clothed the World: The World of South Asian Textiles, 1500–1850* (Leiden, 2009).

7 Frank, *ReOrient*, pp. 126–30.

8 Om Prakash, "Bullion for Goods: International Trade and the Economy of Early Eighteenth Century Bengal," *IESHR*, 13 (1976), pp. 159–87.

9 Richard M. Eaton, *A Social History of the Deccan, 1300–1761: Eight Indian Lives* (Cambridge, 2005), pp. 107–12. The quotation appears on p. 111.

10 P. J. Thomas, *Mercantilism and the East India Trade* (London, 1926), chap. 2; Beverly Lemire, *Fashion's Favourite: The Cotton Trade and the Consumer in Britain, 1660–1800* (Oxford, 1991), chap. 1; Beverly Lemire, "Revising the Historical Narrative: India, Europe, and the Cotton Trade, *c.*1300–1800," in Giorgio Riello and Prasannan Parthasarathi (eds.), *The Spinning World: A Global History of Cotton Textiles, 1200–1850* (Oxford, 2009), pp. 205–26.

11 Marion Johnson, *Anglo-African Trade in the Eighteenth Century*, ed. J. T. Lindblad and Robert Ross (Leiden, 1990), pp. 28–9.

12 Herbert S. Klein, *The Atlantic Slave Trade* (Cambridge, 1999), p. 87. Indian cloths accounted for 63 percent of the value of all the cloths exported, which in turn represented 56 percent of all exports.

13 Robert Louis Stein, *The French Slave Trade in the Eighteenth Century: An Old Regime Business* (Madison, 1979), p. 211.

14 Robert S. DuPlessis, "Cottons Consumption in the Seventeenth- and Eighteenth-Century North Atlantic," in Riello and Parthasarathi, *Spinning World*, pp. 227–46.

15 Marta V. Vicente, "Fashion, Race, and Cotton Textiles in Colonial Spanish America," in Riello and Parthasarathi, *Spinning World*, pp. 247–60.

16 Katsumi Fukasawa, *Toilerie et commerce du Levant: d'Alep à Marseilles* (Paris, 1987), p. 41. The report gives these figures in iz. piastres, which have been converted to livres tournois on the basis of information Fukasawa gives in chap. 4, n. 89, pp. 152–3. One pound sterling has been taken as equal to 23 livres tournois.

17 John Guy, *Woven Cargoes: Indian Textiles in the East* (London, 1998), p. 81.

18 For two examples, see John Darwin, *After Tamerlane: The Global History of Empire since 1405* (New York, 2008), p. 193 and Ronald Findlay and Kevin H. O'Rourke, *Power and Plenty: Trade, War, and the World Economy in the Second Millennium* (Princeton, 2007), p. 355.

19 Guy, *Woven Cargoes*, p. 133.

20 Ibid., p. 10.

21 Lemire, *Fashion's Favourite*, pp. 7–12.

22 Ibid., p. 13.

23 Quoted in K. N. Chaudhuri, *The Trading World of Asia and the East India Company, 1660–1760* (Cambridge, 1978), p. 281.

24 Quoted in Thomas, *Mercantilism and the East India Trade*, p. 28.
25 Lemire, *Fashion's Favourite*, p. 13.
26 John Styles, *The Dress of the People: Everyday Fashion in Eighteenth-Century England* (New Haven, 2007), p. 109.
27 Daniel Roche, *The Culture of Clothing: Dress and Fashion in the Ancien Régime*, trans. Jean Birrell (Cambridge, 1996), Table 10, p. 127 and Table 14, p. 138. Roche's category of cottons includes both lighter cloth akin to Indian goods as well as heavier cotton and linen mixtures such as corduroys and velvets.
28 Jacob Nicolas Moreau, *Examen des effets que doivent produire dans le commerce de France, l'usage & la fabrication des toiles peintes: ou Réponse à l'ouvrage intitulé . . .* (Geneva, 1759), p. 60, quoted in Giorgio Riello, "The Globalization of Cotton Textiles: Indian Cottons, Europe, and the Atlantic World, 1600–1850," in Riello and Parthasarathi, *Spinning World*, p. 267.
29 Quoted in Thomas, *Mercantilism and the East India Trade*, p. 27.
30 Quoted in Styles, *Dress of the People*, p. 111.
31 For a survey, see Prasannan Parthasarathi and Giorgio Riello, "From India to the World: Cotton and Fashionability," in Frank Trentmann (ed.), *The Oxford Handbook of the History of Consumption* (Oxford, forthcoming).
32 Rudiger Klein, "Trade in the Safavid Port City Bandar Abbas and the Persian Gulf Area (*ca.*1600–1680): A Study of Selected Aspects," unpublished Ph.D. dissertation, University of London, 1994, chap. 5; Pedro Machado, "Awash in a Sea of Cloth: Gujarat, Africa, and the Western Indian Ocean, 1300–1800," in Riello and Parthasarathi, *Spinning World*, pp. 173–5; Guy, *Woven Cargoes*, p. 150.
33 Giorgio Riello, "Asian Knowledge and the Development of Calico Printing in Europe in the Seventeenth and Eighteenth Centuries," *Journal of Global History*, 5 (2010), pp. 1–28.
34 Thomas, *Mercantilism and the East India Trade*, pp. 33–4.
35 Ibid.
36 Richard Roberts, "West Africa and the Pondicherry Textile Industry," in Tirthankar Roy (ed.), *Cloth and Commerce: Textiles in Colonial India* (New Delhi, 1996), p. 158.
37 Daniel Defoe, *A Plan of the English Commerce* (London, 1728, repr. Oxford, 1928), pp. 49–50.
38 William Gervase Clarence-Smith, "The Production of Cotton Textiles in Early Modern South-East Asia," in Riello and Parthasarathi, *Spinning World*, p. 131.
39 Fukasawa, *Toilerie et commerce du Levant*, pp. 44–5.

40 Carole Shammas, "The Decline of Textile Prices in England and British America Prior to Industrialization," *Economic History Review*, n.s., 47 (1994), p. 484. Shammas' prices for the late seventeenth century are consistent with those in Margaret Spufford, "The Cost of Apparel in Seventeenth-Century England, and the Accuracy of Gregory King," *Economic History Review*, n.s., 53 (2000), pp. 690–1. For some additional eighteenth-century prices, see Giorgio Riello, "The Indian Apprenticeship: The Trade of Indian Textiles and the Making of European Cottons," in Riello and Roy, *How India Clothed the World*, pp. 344–5.

41 Styles, *Dress of the People*, p. 127.

42 Ibid., pp. 127–32.

43 Alfred P. Wadsworth and Julia de Lacy Mann, *The Cotton Trade and Industrial Lancashire, 1600–1780* (Manchester, 1931, repr. New York, 1968), p. 176.

44 Ibid., p. 176.

45 "First, Second, and Third Reports of the Select Committee, Appointed by the Court of Directors of the East India Company, to take into Consideration the Export Trade from Great Britain to the East Indies: With appendixes, 1793," H/401, p. 43, APAC, BL.

46 Lemire, *Fashion's Favourite*, p. 7.

47 Ibid., p. 14.

48 N. C., a Weaver of London, *The Great Necessity and Advantage of Preserving Our Own Manufactures* (London, 1697).

49 John Smith (ed.), *Chronicon Rusticum-Comerciale*, 2 vols. (London, 1747), vol. I, p. 351.

50 Francisco Pelsaert, *Jahangir's India*, trans. W. H. Moreland and P. Geyl (Cambridge, 1925), p. 60. For the views of other travelers, see W. H. Moreland, *India at the Death of Akbar: An Economic Study* (London, 1920, repr. New Delhi, 1990), pp. 265–70.

51 Mrs. J. Kindersley, *Letters from the Island of Teneriffe, Brazil, the Cape of Good Hope and the East Indies* (London, 1777), no. 43; cited in Tapan Raychaudhuri, "The Mid-Eighteenth Century Background," in Dharma Kumar (ed.), *The Cambridge Economic History of India*, vol. II, c.*1757–c.1970* (Cambridge, 1982), p. 8.

52 W. H. Moreland, *From Akbar to Aurangzeb: A Study in Indian Economic History* (London, 1923, repr. New Delhi, 1993), pp. 197–8; Raychaudhuri, "Mid-Eighteenth Century Background," p. 17; Chaudhuri, *Trading World*, p. 274; Eric Hobsbawm, *Labouring Men* (New York, 1964), p. 87.

53 Some participants in the debate on comparative standards of living fail to recognize the limits of quantification and the critical importance of

qualitative evidence. See, for example, Stephen Broadberry and Bishnu-priya Gupta, "The Early Modern Great Divergence: Wages, Prices and Economic Development in Europe and Asia, 1500–1800," *Economic History Review*, n.s., 59 (2006), pp. 2–31. This bias may stem from a belief that to quantify implies greater objectivity. According to Deirdre McCloskey, "Most economists believe that once you have reduced a question to numbers you have taken it out of human hands." See her *The Rhetoric of Economics* (2nd edn., Madison, 1998), p. 100.

54 Prasannan Parthasarathi, "Rethinking Wages and Competitiveness in the Eighteenth Century: Britain and South India," *P&P*, 158 (1998), pp. 92–101.

55 Ibid., pp. 92–101.

56 Prasannan Parthasarathi, "Productivity in South Indian Agriculture, *c.*1800," paper presented at a Workshop on Agricultural Productivity, University of California, Davis, December 2002.

57 For an occupational breakdown of eighteenth-century Britain, see Peter Mathias, *The Transformation of England: Essays in the Economic and Social History of England in the Eighteenth Century* (New York, 1979), pp. 186–7. While no such data exist for any Indian region, anecdotal evidence points to the importance of the textile trades.

58 The flying shuttle was invented in the 1730s, but it was slow to diffuse. Akos Paulinyi, "John Kay's Flying Shuttle: Some Considerations on His Technical Capacity and Economic Impact," *Textile History*, 17 (1986), pp. 149–66.

59 John Rule, *The Experience of Labour in Eighteenth-Century English Industry* (New York, 1981), p. 57; Hans-Joachim Voth, *Time and Work in England, 1750–1830* (Oxford, 2000). Also see the classic E. P. Thompson, "Time, Work-Discipline, and Industrial Capitalism," *P&P*, 38 (1967), pp. 56–97.

60 For South India, see Prasannan Parthasarathi, *The Transition to a Colonial Economy: Weavers, Merchants and Kings in South India, 1720–1800* (Cambridge, 2001), chap. 1; for Bengal, Hameeda Hossain, *The Company Weavers of Bengal: The East India Company and the Organization of Textile Production in Bengal 1750–1813* (Delhi, 1988), chap. 2; for Gujarat, Ghulam A. Nadri, *Eighteenth-Century Gujarat: The Dynamics of Its Political Economy, 1750–1800* (Leiden, 2009), chap. 2.

61 Parthasarathi, "Rethinking Wages and Competitiveness," pp. 79–109 and Prasannan Parthasarathi, "Agriculture, Labour, and the Standard of Living in Eighteenth-Century India," in Robert C. Allen, Tommy Bengtsson and Martin Dribe (eds.), *Living Standards in the Past: New Perspectives on Well-Being in Asia and Europe* (Oxford, 2005), pp. 99–109.

62 Broadberry and Gupta, "Early Modern Great Divergence," pp. 13–18.

63 Alan Heston, "Review of Shireen Moosvi, *The Economy of the Mughal Empire c.1595: A Statistical Study*," *Economic History Review*, n.s., 41 (1988), p. 671. The A'in-i Akbari is an administrative and statistical volume compiled in the late sixteenth century.

64 Parthasarathi, *Transition to a Colonial Economy*, pp. 15–16.

65 Ibid., p. 14.

66 Robert C. Allen, "India in the Great Divergence," in Timothy J. Hatton, Kevin H. O'Rourke and Alan M. Taylor (eds.), *The New Comparative Economic History: Essays in Honor of Jeffrey G. Williamson* (Cambridge, Mass., 2007), pp. 9–32. The quotation appears on p. 24. Also see Robert C. Allen, *The British Industrial Revolution in Global Perspective* (Cambridge, 2009), pp. 40–1.

67 Sashi Sivramkrishna, "Ascertaining Living Standards in Erstwhile Mysore, Southern India, from Francis Buchanan's *Journey* of 1800–01: An Empirical Contribution to the Great Divergence Debate," *Journal of the Economic and Social History of the Orient*, 52 (2009), pp. 695–733. The quotation appears on p. 720.

68 Frank, *ReOrient*, p. 115; Dennis O. Flynn and Arturo Giráldez, "Born with a 'Silver Spoon': The Origin of World Trade," *Journal of World History*, 6 (1995), p. 202.

69 Richard von Glahn, *Fountain of Fortune: Money and Monetary Policy in China, 1000–1700* (Berkeley, 1996), pp. 231–2.

70 Kenneth Pomeranz, *The Great Divergence: China, Europe and the Making of the Modern World Economy* (Princeton, 2000), p. 160.

71 American production is from Ward Barrett, "World Bullion Flows, 1450–1850," in James D. Tracy (ed.), *The Rise of Merchant Empires: Long-Distance Trade in the Early Modern World, 1350–1750* (Cambridge, 1990), Table 7.2. I have taken an average of the Humboldt, Soetbeer, and Merrill and Ridgway figures. The Japanese figure, which represents not production but an estimate of exports, is from Frank, *ReOrient*, p. 146.

72 For a brief overview, see M. N. Pearson, "Asia and World Precious Metal Flows in the Early Modern Period," in John McGuire, Patrick Bertola and Peter Reeves (eds.), *Evolution of the World Economy, Precious Metals and India* (New Delhi, 2001), pp. 25–31.

73 Frank, *ReOrient*, p. 149.

74 Von Glahn, *Money and Monetary Policy*, p. 232.

75 Chaudhuri, *Trading World*, pp. 174–82; Huw Bowen, *The Business of Empire: The East India Company and Imperial Britain, 1756–1833* (Cambridge, 2006), pp. 222–34.

76 There is a large literature on this topic, but see Om Prakash, "The Dutch and the Indian Ocean Textile Trade," in Riello and Parthasarathi, *Spinning World*, p. 147.

77 Chaudhuri, *Trading World*, pp. 174–82.

78 Om Prakash, "Indian Textiles in the Indian Ocean in the Early Modern Period," unpublished paper, p. 20; Chaudhuri, *Trading World*, p. 180; A. Das Gupta, "Indian Merchants and the Trade in the Indian Ocean," in Tapan Raychaudhuri and Irfan Habib (eds.), *The Cambridge Economic History of India*, vol. I, *c.1200–c.1750* (Cambridge, 1982), p. 433; Om Prakash, *The Dutch East India Company and the Economy of Bengal, 1630–1720* (Princeton, 1985), chap. 5.

79 Najaf Haider notes that this is three times the figure for silver imports into Ming China in the second half of the sixteenth century. See his "Structure and Movement of Wages in the Mughal Empire, 1500–1700," in Jan Lucassen (ed.), *Wages and Currency: Global Comparisons from Antiquity to the Twentieth Century* (Bern, 2007), p. 302.

80 Najaf Haider, "Precious Metal Flows and Currency Circulation in the Mughal Empire," *Journal of the Economic and Social History of the Orient*, 39 (1996), pp. 298–364. See especially pp. 322–3 and 341–2.

81 Artur Attman, *American Bullion in the European World Trade, 1600–1800*, trans. Eva and Allan Green (Göteborg, 1986), p. 77; Om Prakash, "Global Precious Metal Flows and India, 1500–1750," in McGuire, Bertola and Reeves, *Evolution of the World Economy*, p. 62.

82 Bowen, *Business of Empire*, pp. 222–31.

83 For an overview, see Frank Perlin, "Proto-Industrialization and Pre-Colonial South Asia," *P&P*, 98 (1983), pp. 60–86. For some material on the Dutch trade in Japanese copper, see Kristoff Glamann, "The Dutch East India Company's Trade in Japanese Copper, 1645–1736," *Scandinavian Economic History Review*, 1 (1953), pp. 50–5; Prakash, *Dutch East India Company*, chap. 5.

3 Political institutions and economic life

1 Perry Anderson, *Lineages of the Absolutist State* (London, 1974), p. 400. Bernier is cited in the *Wealth of Nations* and Smith's library contained an English translation of his *Voyages* (1710).

2 *De l'Esprit des lois*, vol. I, pp. 244 and 291–2, cited in Anderson, *Lineages of the Absolutist State*, pp. 464–5.

3 Karl Marx, "The Future Results of British Rule in India," in Robert C. Tucker, *The Marx–Engels Reader* (2nd edn., New York, 1978), p. 659.

4 The classic statement is Douglass C. North and Robert Paul Thomas, *The Rise of the Western World: A New Economic History* (Cambridge, 1973). For a more expansive statement, which combines markets with beliefs and state competition, see Douglass C. North, *Understanding the Process of Economic Change* (Princeton, 2005), chap. 10.

5 See Jan Luiten van Zanden, "The Road to the Industrial Revolution: Hypotheses and Conjectures about the Medieval Origins of the 'European Miracle,'" *Journal of Global History*, 3 (2008), pp. 337–59; Jan Luiten van Zanden, *The Long Road to the Industrial Revolution: The European Economy in Global Perspective, 1000–1800* (Leiden, 2009).

6 Quoted in Anderson, *Lineages of the Absolutist State*, p. 397.

7 See ibid., pp. 398–9. The belief in the despotism of Asia gained empirical support from the accounts of European travelers, who described Ottoman and Mughal rule as capricious, brutal and autocratic. For a good summary of European traveler opinion of India in the late sixteenth and seventeenth centuries, see W. H. Moreland, *India at the Death of Akbar: An Economic Study* (London, 1920, repr. New Delhi, 1990), pp. 265–81 and W. H. Moreland, *From Akbar to Aurangzeb: A Study in Indian Economic History* (London, 1923, repr. New Delhi, 1993), pp. 197–204.

8 François Bernier, *The History of the Late Revolution of the Empire of the Great Mogol*, trans. Henry Oldenburg (2nd edn., London, 1676), vol. II, pp. 166–75. The quoted passage appears on p. 168.

9 Irfan Habib, *The Agrarian System of Mughal India* (2nd rev. edn., Delhi, 1999), pp. 369–70. For an alternative perspective, see my "Rethinking Wages and Competitiveness in the Eighteenth Century: Britain and South India," *P&P*, 158 (1998), pp. 79–109.

10 Francisco Pelsaert, *Jahangir's India*, trans. W. H. Moreland and P. Geyl (Cambridge, 1925), p. 60.

11 Moreland, *India at the Death of Akbar* and *From Akbar to Aurangzeb*; Habib, *Agrarian System*.

12 Eric Jones, *The European Miracle: Environments, Economies and Geopolitics in the History of Europe and Asia* (3rd edn., Cambridge, 2003), chap. 10; David S. Landes, *The Wealth and Poverty of Nations: Why Some Are So Rich and Some So Poor* (New York, 1998), chap. 11.

13 C. A. Bayly, *Indian Society and the Making of the British Empire* (Cambridge, 1988), p. 13. Also see Muzaffar Alam and Sanjay Subrahmanyam (eds.), *The Mughal State, 1526–1750* (Delhi, 1998).

14 W. Foster (ed.), *English Factories in India* (Oxford, 1906–27), vol. V, p. 204, quoted in J. C. Heesterman, *The Inner Conflict of Tradition: Essays in Indian Ritual, Kingship, and Society* (Chicago, 1985), p. 160.

15 Karen Barkey, *Bandits and Bureaucrats: The Ottoman Route to State Centralization* (Ithaca, N.Y., 1994), p. 230.

16 Peter C. Perdue, *China Marches West: The Qing Conquest of Central Eurasia* (Cambridge, Mass., 2005), pp. 555–8; Philip A. Kuhn, *Origins of the Modern Chinese State* (Stanford, 2002), pp. 21–2.

17 Jones, *European Miracle*, pp. 118–19.

18 Ibid., p. 109.

19 Muzaffar Alam and Sanjay Subrahmanyam, "Introduction," in Alam and Subrahmanyam, *The Mughal State*, pp. 14–16, 40–2, etc.

20 Muzaffar Alam, "Aspects of Agrarian Uprisings in North India in the Early Eighteenth Century," in Sabyasachi Bhattacharya and Romila Thapar (eds.), *Situating Indian History for Sarvepalli Gopal* (Delhi, 1986), pp. 146–70; Muzaffar Alam, *The Crisis of Empire in Mughal North India* (Delhi, 1986).

21 See Frank Perlin, "State Formation Reconsidered," *MAS*, 19 (1985), pp. 415–80; Burton Stein, "State Formation and Economy Reconsidered," *MAS*, 19 (1985), pp. 387–413.

22 For the Ottoman case, see the pioneering Dina Rizk Khoury, *State and Provincial Society in the Ottoman Empire: Mosul, 1540–1834* (Cambridge, 1997). For China, see R. Bin Wong, *China Transformed: Historical Change and the Limits of European Experience* (Ithaca, N.Y., 1997), chaps. 4–5.

23 Adam Smith, *An Inquiry into the Nature and Causes of the Wealth of Nations*, 2 vols. (Oxford, 1976), vol. II, p. 680.

24 William S. Atwell, "International Bullion Flows and the Chinese Economy circa 1530–1650," *P&P*, 95 (1982), pp. 68–90; Richard von Glahn, *Fountain of Fortune: Money and Monetary Policy in China, 1000–1700* (Berkeley, 1996), chap. 4.

25 See, for instance, Man-houng Lin, *China Upside Down: Currency, Society, and Ideologies, 1808–1856* (Cambridge, Mass., 2006), chap. 1.

26 Smith, *Wealth of Nations*, vol. I, pp. 284–5.

27 North and Thomas, *Rise of the Western World*, p. 1. For a methodological critique of North and Thomas see Alexander James Field, "The Problem with Neoclassical Institutional Economics: A Critique with Special Reference to the North/Thomas Model of Pre-1500 Europe," *Explorations in Economic History*, 18 (1981), pp. 174–98. The North and Thomas conclusions have also found quantitative support from a cross-national study of colonial areas. See Daron Acemoglu, Simon Johnson and James A. Robinson, "The Colonial Origins of Comparative Development: An Empirical Investigation," *American Economic Review*, 91 (2001), pp. 1369–1401.

28 Jones, *European Miracle*, chap. 5.

29 Van Zanden, "Road to the Industrial Revolution," pp. 337–59.

30 See Prasannan Parthasarathi, *The Transition to a Colonial Economy: Weavers, Merchants and Kings in South India, 1720–1800* (Cambridge,

2001), p. 11; David Washbrook, "Land and Labour in Eighteenth-Century South India: The Golden Age of the Pariah?" in Peter Robb (ed.), *Dalit Movements and the Meanings of Labour in India* (Delhi, 1993), pp. 40–59; David Ludden, *Peasant History in South India* (Princeton, 1985), pp. 82–3; Hiroshi Fukazawa, *The Medieval Deccan: Peasants, Social System and States, Sixteenth to Eighteenth Centuries* (Delhi, 1991), pp. 101–3; Ghulam A. Nadri, *Eighteenth-Century Gujarat: The Dynamics of Its Political Economy, 1750–1800* (Leiden, 2009), p. 27; Irfan Habib, "Labourers and Artisans," in J. S. Grewal (ed.), *The State and Society in Medieval India* (New Delhi, 2005), pp. 171–2.

31 Susan Bayly, *Caste, Society and Politics in India from the Eighteenth Century to the Modern Age* (Cambridge, 1999), pp. 42–3. Also see Nicholas B. Dirks, *Castes of Mind: Colonialism and the Making of Modern India* (Princeton, 2001).

32 Gholam Hossein Khan, *A Translation of Seir Mutaqherin, or, Views of Modern Times: Being an History of India, from the Year 1118, to the Year 1194, of the Hedjrah* (Calcutta, 1902, repr. Lahore, 2005), pp. 912–13.

33 David West Rudner, *Caste and Capitalism in Colonial India: The Nattukottai Chettiars* (Berkeley, 1994), chap. 6; C. A. Bayly, "Indian Merchants in a 'Traditional' Setting: Benares, 1780–1830," in Clive Dewey and A. G. Hopkins (eds.), *The Imperial Impact: Studies in the Economic History of Africa and India* (London, 1978), pp. 178–9, 192.

34 Frank Perlin, "Proto-Industrialization and Pre-Colonial South Asia," *P&P*, 98 (1983), pp. 60–86.

35 Pat Hudson, *The Genesis of Industrial Capital: A Study of the West Riding Wool Textile Industry, c.1750–1850* (Cambridge, 1986), pp. 150–4; also see George Hilton, *The Truck System* (Cambridge, 1960), pp. 71–9 and John Rule, *The Experience of Labour in Eighteenth-Century English Industry* (New York, 1981), pp. 138–9. For an alternative explanation for the shortage of small-value coins see Thomas J. Sargent and François R. Velde, *The Big Problem of Small Change* (Princeton, 2002). Sargent and Velde attribute the problem to the inadequacy of monetary theory before the mid-nineteenth century, but this cannot explain why small change was more abundant in the Indian subcontinent. The explanation may lie in the decentralized organization of minting in India which meant that it was shaped by market forces. See Perlin, "Proto-Industrialization and Pre-Colonial South Asia," p. 76.

36 Wong, *China Transformed*, pp. 17–20; Kenneth Pomeranz, *The Great Divergence: China, Europe and the Making of the Modern World Economy* (Princeton, 2000), chap. 2.

37 Om Prakash, "Bullion for Goods: International Trade and the Economy of Early Eighteenth Century Bengal," *IESHR*, 13 (1976), pp. 166–9.

38 Habib, *Agrarian System*, p. 84.
39 Parthasarathi, *Transition to a Colonial Economy*, pp. 62–71. For the trade in cotton in Gujarat, see Nadri, *Eighteenth-Century Gujarat*, chaps. 2–3.
40 Rajat Datta, *Society, Economy and the Market: Commercialisation in Rural Bengal, c.1760–1800* (Delhi, 2000), p. 16.
41 David Ludden, "Agrarian Commercialism in Eighteenth Century South India: Evidence from the 1823 Tirunelveli Census," *IESHR*, 25 (1988), p. 514.
42 Carol H. Shiue and Wolfgang Keller, "Markets in China and Europe on the Eve of the Industrial Revolution," *American Economic Review*, 97 (2007), pp. 1189–1216. Also see Lillian M. Li, *Fighting Famine in North China: State, Market, and Environmental Decline, 1690s–1990s* (Stanford, 2007), chap. 7.
43 Roman Studer, "India and the Great Divergence: Assessing the Efficiency of Grain Markets in Eighteenth- and Nineteenth-Century India," *JEH*, 68 (2008), pp. 393–437. The piece also makes no mention of the very important issue of rice quality, which varied widely, along with the price. Therefore, the reader cannot tell if the prices that are being compared and correlated are for the same variety of grain.
44 P. J. Thomas and B. Nataraja Pillai, *Economic Depression in the Madras Presidency (1820–1854)* (Madras, 1933); Asiya Siddiqi, *Agrarian Change in a North Indian State: Uttar Pradesh, 1819–1833* (Oxford, 1973), pp. 168–78; C. A. Bayly, *Rulers, Townsmen and Bazaars: North Indian Society in the Age of British Expansion, 1770–1870* (Cambridge, 1983), chap. 7; Sumit Guha, *The Agrarian Economy of the Bombay Deccan 1818–1941* (Delhi, 1985), chap. 2.
45 O. H. K. Spate, *India and Pakistan: A General and Regional Geography* (2nd edn., London, 1957), p. 52. In 1769–70, for example, most of Bengal had excellent harvests while several districts suffered droughts. We will examine the consequences of this differential rainfall shortly. See Datta, *Society, Economy and the Market*, p. 259.
46 Bayly, *Rulers, Townsmen and Bazaars*, pp. 234–5; Parthasarathi, *Transition to a Colonial Economy*, p. 69.
47 Irfan Habib, "Banking in Mughal India," in Tapan Raychaudhuri (ed.), *Contributions to Indian Economic History* (1960), vol. I, pp. 8–10, 14. The quotation appears on p. 10.
48 Irfan Habib, "Usury in Medieval India," *CSSH*, 6 (1964), pp. 401–5.
49 Ibid., pp. 402–4; Sidney Homer and Richard Sylla, *A History of Interest Rates* (4th edn., Hoboken, N.J., 2005), p. 129.
50 Bayly, *Rulers, Townsmen and Bazaars*, pp. 233–4.
51 Homer and Sylla, *History of Interest Rates*, pp. 153–62.

52 Habib, "Usury," pp. 396–7 and 399.

53 Bayly, *Rulers, Townsmen and Bazaars*, pp. 44–5; Datta, *Society, Economy and the Market*, p. 259; Parthasarathi, *Transition to a Colonial Economy*, pp. 22–4 and 47–9; Nadri, *Eighteenth-Century Gujarat*, pp. 29–31.

54 Habib, "Usury," p. 395.

55 The classic paper which argues that credit rationing is not due to market imperfections or shortages of capital is Joseph E. Stiglitz and Andrew Weiss, "Credit Rationing in Markets with Imperfect Information," *American Economic Review*, 71 (1981), pp. 393–410.

56 Habib, "Usury," pp. 402–3.

57 See Pat Hudson, "Industrial Organisation and Structure," in Roderick Floud and Paul Johnson (eds.), *The Cambridge Economic History of Modern Britain*, vol. I, *Industrialisation, 1700–1860* (Cambridge, 2004), pp. 53–5; David Rudner, "Banker's Trust and the Culture of Banking among the Nattukottai Chettiars of Colonial South India," *MAS*, 23 (1989), pp. 417–58; Craig Muldrew, *The Economy of Obligation: The Culture of Credit and Social Relations in Early Modern England* (New York, 1998).

58 Habib, "Banking in Mughal India," pp. 15–17.

59 A. H. John, "The London Assurance Company and the Marine Insurance Market of the Eighteenth Century," *Economica*, 25 (1958), p. 138.

60 Jan de Vries and Ad van der Woude, *The First Modern Economy: Success, Failure, and Perseverance of the Dutch Economy, 1500–1815* (Cambridge, 1997), pp. 137–8. In the mid-eighteenth century Amsterdam marine insurance rates were comparable to those of London.

61 Karen Leonard, "The 'Great Firm' Theory of the Decline of the Mughal Empire," *CSSH*, 21 (1979), pp. 151–67. For a critique, see J. F. Richards, "Mughal State Finance and the Premodern World Economy," *CSSH*, 23 (1981), pp. 285–308.

62 Bayly, *Rulers, Townsmen and Bazaars*, p. 172.

63 Antonia Finnane, *Speaking of Yangzhou: A Chinese City, 1550–1850* (Cambridge, Mass., 2004), p. 121.

64 Robert Brenner, "Agrarian Class Structure and Economic Development in Pre-Industrial Europe," in T. H. Aston and C. H. E. Philpin (eds.), *The Brenner Debate: Agrarian Class Structure and Economic Development in Pre-Industrial Europe* (Cambridge, 1985), p. 53.

65 Robert Brenner and Christopher Isett, "England's Divergence from China's Yangzi Delta: Property Relations, Microeconomics, and Patterns of Development," *JAS*, 61 (2002), pp. 609–62.

66 Robert C. Allen, "Agriculture During the Industrial Revolution, 1700–1850," in Floud and Johnson, *Cambridge Economic History of Modern Britain*, vol. I, p. 115.

67 Ibid., p. 115.

68 S. Arasaratnam, "The Rice Trade in Eastern India 1650–1740," *MAS*, 22 (1988), pp. 533–42. Also see Sanjay Subrahmanyam, "The Portuguese, the Port of Basrur and the Rice Trade, 1600–50," *IESHR*, 21 (1984), pp. 433–62.

69 Arasaratnam, "Rice Trade," pp. 536–44.

70 Nadri, *Eighteenth-Century Gujarat*, p. 140. Habib notes that Gujarat imported food grains in the seventeenth century. See his *Agrarian System*, p. 81.

71 For a discussion of property rights in South Indian rice cultivation, see Ludden, *Peasant History*, pp. 84–94. For Bengal, see Willem van Schendel, *Three Deltas: Accumulation and Poverty in Rural Burma, Bengal and South India* (New Delhi, 1991), pp. 41–5.

72 Li Bozhong, *Agricultural Development in Jiangnan, 1620–1850* (New York, 1998), chap. 8; Kaoru Sugihara, "The East Asian Path of Development: A Long-Term Perspective," in G. Arrighi, T. Hamashita and M. Selden (eds.), *The Resurgence of East Asia* (London, 2003), pp. 82–102.

73 See Prasannan Parthasarathi, "Productivity in South Indian Agriculture, *c.*1800," paper presented at a Workshop on Agricultural Productivity, University of California, Davis, December 2002.

74 Datta, *Society, Economy and the Market*, pp. 189–90.

75 Calculated from data in Saraswati Menon, "Social Characteristics of Land Control in Thanjavur District during the 19th Century: A Sociological Study," unpublished Ph.D. dissertation, Jawaharlal Nehru University, 1983, p. 575. An 1855 survey gives the proportion of tenants at a little under 9 percent. The bulk of these would have cultivated with hired labor, however.

76 Dharma Kumar, *Land and Caste in South India: Agricultural Labour in Madras Presidency in the Nineteenth Century* (Cambridge, 1965), p. 54.

77 Joel Mokyr, *The Enlightened Economy: An Economic History of Britain 1700–1850* (New Haven, 2009), p. 15.

78 John Hajnal, "Two Kinds of Preindustrial Household Formation System," *Population and Development Review*, 8 (1982), pp. 449–94.

79 Alan Macfarlane, *The Savage Wars of Peace: England, Japan and the Malthusian Trap* (Oxford, 1997), chap. 1.

80 William Lavely and R. Bin Wong, "Revising the Malthusian Narrative: The Comparative Study of Population Dynamics in Late Imperial China," *JAS*, 57 (1998), pp. 720–4 and 728.

81 James Z. Lee and Wang Feng, *One Quarter of Humanity: Malthusian Mythology and Chinese Realities, 1700–2000* (Cambridge, Mass., 1999), pp. 88–92.

82 Lavely and Wong, "Revising the Malthusian Narrative," pp. 734–8.

83 Hajnal, "Preindustrial Household Formation," p. 481.

84 Sumit Guha, *Health and Population in South Asia: From Earliest Times to the Present* (New Delhi, 2001), chap. 3. For a more general discussion of the historiography on the family, East and West, see Jack Goody, *The East in the West* (Cambridge, 1996), chap. 6.

85 Guha, *Health and Population*, p. 103.

86 Durgaprasad Bhattacharya (ed.), *Census of India 1961: Report on the Population Estimates of India*, vol. III, *1811–1820* (1963), part A, "Eastern Region," p. 22.

87 Durgaprasad Bhattacharya and Bibhavati Bhattacharya (eds.), *Census of India 1961: Report on the Population Estimates of India (1820–1830)* (1963), p. 45.

88 Hajnal, "Preindustrial Household Formation," p. 463. As Hajnal notes, both joint and nuclear families can yield comparable figures for household size, in the former due to the presence of multiple related adults, in the latter due to the inclusion of unrelated servants. The data on the number of adult males per household in India suggest the preponderance of nuclear families, however.

89 Tim Dyson, "The Historical Demography of Berar, 1881–1980," in Tim Dyson (ed.), *India's Historical Demography: Studies in Famine, Disease and Society* (London, 1989), p. 169.

90 Ibid., p. 185.

91 Ibid., p. 185.

92 Monica Das Gupta, "Fertility Decline in Punjab: Parallels with Historical Europe," *Population Studies*, 49 (1995), pp. 481–500.

93 Malavika Kasturi, *Embattled Identities: Rajput Lineages and the Colonial State in Nineteenth-Century North India* (Delhi, 2002), chap. 3.

94 Jones, *European Miracle*, chap. 2.

95 Ibid., p. 30. Our understanding of famine has become more sophisticated since the publication of Amartya Kumar Sen, *Poverty and Famines: An Essay on Entitlement and Deprivation* (Oxford, 1981).

96 Jones, *European Miracle*, p. 31.

97 Ibid., p. 29.

98 Brian J. Murton, "Land and Class: Cultural, Social and Biophysical Integration in Interior Tamilnadu in the Late Eighteenth Century," in Robert E. Frykenberg (ed.), *Land Tenure and Peasant in South Asia* (Delhi, 1977), pp. 90–1.

99 See Parthasarathi, *Transition to a Colonial Economy*, pp. 43–53. For a discussion of the mobility of artisans, see Douglas E. Haynes and Tirthankar Roy, "Conceiving Mobility: Weavers' Migrations in Pre-Colonial and Colonial India," *IESHR*, 36 (1999), pp. 35–67.

100 Parthasarathi, *Transition to a Colonial Economy*, p. 37. Also see Bhaskar Jyoti Basu, "Trading World of Coromandel and the Crisis of the 1730s," *Proceedings of the Indian History Congress*, 42nd Session, Bodh-Gaya (1981), pp. 333–9.

101 Jones, *European Miracle*, p. 29.

102 Datta, *Society, Economy and the Market*, pp. 260–4.

103 Jones, *European Miracle*, p. 30.

104 Datta, *Society, Economy and the Market*, p. 240.

105 Ibid., p. 244.

106 Ibid., p. 257.

107 Ibid., p. 259.

108 Ibid., p. 259.

109 Parthasarathi, *Transition to a Colonial Economy*, p. 37; Datta, *Society, Economy and the Market*, pp. 78–9.

110 Bayly, *Rulers, Townsmen and Bazaars*, p. 37.

111 For a recent affirmation of the Weberian argument, see Margaret C. Jacob and Matthew Kadane, "Missing, Now Found in the Eighteenth Century: Weber's Protestant Capitalist," *American Historical Review*, 108 (2003), pp. 20–49.

112 Max Weber, *The Protestant Ethic and the Spirit of Capitalism*, trans. Talcott Parsons (London, 1992, reprint of 1930 edn.), pp. 13–17.

113 Ibid., p. 24.

114 Ibid., p. 25.

115 H. H. Gerth and C. Wright Mills (eds.), *From Max Weber: Essays in Sociology* (New York, 1946), p. 293.

116 Max Weber, *The Religion of China*, trans. Hans H. Gerth (New York, 1951), pp. 236–7.

117 Gerth and Mills, *From Max Weber*, p. 275.

118 Max Weber, *The Religion of India*, trans. Hans H. Gerth and Don Martindale (New York, 1958), p. 121.

119 Ibid., p. 111.

120 Ibid., p. 112.

121 Gerth and Mills, *From Max Weber*, p. 294.

122 C. A. Bayly, "Pre-Colonial Indian Merchants and Rationality," in Mushirul Hasan and Narayani Gupta (eds.), *India's Colonial Encounter: Essays in Memory of Eric Stokes* (New Delhi, 1993), p. 18.

123 Ibid., p. 18.

124 Parthasarathi, *Transition to a Colonial Economy*, pp. 109–10. Perlin, "Proto-Industrialization and Pre-Colonial South Asia," pp. 77–8.

125 William Rowe, *Hankow: Commerce and Society in a Chinese City, 1796–1889* (Stanford, 1984), pp. 73–6.

126 Bayly, "Pre-Colonial Indian Merchants and Rationality," pp. 17–21.

127 Perlin, "State Formation Reconsidered," pp. 439–43.

128 Ibid., p. 435.

129 Stein, "State Formation and Economy Reconsidered," pp. 400–7; Norbert Peabody, *Hindu Kingship and Polity in Precolonial India* (Cambridge, 2003), pp. 132–3.

130 Acemoglu, Johnson and Robinson, "Colonial Origins of Comparative Development."

131 S. R. Epstein, *Freedom and Growth: The Rise of States and Markets in Europe, 1300–1750* (London, 2000), pp. 172–3.

4 The European response to Indian cottons

1 S. D. Chapman and S. Chassagne, *European Textile Printers in the Eighteenth Century: A Study of Peel and Oberkampf* (London, 1981), p. 204.

2 The potential market for the successful innovator in cotton is a more satisfying explanation for why technical change in the eighteenth-century European textile industry centered on cotton than the well-worn story that cotton was easier to work and, therefore, mechanize than wool. See, for instance, David S. Landes, *The Unbound Prometheus: Technological Change and Industrial Development in Western Europe from 1750 to the Present* (Cambridge, 1969), p. 83. If cotton was easier to work with, we must also ask why it was so difficult for Europeans to spin good-quality warp yarn by hand.

3 Chapman and Chassagne, *European Textile Printers*, pp. 5 and 7.

4 Paul Schwartz, "Textile Printing," in Maurice Daumas (ed.), *A History of Technology and Invention: Progress through the Ages*, vol. III, *The Expansion of Mechanization, 1725–1860*, trans. Eileen B. Hennessy (New York, 1979), p. 633; Maureen Fennell Mazzaoui, *The Italian Cotton Industry in the Later Middle Ages, 1100–1600* (Cambridge, 1981), p. 96.

5 Frank Lewis, *English Chintz: A History of Printed Fabrics from Earliest Times to the Present Day* (Leigh-on-Sea, Essex, 1942), p. 12.

6 Schwartz, "Textile Printing," p. 638.

7 George P. Baker, *Calico Painting and Printing in the East Indies in the XVIIth and XVIIIth Centuries* (London, 1921), p. 43.

8 For further details see ibid., p. 17. Also see Giorgio Riello, "Asian Knowledge and the Development of Calico Printing in Europe in the Seventeenth and Eighteenth Centuries," *Journal of Global History*, 5 (2010), pp. 1–28.

9 Edgard Depitre, *La toile peinte en France au xvii et au xviii siècles; industrie, commerce, prohibitions* (Paris, 1912), Preface. Quoted in Baker, *Calico Painting and Printing*, p. 50.

10 Schwartz, "Textile Printing," pp. 651–2.

11 Ibid., p. 652.
12 Claudius Rey, *The Weavers True Case; or, the Wearing of Printed Callicoes and Linnen Destructive to the Woollen and Silk Manufacturies* (London, 1719), p. 39.
13 J. K. J. Thomson, *A Distinctive Industrialization: Cotton in Barcelona, 1728–1832* (Cambridge, 1992), pp. 64–5.
14 Chapman and Chassagne, *European Textile Printers*, pp. 154–61; Pierre Caspard, "Manufacture and Trade in Calico Printing at Neuchâtel," *Textile History*, 8 (1977), pp. 151–2.
15 P. J. Thomas, *Mercantilism and the East India Trade* (London, 1926), p. 133.
16 Schwartz, "Textile Printing," p. 640.
17 Alfred P. Wadsworth and Julia de Lacy Mann, *The Cotton Trade and Industrial Lancashire, 1600–1780* (Manchester, 1931, repr. New York, 1968), pp. 139–41.
18 Victoria and Albert Museum, *English Printed Textiles 1720–1836* (London, 1960), p. 1. Emphasis added.
19 Wendy Hefford, *The Victoria and Albert Museum's Textile Collection: Design for Printed Textiles in England from 1750 to 1850* (New York, 1992), p. 154.
20 Quoted in Chapman and Chassagne, *European Textile Printers*, p. 105.
21 Florence Montgomery, *Textiles in America, 1650–1870* (New York, 1984), p. 259.
22 Ibid., p. 197.
23 Chapman and Chassagne, *European Textile Printers*, pp. 194–5.
24 Ibid., p. 38.
25 *Journal of the House of Commons*, vol. 34, 5/6/1774, p. 709.
26 Margaret Cater to Mrs. Mary Williamson, 17 October 1776, Bedfordshire and Luton Archives and Record Service, M10/4/34, quoted in John Styles, *The Dress of the People: Everyday Fashion in Eighteenth-Century England* (New Haven, 2007), p. 127.
27 T/70/20, pp. 3, 10–12, 15–17, etc., TNA: PRO.
28 T/70/120, pp. 30 and 44, TNA: PRO; Wadsworth and Mann, *Cotton Trade*, pp. 154–5.
29 The next chapter has a more detailed discussion of French production for West African markets.
30 T/70/1517, Letter from Thomas Melvil, Cape Coast Castle to Committee of the Company of Merchants Trading to Africa, 23 July 1751, TNA: PRO.
31 T/70/22, ff. 2, 4, 48, TNA: PRO.
32 T/70/1518, Letter from Thomas Melvil, Cape Coast Castle to Committee of the Company of Merchants Trading to Africa, 20 August 1752, TNA: PRO.

33 Wadsworth and Mann, *Cotton Trade*, pp. 153–5. On the preference for all-cotton cloths, see also Thomas Norris to William Hollier, Chorley, 3 December 1751, T/70/1517, TNA: PRO; Newdigate and Ford to Sam Poirier, Manchester, 13 August 1754, T/70/1522, TNA: PRO.

34 BT/1/447, Memorial of the Merchants of Liverpool Trading to Africa to the Commissioners of His Majesty's Treasury, 16 March 1765, TNA: PRO. Emphasis added.

35 BT/6/9, The Examination of Samuel Taylor Esquire, 8 March 1788, pp. 309–11, TNA: PRO.

36 Wadsworth and Mann, *Cotton Trade*, pp. 179–81.

37 For an analysis which also emphasizes the centrality of cloth quality for the development of the eighteenth-century British cotton industry, see Maxine Berg, "Quality, Cotton and the Global Luxury Trade," in Giorgio Riello and Tirthankar Roy (eds.), *How India Clothed the World: The World of South Asian Textiles, 1500–1850* (Leiden, 2009), pp. 391–414.

38 This by no means exhausts the explanations for innovation in the British textile industry. Also see Trevor Griffiths, Philip Hunt and Patrick 'O'Brien, "Scottish, Irish, and Imperial Connections: Parliament, the Three Kingdoms, and the Mechanization of Cotton Spinning in Eighteenth-Century Britain," *Economic History Review*, n.s., 61 (2008), pp. 625–50; Robert C. Allen, "The Industrial Revolution in Miniature: The Spinning Jenny in Britain, France, and India," *JEH*, 69 (2009), pp. 901–27; Robert C. Allen, *The British Industrial Revolution in Global Perspective* (Cambridge, 2009), chap. 8. These contributions have yet to receive the wide assent of the challenge and response model, however. In general, the study of technological change in eighteenth-century Britain has moved from the study of individual sectors. See Kristine Bruland, "Industrialization and Technological Change," in Roderick Floud and Paul Johnson (eds.), *The Cambridge Economic History of Modern Britain*, vol. I, *Industrialization, 1700–1860* (Cambridge, 2004), pp. 117–46.

39 Edward Baines, *History of the Cotton Manufacture in Great Britain* (London, 1835), pp. 6 and 7.

40 Ibid., pp. 9, 76–7.

41 Ibid., pp. 9, 77, 81.

42 Ibid., pp. 115–16.

43 Paul Mantoux, *The Industrial Revolution in the Eighteenth Century: An Outline of the Beginnings of the Modern Factory System in England* (Chicago, 1983; reprint of revised edition of London, 1961), pp. 203, 217.

44 Thomas Ellison, *The Cotton Trade of Great Britain* (London, 1886), pp. 13 and 14–15.

45 Wadsworth and Mann, *Cotton Trade*, p. 471. The diffusion of the fly shuttle is also now known to have been limited before the late eighteenth century. See Akos Paulinyi, "John Kay's Flying Shuttle: Some Considerations on His Technical Capacity and Economic Impact," *Textile History*, 17 (1986), pp. 149–66.

46 A similar dropping of the Indian connection happened in calico printing. See Riello, "Asian Knowledge and the Development of Calico Printing."

47 Landes, *Unbound Prometheus*, p. 57; Phyllis Deane, *The First Industrial Revolution* (Cambridge, 1965), pp. 86 and 87; Eric Hobsbawm, *Industry and Empire: The Birth of the Industrial Revolution* (new edn., London, 1999), p. 36.

48 M. J. Daunton, *Progress and Poverty: An Economic and Social History of Britain 1700–1850* (Oxford, 1995), p. 187. Geoffrey Timmins, "Technological Change," in Mary Rose (ed.), *The Lancashire Cotton Industry: A History since 1700* (Preston, 1996), pp. 39–40.

49 Patrick O'Brien, Trevor Griffiths and Philip Hunt, "Political Components of the Industrial Revolution: Parliament and the English Cotton Textile Industry, 1660–1774," *Economic History Review*, n.s., 44 (1991), pp. 395–423.

50 Trevor Griffiths, Philip Hunt and Patrick O'Brien, "The Curious History and Imminent Demise of the Challenge and Response Model," in Maxine Berg and Kristine Bruland (eds.), *Technological Revolutions in Europe: Historical Perspectives* (Cheltenham, 1998), pp. 119–37.

51 Patrick O'Brien, Trevor Griffiths and Philip Hunt, "Technological Change During the First Industrial Revolution: The Paradigm Case of Textiles, 1688–1851," in Robert Fox (ed.), *Technological Change: Methods and Themes in the History of Technology* (Amsterdam, 1996), p. 163. Also see Paulinyi, "John Kay's Flying Shuttle," pp. 149–66.

52 Richard Guest, *A Compendious History of the Cotton Manufacture* (Manchester, 1823), pp. 12–13.

53 John Aikin, *A Description of the Country from Thirty to Forty Miles Round Manchester* (London, 1795), p. 167.

54 "From the time that the original system was changed in the fustian branch, of buying pieces in the grey from the weavers, by delivering them out work, the custom of giving them out weft in the cops, which obtained for a while, grew into disuse, as there was no detecting the knavery of spinners till a piece came in woven; so that the practice was changed, and wool given with warps, the weaver answering for spinning; and the weavers, in a scarcity of spinning, have been paid less for the weft than they gave the spinner, but durst not complain, much less abate the spinner, lest their looms should stand unemployed; but when

jennies were introduced and children could work on them, the case was altered." James Ogden, *A Description of Manchester: Giving an Historical Account of those Limits in which the Town was Formerly Included* (Manchester, 1783), p. 88.

55 Cited in Mantoux, *Industrial Revolution*, p. 215. Yarn shortages at harvest time were not unique to Britain. See Prasannan Parthasarathi, *The Transition to a Colonial Economy: Weavers, Merchants and Kings in South India, 1720–1800* (Cambridge, 2001), pp. 57–8.

56 Sir Henry Trueman Wood, *A History of the Royal Society of the Arts* (London, 1913), p. 259; Derek Hudson and Kenneth W. Luckhurst, *The Royal Society of Arts, 1754–1954* (London, 1954), p. 129.

57 In 1754 and in 1787 Manchester cloth manufacturers reported delays in supplying goods because workers had "mostly gone off into the harvest" and "owing to the hay harvest." The fact that spinners were not specified suggests that many textile manufacturers, including weavers, contributed to the harvest work. It is also notable that the second statement comes after the invention of a variety of spinning machines. See T/70/1522 and C/107/9, TNA: PRO.

58 Robert Dossie, *Memoirs of Agriculture and Other Oeconomical Arts* (London, 1768), vol. I, pp. 93 and 94.

59 Ibid., p. 94.

60 *Premiums Offered by the Society Instituted at London for the Encouragement of Arts, Manufactures and Commerce* (London, 1760), p. 36.

61 Mr. Moore to the Royal Society, no date, no place, Guard Book No. 3, Item No. 19, Archives of the Royal Society of Arts.

62 *Commons Journal*, vol. 34, pp. 496–7, quoted in R. S. Fitton and A. P. Wadsworth, *The Strutts and the Arkwrights* (Manchester, 1958), p. 70.

63 *The Case of Mr. Richard Arkwright and Co. In Relation to Mr. Arkwright's Invention of an Engine for Spinning Cotton, etc. into Yarn* (London, 1782), pp. 1–2.

64 When John Holker, Jr., learned of the water frame he was "ecstatic" because it could "allow the French to imitate some cloths which were now imported from India in huge quantities and which they had been unable to copy successfully." J. R. Harris, *Industrial Espionage and Technology Transfer: Britain and France in the Eighteenth Century* (Aldershot, 1998), p. 366.

65 Letter to McConnel and Kennedy, Bolton, 30 December 1802, ZCR/6/4, Bolton Central Library.

66 Draft of a Letter from Crompton to Sir Joseph Banks, Bolton, 30 October 1807, Egerton MSS, BL. Typescript consulted in the Wadsworth MSS, Eng MSS 1206, Box 1/5, John Rylands Library, Manchester.

67 Letter to the Merchants Manufacturers Cotton Spiners Bleachers Printers, &c. of these United Kingdoms, Bolton, 25 April 1811, ZCR/15/18, Bolton Central Library.

68 Petition from Samuel Crompton to the House of Commons, Bolton, 29 May 1825, Bolton Central Library, ZCR/43/3.

69 *Case of Mr. Richard Arkwright and Co.*, p. 2.

70 Letter from Mrs. Strutt to her husband, Jedediah Strutt, 14 February 1774, in Fitton and Wadsworth, *The Strutts and the Arkwrights*, p. 73.

71 George Walker, *Observations, Founded on Facts, upon the Propriety or Impropriety of Exporting Cotton Twist, for the Purpose of Being Manufactured into Cloth by Foreigners* (London, 1803), p. 30.

72 Mercator, *A Second Letter to the Inhabitants of Manchester on the Exportation of Twist* (Manchester, 1800), pp. 9–11.

73 T. Hawkes, "Observations on the Cotton Trade of Manchester, in a Series of Essays," unpublished manuscript, c.1793, Manuscript B.R.338.1 H3, Manchester Central Library.

74 *Thoughts on the Use of Machines in the Cotton Manufacture: Addressed to the Working People in that Manufacture, and the Poor in General. By a Friend of the Poor* (Manchester, 1780), p. 16.

75 Official Papers of First Earl of Liverpool, Liverpool Papers, Add MS 38342, 1776, ff. 232–37, BL.

76 *The Gentleman's Magazine*, vol. 24 (1754), p. 140.

77 Griffiths, Hunt and O'Brien, "Scottish, Irish, and Imperial Connections," p. 638.

78 Wadsworth and Mann, *Cotton Trade*, p. 447.

79 Ibid., p. 122.

80 Ibid., p. 123; Harris, *Industrial Espionage and Technology Transfer*, p. 32.

81 Quoted in Thomas, *Mercantilism and the East India Trade*, p. 128.

82 Ibid., p. 128.

83 *Considerations on the East India Trade* (London, 1701), in *A Select Collection of Early English Tracts on Commerce*, ed. J. R. McCulloch (London, 1856, repr. Cambridge, 1954), pp. 589–90.

84 Joseph E. Inikori, *Africans and the Industrial Revolution in England: A Study in International Trade and Economic Development* (Cambridge, 2002), pp. 427–51.

85 Trevor Griffiths, Philip Hunt and Patrick O'Brien write, "What pressures [in cotton textile manufacturing] were felt were specific to the spinning of yarn." See their "Scottish, Irish, and Imperial Connections," p. 627.

86 Allen, *British Industrial Revolution in Global Perspective*, chap. 8. Also see Allen, "Industrial Revolution in Miniature."

87 The lecture was published in the Memoirs of the Society in 1819 and reprinted in John Kennedy, *Miscellaneous Papers, On Subjects Connected with the Manufactures of Lancashire* (Manchester, 1849).

88 This was also published in Kennedy, *Miscellaneous Papers*.

89 John Kennedy, "A Brief Memoir of Samuel Crompton," *Miscellaneous Papers*, p. 70.

90 John Kennedy, "Observations," in *Miscellaneous Papers*, pp. 6–8.

91 Adam Smith, *An Inquiry into the Nature and Causes of the Wealth of Nations*, 2 vols. (Oxford, 1976), vol. I, p. 20.

92 Fitton and Wadsworth, *The Strutts and the Arkwrights*, pp. 68–70.

93 John Wright, M.D., *An Address to the Members of Both Houses of Parliament on the Late Tax Laid on Fustian and Other Cotton Goods* (Warrington, 1785), p. 9.

94 Minutes of a General Meeting of the Cotton-Spinners, and Manufacturers . . . residing in Glasgow, Paisley, and the neighbourhood, Glasgow, 13 February 1788, BT/6/140, f. 36, TNA: PRO. This association generated a huge pamphlet, broadside and other literature.

95 Although it should be noted that in 1785 the cotton and woolen manufacturers of Manchester expressed support for free trade in the countries to the east of the Cape of Good Hope. See Broadside dated 24 May 1785, Shelfmark 1856.c.5 (74), BL. For an overview of the rise of free trade ideas in Manchester, see Arthur Redford, *Manchester Merchants and Foreign Trade, 1794–1858* (Manchester, 1934, repr. Manchester 1973), chap. 10; Michael J. Turner, "Before the Manchester School: Economic Theory in Early Nineteenth-Century Manchester," *History*, 79 (1994), pp. 218–29.

96 Letter from Samuel Turner, Secretary of the Provincial Chamber at Nottingham, to John Kearsley, Chairman of the Fustian Manufactures Committee, Manchester, Nottingham, 5 March 1787, Liverpool Papers, Add MS 38376, f. 19, BL. The debate on exports of cotton yarn also inspired a voluminous literature.

97 *At a Special Meeting of Merchants, Manufacturers, and Cotton Spinners, held at Spencer's Tavern in Manchester, on Friday, 2d day of May, 1800*, Shelfmark 937.g.14, BL.

98 Letter to the Committee at Manchester, meeting to oppose the exclusive Trade of the East India Company, Manchester, 15 April 1812, ZCR/19/5, Bolton Central Library. Also see Redford, *Manchester Merchants*, chap. 9.

99 Derek Fraser, "Edward Baines," in Patricia Hollis (ed.), *Pressure from Without in Early Victorian England* (London, 1974), pp. 186–7.

100 *Leeds Mercury*, 13 February 1830, quoted in Fraser, "Edward Baines," p. 187.

5 State and market: Britain, France and the Ottoman Empire

1 Gabor Agoston, *Guns for the Sultan: Military Power and the Weapons Industry in the Ottoman Empire* (Cambridge, 2005).

2 For an example of the Western bias of Ottomanists when it comes to cottons, see Suraiya Faroqhi, "Ottoman Cotton Textiles: The Story of a Success that did not Last, 1500–1800," in Giorgio Riello and Prasannan Parthasarathi (eds.), *The Spinning World: A Global History of Cotton Textiles, 1200–1850* (Oxford, 2009), pp. 89–103. But also see the important articles by Halil İnalcık, "The Ottoman Cotton Market and India: The Role of Labor Cost in Market Competition," in his *The Middle East and the Balkans under the Ottoman Empire: Essays on Economy and Society* (Bloomington, 1993), pp. 264–306; and Gilles Veinstein, "Commercial Relations between India and the Ottoman Empire (Late Fifteenth to Late Eighteenth Centuries): A Few Notes and Hypotheses," in Sushil Chaudhury and Michel Morineau (eds.), *Merchants, Companies and Trade: Europe and Asia in the Early Modern Era* (Cambridge, 1999), pp. 95–115.

3 The publication of Giancarlo Casale's *The Ottoman Age of Exploration* (Oxford, 2010) may mark the beginnings of an Ottoman historical interest in the Indian Ocean, however.

4 See Şevket Pamuk, *A Monetary History of the Ottoman Empire* (Cambridge, 2000).

5 Katsumi Fukasawa, *Toilerie et commerce du Levant: d'Alep à Marseilles* (Paris, 1987), p. 39.

6 K. N. Chaudhuri, *The Trading World of Asia and the East India Company, 1660–1760* (Cambridge, 1978), pp. 246–7.

7 Robert Paris, *Histoire du commerce de Marseille*, vol. V, *De 1660 à 1789; le Levant* (Paris, 1957), pp. 548–56.

8 Fukasawa, *Toilerie et commerce du Levant*, p. 41.

9 Donald Quataert, "Introduction," in Donald Quataert (ed.), *Consumption Studies and the History of the Ottoman Empire, 1550–1922: An Introduction* (Albany, 2000), p. 10.

10 Donald Quataert, "Clothing Laws, State, and Society in the Ottoman Empire, 1720–1829," *International Journal of Middle East Studies*, 29 (1997), p. 411.

11 Ibid., p. 424, note 59. Also see Edhem Eldem, who writes, "As western traders often noted, the *nec plus ultra* in sartorial tastes and expenditures were not these western products but rather eastern fabrics – muslins, shawls – the fineness and beauty of which could never be matched by the coarser and heavier woollens of the West." See Edhem Eldem, *French Trade in Istanbul in the Eighteenth Century* (Leiden, 1999), p. 45.

12 Halil İnalcık, "When and How British Cotton Goods Invaded the Levant Markets," in Huri İslamoğlu-İnan (ed.), *The Ottoman Empire and the World Economy* (Cambridge, 1987), pp. 375 and 376.

13 According to Afaf Marsot, "Egypt had always been a cotton-textile exporting country." *Egypt in the Reign of Muhammad Ali* (Cambridge, 1984), p. 162.

14 André Raymond, *Artisans et commerçants au Caire au xviii siècle*, 2 vols. (Damascus, 1973), vol. I, p. 65.

15 It should be noted that French woolen cloth exports took off in the 1770s. See André Raymond, "L'impact de la pénétration Européenne sur l'économie de l'Égypte au xviii siècle," *Annales islamologiques*, 18 (1982), p. 227.

16 André Raymond, "Les sources de la richesse urbaine au Caire au dix-huitième siècle," in Thomas Naff and Roger Owen (eds.), *Studies in Eighteenth Century Islamic History* (Carbondale, Ill., 1977), p. 199.

17 Ibid., pp. 194–5.

18 Necmi Ülker, "The Emergence of İzmir as a Mediterranean Commercial Center for the French and English Interests, 1698–1740," *International Journal of Turkish Studies*, 4 (1987), pp. 32–3. Elena Frangakis-Syrett, *The Commerce of Smyrna in the Eighteenth Century (1700–1820)* (Athens, 1992), pp. 316–17.

19 Elena Frangakis-Syrett, "The Trade of Cotton and Cloth in İzmir: From the Second Half of the Eighteenth Century to the Early Nineteenth Century," in Çaglar Keyder and Faruk Tabak (eds.), *Landholding and Commercial Agriculture in the Middle East* (Albany, 1991), pp. 97–8.

20 Frangakis-Syrett, *Commerce of Smyrna*, pp. 318–19.

21 A. B. Cunningham (ed.), "The Journal of Christophe Aubin: A Report on the Levant Trade in 1812," *Archivum Ottomanicum*, 7 (1983), p. 68.

22 Ibid., p. 87.

23 İnalcık, "Ottoman Cotton Market and India"; Rudiger Klein, "Trade in the Safavid Port City Bandar Abbas and the Persian Gulf Area (*ca.*1600–1680): A Study of Selected Aspects," unpublished Ph.D. dissertation, University of London, 1994, chap. 5.

24 İnalcık, "Ottoman Cotton Market and India," p. 264.

25 Veinstein, "Commercial Relations," pp. 104–5.

26 Ibid., p. 105.

27 M. de (Charles) Peyssonnel, *Traité sur le commerce de la mer Noire*, 2 vols. (Paris, 1787), vol. I, p. 47.

28 Fukasawa, *Toilerie et commerce du Levant*, pp. 24, 51–2.

29 Ibid., p. 44.

30 İnalcık, "British Cotton Goods," pp. 374–5.

31 İnalcık, "Ottoman Cotton Market and India," p. 272.

32 Quoted in ibid., pp. 272–3.

33 Pamuk, *Monetary History of the Ottoman Empire*, p. 18.

34 Modern trade theory has made the case for free trade less compelling, however. See Paul R. Krugman, "Is Free Trade Passé?" *Journal of Economic Perspectives*, 1 (1987), pp. 131–44 and Paul R. Krugman, "Trade, Accumulation, and Uneven Development," *Journal of Development Economics*, 8 (1981), pp. 149–61.

35 Robert C. Allen, *The British Industrial Revolution in Global Perspective* (Cambridge, 2009); Joel Mokyr, *The Enlightened Economy: An Economic History of Britain 1700–1850* (New Haven, 2009).

36 P. J. Thomas, *Mercantilism and the East India Trade* (London, 1926), p. 66.

37 Ibid., p. 105.

38 Ibid., pp. 105–17.

39 Alfred P. Wadsworth and Julia de Lacy Mann, *The Cotton Trade and Industrial Lancashire, 1600–1780* (Manchester, 1931, repr. New York, 1968), chap. 7.

40 Cited in ibid., pp. 132–3.

41 *Reasons Humbly offer'd to the Honourable House of Commons, against a Duty intended to be laid upon Silks, Manufactured, Printed, or Stained, as far as it concerns Handkerchiefs* (London, 1711).

42 Thomas, *Mercantilism and the East India Trade*, p. 141. Also see Natalie Rothstein, "The Calico Campaign of 1719–1721," *East London Papers*, 7 (1964), pp. 3–21.

43 Thomas, *Mercantilism and the East India Trade*, p. 160.

44 Official Papers of First Earl of Liverpool, Liverpool Papers, Add MS 38342, 1776?, ff. 232–37, BL.

45 Wadsworth and Mann, *Cotton Trade*, p. 144.

46 For a fascinating exploration of the ways in which the operation of the excise supported English manufacturing, see William J. Ashworth, *Customs and Excise: Trade, Production, and Consumption in England, 1640–1845* (Oxford, 2003).

47 Official Papers of First Earl of Liverpool, Liverpool Papers, Add MS 38342, 1776?, ff. 232–37, BL.

48 Patrick O'Brien, Trevor Griffiths and Philip Hunt, "Political Components of the Industrial Revolution: Parliament and the English Cotton Textile Industry, 1660–1774," *Economic History Review*, n.s., 44 (1991), p. 414.

49 Samuel Oldknow Papers, John Rylands Library, Manchester, Eng MSS 751. The English East India Company catalog is Eng MSS 839.

50 See, for instance, BT/6/140, f. 36, TNA: PRO.

51 BT/6/140, f. 36, TNA: PRO.

52 Mehmet Genç, "Ottoman Industry in the Eighteenth Century," in Donald Quataert (ed.), *Manufacturing in the Ottoman Empire and Turkey, 1500–1950* (Albany, N.Y., 1994), p. 60.

53 Ibid., pp. 68–74. The quoted passages are on pp. 69–70 and 73.

54 Ibid., pp. 78–82.

55 Thomas Smith, *A Discourse of the Common Weal of this Realm of England*, ed. Elizabeth Lamond (Cambridge, 1954), p. 65. The spelling of the original has been modernized.

56 See Joan Thirsk, *Economic Policy and Projects: The Development of a Consumer Society in Early Modern England* (Oxford, 1978), p. 31.

57 O'Brien, Griffiths and Hunt, "Political Components of the Industrial Revolution," p. 418.

58 Calculated from figures given in Ralph Davis, "English Foreign Trade, 1700–1774," *Economic History Review*, 2nd ser., 15 (1962), pp. 302–3.

59 Calculated from data in ibid., pp. 302–3 and Joseph E. Inikori, *Africans and the Industrial Revolution in England: A Study in International Trade and Economic Development* (Cambridge, 2002), p. 444.

60 Wadsworth and Mann, *Cotton Trade*, p. 146.

61 Robert S. DuPlessis, "Cloth and the Emergence of the Atlantic Economy," in Peter Coclanis (ed.), *The Atlantic Economy during the Seventeenth and Eighteenth Centuries* (Columbia, S.C., 2005), p. 78; Robert S. DuPlessis, "Cottons Consumption in the Seventeenth- and Eighteenth-Century North Atlantic," in Riello and Parthasarathi, *Spinning World*, pp. 230–1.

62 Elizabeth Schumpeter, *English Overseas Trade Statistics, 1697–1808* (Oxford, 1960), Table xxxvii, p. 67.

63 Davis, "English Foreign Trade," p. 297.

64 David Ormrod, *The Rise of Commercial Empires: England and the Netherlands in the Age of Mercantilism* (Cambridge, 2003), pp. 337–8. In a similar vein, Patrick O'Brien has pointed repeatedly to the key role that the navy played in the economic development of Britain in the eighteenth century. As we will see in the next chapter, the navy protected the coal trade along the east coast, which was critical for the expansion of British coal mining. See Patrick O'Brien, "Mercantilism and Imperialism in the Rise and Decline of the Dutch and British Economies 1585–1815," *De Economist*, 148 (2000), pp. 469–501; and Patrick Karl O'Brien, "Fiscal and Financial Preconditions for the Rise of British Naval Hegemony 1485–1815," London School of Economics, Department of Economic History Working Paper, No. 91/05, November 2005.

65 Paul Butel, *The Atlantic*, trans. Iain Hamilton Grant (London, 1999), chap. 5.

66 Fukasawa, *Toilerie et commerce du Levant*, p. 45.

67 Olivier Raveux, "Spaces and Technologies in the Cotton Industry in the Seventeenth and Eighteenth Centuries: The Example of Printed Calicoes in Marseilles," *Textile History*, 36 (2005), pp. 132–3.

68 Edgard Depitre, *La toile peinte en France au xvii et au xviii siècles; industrie, commerce, prohibitions* (Paris, 1912), pp. 12, 41–2.

69 Raveux, "Spaces and Technologies," p. 134.

70 Olivier Raveux, "The Birth of a New European Industry: *L'Indiennage* in Seventeenth-Century Marseilles," in Riello and Parthasarathi, *Spinning World*, pp. 304–5; Raveux, "Spaces and Technologies," p. 134.

71 Depitre, *Toile peinte*, p. v.

72 Daniel Roche, *The Culture of Clothing: Dress and Fashion in the Ancien Régime*, trans. Jean Birrell (Cambridge, 1994), pp. 127 and 138.

73 Serge Chassagne, *Le coton et ses patrons: France, 1760–1840* (Paris, 1991), pp. 21–2.

74 Raveux, "Spaces and Technologies," p. 134.

75 Chassagne, *Coton et ses patrons*, p. 75.

76 Raveux, "Spaces and Technologies," pp. 134–5.

77 BT/6/140, f. 121, TNA: PRO.

78 Depitre, *Toile peinte*, pp. 48, 61; Fukasawa, *Toilerie et commerce du Levant*, pp. 51–2.

79 Ralph Davis, *The Industrial Revolution and British Overseas Trade* (Leicester, 1979), p. 94.

80 Robert Louis Stein, *The French Slave Trade in the Eighteenth Century: An Old Regime Business* (Madison, 1979), p. 11.

81 David Richardson, "The Eighteenth-Century British Slave Trade: Estimates of its Volume and Coastal Distribution in Africa," *Research in Economic History*, 12 (1989), p. 157.

82 Paul Lovejoy, *Transformations in Slavery: A History of Slavery in Africa* (Cambridge, 1983), p. 48.

83 Gaston Martin, *Nantes au xviiie siècle: L'ère des négriers (1714–1774)* (Paris, 1931), p. 47.

84 Giorgio Riello, "The Globalization of Cotton Textiles: Indian Cottons, Europe, and the Atlantic World, 1600–1850," in Riello and Parthasarathi, *Spinning World*, pp. 282–3.

85 David Geggus, "The French Slave Trade: An Overview," *William and Mary Quarterly*, 58 (2001), p. 122.

86 Pierre H. Boulle, "Slave Trade, Commercial Organization and Industrial Growth in Eighteenth-Century Nantes," *Revue francaise d'histoire d'outre-mer*, 59 (1972), p. 78.

87 Ibid., p. 97.

88 Ibid., p. 99.

89 Ibid., pp. 99 and 102; Depitre, *Toile peinte*, p. 154.

90 Boulle, "Slave Trade," p. 101.

91 Despite the limited export of French cotton cloth in the first three-quarters of the eighteenth century, France imported huge quantities of raw cotton from the Levant and the West Indies. Imports from the Levant to Marseilles alone were larger than the cotton imports of Britain for the first two-thirds of the century. A sizable fraction of Levant cotton was actually not used in France. According to a memorandum of the Marseilles Chamber of Commerce from 1766, cited by Katsumi Fukasawa, French merchants in Marseilles only purchased a third of the raw cotton imported from İzmir. The other two-thirds were shipped to Switzerland and Germany. See Fukasawa, *Toilerie et commerce du Levant*, p. 27.

92 Alexander Gerschenkron, *Economic Backwardness in Historical Perspective: A Book of Essays* (Cambridge, Mass., 1962), p. 20.

93 I reject writings that see state intervention in the economy as primarily rent seeking or redistributing existing wealth and income. State actions could also be creative and expand productive capacities. For views of mercantilism as rent seeking, see Robert B. Ekelund, Jr. and Robert D. Tollison, *Politicized Economies: Monarchy, Monopoly, and Mercantilism* (College Station, Tex., 1997) and Mokyr, *Enlightened Economy*, p. 393.

94 Smith, *Discourse of the Common Weal*, p. 65.

95 Thirsk, *Economic Policy and Projects*, p. 31.

96 Ibid., p. 101.

97 See the following by Patrick K. O'Brien: "Political Preconditions for the Industrial Revolution," in Patrick O'Brien and Roland Quinault (eds.), *The Industrial Revolution and British Society* (Cambridge, 1993), pp. 124–55; "State Formation and the Construction of Institutions for the First Industrial Nation," in Ha-Joon Chang, *Institutional Change and Economic Development* (New York, 2007), pp. 177–97; "The History, Nature and Economic Significance of an Exceptional Fiscal State for the Growth of the British Economy, 1453–1815," London School of Economics, Department of Economic History Working Paper, No. 109/08, October 2008.

98 Ormrod, *Rise of Commercial Empires*, p. 25.

99 M. J. Daunton, *Progress and Poverty: An Economic and Social History of Britain 1700–1850* (Oxford, 1995), chap. 18.

100 George Unwin, *Samuel Oldknow and the Arkwrights: The Industrial Revolution in Stockport and Marple* (2nd edn., New York, 1968), p. 98.

101 See T. S. Ashton, *An Economic History of England: The 18th Century* (London, 1955), chap. 7; John Rule, *The Experience of Labour in*

Eighteenth-Century English Industry (New York, 1981); Peter Linebaugh, *The London Hanged* (Cambridge, 1992).

102 The classic treatment of this dimension of mercantile thinking remains Edgar S. Furniss, *The Position of the Laborer in a System of Nationalism: A Study of the Labor Theories of the Later English Mercantilists* (Boston, 1920).

103 Prasannan Parthasarathi, *The Transition to a Colonial Economy: Weavers, Merchants and Kings in South India, 1720–1800* (Cambridge, 2001), chap. 5.

104 For an elaboration of this comparison, see Prasannan Parthasarathi, "Rethinking Wages and Competitiveness in the Eighteenth Century: Britain and South India," *P&P*, 158 (1998), pp. 79–109.

105 Jeff Horn, *The Path Not Taken: French Industrialization in the Age of Revolution, 1750–1830* (Cambridge, Mass., 2006), p. 22.

106 Florence Montgomery, *Textiles in America, 1650–1870* (New York, 1984), p. 347.

107 Chassagne, *Coton et ses patrons*, p. 22.

108 Ibid., pp. 27–30. The quoted phrase is on p. 30.

109 Ibid., p. 29.

110 Montgomery, *Textiles in America*, p. 347.

111 Ibid., pp. 347–8.

112 J. R. Harris, *Industrial Espionage and Technology Transfer: Britain and France in the Eighteenth Century* (Aldershot, 1998), p. 48. See also Chassagne, *Coton et ses patrons*, p. 46.

113 Harris, *Industrial Espionage and Technology Transfer*, pp. 54–63.

6 From cotton to coal

1 E. A. Wrigley, *Continuity, Chance and Change: The Character of the Industrial Revolution in England* (Cambridge, 1988).

2 Kenneth Pomeranz, *The Great Divergence: China, Europe and the Making of the Modern World Economy* (Princeton, 2000), pp. 62–8.

3 A. B. Cunningham (ed.), "The Journal of Christophe Aubin: A Report on the Levant Trade in 1812," *Archivum Ottomanicum*, 7 (1983), p. 68; Halil İnalcık, "When and How British Cotton Goods Invaded the Levant Markets," in Huri İslamoğlu-İnan (ed.), *The Ottoman Empire and the World Economy* (Cambridge, 1987), pp. 374–83; Joseph E. Inikori, *Africans and the Industrial Revolution in England: A Study in International Trade and Economic Development* (Cambridge, 2002), p. 447.

4 For a discussion of some of these issues in South India, see Prasannan Parthasarathi, "Historical Issues of Deindustrialization in Nineteenth-Century South India," in Giorgio Riello and Tirthankar Roy (eds.),

How India Clothed the World: The World of South Asian Textiles, 1500–1850 (Leiden, 2009), pp. 415–35.

5 N. F. R. Crafts and C. K. Harley, "Output Growth and the British Industrial Revolution: A Restatement of the Crafts–Harley View," *Economic History Review*, n.s. 45 (1992), p. 709.

6 Douglas Farnie, *The English Cotton Industry and the World Market, 1815–1896* (Oxford, 1979), p. 7.

7 Prasannan Parthasarathi, *The Transition to a Colonial Economy: Weavers, Merchants and Kings in South India, 1720–1800* (Cambridge, 2001), p. 77.

8 John Aikin, *A Description of the Country from Thirty to Forty Miles Round Manchester* (London, 1795), pp. 176–8, quoted in A. E. Musson and Eric Robinson, *Science and Technology in the Industrial Revolution* (Manchester, 1969), p. 433.

9 Musson and Robinson, *Science and Technology*, pp. 430–1.

10 Ibid., p. 435.

11 Ibid., p. 435.

12 Raphael Samuel, "Workshop of the World: Steam Power and Hand Technology in mid-Victorian Britain," *History Workshop*, 3 (1977), pp. 18–19.

13 G. N. von Tunzelmann, *Steam Power and British Industrialization to 1860* (Oxford, 1978), pp. 179 and 182–3. Also see the re-evaluation of the steam engine's contribution to British economic growth in Nicholas Crafts, "Productivity Growth in the Industrial Revolution: A New Growth Accounting Perspective," *JEH*, 64 (2004), pp. 521–35.

14 Von Tunzelmann, *Steam Power*, chap. 7.

15 Dolores Greenberg, "Reassessing the Power Patterns of the Industrial Revolution: An Anglo-American Comparison," *American Historical Review*, 87 (1982), pp. 1237–61.

16 Samuel, "Workshop of the World," pp. 46–7.

17 Ibid., p. 43.

18 John F. Richards, *The Unending Frontier: An Environmental History of the Early Modern World* (Berkeley, 2003), p. 4.

19 M. J. G. Leutmann, *Vulcanus Famulans oder Sonderbahre Feuer-Nutzung* (Wittenberg, 1720), cited in Rolf Peter Sieferle, *The Subterranean Forest: Energy Systems and the Industrial Revolution*, trans. Michael P. Osman (Cambridge, 2001), p. 1.

20 Sieferle, *Subterranean Forest*, p. 141.

21 Peter C. Perdue, *Exhausting the Earth: State and Peasant in Hunan, 1500–1850* (Cambridge, Mass., 1987); Robert B. Marks, *Tigers, Rice, Silk, and Silt: Environment and Economy in Late Imperial South China* (Cambridge, 1998); Anne Osborne, "Highlands and Lowlands: Economic

and Ecological Interactions in the Lower Yangzi Region under the Qing," in Mark Elvin and Liu Ts'ui-jung (eds.), *Sediments of Time: Environment and Society in Chinese History* (Cambridge, 1998), pp. 203–34; Conrad Totman, *The Green Archipelago: Forestry in Pre-Industrial Japan* (Athens, Ohio, 1998).

22 Robert Hartwell, "A Revolution in the Iron and Coal Industries during the Northern Sung," *JAS*, 21 (1962), pp. 153–62; Robert Hartwell, "A Cycle of Economic Change in Imperial China: Coal and Iron in Northeast China, 750–1350," *Journal of the Economic and Social History of the Orient*, 10 (1967), pp. 102–59.

23 Sung Ying-hsing, *T'ien Kung K'ai Wu: Chinese Technology in the Seventeenth Century*, trans. E-tu Zen Sun and Shiou-chuan Sun (University Park, Penn., 1966), p. 205.

24 Peter J. Golas, *Science and Civilisation in China*, vol. V, *Chemistry and Chemical Technology*, part 13, "Mining" (Cambridge, 1999), p. 197.

25 Susan Naquin, *Peking: Temples and City Life, 1400–1900* (Berkeley, 2000), pp. 127, 433, 479; Ferdinand, Freiherr von Richthofen, *Baron Richthofen's Letters, 1870–1872* (Shanghai, 1872?), pp. 29–36, 77–82, 94–5.

26 Golas, *Science and Civilisation*, p. 197.

27 Ibid., p. 200.

28 Von Richthofen, *Baron Richthofen's Letters*, p. 6.

29 William T. Rowe, *Hankow: Commerce and Society in a Chinese City, 1796–1889* (Stanford, 1984), pp. 57 and 82.

30 Von Richthofen, *Baron Richthofen's Letters*, p. 6.

31 Conrad Totman, *Early Modern Japan* (Berkeley, 1993), pp. 271–2.

32 Sieferle, *Subterranean Forest*, p. 162.

33 Paolo Malanima, "The Energy Basis for Early Modern Growth, 1650–1820," in Maarten Prak (ed.), *Early Modern Capitalism: Economic and Social Change in Europe, 1400–1800* (London, 2001), p. 57.

34 John Hatcher, *The History of the British Coal Industry*, vol. I, *Before 1700, Towards the Age of Coal* (Oxford, 1993), p. 47.

35 Hatcher, *History of the British Coal Industry*, p. 498.

36 Ibid., p. 409. Michael W. Flinn, *The History of the British Coal Industry*, vol. II, *1700–1830, The Industrial Revolution* (Oxford, 1984), p. 212.

37 For a breakdown of coal consumption by sector from 1700 to 1830, see Flinn, *History of the British Coal Industry*, pp. 252–3.

38 Pomeranz, *Great Divergence*, p. 64.

39 Theodore Walrond (ed.), *Letters and Journals of James, Eighth Earl of Elgin* (London, 1872), p. 298.

40 Osborne, "Highlands and Lowlands," pp. 207, 215. Also see her "Barren Mountains, Raging Rivers: The Ecological and Social Effects

of Changing Land Use on the Lower Yangzi Periphery in Late Imperial China," unpublished Ph.D. dissertation, Columbia University, 1989, pp. 69, 197, 209.

41 Hatcher, *History of the British Coal Industry*, p. 90.

42 John Nef, *The Rise of the British Coal Industry*, 2 vols. (London, 1932), vol. II, p. 201.

43 *The History and Description of Fossil Fuel, the Collieries, and Coal Trade of Great Britain* (London, 1835), pp. 363–4.

44 Nef, *Rise of the British Coal Industry*, vol. II, p. 203.

45 Hatcher, *History of the British Coal Industry*, p. 446; Flinn, *History of the British Coal Industry*, pp. 212–25.

46 Nef, *Rise of the British Coal Industry*, vol. II, pp. 219–20.

47 Ibid., pp. 221–38; T. S. Ashton and Joseph Sykes, *The Coal Industry of the Eighteenth Century* (Manchester, 1929), p. 247.

48 William J. Hausman, "A Model of the London Coal Trade in the Eighteenth Century," *Quarterly Journal of Economics*, 94 (1980), p. 11.

49 Ashton and Sykes, *Coal Industry*, p. 247.

50 Flinn, *History of the British Coal Industry*, p. 283; Nef, *Rise of the British Coal Industry*, vol. II, p. 314.

51 Flinn, *History of the British Coal Industry*, Table 8.1, p. 274.

52 Ibid., p. 27.

53 Edward Hughes, *North Country Life in the Eighteenth Century*, vol. I, *The North-East, 1700–1750* (Oxford, 1952), p. 177.

54 Nef, *Rise of the British Coal Industry*, vol. II, pp. 259–62.

55 Ashton and Sykes, *Coal Industry*, p. 212.

56 Flinn, *History of the British Coal Industry*, Table 8.1, p. 274.

57 *History and Description of Fossil Fuel*, p. 365.

58 Flinn, *History of the British Coal Industry*, p. 173.

59 Nef, *Rise of the British Coal Industry*, vol. II, pp. 296–302. The quotations appear on pp. 298 and 301.

60 Alan Pearsall, "The Royal Navy and the Protection of Trade in the Eighteenth Century," in *Guerres et paix, 1660–1815* (Vincennes, 1987), p. 155.

61 *The Late Measures of the Ship-Owners in the Coal Trade Fully Examined, in a Letter to the Right Honourable William Pitt* (London, 1786), pp. 39–45; *Letters Addressed to the Right Honourable William Pitt, Chancellor of the Exchequer of Great Britain* (London, 1793), pp. 120–1.

62 Joan Thirsk, *Economic Policy and Projects: The Development of a Consumer Society in Early Modern England* (Oxford, 1978), pp. 24–5. H. R. Schubert has written that the Crown was the "driving force" behind the expansion of the Sussex iron industry in the 1540s. See his *History of the British Iron and Steel Industry* (London, 1957), p. 170.

63 G. Hammersley, "The Charcoal Iron Industry and its Fuel, 1540–1750," *Economic History Review*, 2nd ser., 26 (1973), pp. 601–2.

64 Charles K. Hyde, *Technological Change and the British Iron Industry, 1700–1870* (Princeton, 1977), p. 43.

65 M. W. Flinn, "The Growth of the English Iron Industry 1660–1760," *Economic History Review*, 2nd ser., 11 (1958), pp. 151–2.

66 M. J. Daunton, *Progress and Poverty: An Economic and Social History of Britain 1700–1850* (Oxford, 1995), p. 545.

67 Charles K. Hyde, "Technological Change in the British Wrought Iron Industry, 1750–1815: A Reinterpretation," *Economic History Review*, 2nd ser., 27 (1974), pp. 204–5.

68 See T. S. Ashton, *Iron and Steel in the Industrial Revolution* (2nd edn., Manchester, 1951), chap. 5.

69 Hyde, "Technological Change in the British Wrought Iron Industry," pp. 195–6.

70 Mark Elvin, "Skills and Resources in Late Traditional China," in Dwight H. Perkins (ed.), *China's Modern Economy in Historical Perspective* (Stanford, 1975), p. 110.

71 William Rowe, *Saving the World: Chen Hongmou and Elite Consciousness in Eighteenth-Century China* (Stanford, 2001), p. 244. Also see Yoichi Miyazaki, "Seicho Zenki No Sekitangyo: Kanryuki No Tanko Seisaku To Keiei (Coal Mining in Early Qing China: Coal Mining Policies and Administration during the Qianlong Period)," *Shigaku Zasshi*, 100 (1991), pp. 36–63. I am grateful to Rebecca Nedostup for bringing this article to my attention and to Hidetaka Hirota for providing me with a summary translation.

72 Ku Yen-Wu, *T'ien-hsia chün-kuo li-ping shu* (Documents on the Strengths and Weaknesses of the Commanderies and Principates of the Empire) (1639–62), Ssu-k'u shan-pen edition, xxvi 36a–37b, quoted in Mark Elvin, *The Pattern of the Chinese Past* (Stanford, 1973), pp. 299–300.

73 Quoted in Donald B. Wagner, *The Traditional Chinese Iron Industry and its Modern Fate* (Richmond, 1997), pp. 49–50.

74 Wagner, *Traditional Chinese Iron Industry*, p. 36.

75 Von Richthofen, *Baron Richthofen's Letters*, p. 7.

76 Wagner, *Traditional Chinese Iron Industry*, chap. 5.

77 Translation of a passage on iron-smelting by Qu Dajun (1630–97), ibid., p. 65.

78 Qu Dajun, ibid., pp. 66–7.

79 Sarasin Viraphol, *Tribute and Profit: Sino-Siamese Trade, 1652–1853* (Cambridge, Mass., 1977), pp. 39–40, 200, 203. Wagner, *Traditional Chinese Iron Industry*, pp. 58, 73.

80 Pierre-Étienne Will and R. Bin Wong (with James Lee, Jean C. Oi and Peter C. Perdue), *Nourish the People: The State Civilian Granary System in China, 1650–1850* (Ann Arbor, 1991), p. 21.

81 Ibid., pp. 479–84; R. Bin Wong and Peter C. Perdue, "Famine's Foes in Ch'ing China," *Harvard Journal of Asiatic Studies*, 43 (1983), pp. 291–332; Pierre-Étienne Will, *Bureaucracy and Famine in Eighteenth-Century China*, trans. Elborg Forster (Stanford, 1990), chaps. 7–8; Carol H. Shiue, "The Political Economy of Famine Relief in China, 1740–1820," *Journal of Interdisciplinary History*, 36 (2005), pp. 33–55. Also see Lillian M. Li, *Fighting Famine in North China: State, Market, and Environmental Decline, 1690s–1990s* (Stanford, 2007), chap. 6.

82 R. Bin Wong, "Food Riots in the Qing Dynasty," *JAS*, 41 (1982), p. 773.

83 Ibid., p. 767.

84 Will and Wong, *Nourish the People*, pp. 14–15.

85 R. Bin Wong, *China Transformed: Historical Change and the Limits of European Experience* (Ithaca, N.Y., 1997), p. 134.

86 R. Bin Wong, "Taxation and Good Governance in China, 1500–1914," unpublished paper presented at the Harvard Economic History Workshop, 23 September 2005. In the eighteenth century the Qing state was also preoccupied by its great westward expansion. See Peter C. Perdue, *China Marches West: The Qing Conquest of Central Eurasia* (Cambridge, Mass., 2005).

87 Osborne, "Highlands and Lowlands," pp. 215–16.

88 Anne Osborne, "The Local Politics of Land Reclamation in the Lower Yangzi Highlands," *Late Imperial China*, 15 (1994), p. 14.

89 Ibid., p. 12. Flooding was also caused by land reclamation in the lowlands, particularly the filling in of bodies of water. Chinese political authorities had little success in stopping this as well. See Perdue, *Exhausting the Earth*, chap. 7 and R. Keith Schoppa, *Xiang Lake – Nine Centuries of Chinese Life* (New Haven, 1989), chaps. 5 and 6.

90 Osborne, "Local Politics of Land Reclamation," pp. 14–30.

91 Ibid., pp. 30–6.

92 Ibid., p. 35.

93 Ibid., pp. 38–9.

94 Totman, *Green Archipelago*, chap. 3.

95 Ibid., p. 84.

96 Quoted in ibid., p. 96.

97 For more details see ibid., chap. 4 and Conrad Totman, *The Origins of Japan's Modern Forests: The Case of Akita* (Honolulu, 1985), chap. 3.

98 Totman, *Green Archipelago*, p. 114.

99 Ibid., pp. 117, 119.

100 Ibid., p. 168.

101 Osborne, "Barren Mountains, Raging Rivers," p. 297.
102 Mark Elvin, "Three Thousand Years of Unsustainable Growth: China's Environment from Archaic Times to the Present," *East Asian History*, 6 (1993), p. 29. Also see Osamu Saito, "Forest History and the Great Divergence: China, Japan, and the West Compared," *Journal of Global History*, 4 (2009), pp. 379–404.
103 Conrad Totman, *A History of Japan* (Malden, Mass., 2000), p. 247.
104 Ibid., p. 304.
105 Penelope Francks, *Rural Economic Development in Japan from the Nineteenth Century to the Pacific War* (London, 2006), pp. 26–36.
106 Michael Mann, "Ecological Change in North India: Deforestation and Agrarian Distress in the Ganga-Yamuna Doab 1800–1850," in Richard H. Grove, Vinita Damodaran and Satpal Sangwan (eds.), *Nature and the Orient: The Environmental History of South and Southeast Asia* (Delhi, 1998), pp. 403 and 405.
107 Richards, *Unending Frontier*, pp. 32–3.
108 Ibid., pp. 33–8; Richard M. Eaton, *The Rise of Islam and the Bengal Frontier, 1204–1760* (Berkeley, 1993), pp. 207–19.
109 The Paterson Diaries, MSS Eur E379, APAC, BL; Francis Buchanan, *A Journey from Madras through the Countries of Mysore, Canara and Malabar*, 3 vols. (London, 1807); Hugh Cleghorn, *The Forests and Gardens of South India* (London, 1861), p. 2.
110 Mann, "Ecological Change," p. 411.
111 Madhav Gadgil and Ramachandra Guha, *This Fissured Land: An Ecological History of India* (Berkeley, 1993), p. 120.
112 K. N. Chaudhuri, *The Trading World of Asia and the East India Company, 1660–1760* (Cambridge, 1978), p. 221; Tapan Raychaudhuri, "Non-Agricultural Production: Mughal India," in Tapan Raychaudhuri and Irfan Habib (eds.), *The Cambridge Economic History of India*, vol. I, c.1200–c.1750 (Cambridge, 1982), p. 275; Henry Wilkinson, "On the Cause of the External Pattern: or, Watering of the Damascus Sword-Blades," *Journal of the Royal Asiatic Society of Great Britain and Ireland*, 4 (1837), pp. 187–93.

7 Science and technology in India, 1600–1800

1 Margaret C. Jacob, *Scientific Culture and the Making of the Industrial West* (Oxford, 1997), p. 2. Also see her "Mechanical Science on the Factory Floor: The Early Industrial Revolution in Leeds," *History of Science*, 45 (2007), pp. 197–221.
2 Joel Mokyr, *The Gifts of Athena: Historical Origins of the Knowledge Economy* (Princeton, 2002), p. 297. Also see Joel Mokyr, *The*

Enlightened Economy: An Economic History of Britain 1700–1850 (New Haven, 2009), chaps. 3 and 5.

3 Jacob, *Scientific Culture*, p. 205.

4 Mokyr, *Gifts of Athena*, p. 35. Also see Ian Inkster, "Potentially Global: 'Useful and Reliable Knowledge' and Material Progress in Europe, 1474–1914," *International History Review*, 27 (2006), pp. 237–86. For a trenchant critique of Mokyr's *Gifts of Athena*, see William J. Ashworth, "The Ghost of Rostow: Science, Culture and the British Industrial Revolution," *History of Science*, 46 (2008), pp. 249–74.

5 Mokyr, *Gifts of Athena*, pp. 38–9.

6 Joel Mokyr, "The Intellectual Origins of Modern Economic Growth," *JEH*, 65 (2005), p. 287.

7 Ibid., p. 323.

8 Joel Mokyr, *The Lever of Riches: Technological Creativity and Economic Progress* (New York, 1990), p. 81.

9 David S. Landes, *The Wealth and Poverty of Nations: Why Some Are So Rich and Some So Poor* (New York, 1998), p. 228.

10 Ibid., pp. 341 and 342.

11 Nathan Sivin, "Why the Scientific Revolution Did Not Take Place in China – Or Didn't It?" *Chinese Science*, 5 (1982), p. 58. To focus on the scientific revolution problem also restricts science to the experimental and lab-based disciplines. The bulk of science in the seventeenth and eighteenth centuries, however, was based on observation. And in these observational fields, Asians contributed much to the creation of knowledge of the natural world. See, for instance, Kapil Raj, *Relocating Modern Science: Circulation and the Construction of Scientific Knowledge in South Asia and Europe* (Delhi, 2006), "Introduction."

12 Mokyr, *Gifts of Athena*, pp. 36–41.

13 Steven Shapin, *The Scientific Revolution* (Chicago, 1996), p. 3.

14 Andrew Cunningham and Perry Williams, "De-centering the 'Big Picture': *The Origins of Modern Science* and the Modern Origins of Science," *British Journal of the History of Science*, 26 (1993), p. 412.

15 Shapin, *Scientific Revolution*, pp. 3–4.

16 See, for example, Harold J. Cook, *Matters of Exchange: Commerce, Medicine, and Science in the Dutch Golden Age* (New Haven, 2007).

17 Ibid., pp. 310 and 314. Also see H. Y. Mohan Ram, "On the English Edition of Van Rheede's *Hortus Malabaricus* by K. S. Manilal (2003)," *Current Science*, 89 (2005), pp. 1672–80.

18 Richard Grove, "The Transfer of Botanical Knowledge between Europe and Asia, 1498–1800," *Journal of the Japan–Netherlands Institute*, 3 (1991), p. 163. Cook, however, finds insufficient evidence for Grove's claims. See Cook, *Matters of Exchange*, p. 313.

19 Raj, *Relocating Modern Science*, p. 44.

20 Ibid., pp. 42–3.

21 Ibid., p. 63.

22 Lawrence McCrea, "Playing with the System: Fragmentation and Individualization in Late Pre-colonial Mimamsa," *Journal of Indian Philosophy*, 36 (2008), pp. 579 and 581. Also see Lawrence McCrea, "Novelty of Form and Novelty of Substance in Seventeenth-Century Mimamsa," *Journal of Indian Philosophy*, 30 (2002), pp. 481–94.

23 Sheldon Pollock, "Is There an Indian Intellectual History? Introduction to 'Theory and Method in Indian Intellectual History,'" *Journal of Indian Philosophy*, 36 (2008), p. 541.

24 Dominik Wujastyk, "The Questions of King Tukkoji: Medicine at an Eighteenth-Century South Indian Court," *Indian Journal of History of Science*, 41 (2006), pp. 362–3.

25 Ibid., p. 365. For improvement in the European Enlightenment, see Mokyr, "Intellectual Origins," p. 291.

26 Sheldon Pollock, *The Ends of Man at the End of Premodernity* (Amsterdam, 2005), pp. 78–9.

27 Ibid., p. 80.

28 Ibid., p. 79.

29 Iqbal Ghani Khan has dated a shift in thinking about technology in Mughal India to 1992 when Irfan Habib delivered a lecture entitled "Akbar and Technology," which argued that Akbar had a keen interest in technical matters and interacted with technical experts. See Iqbal Ghani Khan, "Technology and the Question of Elite Intervention in Eighteenth-Century North India," in Richard B. Barnett (ed.), *Rethinking Early Modern India* (New Delhi, 2002), p. 264.

30 Sreeramula Rajeswara Sarma, "Indian Astronomical and Time-Measuring Instruments: A Catalogue in Preparation," *Indian Journal of History of Science*, 29 (1994), p. 519.

31 Iqbal Ghani Khan, "The Awadh Scientific Renaissance and the Role of the French: *c.*1750–1820," *Indian Journal of History of Science*, 38 (2003), p. 275.

32 Virendra Nath Sharma, *Sawai Jai Singh and His Astronomy* (Delhi, 1995), pp. 36–45, 137.

33 Ibid., pp. 187–90.

34 Ibid., p. 243. Also see pp. 309–11.

35 Ibid., pp. 19–20, 252.

36 G. Sobirov, "Samarkand Scientific School of Ulugh Begh," *Dushanbe*, 1975, quoted in Deepak Kumar, "India," in Roy Porter (ed.), *The Cambridge History of Science*, vol. IV, *Eighteenth-Century Science* (Cambridge, 2003), p. 676. An eighteenth-century commentator, Mirza

Khairullah Khan, wrote of the astronomical tables that were compiled under Jai Singh: "Whenever we calculate the different positions of the Sun and other planets in accordance with equations of the circle, they do not conform with the actually observed ones. On the contrary, when the equations are derived, taking the orbits elliptical and calculating the positions, they generally conform with observations. Hence the orbits must be elliptical." Quoted in Kumar, "India," p. 677.

37 Sharma, *Sawai Jai Singh*, pp. 253–6, 286–302, 329–31, 333–4.

38 William Hunter, "Some Account of the Astronomical Labours of Jayasinha, Rajah of Ambhere, or Jayanagar," *Asiatic Researches*, 5 (1799), pp. 209–10.

39 Sharma, *Sawai Jai Singh*, p. 276.

40 Khan, "Awadh Scientific Renaissance," pp. 276–7.

41 Charles Stewart, *A Descriptive Catalogue of the Oriental Library of the Late Tippoo Sultan of Mysore. To which are Prefixed, Memoirs of Hyder Aly Khan, and His Son Tippoo Sultan* (London, 1809).

42 Andrew Bell, *The Madras School or, Elements of Tuition* (London, 1808, repr. London, 1993), pp. 234–5.

43 Savithri Preetha Nair, "Native Collecting and Natural Knowledge (1798–1832): Raja Serfoji II of Tanjore as a 'Centre of Calculation,'" *Journal of the Royal Asiatic Society*, series 3, 15 (2005), p. 291. Also see Indira Viswanathan Peterson, "The Cabinet of King Serfoji of Tanjore: A European Collection in Early Nineteenth-Century India," *Journal of the History of Collections*, 11 (1999), pp. 71–93.

44 R. Jayaraman, *Sarasvati Mahal: A Short History and Guide* (Thanjavur, 1981), pp. 3–4.

45 Ibid., p. 21.

46 Ibid., p. 23.

47 Nair, "Native Collecting," p. 285.

48 Khan, "Awadh Scientific Renaissance," p. 281.

49 Ibid., pp. 297–8.

50 Ibid., pp. 287–93; Iqbal Ghani Khan, "Revenue, Warfare and Agriculture in North India: Technical Knowledge and the Post-Mughal Elites from the Mid-18th to the Early 19th Century," unpublished Ph.D. dissertation, University of London, 1990, chap. 1.

51 Khan, "Awadh Scientific Renaissance," p. 280.

52 Sheldon Pollock, "Literary Culture and Manuscript Culture in Precolonial India," in Simon Eliot, Andrew Nash and Ian Willison (eds.), *Literary Cultures and the Material Book* (London, 2007), p. 87.

53 Raj, *Relocating Modern Science*, pp. 40–1. Also see Cook, *Matters of Exchange*, p. 98.

54 N. K. Panikkar and T. M. Srinivasan, "*Kappal Sattiram*: A Tamil Treatise on Shipbuilding during the Seventeenth Century," *Indian Journal of the History of Science*, 7 (1972), p. 20.

55 Raj, *Relocating Modern Science*, p. 80.

56 See, for instance, Christopher Z. Minkowski, "Competing Cosmologies in Early Modern Indian Astronomy," in Charles Burnett, Jan P. Hogendijk, Kim Plofker and Michio Yano (eds.), *Studies in the History of the Exact Sciences in Honour of David Pingree* (Leiden, 2004), pp. 349–85.

57 Irfan Habib, "Akbar and Technology," in Irfan Habib (ed.), *Akbar and His India* (Delhi, 1997), pp. 129–32, 143.

58 Ibid., pp. 134–5.

59 Ibid., pp. 144–6.

60 Ibid., pp. 137–41. The quotation is on p. 141. What appear to be similar horse-powered boring machines were in use in the Woolwich Arsenal till 1842. See H. A. Young, *The East India Company's Arsenals and Manufactories* (Oxford, 1937), p. 140.

61 Habib, "Akbar and Technology," pp. 133–4.

62 Joseph E. Schwartzberg, "South Asian Cartography: Geographical Mapping," in J. B. Harley and David Woodward (eds.), *The History of Cartography*, vol. II, bk. 1, *Cartography in the Traditional Islamic and South Asian Societies* (Chicago, 1992), pp. 408–9.

63 Irfan Habib, "Cartography in Mughal India," *The Indian Archives*, 28 (1979), pp. 90–5. The quotation appears on p. 90.

64 *The Commentary of Father Monserrate, S.J. on his Journey to the Court of Akbar*, trans. John S. Hoyland and S. N. Banerjee (Cuttack and London, 1922), quoted in Raj, *Relocating Modern Science*, p. 70.

65 Khan, "Revenue, Warfare and Agriculture in North India," chap. 1.

66 Khan, "Technology and the Question of Elite Intervention," p. 260.

67 Khan, "Revenue, Warfare and Agriculture in North India," chaps. 1–3. For more on Indo-Persian travel literature, see Muzaffar Alam and Sanjay Subrahmanyam, *Indo-Persian Travels in the Age of Discoveries, 1400–1800* (Cambridge, 2007).

68 Norbert Peabody, *Hindu Kingship and Polity in Precolonial India* (Cambridge, 2003), pp. 131–2.

69 See Irfan Habib (ed.), *State and Diplomacy under Tipu Sultan: Documents and Essays* (New Delhi, 2001), pp. 70–9.

70 Ibid., pp. 76–9; Francis Buchanan, *A Journey from Madras through the Countries of Mysore, Canara and Malabar*, 3 vols. (London, 1807), vol. I, p. 70.

71 Irfan Habib, "Introduction: An Essay on Haidar Ali and Tipu Sultan," in Irfan Habib (ed.), *Confronting Colonialism: Resistance and Modernization under Haidar Ali and Tipu Sultan* (New Delhi, 1999), p. xliv, n. 47.

72 Buchanan, *Journey*, vol. I, p. 70.

73 Habib, *State and Diplomacy under Tipu Sultan*, pp. 25–42.

74 *The Travels of Ludovico di Varthema, 1503–1508*, trans. J. W. Jones and G. P. Badger (London, 1863), p. 152, quoted in Ahsan Jan Qaisar, *The Indian Response to European Technology and Culture* (Delhi, 1982), p. 22.

75 *English Factories in India, 1688–89*, p. 79, quoted in Qaisar, *Indian Response*, p. 22.

76 K. N. Chaudhuri, *Trade and Civilisation in the Indian Ocean: An Economic History from the Rise of Islam to 1750* (Cambridge, 1985), pp. 149–50.

77 Satpal Sangwan, "The Sinking Ships: Colonial Policy and the Decline of Indian Shipping, 1735–1835," in Roy MacLeod and Deepak Kumar (eds.), *Technology and the Raj: Western Technology and Technical Transfers to India 1700–1947* (New Delhi, 1995), pp. 138–44. Also see Sanjay Subrahmanyam, "A Note on Narsapur Peta: A 'Syncretic' Shipbuilding Centre in South India, 1570–1700," *Journal of the Economic and Social History of the Orient*, 31 (1988), pp. 305–11. K. N. Chaudhuri notes that iron nails may have been used even before the arrival of Europeans for a type of flat-bottomed ship. See his *Trade and Civilisation in the Indian Ocean*, p. 150.

78 Chaudhuri, *Trade and Civilisation in the Indian Ocean*, p. 150.

79 J. H. Grose, *A Voyage to the East Indies* (London, 1778), vol. I, pp. 107–8, quoted in Sangwan, "Sinking Ships," p. 140.

80 *British Parliamentary Papers*, 1813–14, vol. VIII.I (115), *Minutes of the Evidence taken before the Select Committee of the House of Commons on petitions relating to East-India-built shipping*, p. 40.

81 Quoted in Satpal Sangwan, *Science, Technology and Colonisation: An Indian Experience, 1757–1857* (Delhi, 1991), p. 108, n. 30. For the Solvyns work on the boats of Bengal, see Robert L. Hardgrave, Jr., *A Portrait of the Hindus: Balthazar Solvyns and the European Image of India 1760–1824* (Ahmedabad, 2004), pp. 465–508.

82 *British Parliamentary Papers*, 1813–14, vol. VIII.I (115), *Minutes of the Evidence taken before the Select Committee of the House of Commons on petitions relating to East-India-built shipping*, p. 121. *Gulgul* was a mixture of crushed sea shells and a drying oil. In the seventeenth century planks were smeared with pitch or tar and lime, and on occasion fish-oil, most likely mixed with other ingredients. See Qaisar, *Indian Response*, p. 22.

83 *British Parliamentary Papers*, 1813–14, vol. VIII.I (115), *Minutes of the Evidence taken before the Select Committee of the House of Commons on petitions relating to East-India-built shipping*, p. 515.

84 Ibid., pp. 535–6.

85 Sangwan, "Sinking Ships," pp. 145–6.

86 *The Fann-Makers Grievance by the Importation of Fanns from the East-Indies*, Shelfmark 816.m.12 (97), BL.

87 *The Case of the Joyners Company Against the Importation of Manufactured Cabinet Work from the East Indies*, Shelfmark 816.m.13 (2), BL.

88 Jean-Baptiste Tavernier, *Travels in India*, trans. V. Ball, 2 vols. (New York, 1889), vol. I, p. 157. Tavernier also wrote that the ruler of Golconda "passionately loves all those who are proficient in mathematics, and he understands them fairly well; it is the reason why, although a Muhammadan, he favours all Christians who are learned in this science." See his *Travels*, vol. I, p. 163.

89 Randolf G. S. Cooper, *The Anglo-Maratha Campaigns and the Contest for India: The Struggle for Control of the South Asian Military Economy* (Cambridge, 2003), p. 40.

90 Young, *East India Company's Arsenals*, pp. 223–4.

91 Cooper, *Anglo-Maratha Campaigns*, pp. 37–41.

92 Ibid., p. 297.

93 Ibid., p. 184. On the elevating screw, also see R. G. S. Cooper and N. K. Wagle, "Maratha Artillery: From Dabhoi to Assaye," *Journal of the Ordnance Society*, 7 (1995), p. 66.

94 Cooper, *Anglo-Maratha Campaigns*, pp. 296–7.

95 Roddam Narasimha, "Rockets in Mysore and Britain, 1750–1850 A.D.," lecture delivered on 2 April 1985 at the inauguration of the Centre for History and Philosophy of Science, Indian Institute of World Culture, Bangalore, National Aeronautical Laboratory, Project Document DU 8503; Wernher von Braun and Frederick I. Ordway, III, *History of Rocketry and Space Travel* (New York, 1967), pp. 30–1. The Royal Artillery Museum in Woolwich has on display Mysorean rockets which Congreve studied.

96 Mokyr, "Intellectual Origins," p. 287.

97 Ibid., p. 295.

98 See Eltjo Buringh and Jan Luiten van Zanden, "Charting the 'Rise of the West': Manuscripts and Printed Books in Europe, A Long-Term Perspective from the Sixth through Eighteenth Centuries," *JEH*, 69 (2009), pp. 409–45. Recall the estimate that there are some 30 million Indic manuscripts extant today, which indicates that manuscript production could reach staggering proportions. Sheldon Pollock also gives a striking example of the speed with which manuscripts could circulate in the seventeenth and eighteenth centuries. See his "Literary Culture and Manuscript Culture," p. 87.

99 Mokyr, "Intellectual Origins," pp. 298, 300.

100 Adrian Johns, "How to Acknowledge a Revolution," *American Historical Review*, 107 (2002), pp. 106–25. The quotation appears on p. 118. Also see his *The Nature of the Book: Print and Knowledge in the Making* (Chicago, 1998), chap. 9.

101 Simon Schaffer, "Introduction to Part IV," in Lissa Roberts, Simon Schaffer and Peter Dear (eds.), *The Mindful Hand: Inquiry and Invention from the Late Renaissance to Early Industrialization* (Amsterdam, 2007), p. 313.

102 The worker was the repository of skill with respect to coal. See J. R. Harris, "Skills, Coal and British Industry in the Eighteenth Century," *History*, 61 (1976), pp. 167–82.

103 Nicolas Desmarest, 'Second mémoire sur la papeterie,' *Memoires de l'Academie Royale des Sciences* (1774, pb. 1778), quoted in Simon Schaffer, "Introduction to Part IV," in Roberts, Schaffer and Dear, *Mindful Hand*, p. 313.

104 Bundla Ramaswamy Naidu, *Memoirs on the Internal Revenue System of the Madras Presidency* (Madras, 1820, repr. 1870), p. 43.

105 C. A. Bayly, *Empire and Information: Intelligence Gathering and Social Communication in India, 1780–1870* (Cambridge, 1996).

106 Mokyr, "Intellectual Origins," p. 311.

107 See, for example, Liliane Hilaire-Perez, "Invention and the State in 18th-Century France," *Technology and Culture*, 32 (1991), pp. 911–31. Also see J. R. Harris, *Industrial Espionage and Technology Transfer: Britain and France in the Eighteenth Century* (Aldershot, 1998).

108 The classic work is Christine MacLeod, *Inventing the Industrial Revolution: The English Patent System, 1660–1800* (Cambridge, 1988).

109 Mokyr, "Intellectual Origins," p. 297.

110 Liliane Hilaire-Perez, "Technology as a Public Culture in the Eighteenth Century: The Artisans' Legacy," *History of Science*, 45 (2007), pp. 137 and 139. Also see S. R. Epstein, "Property Rights to Technical Knowledge in Premodern Europe, 1300–1800," *American Economic Review*, 94 (2004), pp. 384–6 and S. R. Epstein, "Craft Guilds, Apprenticeship, and Technological Change in Pre-Industrial Europe," *JEH*, 58 (1998), pp. 684–713. And, as already mentioned, in coal skill was embodied in workers. See Harris, "Skills, Coal and British Industry."

111 Thomas Bowrey, *A Geographical Account of Countries Round the Bay of Bengal, 1669 to 1679*, ed. Sir Richard Carnac Temple (London, 1905, repr. Nendeln, Liechtenstein, 1967), p. 102.

112 Ibid., p. 102.

113 This view is contrary to that of Tirthankar Roy. See his "Knowledge and Divergence from the Perspective of Early Modern India," *Journal of Global History*, 3 (2008), pp. 361–87. Despite the title, Tirthankar

Roy relies largely upon evidence from the nineteenth century, which is then projected into the early-modern period. The next chapter should make evident why this is a problematic procedure.

114 Roxburgh Papers, MSS Eur D809, no date but from late eighteenth century, APAC, BL.

115 "Observations of Major James Franklin on Iron," *c.*1825, MSS Eur D154.155, p. 15, APAC, BL.

116 Habib, "Akbar and Technology," pp. 146–7.

117 Charles C. Gillispie, "The Natural History of Industry," *Isis*, 48 (1957), p. 399.

118 D. S. L. Cardwell, *From Watt to Clausius: The Rise of Thermodynamics in the Early Industrial Age* (Ithaca, N.Y., 1971), p. 292.

119 A. E. Musson and Eric Robinson, *Science and Technology in the Industrial Revolution* (Manchester, 1969), p. 7.

120 Lissa Roberts and Simon Schaffer, "Preface," in Roberts, Schaffer and Dear, *Mindful Hand*, pp. xvi and xvii.

121 Ibid., p. xxiii.

8 Modern industry in early nineteenth-century India

1 Barry Supple, "The State and the Industrial Revolution 1700–1914," in Carlo M. Cipolla (ed.), *The Fontana Economic History of Europe: The Industrial Revolution* (London, 1973), p. 324.

2 The classic study for the eighteenth century is J. R. Harris, *Industrial Espionage and Technology Transfer: Britain and France in the Eighteenth Century* (Aldershot, 1998). Also see Jeff Horn, *The Path Not Taken: French Industrialization in the Age of Revolution, 1750–1830* (Cambridge, Mass., 2006), chaps. 3 and 7.

3 Friedrich List, *National System of Political Economy* (1904 edn.), pp. 168–9, quoted in Supple, "State and the Industrial Revolution," pp. 322–3.

4 Anne Rankin Osborne, "Barren Mountains, Raging Rivers: The Ecological and Social Effects of Changing Land Use on the Lower Yangzi Periphery in Late Imperial China," unpublished Ph.D. dissertation, Columbia University, 1989, p. 297.

5 Mike Davis, *Late Victorian Holocausts: El Niño Famines and the Making of the Third World* (London, 2002), p. 7.

6 Romesh Dutt, *The Economic History of India*, vol. II, *In the Victorian Age 1837–1900* (2nd edn., London, 1906, repr. Delhi, 1990), p. 388.

7 Vera Anstey, *The Economic Development of India* (3rd edn., London, 1936), p. 471.

8 Tirthankar Roy, "Economic History and Modern India: Redefining the Link," *Journal of Economic Perspectives*, 16 (2002), p. 128.

9 Niall Ferguson, *Empire: The Rise and Demise of the British World Order and the Lessons for Global Power* (New York, 2003), p. 164. This statement abounds in historical inaccuracies. The bulk of the capital invested in cotton was Indian. The first steel mill, TISCO, was built in the early twentieth century and financed and built by the Tatas.

10 D. R. Gadgil, *The Industrial Evolution of India in Recent Times* (London, 1924); Amiya Kumar Bagchi, *Private Investment in India, 1900–1939* (Cambridge, 1972); Rajnarayan Chandavarkar, *The Origins of Industrial Capitalism in India: Business Strategies and the Working Classes in Bombay, 1900–1940* (Cambridge, 1994).

11 On this point see C. A. Bayly, *Rulers, Townsmen and Bazaars: North Indian Society in the Age of British Expansion, 1770–1870* (Cambridge, 1983), pp. 268–83.

12 K. N. Chaudhuri, "India's Foreign Trade and the Cessation of the East India Company's Trading Activities, 1828–1840," *Economic History Review*, 2nd ser., 19 (1966), pp. 354–5; Prasannan Parthasarathi, "Historical Issues of Deindustrialization in Nineteenth-Century South India," in Giorgio Riello and Tirthankar Roy (eds.), *How India Clothed the World: The World of South Asian Textiles, 1500–1850* (Leiden, 2009), pp. 423–34. For a classic analysis of the consequences of this import trade, see Amiya Kumar Bagchi, "De-industrialization in India in the Nineteenth Century: Some Theoretical Implications," *Journal of Development Studies*, 12 (1976), pp. 135–64.

13 Dharma Kumar, *Land and Caste in South India: Agricultural Labour in Madras Presidency in the Nineteenth Century* (Cambridge, 1965), p. 139.

14 P. J. Thomas and B. Nataraja Pillai, *Economic Depression in the Madras Presidency (1820–1854)* (Madras, 1933); Asiya Siddiqi, *Agrarian Change in a North Indian State: Uttar Pradesh, 1819–1833* (Oxford, 1973), pp. 168–78; Bayly, *Rulers, Townsmen and Bazaars*, chap. 7; David Washbrook, "Economic Depression and the Making of 'Traditional' Society in Colonial India," *Transactions of the Royal Historical Society*, 6th series, III (London, 1993), pp. 237–63.

15 *Irish University Press Series of British Parliamentary Papers. Colonies: East India* (Shannon, 1970), vol. VIII, pp. 115–16. The quotations appear on p. 116.

16 Richard Roberts, "West Africa and the Pondicherry Textile Industry," in Tirthankar Roy (ed.), *Cloth and Commerce: Textiles in Colonial India* (New Delhi, 1996), pp. 152–3.

17 Ibid., p. 150.

18 Ibid., p. 151.

19 Mireille Lobligeois, "Atelier publics et filatures privées à Pondichéry après 1816," *Bulletin de l'École française d'Extrême Orient*, 59 (1972), pp. 52, 53 and 57.

20 Ibid., p. 74.

21 Ibid., p. 75.

22 Ibid., p. 52.

23 Jennifer Tann and M. M. Breckin, "The International Diffusion of the Watt Engine, 1775–1825," *Economic History Review*, n.s., 31 (1978), p. 545; Jennifer Tann and John Aitken, "The Diffusion of the Stationary Steam Engine from Britain to India 1790–1830," *IESHR*, 29 (1992), p. 211.

24 Tann and Aitken, "Diffusion of the Stationary Steam Engine," pp. 205–6.

25 Ibid., p. 207.

26 Ibid., pp. 206 and 212–13.

27 Ibid., pp. 209–10.

28 Ibid., p. 214.

29 Tann and Breckin, "International Diffusion," pp. 545, 547.

30 Blair B. Kling, *Partner in Empire: Dwarkanath Tagore and the Age of Enterprise in Eastern India* (Berkeley, 1976), p. 65.

31 *Irish University Press Series of British Parliamentary Papers. Colonies: East India* (Shannon, 1970), vol. VIII, p. 114.

32 Kling, *Partner in Empire*, p. 65.

33 *Irish University Press Series of British Parliamentary Papers. Colonies: East India* (Shannon, 1970), vol. VIII, pp. 471–2; Kling, *Partner in Empire*, pp. 94–9.

34 *British Parliamentary Papers*, 1813–14, vol. VIII.I (115), *Minutes of the Evidence taken before the Select Committee of the House of Commons on petitions relating to East-India-built shipping*, pp. 137, 335–6; Andrew Lambert, "Empire and Seapower: Shipbuilding by the East India Company at Bombay for the Royal Navy 1805–1850," in Philippe Haudrère, René Estienne and Gérard Le Bouëdec (eds.), *Les flottes des Compagnies des Indes 1600–1857* (Vincennes, 1996), p. 158.

35 *British Parliamentary Papers*, 1813–14, vol. VIII.I (115), *Minutes of the Evidence taken before the Select Committee of the House of Commons on petitions relating to East-India-built shipping*, pp. 122, 569.

36 Ibid., pp. 127–8, 338–9.

37 Kling, *Partner in Empire*, pp. 62 and 65.

38 Satpal Sangwan, *Science, Technology and Colonisation: An Indian Experience, 1757–1857* (Delhi, 1991), p. 127. Also see W. H. Carey, *The Good Old Days of Honorable John Company*, 2 vols. (Calcutta, 1907), vol. II, p. 26.

39 Bishop Reginald Heber, *Narrative of a Journey through the Upper Provinces of India, 1824–1825* (Philadelphia, 1828), vol. II, pp. 289–90,

quoted in B. N. Ganguli, *Indian Economic Thought: Nineteenth Century Perspectives* (New Delhi, 1977), p. 34.

40 Sangwan, *Science, Technology and Colonisation*, p. 127; *Irish University Press Series of British Parliamentary Papers. Colonies: East India* (Shannon, 1970), vol. VIII, p. 285.

41 Daniel R. Headrick, *The Tentacles of Progress: Technology Transfer in the Age of Imperialism, 1850–1940* (Oxford, 1988), p. 367, quoted in Satpal Sangwan, "The Sinking Ships: Colonial Policy and the Decline of Indian Shipping, 1735–1835," in Roy MacLeod and Deepak Kumar (eds.), *Technology and the Raj: Western Technology and Technical Transfers to India, 1700–1947* (New Delhi, 1995), p. 144. Also see Asiya Siddiqi, "The Business World of Jamsetjee Jejeebhoy," in Asiya Siddiqi (ed.), *Trade and Finance in Colonial India, 1750–1860* (Delhi, 1995), pp. 211–15.

42 Sangwan, "Sinking Ships," p. 145.

43 For details of the Act, see ibid., p. 152, n. 81.

44 *Irish University Press Series of British Parliamentary Papers. Colonies: East India* (Shannon, 1970), vol. VIII, p. 286.

45 Headrick, *Tentacles of Progess*, p. 24.

46 Ibid., p. 367; Sangwan, "Sinking Ships," pp. 145–7.

47 Arun Kumar Biswas, *Minerals and Metals in Pre-Modern India* (New Delhi, 2001), pp. 121–2.

48 Board's Collections, F/4/384, Item 9796, pp. 1–2, APAC, BL.

49 Board's Collections, F/4/511, Item 12281, p. 54, APAC, BL.

50 Board's Collections, F/4/511, Item 12281, p. 85, APAC, BL.

51 Board's Collections, F/4/825, Item 21927, pp. 3–4, 24, APAC, BL.

52 Board's Collections, F/4/1079, Item 29444, p. 2; F/4/1464, Item 57536A, pp. 38A–39A, APAC, BL.

53 Board's Collections, F/4/1079, Item 29444, pp. 14–15. Also see F/4/1734, Item 70221b, pp. 103–9, APAC, BL.

54 Board's Collections, F/4/1464, Item 57536A, p. 104, APAC, BL.

55 Board's Collections, F/4/1464, Item 57536A, pp. 146–7, 151–2, 179–80, APAC, BL.

56 Board's Collections, F/4/1734, Item 70221c, pp. 33–5, APAC, BL.

57 Board's Collections, F/4/1734, Item 70221b, pp. 139–40; Item 70221c, p. 40, APAC, BL.

58 Board's Collections, F/4/1821, Item 75084, p. 15, APAC, BL.

59 H. C. Bhardwaj, "Development of Iron and Steel Technology in India during 18th and 19th Centuries," *Indian Journal of History of Science*, 17 (1982), p. 230.

60 Board's Collections, F/4/1734, Item 70221c, p. 46, APAC, BL.

61 Board's Collections, F/4/1734, Item 70221b, pp. 53–4, APAC, BL.

62 Board's Collections, F/4/1734, Item 70221b, pp. 26, 55; Item 70221c, pp. 32–4; Item 70221b, pp. 133–5, APAC, BL.

63 Board's Collections, F/4/1734, Item 70221c, pp. 47, 52–3, 59, APAC, BL.

64 Board's Collections, F/4/1734, Item 70221a, Public Department to Fort St. George Council, 5 June 1839, paras. 10–12, 14, 16, 18 (no page numbers), APAC, BL.

65 Board's Collections, F/4/1464, Item 57536A, pp. 7, 44–5, APAC, BL.

66 Board's Collections, F/4/1734, Item 70221c, pp. 62–3; F/4/825, Item 21927, pp. 26–7, APAC, BL.

67 Benjamin Heyne, "On the Establishment of Copper and Iron Works in India," 1814, Home Miscellaneous Series, H/258, p. 562, APAC, BL.

68 Board's Collections, F/4/825, Item 21927, pp. 26–7; F/4/1734, Item 70221c, p. 87.

69 Pedro Machado, "Awash in a Sea of Cloth: Gujarat, Africa, and the Western Indian Ocean, 1300–1800," in Giorgio Riello and Prasannan Parthasarathi (eds.), *The Spinning World: A Global History of Cotton Textiles, 1200–1850* (Oxford, 2009), pp. 175–6. The Gujarati mercantile advantage over Europeans was a longstanding feature of the western Indian Ocean. See H. W. van Santen, "Trade between Mughal India and the Middle East, and Mughal Monetary Policy, *c.*1600–1660," in Karl Reinhold Haellquist (ed.), *Asian Trade Routes* (London, 1991), pp. 88–9.

70 Report on External Commerce of Bengal, from Bengal Commercial Reports, 1802–3, cited in Amales Tripathi, *Trade and Finance in the Bengal Presidency* (new edn., Calcutta, 1979), p. 117.

71 Siddiqi, "Business World of Jamsetjee Jejeebhoy," pp. 215–16. For more evidence of the entrepreneurial savvy of Indian merchants, see Claude Markovits, *The Global World of Indian Merchants, 1750–1947: Traders of Sind from Bukhara to Panama* (Cambridge, 2000), chap. 1.

72 See, for example, Rondo E. Cameron, "Some French Contributions to the Industrial Development of Germany, 1840–1870," *JEH*, 16 (1956), pp. 281–321.

73 For a brief overview of the issues, see Pat Hudson, *The Genesis of Industrial Capital: A Study of the West Riding Wool Textile Industry, c.1750–1850* (Cambridge, 1986), pp. 14–24.

74 Radhe Shyam Rungta, *The Rise of Business Corporations in India* (Cambridge, 1970), pp. 27–8.

75 Ibid., pp. 28–9.

76 H. Prinsep's Minute on Banking, 4 January 1837, in Narendra Krishna Sinha, *The Economic History of Bengal*, vol. III, *1793–1848* (Calcutta, 1970), p. 143.

77 R. H. Phillimore, *Historical Records of the Survey of India*, vol. I, *18th Century* (Dehra Dun, 1945), pp. 198–9; vol. II, *1800 to 1815* (Dehra Dun, 1950), p. 228; vol. III, *1815 to 1830* (Dehra Dun, 1954), p. 219.

78 Ibid., vol. II, p. 225.
79 Ibid., vol. IV, *1830 to 1843 George Everest* (Dehra Dun, 1958), p. 122.
80 Ibid., vol. IV, p. 124.
81 Ibid., vol. IV, p. 125.
82 Ibid., vol. IV, pp. 129–31. The quotation is on p. 130.
83 Ibid., vol. IV, p. 134.
84 Ibid., vol. IV, pp. 126–7, 129–30.
85 Ibid., vol. IV, p. 127.
86 Montgomery Martin, *Eastern India* (London, 1838), vol. III, Introduction, quoted in Romesh Dutt, *The Economic History of India*, vol. I, *Under Early British Rule* (2nd edn., London, 1906, repr. Delhi, 1990), p. 207.
87 M. J. Daunton, *Progress and Poverty: An Economic and Social History of Britain 1700–1850* (Oxford, 1995), p. 217.
88 Horn, *Path Not Taken*, pp. 223 and 226.
89 Ibid., pp. 241–2.
90 Rainer Fremdling, "Continental Responses to British Innovations in the Iron Industry during the Eighteenth and Early Nineteenth Centuries," in Leandro Prados de la Escosura (ed.), *Exceptionalism and Industrialisation: Britain and its European Rivals, 1688–1815* (Cambridge, 2004), p. 158.
91 Ibid., pp. 162–3.
92 Ibid., p. 159.
93 J. H. Clapham, *Economic Development of France and Germany 1815– 1914* (4th edn., Cambridge, 1936), p. 102.
94 Fremdling, "Continental Responses to British Innovations," p. 157. On some of the problems with European coal, see David S. Landes, *The Unbound Prometheus: Technological Change and Industrial Development in Western Europe from 1750 to the Present* (Cambridge, 1969), p. 139.
95 Christine MacLeod, "The European Origins of British Technological Predominance," in Prados de la Escosura, *Exceptionalism and Industrialisation*, p. 113.
96 Ibid., p. 119.
97 Harris, *Industrial Espionage and Technology Transfer*, p. 9.
98 Horn, *Path Not Taken*, p. 245.
99 John Macgregor, Secretary to the Board of Trade, cited in Supple, "State and the Industrial Revolution," p. 322.
100 Eric Dorn Brose, *The Politics of Technological Change in Prussia: Out of the Shadow of Antiquity, 1809–1848* (Princeton, 1993), p. 155.

101 Frank Tipton, "Government and Economy in the Nineteenth Century," in Sheilagh Ogilvie and Richard Overy (eds.), *Germany: A New Social and Economic History*, vol. III, *Since 1800* (London, 2003), p. 117.

102 R. Fremdling and B. Gales, "Ironmasters and Iron Production during the Belgian Industrial Revolution: The 'Enquete' of 1828," in Paul Klep and Eddy van Cauwenberghe (eds.), *Entrepreneurship and the Transformation of the Economy (10th–20th Centuries): Essays in Honour of Herman van der Wee* (Leuven, 1994), pp. 247–8.

103 Landes, *Unbound Prometheus*, pp. 150–1.

104 Supple, "State and the Industrial Revolution," pp. 311–12.

105 Brose, *Politics of Technological Change in Prussia*, pp. 145–7. The quotation appears on p. 147.

106 Supple, "State and the Industrial Revolution," p. 324.

107 Fremdling, "Continental Responses to British Innovations," p. 155.

108 Brose, *Politics of Technological Change in Prussia*, p. 155.

109 Supple, "State and the Industrial Revolution," pp. 324–5.

110 Clapham, *Economic Development of France and Germany*, p. 140.

111 Quoted in ibid., p. 143.

112 Supple, "State and the Industrial Revolution," pp. 328–30.

113 Ibid., p. 327. Also see Fremdling and Gales, "Ironmasters and Iron Production," p. 258.

114 Rainer Fremdling, "Transfer Patterns of British Technology to the Continent: The Case of the Iron Industry," *European Review of Economic History*, 4 (2000), p. 216.

115 Ibid., p. 217.

116 Rainer Fremdling, "Foreign Competition and Technological Change: British Exports and the Modernisation of the German Iron Industry from the 1820s to the 1860s," in W. R. Lee (ed.), *German Industry and German Industrialization: Essays in German Economic and Business History in the Nineteenth and Twentieth Centuries* (London, 1991), p. 52.

117 Brose, *Politics of Technological Change in Prussia*, p. 168.

118 Ibid., p. 170.

119 Ibid., chap. 5.

120 Quoted in S. Bhattacharya, "Regional Economy (1757–1857): Eastern India I," in Dharma Kumar (ed.), *The Cambridge Economic History of India*, vol. II, c.1757–c.1970 (Cambridge, 1982), pp. 276–7. For a detailed discussion, see Jitendra G. Borpujari, "The Impact of the Transit Duty System in British India," in Asiya Siddiqi (ed.), *Trade and Finance in Colonial India, 1750–1860* (Delhi, 1995), pp. 321–44.

121 *Irish University Press Series of British Parliamentary Papers. Colonies: East India* (Shannon, 1970), vol. VIII, pp. 274–5.

122 *Irish University Press Series of British Parliamentary Papers. Colonies: East India* (Shannon, 1970), vol. VI, p. 484.

123 Ibid., p. 484.

124 Ibid., p. 267.

125 Ibid., p. 279.

126 H. A. Young, *The East India Company's Arsenals and Manufactories* (Oxford, 1937), p. 147.

127 Bayly, *Rulers, Townsmen and Bazaars*, pp. 268–83.

128 For a first step towards such a broader analysis, see K. N. Panikkar, "Cultural Trends in Precolonial India: An Overview," in S. Irfan Habib and Dhruv Raina (eds.), *Social History of Science in Colonial India* (Delhi, 2007), pp. 1–24.

129 Young, *East India Company's Arsenals*, p. 133.

130 Ibid., p. 139.

131 Ibid., pp. 148–50.

132 Ibid., p. 222.

133 Ibid., p. 224.

134 John M. Hurd, "Railways," in Kumar, *Cambridge Economic History of India*, vol. II, p. 749.

135 C. A. Bayly, *Indian Society and the Making of the British Empire* (Cambridge, 1988), pp. 120–3.

136 Young, *East India Company's Arsenals*, pp. 133 and 138.

137 Phillimore, *Historical Records of the Survey of India*, vol. II, p. 340.

138 BT/6/140, ff. 42, 53, TNA: PRO.

139 Evidence of Robert Rickards, 30 June 1820, Select Committee of the House of Lords, 1820–1, quoted in Tripathi, *Trade and Finance*, p. 155.

140 Quoted in Tann and Aitken, "Diffusion of the Stationary Steam Engine," p. 201.

141 *Irish University Press Series of British Parliamentary Papers. Colonies: East India* (Shannon, 1970), vol. VIII, pp. 573–4. The petition was dated 1 September 1831.

142 Ibid., p. 609. The petition was dated 13 October 1832.

143 Landes, *Unbound Prometheus*, p. 146.

144 Joel Mokyr, *The Enlightened Economy: An Economic History of Britain 1700–1850* (New Haven, 2009), p. 393. Emphasis added.

145 For more on this point, see Ha-Joon Chang, "Breaking the Mould: An Institutionalist Political Economy Alternative to the Neo-Liberal Theory of the Market and the State," *Cambridge Journal of Economics*, 26 (2002), pp. 539–59.

146 S. R. Epstein, *Freedom and Growth: The Rise of States and Markets in Europe, 1300–1750* (London, 2000), pp. 172 and 167.

9 Conclusion

1 James Mill, *The History of British India*, 10 vols. (5th edn., London, 1858, repr. London, 1997), vol. I, p. 118.
2 Karl Marx, "The British Rule in India," in Robert C. Tucker (ed.), *The Marx–Engels Reader* (2nd edn., New York, 1978), p. 656.

Bibliography

Primary sources

Manuscript

Archives of the Royal Society of Arts
Guard Book Number 3.

Bolton Central Library, Bolton
Samuel Crompton Papers, ZCR/6/4, ZCR/15/18, ZCR/19/5, ZCR/43/3.

British Library, London
Asia, Pacific and Africa Collections
Board's Collections, F/4/384, F/4/511, F/4/825, F/4/1079, F/4/1464, F/4/1734, F/4/1821.
Home Miscellaneous Series, H/258, H/401.
The Paterson Diaries, MSS Eur E379.
Roxburgh Papers, MSS Eur D809.
"Observations of Major James Franklin on Iron," *c.*1825, MSS Eur D154.155.

Department of Manuscripts
Liverpool Papers, Add MS 38342, 38376.

John Rylands Library, Manchester
Samuel Oldknow Papers, Eng MSS 751 and Eng MSS 839.
Wadsworth Manuscripts, Eng MSS 1206.

Manchester Central Library

T. Hawkes, "Observations on the Cotton Trade of Manchester, in a Series of Essays," *c.*1793, Manuscript B.R.338.1 H3.

National Archives of the United Kingdom: Public Record Office, Kew

Papers of the Board of Trade, BT/1, BT/6.

Papers of the English African Companies, T/70, C/107.

Printed

Aikin, John. *A Description of the Country from Thirty to Forty Miles Round Manchester* (London, 1795).

Bell, Andrew. *The Madras School or, Elements of Tuition* (London, 1808, repr. London, 1993).

Bernier, François. *The History of the Late Revolution of the Empire of the Great Mogol*, trans. Henry Oldenburg (2nd edn., London, 1676).

Bowrey, Thomas. *A Geographical Account of Countries Round the Bay of Bengal, 1669 to 1679*, ed. Sir Richard Carnac Temple (London, 1905, repr. Nendeln, Liechtenstein, 1967).

British Parliamentary Papers, 1813–14, vol. VIII.I (115), *Minutes of the Evidence taken before the Select Committee of the House of Commons on petitions relating to East-India-built shipping.*

Buchanan, Francis. *A Journey from Madras through the Countries of Mysore, Canara and Malabar*, 3 vols. (London, 1807).

The Case of the Joyners Company Against the Importation of Manufactured Cabinet Work from the East Indies, Shelfmark 816.m.13 (2), BL.

The Case of Mr. Richard Arkwright and Co. In Relation to Mr. Arkwright's Invention of an Engine for Spinning Cotton, etc. into Yarn (London, 1782).

Cleghorn, Hugh. *The Forests and Gardens of South India* (London, 1861).

Considerations on the East India Trade (London, 1701), in *A Select Collection of Early English Tracts on Commerce*, ed. J. R. McCulloch (London, 1856, repr. Cambridge, 1954).

Cunningham, A. B. (ed.). "The Journal of Christophe Aubin: A Report on the Levant Trade in 1812," *Archivum Ottomanicum*, 7 (1983), pp. 5–127.

Defoe, Daniel. *A Plan of the English Commerce* (London, 1728, repr. Oxford, 1928).

Dossie, Robert. *Memoirs of Agriculture and Other Oeconomical Arts*, 3 vols. (London, 1768–82).

The Fann-Makers Grievance by the Importation of Fanns from the East-Indies, Shelfmark 816.m.12 (97), BL.

The Gentleman's Magazine, 24 (1754).

Guest, Richard. *A Compendious History of the Cotton Manufacture* (Manchester, 1823).

Hunter, William. "Some Account of the Astronomical Labours of Jayasinha, Rajah of Ambhere, or Jayanagar," *Asiatic Researches*, 5 (1799), pp. 177–211.

Irish University Press Series of British Parliamentary Papers. Colonies: East India, 22 vols. (Shannon, 1968–71).

Journal of the House of Commons, vol. 34 (1774).

Kennedy, John. *Miscellaneous Papers, On Subjects Connected with the Manufactures of Lancashire* (Manchester, 1849).

Khan, Gholam Hossein. *A Translation of Seir Mutaqherin, or, Views of Modern Times: Being an History of India, from the Year 1118, to the Year 1194, of the Hedjrah* (Calcutta, 1902, repr. Lahore, 2005).

The Late Measures of the Ship-Owners in the Coal Trade Fully Examined, in a Letter to the Right Honourable William Pitt (London, 1786).

Letters Addressed to the Right Honourable William Pitt, Chancellor of the Exchequer of Great Britain (London, 1793).

Marx, Karl. "The British Rule in India," in Robert C. Tucker (ed.), *The Marx-Engels Reader* (2nd edn., New York, 1978), pp. 653–8.

    "The Future Results of British Rule in India," in Robert C. Tucker (ed.), *The Marx-Engels Reader* (2nd. edn., New York, 1978), pp. 659–64.

Mercator. *A Second Letter to the Inhabitants of Manchester on the Exportation of Twist* (Manchester, 1800).

Mill, James. *The History of British India*, 10 vols. (5th edn., London, 1858, repr. London, 1997).

N. C., a Weaver of London. *The Great Necessity and Advantage of Preserving Our Own Manufactures* (London, 1697).

Naidu, Bundla Ramaswamy. *Memoirs on the Internal Revenue System of the Madras Presidency* (Madras, 1820, repr. 1870).

Ogden, James. *A Description of Manchester: Giving an Historical Account of those Limits in which the Town was Formerly Included* (Manchester, 1783).

Pelsaert, Francisco. *Jahangir's India*, trans. W. H. Moreland and P. Geyl (Cambridge, 1925).

Peyssonnel, M. de (Charles). *Traité sur le commerce de la mer Noire*, 2 vols. (Paris, 1787).

Premiums Offered by the Society Instituted at London for the Encouragement of Arts, Manufactures and Commerce (London, 1760).

Reasons Humbly offer'd to the Honourable House of Commons, against a Duty intended to be laid upon Silks, Manufactured, Printed, or Stained, as far as it concerns Handkerchiefs (London, 1711).

Rey, Claudius. *The Weavers True Case; or, the Wearing of Printed Callicoes and Linnen Destructive to the Woollen and Silk Manufactures* (London, 1719).

Smith, Adam. *An Inquiry into the Nature and Causes of the Wealth of Nations*, 2 vols. (Oxford, 1976).

Smith, John. *Chronicon Rusticum-Comerciale*, 2 vols. (London, 1747).

Smith, Thomas. *A Discourse of the Common Weal of this Realm of England*, ed. Elizabeth Lamond (Cambridge, 1954).

Stewart, Charles. *A Descriptive Catalogue of the Oriental Library of the Late Tippoo Sultan of Mysore. To which are Prefixed, Memoirs of Hyder Aly Khan, and His Son Tippoo Sultan* (London, 1809).

Tavernier, Jean-Baptiste. *Travels in India*, trans. V. Ball, 2 vols. (New York, 1889).

Thoughts on the Use of Machines in the Cotton Manufacture: Addressed to the Working People in that Manufacture, and the Poor in General. By a Friend of the Poor (Manchester, 1780).

von Richthofen, Ferdinand, Freiherr. *Baron Richthofen's Letters, 1870–1872* (Shanghai, 1872?)

Walker, George. *Observations, Founded on Facts, upon the Propriety or Impropriety of Exporting Cotton Twist, for the Purpose of Being Manufactured into Cloth by Foreigners* (London, 1803).

Walrond, Theodore (ed.). *Letters and Journals of James, Eighth Earl of Elgin* (London, 1872).

Wilkinson, Henry. "On the Cause of the External Pattern: or, Watering of the Damascus Sword-Blades," *Journal of the Royal Asiatic Society of Great Britain and Ireland*, 4 (1837), pp. 187–93.

Wright, M. D., John. *An Address to the Members of Both Houses of Parliament on the Late Tax Laid on Fustian and Other Cotton Goods* (Warrington, 1785).

Ying-hsing, Sung. *T'ien Kung K'ai Wu: Chinese Technology in the Seventeenth Century*, trans. E-tu Zen Sun and Shiou-chuan Sun (University Park, Penn., 1966).

Secondary works

Acemoglu, Daron, Simon Johnson and James A. Robinson. "The Colonial Origins of Comparative Development: An Empirical Investigation," *American Economic Review*, 91 (2001), pp. 1369–1401.

Agoston, Gabor. *Guns for the Sultan: Military Power and the Weapons Industry in the Ottoman Empire* (Cambridge, 2005).

Alam, Muzaffar. "Aspects of Agrarian Uprisings in North India in the Early Eighteenth Century," in Sabyasachi Bhattacharya and Romila Thapar (eds.), *Situating Indian History for Sarvepalli Gopal* (Delhi, 1986), pp. 146–70.

The Crisis of Empire in Mughal North India (Delhi, 1986).

Alam, Muzaffar and Sanjay Subrahmanyam. *Indo-Persian Travels in the Age of Discoveries, 1400–1800* (Cambridge, 2007).

(eds.). *The Mughal State, 1526–1750* (Delhi, 1998).

Allen, Robert C. "Agriculture During the Industrial Revolution, 1700–1850," in Roderick Floud and Paul Johnson (eds.), *The Cambridge Economic History of Modern Britain*, vol. I, *Industrialisation, 1700–1860* (Cambridge, 2004), pp. 96–116.

The British Industrial Revolution in Global Perspective (Cambridge, 2009).

"India in the Great Divergence," in Timothy J. Hatton, Kevin H. O'Rourke and Alan M. Taylor (eds.), *The New Comparative Economic History: Essays in Honor of Jeffrey G. Williamson* (Cambridge, Mass., 2007), pp. 9–32.

"The Industrial Revolution in Miniature: The Spinning Jenny in Britain, France, and India," *JEH*, 69 (2009), pp. 901–27.

Anderson, Perry. *Lineages of the Absolutist State* (London, 1974).

Anstey, Vera. *The Economic Development of India* (3rd edn., London, 1936).

Arasaratnam, S. "The Rice Trade in Eastern India 1650–1740," *MAS*, 22 (1988), pp. 531–49.

Ashton, T. S. *An Economic History of England: The 18th Century* (London, 1955).

Iron and Steel in the Industrial Revolution (2nd edn., Manchester, 1951).

Ashton, T. S. and Joseph Sykes. *The Coal Industry of the Eighteenth Century* (Manchester, 1929).

Ashworth, William J. *Customs and Excise: Trade, Production, and Consumption in England, 1640–1845* (Oxford, 2003).

"The Ghost of Rostow: Science, Culture and the British Industrial Revolution," *History of Science*, 46 (2008), pp. 249–74.

Attman, Artur. *American Bullion in the European World Trade, 1600–1800*, trans. Eva and Allan Green (Göteborg, 1986).

Atwell, William S. "International Bullion Flows and the Chinese Economy circa 1530–1650," *P&P*, 95 (1982), pp. 68–90.

Bagchi, Amiya Kumar. "De-industrialization in India in the Nineteenth Century: Some Theoretical Implications," *Journal of Development Studies*, 12 (1976), pp. 135–64.

Private Investment in India, 1900–1939 (Cambridge, 1972).

Baines, Edward. *History of the Cotton Manufacture in Great Britain* (London, 1835).

Baker, George P. *Calico Painting and Printing in the East Indies in the XVIIth and XVIIIth Centuries* (London, 1921).

Barkey, Karen. *Bandits and Bureaucrats: The Ottoman Route to State Centralization* (Ithaca, N.Y., 1994).

Barrett, Ward. "World Bullion Flows, 1450–1850," in James D. Tracy (ed.), *The Rise of Merchant Empires: Long-Distance Trade in the Early Modern World, 1350–1750* (Cambridge, 1990), pp. 224–54.

Basu, Bhaskar Jyoti. "Trading World of Coromandel and the Crisis of the 1730s," *Proceedings of the Indian History Congress*, 42nd Session, Bodh-Gaya (1981), pp. 333–9.

Bayly, C. A. *Empire and Information: Intelligence Gathering and Social Communication in India, 1780–1870* (Cambridge, 1996).

   "Indian Merchants in a 'Traditional' Setting: Benares, 1780–1830," in Clive Dewey and A. G. Hopkins (eds.), *The Imperial Impact: Studies in the Economic History of Africa and India* (London, 1978), pp. 171–93.

   Indian Society and the Making of the British Empire (Cambridge, 1988).

   "Pre-Colonial Indian Merchants and Rationality," in Mushirul Hasan and Narayani Gupta (eds.), *India's Colonial Encounter: Essays in Memory of Eric Stokes* (New Delhi, 1993), pp. 3–24.

   Rulers, Townsmen and Bazaars: North Indian Society in the Age of British Expansion, 1770–1870 (Cambridge, 1983).

Bayly, Susan. *Caste, Society and Politics in India from the Eighteenth Century to the Modern Age* (Cambridge, 1999).

Berg, Maxine. *Luxury and Pleasure in Eighteenth-Century Britain* (Oxford, 2005).

   "In Pursuit of Luxury: Global Origins of British Consumer Goods in the Eighteenth Century," *P&P*, 182 (2004), pp. 85–142.

   "Quality, Cotton and the Global Luxury Trade," in Riello and Roy, *How India Clothed the World*, pp. 391–414.

Bhardwaj, H. C. "Development of Iron and Steel Technology in India during 18th and 19th Centuries," *Indian Journal of History of Science*, 17 (1982), pp. 223–33.

Bhattacharya, Durgaprasad (ed.). *Census of India 1961: Report on the Population Estimates of India*, vol. III, 1811–1820, part A, "Eastern Region" (1963).

Bhattacharya, Durgaprasad and Bibhavati Bhattacharya (eds.). *Census of India 1961: Report on the Population Estimates of India (1820–1830)* (1963).

Bhattacharya, S. "Regional Economy (1757–1857): Eastern India I," in Dharma Kumar (ed.), *The Cambridge Economic History of India*, vol. II, c.1757–c.1970 (Cambridge, 1982), pp. 270–95.

Biswas, Arun Kumar. *Minerals and Metals in Pre-Modern India* (New Delhi, 2001).

Borpujari, Jitendra G. "The Impact of the Transit Duty System in British India," in Asiya Siddiqi (ed.), *Trade and Finance in Colonial India, 1750–1860* (Delhi, 1995), pp. 321–44.

Boulle, Pierre H. "Slave Trade, Commercial Organization and Industrial Growth in Eighteenth-Century Nantes," *Revue francaise d'histoire d'outre-mer*, 59 (1972), pp. 70–112.

Bowen, Huw. *The Business of Empire: The East India Company and Imperial Britain, 1756–1833* (Cambridge, 2006).

Bowles, Samuel and Herbert Gintis. "Walrasian Economics in Retrospect," *Quarterly Journal of Economics*, 115 (2000), pp. 1411–39.

Brenner, Robert. "Agrarian Class Structure and Economic Development in Pre-Industrial Europe," in T. H. Aston and C. H. E. Philpin (eds.), *The Brenner Debate: Agrarian Class Structure and Economic Development in Pre-Industrial Europe* (Cambridge, 1985), pp. 10–63.

Brenner, Robert and Christopher Isett. "England's Divergence from China's Yangzi Delta: Property Relations, Microeconomics, and Patterns of Development," *JAS*, 61 (2002), pp. 609–62.

Broadberry, Stephen and Bishnupriya Gupta. "The Early Modern Great Divergence: Wages, Prices and Economic Development in Europe and Asia, 1500–1800," *Economic History Review*, n.s., 59 (2006), pp. 2–31.

Brose, Eric Dorn. *The Politics of Technological Change in Prussia: Out of the Shadow of Antiquity, 1809–1848* (Princeton, 1993).

Bruland, Kristine. "Industrialization and Technological Change," in Roderick Floud and Paul Johnson (eds.), *The Cambridge Economic History of Modern Britain*, vol. I, *Industrialization, 1700–1860* (Cambridge, 2004), pp. 117–46.

Buringh, Eltjo and Jan Luiten van Zanden. "Charting the 'Rise of the West': Manuscripts and Printed Books in Europe, A Long-Term Perspective from the Sixth through Eighteenth Centuries," *JEH*, 69 (2009), pp. 409–45.

Butel, Paul. *The Atlantic*, trans. Iain Hamilton Grant (London, 1999).

Cameron, Rondo E. "Some French Contributions to the Industrial Development of Germany, 1840–1870," *JEH*, 16 (1956), pp. 281–321.

Cardwell, D. S. L. *From Watt to Clausius: The Rise of Thermodynamics in the Early Industrial Age* (Ithaca, N.Y., 1971).

Carey, W. H. *The Good Old Days of Honorable John Company*, 2 vols. (Calcutta, 1906–7).

Casale, Giancarlo. *The Ottoman Age of Exploration* (Oxford, 2010).

Caspard, Pierre. "Manufacture and Trade in Calico Printing at Neuchâtel," *Textile History*, 8 (1977), pp. 149–62.

Chandavarkar, Rajnarayan. "Industrialization in India before 1947: Conventional Approaches and Alternative Perspectives," *MAS*, 19 (1985), pp. 623–68.

The Origins of Industrial Capitalism in India: Business Strategies and the Working Classes in Bombay, 1900–1940 (Cambridge, 1994).

Chang, Ha-Joon. "Breaking the Mould: An Institutionalist Political Economy Alternative to the Neo-Liberal Theory of the Market and the State," *Cambridge Journal of Economics*, 26 (2002), pp. 539–59.

Chapman, S. D. and S. Chassagne. *European Textile Printers in the Eighteenth Century: A Study of Peel and Oberkampf* (London, 1981).

Chassagne, Serge. *Le coton et ses patrons: France, 1760–1840* (Paris, 1991).

Chaudhuri, K. N. *Asia Before Europe: Economy and Civilisation of the Indian Ocean from the Rise of Islam to 1750* (Cambridge, 1990).

"India's Foreign Trade and the Cessation of the East India Company's Trading Activities, 1828–1840," *Economic History Review*, 2nd ser., 19 (1966), pp. 345–63.

Trade and Civilisation in the Indian Ocean: An Economic History from the Rise of Islam to 1750 (Cambridge, 1985).

The Trading World of Asia and the East India Company, 1660–1760 (Cambridge, 1978).

Clapham, J. H. *Economic Development of France and Germany 1815–1914* (4th edn., Cambridge, 1936).

Clarence-Smith, William Gervase. "The Production of Cotton Textiles in Early Modern South-East Asia," in Riello and Parthasarathi, *Spinning World*, pp. 127–42.

Clark, Gregory. *A Farewell to Alms: A Brief Economic History of the World* (Princeton, 2007).

Cook, Harold J. *Matters of Exchange: Commerce, Medicine, and Science in the Dutch Golden Age* (New Haven, 2007).

Cooper, Randolf G. S. *The Anglo-Maratha Campaigns and the Contest for India: The Struggle for Control of the South Asian Military Economy* (Cambridge, 2003).

Cooper, R. G. S. and N. K. Wagle. "Maratha Artillery: From Dabhoi to Assaye," *Journal of the Ordnance Society*, 7 (1995), pp. 58–78.

Crafts, Nicholas. "Productivity Growth in the Industrial Revolution: A New Growth Accounting Perspective," *JEH*, 64 (2004), pp. 521–35.

Crafts, N. F. R. and C. K. Harley. "Output Growth and the British Industrial Revolution: A Restatement of the Crafts–Harley View," *Economic History Review*, n.s. 45 (1992), pp. 703–30.

Cunningham, Andrew and Perry Williams. "De-centering the 'Big Picture': *The Origins of Modern Science* and the Modern Origins of Science," *British Journal of the History of Science*, 26 (1993), pp. 407–32.

Darwin, John. *After Tamerlane: The Global History of Empire since 1405* (New York, 2008).

Das Gupta, A. "Indian Merchants and the Trade in the Indian Ocean," in Tapan Raychaudhuri and Irfan Habib (eds.), *The Cambridge Economic History of India*, vol. I, c.*1200–c.1750* (Cambridge, 1982), pp. 407–33.

Das Gupta, Ashin and M. N. Pearson (eds.). *India and the Indian Ocean 1500–1800* (Calcutta, 1987).

Das Gupta, Monica. "Fertility Decline in Punjab: Parallels with Historical Europe," *Population Studies*, 49 (1995), pp. 481–500.

Datta, Rajat. *Society, Economy and the Market: Commercialisation in Rural Bengal, c.1760–1800* (Delhi, 2000).

Daunton, M. J. *Progress and Poverty: An Economic and Social History of Britain 1700–1850* (Oxford, 1995).

Davis, Mike. *Late Victorian Holocausts: El Niño Famines and the Making of the Third World* (London, 2002).

Davis, Ralph. "English Foreign Trade, 1700–1774," *Economic History Review*, 2nd ser., 15 (1962), pp. 285–303.

The Industrial Revolution and British Overseas Trade (Leicester, 1979).

Deane, Phyllis. *The First Industrial Revolution* (Cambridge, 1965).

Depitre, Edgard. *La toile peinte en France au xvii et au xviii siècles; industrie, commerce, prohibitions* (Paris, 1912).

Dirks, Nicholas B. *Castes of Mind: Colonialism and the Making of Modern India* (Princeton, 2001).

DuPlessis, Robert S. "Cloth and the Emergence of the Atlantic Economy," in Peter Coclanis (ed.), *The Atlantic Economy during the Seventeenth and Eighteenth Centuries* (Columbia, S.C., 2005), pp. 72–94.

"Cottons Consumption in the Seventeenth- and Eighteenth-Century North Atlantic," in Riello and Parthasarathi, *Spinning World*, pp. 227–46.

Dutt, Romesh. *The Economic History of India*, vol. I, *Under Early British Rule* (2nd edn., London, 1906, repr. Delhi, 1990).

The Economic History of India, vol. II, *In the Victorian Age 1837–1900* (2nd edn., London, 1906, repr. Delhi, 1990).

Dyson, Tim. "The Historical Demography of Berar, 1881–1980," in Tim Dyson (ed.), *India's Historical Demography: Studies in Famine, Disease and Society* (London, 1989), pp. 150–96.

Eaton, Richard M. *The Rise of Islam and the Bengal Frontier, 1204–1760* (Berkeley, 1993).

A Social History of the Deccan, 1300–1761: Eight Indian Lives (Cambridge, 2005).

Ekelund, Jr., Robert B. and Robert D. Tollison. *Politicized Economies: Monarchy, Monopoly, and Mercantilism* (College Station, Tex., 1997).

Eldem, Edhem. *French Trade in Istanbul in the Eighteenth Century* (Leiden, 1999).

Ellison, Thomas. *The Cotton Trade of Great Britain* (London, 1886).

Elvin, Mark. *The Pattern of the Chinese Past* (Stanford, 1973).

"Skills and Resources in Late Traditional China," in Dwight H. Perkins (ed.), *China's Modern Economy in Historical Perspective* (Stanford, 1975), pp. 85–113.

"Three Thousand Years of Unsustainable Growth: China's Environment from Archaic Times to the Present," *East Asian History*, 6 (1993), pp. 7–46.

Epstein, S. R. "Craft Guilds, Apprenticeship, and Technological Change in Pre-Industrial Europe," *JEH*, 58 (1998), pp. 684–713.

Freedom and Growth: The Rise of States and Markets in Europe, 1300–1750 (London, 2000).

"Property Rights to Technical Knowledge in Premodern Europe, 1300–1800," *American Economic Review*, 94 (2004), pp. 382–7.

Farnie, Douglas. *The English Cotton Industry and the World Market, 1815–1896* (Oxford, 1979).

Faroqhi, Suraiya. "Ottoman Cotton Textiles: The Story of a Success that did not Last, 1500–1800," in Riello and Parthasarathi, *Spinning World*, pp. 89–103.

Febvre, Lucien. *The Problem of Unbelief in the Sixteenth Century: The Religion of Rabelais*, trans. Beatrice Gottlieb (Cambridge, Mass., 1982).

Ferguson, Niall. *Empire: The Rise and Demise of the British World Order and the Lessons for Global Power* (New York, 2003).

Field, Alexander James. "The Problem with Neoclassical Institutional Economics: A Critique with Special Reference to the North/Thomas Model of Pre-1500 Europe," *Explorations in Economic History*, 18 (1981), pp. 174–98.

Findlay, Ronald and Kevin H. O'Rourke. *Power and Plenty: Trade, War, and the World Economy in the Second Millennium* (Princeton, 2007).

Finnane, Antonia. *Speaking of Yangzhou: A Chinese City, 1550–1850* (Cambridge, Mass., 2004).

Fitton, R. S. and A. P. Wadsworth. *The Strutts and the Arkwrights* (Manchester, 1958).

Flinn, Michael W. "The Growth of the English Iron Industry 1660–1760," *Economic History Review*, 2nd ser., 11 (1958), pp. 144–53.

The History of the British Coal Industry, vol. II, *1700–1830, The Industrial Revolution* (Oxford, 1984).

Flynn, Dennis O. and Arturo Giráldez. "Born with a 'Silver Spoon': The Origin of World Trade," *Journal of World History*, 6 (1995), pp. 201–21.

Francks, Penelope. *Rural Economic Development in Japan from the Nineteenth Century to the Pacific War* (London, 2006).

Frangakis-Syrett, Elena. *The Commerce of Smyrna in the Eighteenth Century (1700–1820)* (Athens, 1992).

"The Trade of Cotton and Cloth in İzmir: From the Second Half of the Eighteenth Century to the Early Nineteenth Century," in Çaglar Keyder and Faruk Tabak (eds.), *Landholding and Commercial Agriculture in the Middle East* (Albany, 1991), pp. 97–111.

Frank, Andre Gunder. *ReOrient: Global Economy in the Asian Age* (Berkeley, 1998).

Fraser, Derek. "Edward Baines," in Patricia Hollis (ed.), *Pressure from Without in Early Victorian England* (London, 1974), pp. 183–209.

Fremdling, Rainer. "Continental Responses to British Innovations in the Iron Industry during the Eighteenth and Early Nineteenth Centuries," in Leandro Prados de la Escosura (ed.), *Exceptionalism and Industrialisation: Britain and its European Rivals, 1688–1815* (Cambridge, 2004), pp. 145–69.

"Foreign Competition and Technological Change: British Exports and the Modernisation of the German Iron Industry from the 1820s to the 1860s," in W. R. Lee (ed.), *German Industry and German Industrialization: Essays in German Economic and Business History in the Nineteenth and Twentieth Centuries* (London, 1991), pp. 47–76.

"Transfer Patterns of British Technology to the Continent: The Case of the Iron Industry," *European Review of Economic History*, 4 (2000), pp. 195–222.

Fremdling, R. and B. Gales. "Ironmasters and Iron Production during the Belgian Industrial Revolution: The 'Enquete' of 1828," in Paul Klep and Eddy van Cauwenberghe (eds.), *Entrepreneurship and the Transformation of the Economy (10th–20th Centuries): Essays in Honour of Herman van der Wee* (Leuven, 1994), pp. 247–58.

Fukasawa, Katsumi. *Toilerie et commerce du Levant: d'Alep à Marseilles* (Paris, 1987).

Fukazawa, Hiroshi. *The Medieval Deccan: Peasants, Social System and States, Sixteenth to Eighteenth Centuries* (Delhi, 1991).

Furniss, Edgar S. *The Position of the Laborer in a System of Nationalism: A Study of the Labor Theories of the Later English Mercantilists* (Boston, 1920).

Gadgil, D. R. *The Industrial Evolution of India in Recent Times* (London, 1924).

Gadgil, Madhav and Ramachandra Guha. *This Fissured Land: An Ecological History of India* (Berkeley, 1993).

Ganguli, B. N. *Indian Economic Thought: Nineteenth Century Perspectives* (New Delhi, 1977).

Geggus, David. "The French Slave Trade: An Overview," *William and Mary Quarterly*, 58 (2001), pp. 119–38.

Genç, Mehmet. "Ottoman Industry in the Eighteenth Century," in Donald Quataert (ed.), *Manufacturing in the Ottoman Empire and Turkey, 1500–1950* (Albany, N.Y., 1994), pp. 59–86.

Gerschenkron, Alexander. *Economic Backwardness in Historical Perspective: A Book of Essays* (Cambridge, Mass., 1962).

Gerth, H. H. and C. Wright Mills (eds.). *From Max Weber: Essays in Sociology* (New York, 1946).

Gillispie, Charles C. "The Natural History of Industry," *Isis*, 48 (1957), pp. 398–407.

Glamann, Kristoff. "The Dutch East India Company's Trade in Japanese Copper, 1645–1736," *Scandinavian Economic History Review*, 1 (1953), pp. 41–79.

Golas, Peter J. *Science and Civilisation in China,* vol. V, *Chemistry and Chemical Technology,* part 13, "Mining" (Cambridge, 1999).

Goldstone, Jack A. "Efflorescences and Economic Growth in World History: Rethinking the 'Rise of the West' and the Industrial Revolution," *Journal of World History*, 13 (2002), pp. 323–89.

Goody, Jack. *The East in the West* (Cambridge, 1996).

Greenberg, Dolores. "Reassessing the Power Patterns of the Industrial Revolution: An Anglo-American Comparison," *American Historical Review*, 87 (1982), pp. 1237–61.

Griffiths, Trevor, Philip Hunt and Patrick O'Brien. "The Curious History and Imminent Demise of the Challenge and Response Model," in Maxine Berg and Kristine Bruland (eds.), *Technological Revolutions in Europe: Historical Perspectives* (Cheltenham, 1998), pp. 119–37.

"Scottish, Irish, and Imperial Connections: Parliament, the Three Kingdoms, and the Mechanization of Cotton Spinning in Eighteenth-Century Britain," *Economic History Review*, n.s., 61 (2008), pp. 625–50.

Grove, Richard. "The Transfer of Botanical Knowledge between Europe and Asia, 1498–1800," *Journal of the Japan–Netherlands Institute*, 3 (1991), pp. 160–76.

Guha, Sumit. *The Agrarian Economy of the Bombay Deccan 1818–1941* (Delhi, 1985).

Health and Population in South Asia: From Earliest Times to the Present (New Delhi, 2001).

Guy, John. *Woven Cargoes: Indian Textiles in the East* (London, 1998).

Habakkuk, H. J. "The Historical Experience of Economic Development," in E. A. G. Robinson (ed.), *Problems in Economic Development:*

Proceedings of a Conference held by the International Economic Association (London, 1965), pp. 112–38.

Habib, Irfan. *The Agrarian System of Mughal India* (2nd rev. edn., Delhi, 1999).

"Akbar and Technology," in Irfan Habib (ed.), *Akbar and His India* (Delhi, 1997), pp. 129–48.

"Banking in Mughal India," in Tapan Raychaudhuri (ed.), *Contributions to Indian Economic History*, vol. I (1960), pp. 1–20.

"Cartography in Mughal India," *The Indian Archives*, 28 (1979), pp. 90–5.

"Labourers and Artisans," in J. S. Grewal (ed.), *The State and Society in Medieval India* (New Delhi, 2005), pp. 166–73.

"Usury in Medieval India," *CSSH*, 6 (1964), pp. 393–419.

(ed.). *Confronting Colonialism: Resistance and Modernization under Haidar Ali and Tipu Sultan* (New Delhi, 1999).

(ed.). *State and Diplomacy under Tipu Sultan: Documents and Essays* (New Delhi, 2001).

Haider, Najaf. "Precious Metal Flows and Currency Circulation in the Mughal Empire," *Journal of the Economic and Social History of the Orient*, 39 (1996), pp. 298–364.

"Structure and Movement of Wages in the Mughal Empire, 1500–1700," in Jan Lucassen (ed.), *Wages and Currency: Global Comparisons from Antiquity to the Twentieth Century* (Bern, 2007), pp. 293–321.

Hajnal, John. "Two Kinds of Preindustrial Household Formation System," *Population and Development Review*, 8 (1982), pp. 449–94.

Hammersley, G. "The Charcoal Iron Industry and its Fuel, 1540–1750," *Economic History Review*, 2nd ser., 26 (1973), pp. 593–613.

Hardgrave, Jr., Robert L. *A Portrait of the Hindus: Balthazar Solvyns and the European Image of India 1760–1824* (Ahmedabad, 2004).

Harley, C. Knick. "Reassessing the Industrial Revolution: A Macro View," in Joel Mokyr (ed.), *The British Industrial Revolution: An Economic Perspective* (2nd edn., Boulder, Colo., 1999), pp. 160–205.

Harris, J. R. *Industrial Espionage and Technology Transfer: Britain and France in the Eighteenth Century* (Aldershot, 1998).

"Skills, Coal and British Industry in the Eighteenth Century," *History*, 61 (1976), pp. 167–82.

Hartwell, Robert. "A Cycle of Economic Change in Imperial China: Coal and Iron in Northeast China, 750–1350," *Journal of the Economic and Social History of the Orient*, 10 (1967), pp. 102–59.

"A Revolution in the Iron and Coal Industries during the Northern Sung," *JAS*, 21 (1962), pp. 153–62.

Hatcher, John. *The History of the British Coal Industry*, vol. I, *Before 1700, Towards the Age of Coal* (Oxford, 1993).

Hausman, William J. "A Model of the London Coal Trade in the Eighteenth Century," *Quarterly Journal of Economics*, 94 (1980), pp. 1–14.

Haynes, Douglas E. and Tirthankar Roy. "Conceiving Mobility: Weavers' Migrations in Pre-Colonial and Colonial India," *IESHR*, 36 (1999), pp. 35–67.

Headrick, Daniel R. *The Tentacles of Progess: Technology Transfer in the Age of Imperialism, 1850–1940* (Oxford, 1988).

Heesterman, J. C. *The Inner Conflict of Tradition: Essays in Indian Ritual, Kingship, and Society* (Chicago, 1985).

Hefford, Wendy. *The Victoria and Albert Museum's Textile Collection: Design for Printed Textiles in England from 1750 to 1850* (New York, 1992).

Heston, Alan. "Review of Shireen Moosvi, *The Economy of the Mughal Empire c.1595: A Statistical Study*," *Economic History Review*, n.s., 41 (1988), pp. 670–2.

Hilaire-Perez, Liliane. "Invention and the State in 18th-Century France," *Technology and Culture*, 32 (1991), pp. 911–31.

"Technology as a Public Culture in the Eighteenth Century: The Artisans' Legacy," *History of Science*, 45 (2007), pp. 135–53.

Hilton, George. *The Truck System* (Cambridge, 1960).

The History and Description of Fossil Fuel, the Collieries, and Coal Trade of Great Britain (London, 1835).

Hobsbawm, Eric. *Industry and Empire: The Birth of the Industrial Revolution* (new edn., London, 1999).

Labouring Men (New York, 1964).

Homer, Sidney and Richard Sylla. *A History of Interest Rates* (4th edn., Hoboken, N.J., 2005).

Horn, Jeff. *The Path Not Taken: French Industrialization in the Age of Revolution, 1750–1830* (Cambridge, Mass., 2006).

Hossain, Hameeda. *The Company Weavers of Bengal: The East India Company and the Organization of Textile Production in Bengal 1750–1813* (Delhi, 1988).

Hudson, Derek and Kenneth W. Luckhurst. *The Royal Society of Arts, 1754–1954* (London, 1954).

Hudson, Pat. *The Genesis of Industrial Capital: A Study of the West Riding Wool Textile Industry, c.1750–1850* (Cambridge, 1986).

"Industrial Organisation and Structure," in Roderick Floud and Paul Johnson (eds.), *The Cambridge Economic History of Modern Britain*, vol. I, *Industrialisation, 1700–1860* (Cambridge, 2004), pp. 28–56.

Hughes, Edward. *North Country Life in the Eighteenth Century*, vol. I, *The North-East, 1700–1750* (Oxford, 1952).

Hurd, John M. "Railways," in Dharma Kumar (ed.), *Cambridge Economic History of India*, vol. II, c.*1757–c.1970* (Cambridge, 1982), pp. 737–61.

Hyde, Charles K. *Technological Change and the British Iron Industry, 1700–1870* (Princeton, 1977).

"Technological Change in the British Wrought Iron Industry, 1750–1815: A Reinterpretation," *Economic History Review*, 2nd ser., 27 (1974), pp. 190–206.

İnalcık, Halil. "The Ottoman Cotton Market and India: The Role of Labor Cost in Market Competition," in Halil İnalcık, *The Middle East and the Balkans under the Ottoman Empire: Essays on Economy and Society* (Bloomington, 1993), pp. 264–306.

"When and How British Cotton Goods Invaded the Levant Markets," in Huri İslamoğlu-İnan (ed.), *The Ottoman Empire and the World Economy* (Cambridge, 1987), pp. 374–83.

Inikori, Joseph E. *Africans and the Industrial Revolution in England: A Study in International Trade and Economic Development* (Cambridge, 2002).

Inkster, Ian. "Potentially Global: 'Useful and Reliable Knowledge' and Material Progress in Europe, 1474–1914," *International History Review*, 27 (2006), pp. 237–86.

Jacob, Margaret C. "Mechanical Science on the Factory Floor: The Early Industrial Revolution in Leeds," *History of Science*, 45 (2007), pp. 197–221.

Scientific Culture and the Making of the Industrial West (Oxford, 1997).

Jacob, Margaret C. and Matthew Kadane. "Missing, Now Found in the Eighteenth Century: Weber's Protestant Capitalist," *American Historical Review*, 108 (2003), pp. 20–49.

Jayaraman, R. *Sarasvati Mahal: A Short History and Guide* (Thanjavur, 1981).

John, A. H. "The London Assurance Company and the Marine Insurance Market of the Eighteenth Century," *Economica*, 25 (1958), pp. 126–41.

Johns, Adrian. "How to Acknowledge a Revolution," *American Historical Review*, 107 (2002), pp. 106–25.

The Nature of the Book: Print and Knowledge in the Making (Chicago, 1998).

Johnson, Marion. *Anglo-African Trade in the Eighteenth Century*, ed. J. T. Lindblad and Robert Ross (Leiden, 1990).

Jones, Eric. *The European Miracle: Environments, Economies and Geopolitics in the History of Europe and Asia* (3rd edn., Cambridge, 2003).

Kasturi, Malavika. *Embattled Identities: Rajput Lineages and the Colonial State in Nineteenth-Century North India* (Delhi, 2002).

Khan, B. Zorina and Kenneth L. Sokoloff. "A Tale of Two Countries: Innovation and Incentive among Great Inventors in Britain and the United States, 1750–1930," in Roger E. A. Farmer (ed.), *Macroeconomics in the Small and the Large: Essays on Microfoundations, Macroeconomic Applications and Economic History in Honor of Axel Leijonhufvud* (Cheltenham, 2008), pp. 140–55.

Khan, Iqbal Ghani. "The Awadh Scientific Renaissance and the Role of the French: *c.*1750–1820," *Indian Journal of History of Science*, 38 (2003), pp. 273–301.

"Technology and the Question of Elite Intervention in Eighteenth-Century North India," in Richard B. Barnett (ed.), *Rethinking Early Modern India* (New Delhi, 2002), pp. 257–88.

Khoury, Dina Rizk. *State and Provincial Society in the Ottoman Empire: Mosul, 1540–1834* (Cambridge, 1997).

Klein, Herbert S. *The Atlantic Slave Trade* (Cambridge, 1999).

Kling, Blair B. *Partner in Empire: Dwarkanath Tagore and the Age of Enterprise in Eastern India* (Berkeley, 1976).

Krugman, Paul R. "Is Free Trade Passé?" *Journal of Economic Perspectives*, 1 (1987), pp. 131–44.

"Trade, Accumulation, and Uneven Development," *Journal of Development Economics*, 8 (1981), pp. 149–61.

Kuhn, Philip A. *Origins of the Modern Chinese State* (Stanford, 2002).

Kumar, Deepak. "India," in Roy Porter (ed.), *The Cambridge History of Science*, vol. IV, *Eighteenth-Century Science* (Cambridge, 2003), pp. 669–87.

Kumar, Dharma. *Land and Caste in South India: Agricultural Labour in Madras Presidency in the Nineteenth Century* (Cambridge, 1965).

Lambert, Andrew. "Empire and Seapower: Shipbuilding by the East India Company at Bombay for the Royal Navy 1805–1850," in Philippe Haudrère, René Estienne and Gérard Le Bouëdec (eds.), *Les flottes des Compagnies des Indes 1600–1857* (Vincennes, 1996), pp. 149–71.

Landes, David S. *The Unbound Prometheus: Technological Change and Industrial Development in Western Europe from 1750 to the Present* (Cambridge, 1969).

The Wealth and Poverty of Nations: Why Some Are So Rich and Some So Poor (New York, 1998).

Lavely, William and R. Bin Wong. "Revising the Malthusian Narrative: The Comparative Study of Population Dynamics in Late Imperial China," *JAS*, 57 (1998), pp. 714–48.

Lee, James Z. and Wang Feng. *One Quarter of Humanity: Malthusian Mythology and Chinese Realities, 1700–2000* (Cambridge, Mass., 1999).

Lemire, Beverly. *Fashion's Favourite: The Cotton Trade and the Consumer in Britain, 1660–1800* (Oxford, 1991).

"Revising the Historical Narrative: India, Europe, and the Cotton Trade, *c.*1300–1800," in Riello and Parthasarathi, *Spinning World*, pp. 205–26.

Leonard, Karen. "The 'Great Firm' Theory of the Decline of the Mughal Empire," *CSSH*, 21 (1979), pp. 151–67.

Lewis, Frank. *English Chintz: A History of Printed Fabrics from Earliest Times to the Present Day* (Leigh-on-Sea, Essex, 1942).

Li, Bozhong. *Agricultural Development in Jiangnan, 1620–1850* (New York, 1998).

Li, Lillian M. *Fighting Famine in North China: State, Market, and Environmental Decline, 1690s–1990s* (Stanford, 2007).

Lin, Man-houng. *China Upside Down: Currency, Society, and Ideologies, 1808–1856* (Cambridge, Mass., 2006).

Linebaugh, Peter. *The London Hanged* (Cambridge, 1992).

Lobligeois, Mireille. "Atelier publics et filatures privées à Pondichéry après 1816," *Bulletin de l'École française d'Extrême Orient*, 59 (1972), pp. 3–99.

Lovejoy, Paul. *Transformations in Slavery: A History of Slavery in Africa* (Cambridge, 1983).

Ludden, David. "Agrarian Commercialism in Eighteenth-Century South India: Evidence from the 1823 Tirunelveli Census," *IESHR*, 25 (1988), pp. 493–519.

Peasant History in South India (Princeton, 1985).

Macfarlane, Alan. *The Savage Wars of Peace: England, Japan and the Malthusian Trap* (Oxford, 1997).

Machado, Pedro. "Awash in a Sea of Cloth: Gujarat, Africa, and the Western Indian Ocean, 1300–1800," in Riello and Parthasarathi, *Spinning World*, pp. 161–79.

MacLeod, Christine. "The European Origins of British Technological Predominance," in Leandro Prados de la Escosura (ed.), *Exceptionalism and Industrialisation: Britain and its European Rivals, 1688–1815* (Cambridge, 2004), pp. 111–26.

Inventing the Industrial Revolution: The English Patent System, 1660–1800 (Cambridge, 1988).

Malanima, Paolo. "The Energy Basis for Early Modern Growth, 1650–1820," in Maarten Prak (ed.), *Early Modern Capitalism: Economic and Social Change in Europe, 1400–1800* (London, 2001), pp. 51–68.

Mann, Michael. "Ecological Change in North India: Deforestation and Agrarian Distress in the Ganga-Yamuna Doab 1800–1850," in Richard H. Grove, Vinita Damodaran and Satpal Sangwan (eds.), *Nature and* the Orient: The Environmental History of South and Southeast Asia (Delhi, 1998), pp. 396–420.

Mantoux, Paul. The Industrial Revolution in the Eighteenth Century: An Outline of the Beginnings of the Modern Factory System in England (Chicago, 1983; reprint of revised edition of London, 1961).

Markovits, Claude. The Global World of Indian Merchants, 1750–1947: Traders of Sind from Bukhara to Panama (Cambridge, 2000).

Marks, Robert B. Tigers, Rice, Silk, and Silt: Environment and Economy in Late Imperial South China (Cambridge, 1998).

Marshall, P. J. "The Company and the Coolies: Labour in Early Calcutta," in P. Sinha (ed.), The Urban Experience, Calcutta: Essays in Honour of Professor Nisith R. Ray (Calcutta, 1987), pp. 23–38.

Marsot, Afaf Lutfi al-Sayyid. Egypt in the Reign of Muhammad Ali (Cambridge, 1984).

Martin, Gaston. Nantes au xviiie siècle: L'ère des négriers (1714–1774) (Paris, 1931).

Marx, Karl. The Eighteenth Brumaire of Louis Bonaparte (New York, 1963).

Mathias, Peter. The Transformation of England: Essays in the Economic and Social History of England in the Eighteenth Century (New York, 1979).

Mazzaoui, Maureen Fennell. The Italian Cotton Industry in the Later Middle Ages, 1100–1600 (Cambridge, 1981).

McCloskey, Deirdre. The Rhetoric of Economics (2nd edn., Madison, 1998).

McCrea, Lawrence. "Novelty of Form and Novelty of Substance in Seventeenth-Century Mimamsa," Journal of Indian Philosophy, 30 (2002), pp. 481–94.

"Playing with the System: Fragmentation and Individualization in Late Pre-colonial Mimamsa," Journal of Indian Philosophy, 36 (2008), pp. 575–85.

Minkowski, Christopher Z. "Competing Cosmologies in Early Modern Indian Astronomy," in Charles Burnett, Jan P. Hogendijk, Kim Plofker and Michio Yano (eds.), Studies in the History of the Exact Sciences in Honour of David Pingree (Leiden, 2004), pp. 349–85.

Mitra, D. B. The Cotton Weavers of Bengal, 1757–1833 (Calcutta, 1978).

Miyazaki, Yoichi. "Seicho Zenki No Sekitangyo: Kanryuki No Tanko Seisaku To Keiei (Coal Mining in Early Qing China: Coal Mining Policies and Administration during the Qianlong Period)," Shigaku Zasshi, 100 (1991), pp. 36–63.

Mokyr, Joel. The Enlightened Economy: An Economic History of Britain 1700–1850 (New Haven, 2009).

The Gifts of Athena: Historical Origins of the Knowledge Economy (Princeton, 2002).

"The Intellectual Origins of Modern Economic Growth," *JEH*, 65 (2005), pp. 285–351.

The Lever of Riches: Technological Creativity and Economic Progress (New York, 1990).

Montgomery, Florence. *Textiles in America, 1650–1870* (New York, 1984).

Moreland, W. H. *From Akbar to Aurangzeb: A Study in Indian Economic History* (London, 1923, repr. New Delhi, 1993).

India at the Death of Akbar: An Economic Study (London, 1920, repr. New Delhi, 1990).

Muldrew, Craig. *The Economy of Obligation: The Culture of Credit and Social Relations in Early Modern England* (New York, 1998).

Murton, Brian J. "Land and Class: Cultural, Social and Biophysical Integration in Interior Tamilnadu in the Late Eighteenth Century," in Robert E. Frykenberg (ed.), *Land Tenure and Peasant in South Asia* (Delhi, 1977), pp. 81–99.

Musson, A. E. and Eric Robinson. *Science and Technology in the Industrial Revolution* (Manchester, 1969).

Nadri, Ghulam A. *Eighteenth-Century Gujarat: The Dynamics of Its Political Economy, 1750–1800* (Leiden, 2009).

Nair, Savithri Preetha. "Native Collecting and Natural Knowledge (1798–1832): Raja Serfoji II of Tanjore as a 'Centre of Calculation,'" *Journal of the Royal Asiatic Society*, series 3, 15 (2005), pp. 279–302.

Naquin, Susan. *Peking: Temples and City Life, 1400–1900* (Berkeley, 2000).

Nef, John. *The Rise of the British Coal Industry*, 2 vols. (London, 1932).

North, Douglass C. *Understanding the Process of Economic Change* (Princeton, 2005).

North, Douglass C. and Robert Paul Thomas. *The Rise of the Western World: A New Economic History* (Cambridge, 1973).

O'Brien, Patrick. "Mercantilism and Imperialism in the Rise and Decline of the Dutch and British Economies 1585–1815," *De Economist*, 148 (2000), pp. 469–501.

"Political Preconditions for the Industrial Revolution," in Patrick O'Brien and Roland Quinault (eds.), *The Industrial Revolution and British Society* (Cambridge, 1993), pp. 124–55.

"State Formation and the Construction of Institutions for the First Industrial Nation," in Ha-Joon Chang, *Institutional Change and Economic Development* (New York, 2007), pp. 177–97.

O'Brien, Patrick, Trevor Griffiths and Philip Hunt. "Political Components of the Industrial Revolution: Parliament and the English Cotton Textile Industry, 1660–1774," *Economic History Review*, n.s., 44 (1991), pp. 395–423.

"Technological Change During the First Industrial Revolution: The Paradigm Case of Textiles, 1688–1851," in Robert Fox (ed.), *Technological Change: Methods and Themes in the History of Technology* (Amsterdam, 1996), pp. 155–76.

Ormrod, David. *The Rise of Commercial Empires: England and the Netherlands in the Age of Mercantilism* (Cambridge, 2003).

Osborne, Anne. "Highlands and Lowlands: Economic and Ecological Interactions in the Lower Yangzi Region under the Qing," in Mark Elvin and Liu Ts'ui-jung (eds.), *Sediments of Time: Environment and Society in Chinese History* (Cambridge, 1998), pp. 203–34.

"The Local Politics of Land Reclamation in the Lower Yangzi Highlands," *Late Imperial China*, 15 (1994), pp. 1–46.

Pamuk, Şevket. *A Monetary History of the Ottoman Empire* (Cambridge, 2000).

Panikkar, K. N. "Cultural Trends in Precolonial India: An Overview," in S. Irfan Habib and Dhruv Raina (eds.), *Social History of Science in Colonial India* (Delhi, 2007), pp. 1–24.

Panikkar, N. K. and T. M. Srinivasan. "*Kappal Sattiram*: A Tamil Treatise on Shipbuilding during the Seventeenth Century," *Indian Journal of the History of Science*, 7 (1972), pp. 16–26.

Paris, Robert. *Histoire du commerce de Marseille*, vol. V, *De 1660 à 1789; le Levant* (Paris, 1957).

Parthasarathi, Prasannan. "Agriculture, Labour, and the Standard of Living in Eighteenth-Century India," in Robert C. Allen, Tommy Bengtsson and Martin Dribe (eds.), *Living Standards in the Past: New Perspectives on Well-Being in Asia and Europe* (Oxford, 2005), pp. 99–109.

"Historical Issues of Deindustrialization in Nineteenth-Century South India," in Riello and Roy, *How India Clothed the World*, pp. 415–35.

"Rethinking Wages and Competitiveness in the Eighteenth Century: Britain and South India," *P&P*, 158 (1998), pp. 79–109.

The Transition to a Colonial Economy: Weavers, Merchants and Kings in South India, 1720–1800 (Cambridge, 2001).

Parthasarathi, Prasannan and Giorgio Riello. "From India to the World: Cotton and Fashionability," in Frank Trentmann (ed.), *The Oxford Handbook of the History of Consumption* (Oxford, forthcoming).

Paulinyi, Akos. "John Kay's Flying Shuttle: Some Considerations on His Technical Capacity and Economic Impact," *Textile History*, 17 (1986), pp. 149–66.

Peabody, Norbert. *Hindu Kingship and Polity in Precolonial India* (Cambridge, 2003).

Pearsall, Alan. "The Royal Navy and the Protection of Trade in the Eighteenth Century," in *Guerres et paix, 1660–1815* (Vincennes, 1987), pp. 149–62.

Pearson, M. N. "Asia and World Precious Metal Flows in the Early Modern Period," in John McGuire, Patrick Bertola and Peter Reeves (eds.), *Evolution of the World Economy, Precious Metals and India* (New Delhi, 2001), pp. 21–57.

Perdue, Peter C. *China Marches West: The Qing Conquest of Central Eurasia* (Cambridge, Mass., 2005).

  Exhausting the Earth: State and Peasant in Hunan, 1500–1850 (Cambridge, Mass., 1987).

Perlin, Frank. "Proto-Industrialization and Pre-Colonial South Asia," *P&P*, 98 (1983), pp. 30–95.

  "State Formation Reconsidered," *MAS*, 19 (1985), pp. 415–80.

Peterson, Indira Viswanathan. "The Cabinet of King Serfoji of Tanjore: A European Collection in Early Nineteenth-Century India," *Journal of the History of Collections*, 11 (1999), pp. 71–93.

Phillimore, R. H. *Historical Records of the Survey of India*, 4 vols. (Dehra Dun, 1945–1958).

Pollock, Sheldon. *The Ends of Man at the End of Premodernity* (Amsterdam, 2005).

  "Is There an Indian Intellectual History? Introduction to 'Theory and Method in Indian Intellectual History,'" *Journal of Indian Philosophy*, 36 (2008), pp. 533–42.

  "Literary Culture and Manuscript Culture in Precolonial India," in Simon Eliot, Andrew Nash and Ian Willison (eds.), *Literary Cultures and the Material Book* (London, 2007), pp. 77–94.

Pomeranz, Kenneth. *The Great Divergence: China, Europe and the Making of the Modern World Economy* (Princeton, 2000).

Prakash, Om. "Bullion for Goods: International Trade and the Economy of Early Eighteenth-Century Bengal," *IESHR*, 13 (1976), pp. 159–87.

  "The Dutch and the Indian Ocean Textile Trade," in Riello and Parthasarathi, *Spinning World*, pp. 145–60.

  The Dutch East India Company and the Economy of Bengal, 1630–1720 (Princeton, 1985).

  "Global Precious Metal Flows and India, 1500–1750," in John McGuire, Patrick Bertola and Peter Reeves (eds.), *Evolution of the World Economy, Precious Metals and India* (New Delhi, 2001), pp. 59–76.

Qaisar, Ahsan Jan. *The Indian Response to European Technology and Culture* (Delhi, 1982).

Quataert, Donald. "Clothing Laws, State, and Society in the Ottoman Empire, 1720–1829," *International Journal of Middle East Studies,* 29 (1997), pp. 403–25.

(ed.). *Consumption Studies and the History of the Ottoman Empire, 1550–1922: An Introduction* (Albany, 2000).

Raj, Kapil. *Relocating Modern Science: Circulation and the Construction of Scientific Knowledge in South Asia and Europe* (Delhi, 2006).

Ram, H. Y. Mohan. "On the English Edition of Van Rheede's *Hortus Malabaricus* by K. S. Manilal (2003)," *Current Science,* 89 (2005), pp. 1672–80.

Raveux, Olivier. "The Birth of a New European Industry: *L'Indiennage* in Seventeenth-Century Marseilles," in Riello and Parthasarathi, *Spinning World,* pp. 291–306.

"Spaces and Technologies in the Cotton Industry in the Seventeenth and Eighteenth Centuries: The Example of Printed Calicoes in Marseilles," *Textile History,* 36 (2005), pp. 131–45.

Ray, Rajat Kanta. "Asian Capital in the Age of European Domination: The Rise of the Bazaar, 1800–1914," *MAS,* 29 (1995), pp. 449–554.

Raychaudhuri, Tapan. "The Mid-Eighteenth Century Background," in Dharma Kumar (ed.), *The Cambridge Economic History of India,* vol. II, c.*1757–c.1970* (Cambridge, 1982), pp. 3–35.

"Non-Agricultural Production: Mughal India," in Tapan Raychaudhuri and Irfan Habib (eds.), *The Cambridge Economic History of India,* vol. I, c.*1200–c.1750* (Cambridge, 1982), pp. 261–307.

Raymond, André. *Artisans et commerçants au Caire au xviii siècle,* 2 vols. (Damascus, 1973).

"Les sources de la richesse urbaine au Caire au dix-huitième siècle," in Thomas Naff and Roger Owen (eds.), *Studies in Eighteenth Century Islamic History* (Carbondale, Ill., 1977), pp. 184–204.

"L'impact de la pénétration Européenne sur l'économie de l'Égypte au xviii siècle," *Annales islamologiques,* 18 (1982), pp. 217–35.

Redford, Arthur. *Manchester Merchants and Foreign Trade, 1794–1858* (Manchester, 1934, repr. Manchester 1973).

Richards, John F. "Mughal State Finance and the Premodern World Economy," *CSSH,* 23 (1981), pp. 285–308.

The Unending Frontier: An Environmental History of the Early Modern World (Berkeley, 2003).

Richardson, David. "The Eighteenth-Century British Slave Trade: Estimates of its Volume and Coastal Distribution in Africa," *Research in Economic History,* 12 (1989), pp. 151–95.

Riello, Giorgio. "Asian Knowledge and the Development of Calico Printing in Europe in the Seventeenth and Eighteenth Centuries," *Journal of Global History,* 5 (2010), pp. 1–28.

"The Globalization of Cotton Textiles: Indian Cottons, Europe, and the Atlantic World, 1600–1850", in Riello and Parthasarathi, *Spinning World*, pp. 261–87.

"The Indian Apprenticeship: The Trade of Indian Textiles and the Making of European Cottons," in Riello and Roy, *How India Clothed the World*, pp. 309–46.

Riello, Giorgio and Prasannan Parthasarathi (eds.). *The Spinning World: A Global History of Cotton Textiles, 1200–1850* (Oxford, 2009).

Riello, Giorgio and Tirthankar Roy (eds.). *How India Clothed the World: The World of South Asian Textiles, 1500–1850* (Leiden, 2009).

Roberts, Lissa, Simon Schaffer and Peter Dear (eds.). *The Mindful Hand: Inquiry and Invention from the Late Renaissance to Early Industrialization* (Amsterdam, 2007).

Roberts, Richard. "West Africa and the Pondicherry Textile Industry," in Tirthankar Roy (ed.), *Cloth and Commerce: Textiles in Colonial India* (New Delhi, 1996), pp. 142–74.

Roche, Daniel. *The Culture of Clothing: Dress and Fashion in the Ancien Régime*, trans. Jean Birrell (Cambridge, 1994).

Rothstein, Natalie. "The Calico Campaign of 1719–1721," *East London Papers*, 7 (1964), pp. 3–21.

Rowe, William T. *Hankow: Commerce and Society in a Chinese City, 1796–1889* (Stanford, 1984).

Saving the World: Chen Hongmou and Elite Consciousness in Eighteenth-Century China (Stanford, 2001).

Roy, Tirthankar. "Economic History and Modern India: Redefining the Link," *Journal of Economic Perspectives*, 16 (2002), pp. 109–30.

"Knowledge and Divergence from the Perspective of Early Modern India," *Journal of Global History*, 3 (2008), pp. 361–87.

Rudner, David West. "Banker's Trust and the Culture of Banking among the Nattukottai Chettiars of Colonial South India," *MAS*, 23 (1989), pp. 417–58.

Caste and Capitalism in Colonial India: The Nattukottai Chettiars (Berkeley, 1994).

Rule, John. *The Experience of Labour in Eighteenth-Century Industry* (New York, 1981).

Rungta, Radhe Shyam. *The Rise of Business Corporations in India* (Cambridge, 1970).

Said, Edward. *Orientalism* (New York, 1978).

Saito, Osamu. "Forest History and the Great Divergence: China, Japan, and the West Compared," *Journal of Global History*, 4 (2009), pp. 379–404.

Samuel, Raphael. "Workshop of the World: Steam Power and Hand Technology in mid-Victorian Britain," *History Workshop*, 3 (1977), pp. 6–72.

Sangwan, Satpal. *Science, Technology and Colonisation: An Indian Experience, 1757–1857* (Delhi, 1991).

"The Sinking Ships: Colonial Policy and the Decline of Indian Shipping, 1735–1835," in Roy MacLeod and Deepak Kumar (eds.), *Technology and the Raj: Western Technology and Technical Transfers to India 1700–1947* (New Delhi, 1995), pp. 137–52.

Sargent, Thomas J. and François R. Velde. *The Big Problem of Small Change* (Princeton, 2002).

Sarma, Sreeramula Rajeswara. "Indian Astronomical and Time-Measuring Instruments: A Catalogue in Preparation," *Indian Journal of History of Science*, 29 (1994), pp. 507–28.

Schoppa, R. Keith. *Xiang Lake – Nine Centuries of Chinese Life* (New Haven, 1989).

Schubert, H. R. *History of the British Iron and Steel Industry* (London, 1957).

Schumpeter, Elizabeth. *English Overseas Trade Statistics, 1697–1808* (Oxford, 1960).

Schwartz, Paul. "Textile Printing," in Maurice Daumas (ed.), *A History of Technology and Invention: Progress through the Ages*, vol. III, *The Expansion of Mechanization, 1725–1860*, trans. Eileen B. Hennessy (New York, 1979), pp. 633–54.

Schwartzberg, Joseph E. "South Asian Cartography: Geographical Mapping," in J. B. Harley and David Woodward (eds.), *The History of Cartography*, vol. II, bk. 1, *Cartography in the Traditional Islamic and South Asian Societies* (Chicago, 1992), pp. 388–493.

Sen, Amartya Kumar. *Poverty and Famines: An Essay on Entitlement and Deprivation* (Oxford, 1981).

Shammas, Carole. "The Decline of Textile Prices in England and British America Prior to Industrialization," *Economic History Review*, n.s., 47 (1994), pp. 483–507.

Shapin, Steven. *The Scientific Revolution* (Chicago, 1996).

Sharma, Virendra Nath. *Sawai Jai Singh and his Astronomy* (Delhi, 1995).

Shiue, Carol H. "The Political Economy of Famine Relief in China, 1740–1820," *Journal of Interdisciplinary History*, 36 (2005), pp. 33–55.

Shiue, Carol H. and Wolfgang Keller. "Markets in China and Europe on the Eve of the Industrial Revolution," *American Economic Review*, 97 (2007), pp. 1189–1216.

Siddiqi, Asiya. *Agrarian Change in a North Indian State: Uttar Pradesh, 1819–1833* (Oxford, 1973).

"The Business World of Jamsetjee Jejeebhoy," in Asiya Siddiqi (ed.), *Trade and Finance in Colonial India, 1750–1860* (Delhi, 1995), pp. 186–217.

Sieferle, Rolf Peter. *The Subterranean Forest: Energy Systems and the Industrial Revolution*, trans. Michael P. Osman (Cambridge, 2001).

Sinha, N. K. *The Economic History of Bengal*, vol. I, *From Plassey to the Permanent Settlement* (2nd edn., Calcutta, 1961).

The Economic History of Bengal, vol. III, *1793–1848* (Calcutta, 1970).

Sivin, Nathan. "Why the Scientific Revolution Did Not Take Place in China – Or Didn't It?" *Chinese Science*, 5 (1982), pp. 45–66.

Sivramkrishna, Sashi. "Ascertaining Living Standards in Erstwhile Mysore, Southern India, from Francis Buchanan's *Journey* of 1800–01: An Empirical Contribution to the Great Divergence Debate," *Journal of the Economic and Social History of the Orient*, 52 (2009), pp. 695–733.

Spate, O. H. K. *India and Pakistan: A General and Regional Geography* (2nd edn., London, 1957).

Spufford, Margaret. "The Cost of Apparel in Seventeenth-Century England, and the Accuracy of Gregory King," *Economic History Review*, n.s., 53 (2000), pp. 677–705.

Stein, Burton. "State Formation and Economy Reconsidered," *MAS*, 19 (1985), pp. 387–413.

Stein, Robert Louis. *The French Slave Trade in the Eighteenth Century: An Old Regime Business* (Madison, 1979).

Stiglitz, Joseph E. "The Contributions of the Economics of Information to Twentieth Century Economics," *Quarterly Journal of Economics*, 115 (2000), pp. 1441–78.

Stiglitz, Joseph E. and Andrew Weiss. "Credit Rationing in Markets with Imperfect Information," *American Economic Review*, 71 (1981), pp. 393–410.

Studer, Roman. "India and the Great Divergence: Assessing the Efficiency of Grain Markets in Eighteenth- and Nineteenth-Century India," *JEH*, 68 (2008), pp. 393–437.

Styles, John. *The Dress of the People: Everyday Fashion in Eighteenth-Century England* (New Haven, 2007).

Subrahmanyam, Sanjay. "A Note on Narsapur Peta: A 'Syncretic' Shipbuilding Centre in South India, 1570–1700," *Journal of the Economic and Social History of the Orient*, 31 (1988), pp. 305–11.

The Political Economy of Commerce: Southern India, 1500–1650 (Cambridge, 1990).

"The Portuguese, the Port of Basrur and the Rice Trade, 1600–50," *IESHR*, 21 (1984), pp. 433–62.

Sugihara, Kaoru. "The East Asian Path of Development: A Long-Term Perspective," in G. Arrighi, T. Hamashita and M. Selden (eds.), *The Resurgence of East Asia* (London, 2003), pp. 82–102.

Supple, Barry. "The State and the Industrial Revolution 1700–1914," in Carlo M. Cipolla (ed.), *The Fontana Economic History of Europe: The Industrial Revolution* (London, 1973), pp. 301–57.

Tann, Jennifer and John Aitken. "The Diffusion of the Stationary Steam Engine from Britain to India 1790–1830," *IESHR*, 29 (1992), pp. 199–214.

Tann, Jennifer and M. M. Breckin. "The International Diffusion of the Watt Engine, 1775–1825," *Economic History Review*, n.s., 31 (1978), pp. 541–64.

Thirsk, Joan. *Economic Policy and Projects: The Development of a Consumer Society in Early Modern England* (Oxford, 1978).

Thomas, P. J. *Mercantilism and the East India Trade* (London, 1926).

Thomas, P. J. and B. Nataraja Pillai. *Economic Depression in the Madras Presidency (1820–1854)* (Madras, 1933).

Thompson, E. P. "Time, Work-Discipline, and Industrial Capitalism," *P&P*, 38 (1967), pp. 56–97.

Thomson, J. K. J. *A Distinctive Industrialization: Cotton in Barcelona, 1728–1832* (Cambridge, 1992).

Timmins, Geoffrey. "Technological Change," in Mary Rose (ed.), *The Lancashire Cotton Industry: A History since 1700* (Preston, 1996), pp. 29–62.

Tipton, Frank. "Government and Economy in the Nineteenth Century," in Sheilagh Ogilvie and Richard Overy (eds.), *Germany: A New Social and Economic History*, vol. III, *Since 1800* (London, 2003), pp. 106–51.

Totman, Conrad. *Early Modern Japan* (Berkeley, 1993).

  The Green Archipelago: Forestry in Pre-Industrial Japan (Athens, Ohio, 1998).

  A History of Japan (Malden, Mass., 2000).

  The Origins of Japan's Modern Forests: The Case of Akita (Honolulu, 1985).

Tripathi, Amales. *Trade and Finance in the Bengal Presidency* (new edn., Calcutta, 1979).

Turner, Michael J. "Before the Manchester School: Economic Theory in Early Nineteenth-Century Manchester," *History*, 79 (1994), pp. 216–41.

Tversky, Amos and Daniel Kahneman. "Loss Aversion in Riskless Choice: A Reference-Dependent Model," *Quarterly Journal of Economics*, 106 (1991), pp. 1039–61.

Ülker, Necmi. "The Emergence of İzmir as a Mediterranean Commercial Center for the French and English Interests, 1698–1740," *International Journal of Turkish Studies*, 4 (1987), pp. 1–37.

Unwin, George. *Samuel Oldknow and the Arkwrights: The Industrial Revolution in Stockport and Marple* (2nd edn., New York, 1968).

van Santen, H. W. "Trade between Mughal India and the Middle East, and Mughal Monetary Policy, *c.*1600–1660," in Karl Reinhold Haellquist (ed.), *Asian Trade Routes* (London, 1991), pp. 87–95.

van Schendel, Willem. *Three Deltas: Accumulation and Poverty in Rural Burma, Bengal and South India* (New Delhi, 1991).

van Zanden, Jan Luiten. *The Long Road to the Industrial Revolution: The European Economy in Global Perspective, 1000–1800* (Leiden, 2009).

   "The Road to the Industrial Revolution: Hypotheses and Conjectures about the Medieval Origins of the 'European Miracle,'" *Journal of Global History*, 3 (2008), pp. 337–59.

Veinstein, Gilles. "Commercial Relations between India and the Ottoman Empire (Late Fifteenth to Late Eighteenth Centuries): A Few Notes and Hypotheses," in Sushil Chaudhury and Michel Morineau (eds.), *Merchants, Companies and Trade: Europe and Asia in the Early Modern Era* (Cambidge, 1999), pp. 95–115.

Vicente, Marta V. "Fashion, Race, and Cotton Textiles in Colonial Spanish America," in Riello and Parthasarathi, *Spinning World*, pp.247–60.

Victoria and Albert Museum. *English Printed Textiles 1720–1836* (London, 1960).

Viraphol, Sarasin. *Tribute and Profit: Sino-Siamese Trade, 1652–1853* (Cambridge, Mass., 1977).

von Braun, Wernher and Frederick I. Ordway, III. *History of Rocketry and Space Travel* (New York, 1967).

von Glahn, Richard. *Fountain of Fortune: Money and Monetary Policy in China, 1000–1700* (Berkeley, 1996).

von Tunzelmann, G. N. *Steam Power and British Industrialization to 1860* (Oxford, 1978).

Voth, Hans-Joachim. *Time and Work in England, 1750–1830* (Oxford, 2000).

Vries, Jan de and Ad van der Woude. *The First Modern Economy: Success, Failure, and Perseverance of the Dutch Economy, 1500–1815* (Cambridge, 1997).

Wadsworth, Alfred P. and Julia de Lacy Mann. *The Cotton Trade and Industrial Lancashire, 1600–1780* (Manchester, 1931, repr. New York, 1968).

Wagner, Donald B. *The Traditional Chinese Iron Industry and its Modern Fate* (Richmond, 1997).

Wallerstein, Immanuel. *The Modern World System II: Mercantilism and the Consolidation of the European World-Economy, 1600–1750* (New York, 1980).

Washbrook, David. "Economic Depression and the Making of 'Traditional' Society in Colonial India," *Transactions of the Royal Historical Society*, 6th series, III (London, 1993), pp. 237–63.

"Land and Labour in Eighteenth-Century South India: The Golden Age of the Pariah?" in Peter Robb (ed.), *Dalit Movements and the Meanings of Labour in India* (Delhi, 1993), pp. 40–59.

"Progress and Problems: South Asian Economic and Social History c.1720–1860," *MAS*, 22 (1988), pp. 57–96.

Weber, Max. *The Protestant Ethic and the Spirit of Capitalism*, trans. Talcott Parsons (London, 1992, reprint of 1930 edn.).

The Religion of China, trans. Hans H. Gerth (New York, 1951).

The Religion of India, trans. Hans H. Gerth and Don Martindale (New York, 1958).

Will, Pierre-Étienne. *Bureaucracy and Famine in Eighteenth-Century China*, trans. Elborg Forster (Stanford, 1990).

Will, Pierre-Étienne and R. Bin Wong (with James Lee, Jean C. Oi and Peter C. Perdue). *Nourish the People: The State Civilian Granary System in China, 1650–1850* (Ann Arbor, 1991).

Williams, Raymond. *Keywords: A Vocabulary of Culture and Society* (London, 1976).

Wong, R. Bin. *China Transformed: Historical Change and the Limits of European Experience* (Ithaca, N.Y., 1997).

"Food Riots in the Qing Dynasty," *JAS*, 41 (1982), pp. 767–88.

Wong, R. Bin and Peter C. Perdue. "Famine's Foes in Ch'ing China," *Harvard Journal of Asiatic Studies*, 43 (1983), pp. 291–332.

Wood, Sir Henry Trueman. *A History of the Royal Society of the Arts* (London, 1913).

Wrigley, E. A. *Continuity, Chance and Change: The Character of the Industrial Revolution in England* (Cambridge, 1988).

Wujastyk, Dominik. "The Questions of King Tukkoji: Medicine at an Eighteenth-Century South Indian Court," *Indian Journal of History of Science*, 41 (2006), pp. 357–69.

Young, H. A. *The East India Company's Arsenals and Manufactories* (Oxford, 1937).

Unpublished

Khan, Iqbal Ghani. "Revenue, Warfare and Agriculture in North India: Technical Knowledge and the Post-Mughal Elites from the Mid-18th to the Early 19th Century," unpublished Ph.D. dissertation, University of London, 1990.

Klein, Rudiger. "Trade in the Safavid Port City Bandar Abbas and the Persian Gulf Area (*ca.*1600–1680): A Study of Selected Aspects," unpublished Ph.D. dissertation, University of London, 1994.

Menon, Saraswati. "Social Characteristics of Land Control in Thanjavur District during the 19th Century: A Sociological Study," unpublished Ph.D. dissertation, Jawaharlal Nehru University, 1983.

Narasimha, Roddam. "Rockets in Mysore and Britain, 1750–1850 A.D.," lecture delivered on 2 April 1985 at the inauguration of the Centre for History and Philosophy of Science, Indian Institute of World Culture, Bangalore, National Aeronautical Laboratory, Project Document DU 8503.

O'Brien, Patrick Karl. "Fiscal and Financial Preconditions for the Rise of British Naval Hegemony 1485–1815," London School of Economics, Department of Economic History Working Paper, No. 91/05, November 2005.

   "The History, Nature and Economic Signficance of an Exceptional Fiscal State for the Growth of the British Economy, 1453–1815," London School of Economics, Department of Economic History Working Paper, No. 109/08, October 2008.

Osborne, Anne Rankin. "Barren Mountains, Raging Rivers: The Ecological and Social Effects of Changing Land Use on the Lower Yangzi Periphery in Late Imperial China," unpublished Ph.D. dissertation, Columbia University, 1989.

Parthasarathi, Prasannan. "Productivity in South Indian Agriculture, *c.*1800," paper presented at a Workshop on Agricultural Productivity, University of California, Davis, December 2002.

Prakash, Om. "Indian Textiles in the Indian Ocean in the Early Modern Period," unpublished paper.

Wong, R. Bin. "Taxation and Good Governance in China, 1500–1914," unpublished paper presented at the Harvard Economic History Workshop, 23 September 2005.

Index

Aabidin, Zein al, 199
Abbas, Shah, 199
accountancy, 82–4
Achuden, Itty, 191
agriculture
  in China, 76
  crop failures, 76–9
  in England, 68, 71
  financial support for, 79–80
  in India, 41, 53, 61, 68–71,
    76–8, 267
  and industrialization, 67–9
  manuals, 206
  and manufacturing, 68
  and property rights, 66–71
  state support for, 206–7, 267
Aikin, John, 103, 153
A'in-i Akbari, 42
air cooling, 203–4
Aitken, John, 230
Akbar (Mughal Emperor), 203–5, 218
Alexander the Great (Alexander of
    Macedon), 265
Ali, Haider, 207
Allah, Lutif, 199
Allen, Robert, 45, 68, 109, 126
Althen, Johann, 91
Anatolia, 122–3
Anstey, Vera, 225
Archimedes, 200
architecture, 196
Arkwright, Richard, 95, 98, 104–6,
    109, 111–12, 131, 218
armaments, 206–7, 211–13, 251,
    255–6
Art de faire l'indienne, L', 92
Art de la teinture des fils et étoffes de
    coton, L', 92
Art de peindre les toiles, L', 92
artisans, 216–19

Artisans et commerçants au Caire au
    xviii siècle, 120
Ashton, Thomas Southcliffe, 167
Asia
  and Europe, 1, 7, 10–11, 51–3
  markets in, 3–5
  population balance in, 4, 51
  property rights in, 5
  rationality in, 4, 6, 52, 80–4
  and scientific revolution problem,
    189–90
astronomy, 195–7
Atlantic market, 116, 133–42
  and Britain, 134–7
  and France, 140–2
  Indian cottons, 25–6
  and Ottoman Empire, 137
  and slave trade, 140–1
Attman, Artur, 49
Aubin, Christophe, 122–3, 152
Aurangzeb (Mughal Emperor), 33

Bacon, Francis, 53
badams, 50
Bagchi, Amiya, 226
Baines, Edward, 99, 100–3,
    109–11, 113
Bancroft, Edward, 92
bargaining power, 40
Barnes, Elias, 108
Basset, John, 38
Bayly, Christopher, 54, 60, 64, 67, 79,
    82–3, 215, 255–6
Bayly, Susan, 59
Belgium, 246, 248–50
Bell, Andrew, 208
Bengal, 15, 61, 69–70
  famine of 1769–70, 78–9
Bernier, François, 51, 53–4, 58, 66,
    198, 264

Bertin, M., 91
blue cloth trade, 34
Bodin, Jean, 53
Bomanji, Jamsetji, 233
botany, 191–2
Boulle, Pierre, 141–2
Boulton, Matthew, 229
Bowrey, Thomas, 217
Bozhong, Li, 69
Breckin, M. M., 230
Brenner, Robert, 3, 5, 67–8, 71
Brief Memoir of Samuel Crompton,
    A, 110
Britain, 14
    agriculture in, 68
    and Atlantic market, 134–7
    capital markets in, 240–1
    cloth printing in, 127
    coal in, 11, 18, 152, 161–8
    coin shortages in, 60
    economy policy, 144–5
    family and household structures, 74
    and France, 116, 133–4, 247–8
    grain markets in, 62
    Indian cloth in, 2, 23–4, 31–2,
        35, 211
    industrialization of, 223
    interest rates in, 64–5
    iron industry in, 161, 168–70,
        246, 267
    labor in, 41, 69, 146–7
    manufacturing in, 11–12
    property rights in, 3–4, 67–8
    shipbuilding costs in, 232
    and slave trade, 24, 140–1
    spinning and weaving in, 41
    state actions in, 12–13, 144
    technological innovation in, 2–3, 90,
        98–103, 221, 260
    and trade, 112, 151–4, 267
    unemployment in, 40
    wages in, 38–9
    woolen manufacturers in, 127–8
    worker bargaining power in, 40
    working hours in, 41–2
British colonial policies, 256–8
    education, 254
    government, 13, 18, 78–80
    and Indian industry, 224–7, 244–5,
        252–61, 266–7

and Indian science and technology,
    201–2, 253–4, 257
and trade, 244, 258
British cotton industry, 12, 17–18, 37
    and Atlantic market, 134–5
    and excise taxes, 111–12
    expansion of, 151–4
    and free trade, 112–13
    histories of, 98–103
    and Indian competition, 98, 104,
        106–9, 112, 127–31, 267
    and machinery industry, 153–4
    muslin tariff, 130–1
    and North American market,
        137, 140
    and Ottoman markets, 118–19,
        122–3
    protectionism, 125–31, 133, 145,
        245, 267
    and raw cotton imports, 133, 257–8
    and Smithian political economy,
        109–14
    and state policy, 125–31
    and steam power, 154–5
    technological innovations in, 90,
        98–103, 221
    water frame and, 95, 105
    and West Africa trade, 95–8,
        134–6, 141
    and yarn shortages, 98, 100–4
British Industrial Revolution in Global
    Perspective, The, 126
Broadberry, Stephen, 42–5
Brose, Eric, 249
Buchanan, Francis, 45, 69, 181, 208
Buffon, Georges-Louis Leclerc Comte
    de, 200
bullion, 46–50
Burdwan coal, 231–2

calendars, 197
Calico Act of 1700, 130
calico craze, 23
calico printing, 90–5
Cambridge Economic History of India,
    The, 226
cannibalism, 76
cannons, 212–13
capitalism, 80
capital markets, 240–1, 260

Cardwell, D. S. L., 220
Carey, W. H., 233
Carter, Charles, 210
cartography, 204–5
Cary, John, 108
caste system, 6
  and commerce, 59–60
  and long-distance trading, 60
  and occupational and social mobility,
    59–60
  and property rights, 58
  and rationality, 81
cataclysmic events, 76
caulking, marine, 209
challenge and response model, 98–9,
  101–2, 113
Chandavarkar, Rajnarayan, 226
Chapman, Stanley, 90, 95
charcoal, 169, 172
Charles I, 164
Charles II, 31
Chassagne, Serge, 90–1, 95, 139, 148
Chaudhuri, Kirti Narayan, 21, 38, 48,
  209–10
chemistry, 217–18
China
  accounting in, 83
  agriculture in, 76
  coal in, 3–4, 11, 152, 158–60, 162,
    170–5
  deforestation in, 13, 174–6, 179
  economic growth in, 5
  and Europe, 6
  and foreign trade, 57–8
  grain markets in, 62
  granary system in, 173–4, 267
  highland reclamation in, 175–6
  iron production in, 171–3
  population checks in, 72
  rationality in, 81
  salt merchants in, 67
  scientific culture in, 189
  and silver imports, 46–7, 58
  state institutions in, 55, 57, 67
  state policy in, 173–6
  and world economy, 21–2
China Transformed, 5
chintz, 27
Clapham, John, 250
Cleghorn, Hugh, 181

clock making, 218
cloth printing, 90–5, 127–9
  in Britain, 127
  France, 138–40, 142
  linen, 91, 129
coal industry, 2–3, 11, 18, 151, 221
  anti-combination measures, 167
  in Britain, 11, 18, 152, 161–8
  in China, 3–4, 11, 152, 158–60, 162,
    170–5
  duties and taxes on, 165–6
  in Europe, 160–1
  and India, 182, 231–2
  and industrialization, 161
  and iron production, 169–70, 172
  in Japan, 158, 160
  knowledge transmission, 215
  and shipping protection, 167–8
  and state policies, 164–8, 170–5
  and technological advances, 151–2
  transportation of, 163, 167–8
Cochin, Raja of, 191, 195
coke, 172
*Colloquios dos simples e drogas a
  cousas medicinas da India*, 192
colonialism. *See* British colonial policies
color fastness, 33, 94, 96
Complete Equestrian, The, 198
Confucianism, 81
Congreve, William, 213
conservation, 158
Constable, George, 213
Cook, Harold, 191–2
Cooper, Randolf, 212
copper, 49–50
cotton textiles, 5, 10. *See also* British
    cotton industry; European cottons;
    Indian cottons
  Asian markets for, 26
  cotton–linen mix, 93–4, 97,
    129, 148
  cultivation manuals, 206
  in France, 116, 138–40, 148–50
  Ottoman, 50, 123–5
  prices, 34–7, 119–21
  qualities of, 23–4
  and slave trade, 24
  in South America, 26
  and trading network, 23–7, 61
  and wages, 34, 37–46

cowries, 50
Crafts, Nicholas, 11, 68, 153
credit systems, 64–5
Crompton, Samuel, 98, 104–6,
    109–10, 130–1, 154, 218
Cunningham, Andrew, 190

Dacca muslin, 33–4
D'Aligny, Théodore Caruelle, 92
Darby, Abraham, 169
Datta, Rajat, 61, 78–9
Daunton, Martin, 102, 144–5
Davis, Ralph, 137
Deane, Phyllis, 101
Defoe, Daniel, 31, 34
deforestation
    in China, 13, 174–6, 179
    in Europe, 2–3
    in India, 11, 180–2
    in Japan, 177–80
Delormois, Charles, 92
demographic regimes, 4, 6, 71–80
    and economic divergence, 72
    and family structures, 73–4
    population checks, 71–2, 75
Denmark, 74
Depitre, Edgard, 92, 139
despotism, 53–4
de Vries, Jan, 66
dictionaries, 206
divergence, economic, 2, 7, 12
    and agency, 268–9
    anachronistic views of, 268
    challenge and response model, 98–9,
        101–2, 113
    and context, 9, 13–14
    and empirical data, 263–4
    explanations for, 84–5, 221–2
    and historical categories, 264
    and Industrial Enlightenment, 189
    and scientific culture, 186
division of labor, 110–11
d'Orta, Garcia, 192
Dossie, Robert, 104
Duncan, Andrew, 235
Dundas, Henry, 211
Dutch East India Company, 26
Dutt, Romesh, 224, 244
dyeing, 91, 96–8, 218
Dyson, Tim, 74–5

earnings. *See* wages
Earnshaw, Lawrence, 107
East Africa, 23–4
Eaton, Richard, 23
ecological change, 157–62
    China, 13, 174–6, 179
    Europe, 2–3, 10, 157–8
    India, 180–2
    Japan, 177–80
education, 248–9
    in colonial India, 254
    European university system, 215–16
    and industrialization, 216
    and technological innovation, 260
Egypt, 119–21
*Eighteenth Brumaire of Louis
    Bonaparte, The*, 12
Elements, 197
Elgin, Lord (Thomas Bruce), 159, 162
Eliot, George (Mary Anne Evans), 27
Ellison, Thomas, 100–1, 113
Elvin, Mark, 179
Empire and Information, 215
England. *See* Britain
English East India Company, 31, 37, 47
    and Bengal famine, 78–9
    colonial policies, 256–8
    and Indian imports, 126–7
    and protectionism, 239, 252–3
    and trade monopoly, 112
Enlightened Economy, The, 126
Enlightenment, 4
Epstein, S. R., 85, 262
essentialization, 82
Euclid, 197
Europe
    and Asia, 1, 7, 10–11, 51–3
    and China, 6
    coal use in, 160–1
    and competitive trade, 10
    cotton industry in, 36–7
    demographic regime in, 75–6
    grain markets in, 62
    and India, 6–7, 221–2
    industrialization of, 1
    instrumental rationality in, 4
    markets in, 3
    population balance in, 4
    property rights in, 3–4
    protectionism in, 132–3, 245–7

scientific culture in, 186
and Smithian economics, 114
and technological change, 247–9
trade policy in, 245–7
university system in, 215–16
European cottons, 89–114.
    See also British cotton industry
and Asian expertise, 91–2
calico printing, 90–5
color fastness of, 94, 96
consumption of, 92–3
fustians, 93–4
and Indian imports, 89, 93
linen–cotton blends, 97, 129
and Ottoman imports, 119, 122
quality of, 96–7
technical literature on, 92
technological innovations, 98
and West Africa trade, 95–8
European Miracle, 52
Everest, George, 242
*Experimental Researches Concerning
    the Philosophy of Permanent
    Colours*, 92

factory system, 146
family structures, 73–4
famines, 77–9, 224
Faraday, Michael, 235
Farmer, Roger E. A., 260
fashion, 30–3
Fazl, Abu'l, 204
Febvre, Lucien, 8
female fertility, 71–2
Ferguson, Niall, 225
fertility rates, 6, 71–2, 74–5
Finnane, Antonia, 67
Flinn, Michael, 152, 161, 166–7, 169
flying shuttle, 101–2
Flynn, Dennis O., 46
food consumption, 44–5, 68
forest management, 158, 177–80
Foucault, Michel, 264
Fourcroy, Antoine François Comte de,
    200
France, 158
and Atlantic market, 140–2
and Barnes project, 108
and blue cloth trade, 34
and Britain, 116, 133–4, 247–8

cloth printing in, 138–40, 142
cotton manufacturing in, 116,
    138–40, 148
heavy cotton in, 148–50
and Indian cottons, 32, 140
industrialization in, 223
iron industry in, 168–9, 246
labor in, 146–7
and Ottoman trade, 118–19,
    121, 124
and Pondicherry spinning works,
    228–9
protectionism in, 138–9, 245–6
railways in, 250
silks in, 31
and slave trade, 24, 140–2
state enterprises in, 249
technological capability in, 247–8
and West Africa trade, 140–2
Frank, Andre Gunder, 22, 46–8
Franklin, James, 218
Fraser, Derek, 113
Fremdling, Rainer, 246
fustians, 93–4, 129, 150

Gadgil, Dhananjay Ramchandra, 226
Genç, Mehmet, 131–2
Geodefroy, Thomas, 228
Gerschenkron, Alexander, 143
Ghos of Gwalior, Mohammed, 198
Gillispie, Charles, 219
Giráldez, Arturo, 46
Glahn, Richard von, 46–7
global economy, 21. *See also* trade
Golas, Peter, 159
gold, 47
Gonfreville, Michael, 228
grain
    earnings from, 42–3
    markets, 61–2
    shortages, 76–7
    surpluses, 69–71
Great Divergence, The, 5
Griffiths, Trevor, 102, 130, 133
Grove, Richard, 191–2
Guest, Richard, 102–3, 109, 111
Guha, Sumit, 73–4
Gujarat, 69
gulgul, 210
gum Arabic, 34

Gupta, Ashin Das, 48
Gupta, Bishnupriya, 42–5
Guy, John, 27, 29–30

Habib, Irfan, 54, 59, 61, 63–4, 204–5,
    207, 218
Haider, Najaf, 48–9
Hajnal, John, 71–3
handkerchiefs, 127–8
Hargreaves, James, 98
Harley, C. Knick, 11, 12, 153
Harrington, James, 53
Harris, John R., 108
Hartwell, Robert, 158
Hasan, Abu'l, 204
Hatcher, John, 161, 163
Hausman, William J., 165
Headrick, Daniel, 234
Heath, J. M., 235–8, 244, 252
Heber, Reginald, 233
Henry VIII, 168, 247
Heston, Alan, 42
Heyne, Benjamin, 239
Hilaire-Perez, Liliane, 216
Hipparchus, 197
History of British India, The, 265
History of the British Coal Industry,
    152
*History of the Cotton Manufacture in
    Great Britain*, 99
*History of the County Palatine of
    Lancaster*, 99
Hobsbawm, Eric, 38, 101, 264
Holker, John, 94, 149–50, 248
Holland, 23
Horn, Jeff, 245
horticulture, 205
Hortus Malabaricus, 191–2, 195
hundis, 63
Hunt, Philip, 102, 130, 133
Hunter, William, 197
Husain, Said Mohsin, 242
Hyde, Charles, 170

Imperial Book of Regulations, 205
İnalcık, Halil, 118, 123–4
*Index to Wills of Lancashire and
    Cheshire Record Society*, 154
India. *See also* Indian cottons; Indian
    industry; Indian science and

technology; Mughal India; South
    India
agriculture in, 41, 68–71, 76–8, 267
bullion imports, 46–9
caste system, 6, 58–60, 81
coal in, 182, 231–2
coinage in, 47–50, 60
colonial government in, 13, 18, 78–80
contracting system in, 40
cotton industry in, 2, 17, 22–46
economic regions of, 14–15
and Europe, 6–7, 221–2
family and household structures,
    73–4
famine in, 224
forests in, 180–2
grain markets in, 62–3
iron industry in, 182, 207, 234–9
labor in, 41, 146
literature in, 253–4
occupational distributions, 70
in Orientalist writings, 264–5
population controls, 6
pre-colonial, 185–6
property rights, 5
railways in, 256
scientific culture in, 6–7, 18
spinning and weaving in, 41
standard of living in, 38, 45
technological innovation in, 15–16,
    203–13
and trade, 13, 21–7, 239–40, 265–6
unemployment in, 40
working hours in, 41–2
Indian cottons, 2, 17, 22–46
aesthetic qualities of, 27–33
and Atlantic trade, 25–6
and British competition, 153, 226–7
British import restrictions on,
    127–31, 267
and Egypt, 121
in England, 2, 23–4, 31–2, 35, 211
and fashion, 30–3
and France, 32, 140
imitation of, 34–5, 37, 50, 90–7,
    106, 123–5
and Middle East trade, 117–18
muslins, 33–4
and Ottoman Empire, 115–19,
    122–5

price of, 34–7, 42
quality of, 33–6
and silks, 31, 37
and social status, 30, 32
in Southeast Asia, 30, 35
and spinning innovations, 98–100,
104, 106, 108–9, 227–9
types of, 27, 33
and wages, 34, 37–46
and West Africa trade, 95–8, 134
Indian industry, 224–44
armaments, 206–7, 211–13, 255–6
and British imports, 252–3, 256–8,
266
and capital markets, 240–1
coal mining, 231–2
and colonial policy, 224–7, 244–5,
252–61, 266–7
cotton-spinning, 227–9
decline in, 265–6
early nineteenth century, 226–7, 265
exports, 237–9, 253, 266
and Indian entrepreneurs, 239–40
iron working, 182, 207, 234–9
and labor shortages, 230
and protectionism, 236, 239,
252–3, 258
and resource endowments, 225
shipbuilding, 232–4
and skilled workers, 241–4
and steam engines, 229–31
Indian science and technology, 185–222
administrative and technical
manuals, 205–6
architecture, 196
armaments, 206–7, 211–13
astronomy, 195–7
botany, 191–2
cartography, 204–5
chemistry, 217–18
clock making, 218
and colonial government, 201–2,
253–4, 257
and early-modern science, 191,
194–5
and European cooperation, 192,
197–8, 208, 217
and global science, 191
instrument-making, 195–6
inventions, 203–4

and knowledge transmission, 214–19
libraries, 198–203
loss of knowledge, 266
machinery, 204, 218
mathematics and geometry, 199
medicine, 194
natural history, 202
and Persian, 193
prevalence of texts, 202–3
products of, 187–8
and Sanskrit intellectual tradition,
193–4
shipbuilding, 204, 208–11, 221
and skilled workers, 208, 216–19
state patronage of, 187, 195, 201,
206–7, 221, 255, 267
surveying, 192, 202
translations from European
languages, 198–200
views of, 189
individual decision-making, 14
Industrial Enlightenment, 188–9
*Industrial Evolution of India in Recent
Times*, 226
industrialization, 1. *See also* Indian
industry
and agriculture, 67–9
in Britain, 223
and coal, 161
and comparisons with Asia, 8–10,
268
and education, 216
in France, 223
and property rights, 67–8
and science, 188, 219–20
and state support, 223–4, 251–2, 259
and technological change, 85
Inikori, Joseph, 108–9, 136
institutions. *See* state institutions
instrument-making, 195–6, 242–3
insurance rates, 65–6
interest rates, 5
early nineteenth-century India, 241
Mughal India, 63–5
Invention of Tradition, 264
Iran, 32, 35, 50, 123
iron industry
in Britain, 161, 168–70, 246, 267
in China, 171–3
and coal, 169–70, 172

iron industry (cont.)
  and dead weight cargo, 235
  in France, 168–9, 246
  in India, 182, 207, 234–9, 244
  and protectionism, 247
  and railway construction, 250–1
  and shipbuilding, 234
  state enterprises, 249–50
  state policy, 168–70, 173
iron nails, 209
Isett, Christopher, 68

Jacob, Margaret, 186, 188–90, 220
Jami al Ulum, 198
Japan, 13, 69, 224
  coal in, 158, 160
  forest management in, 177–80, 267
Jardin de Lorixa, 192
Jejeebhoy, Jamsetjee, 240
Jessop, George, 258
Johns, Adrian, 215
Johnson, James, 107
Johnson, Marion, 141
Jones, Eric, 14, 52, 54–6, 58, 76, 78
Journal of the Royal Asiatic Society,
  235

Kahneman, Daniel, 14
karma, 81
Keller, Wolfgang, 62
Kennedy, John, 110, 112–13, 154
Key, Francis Scott, 213
Khan, B. Zorina, 260
Khan, Gholam Hossein, 60
Khan, Iqbal Ghani, 196, 202, 205–6
Khan, Khaliluddin, 201
Klein, Rudiger, 32
knowledge transmission, 214–19, 221,
  247–9
Kuhn, Philip, 55
Kyd, James, 233

labor
  in Britain, 41, 69, 146–7
  hand labor, 156
  in India, 41, 146
  productivity, 41, 69
  shortages, 230
  specialization of, 154
  and state policies, 146–7

Landes, David, 52, 54, 101, 189,
  249, 260
Lardner, Dionysus, 250
Lavoisier, Antoine, 200
Lee, George, 112
Lee, James, 5
Lemire, Beverly, 31, 37, 130
L'Empereur, Nicolas, 192
Leonard, Karen, 66
linen, 35
  cotton–linen mix, 93–4, 97, 129, 148
  printed, 91, 129
Linnaeus, Carl, 200
List, Friedrich, 223
London, 164–7
looms, 41
loss aversion, 14
Lu Chen-fei, 171
Lucknow library, 201

Macfarlane, Alan, 72
Machado, Pedro, 33, 239
Machiavelli, Niccolò di Bernardo dei,
  53
machinery, 204, 218
Madras perambulators, 242
Maistry, Pallikondan, 200
Malanima, Paolo, 161
Malthus, Thomas, 4, 51–2, 71–3
Manchester cotton, 97
Manila silver trade, 48
Mann, Julia de Lacy, 101, 108, 129
Mann, Michael, 180–1
Mantoux, Paul, 100, 103
mapping, 204–5
Maratha technology, 212–13
market economy
  in Asia, 3–5
  capital markets, 240–1, 260
  and efficiency, 62–3
  in Europe, 3
  grain, 61–2
  and Indian trading, 61
  and insurance rates, 65–6
  and interest rates, 5, 63–5
  and productivity, 61–2
  and state policies, 143–5, 259,
    261–2, 266–7
  and technological innovation, 111,
    113–14

Marks, Robert, 158
Marseilles, 139
Martin, Claude, 201
Martin, Gaston, 141
Martin, Robert Montgomery, 234, 244
Marx, Karl, 7, 8, 12, 52, 114, 265
Mary II, Queen, 31
Matters of Exchange, 192
McCrea, Lawrence, 193
McCulloch, John Ramsay, 99
Melvil, Thomas, 96
mercantilism, 133. *See also* state policy
metallurgy, 218
metal working, 256
military. *See* armaments
military fiscalism, 56–7
Mill, James, 265
mindful hand, 186, 219–22
mining, 231–2, 249
minting, 229–30
Minto, Lord, 253–4
Mokyr, Joel, 126, 186, 188–90,
    213–16, 220, 261
Monserrate, António, 205
Montaran, Michau de, 94
Montesquieu, Charles-Louis de
    Secondat, 51–2, 215
Montgomery, Florence, 94, 149
Moreau, Jacob Nicolas, 32
Moreland, William Harrison, 38, 54
Morris, Morris D., 226
mortality rates, 72
Mozambique, 33
Mughal India
    agriculture in, 53, 61
    capital markets in, 63–4
    cartography in, 204–5
    commercial life in, 53–4, 61, 66–7
    credit systems in, 64
    horticulture in, 205
    interest rates in, 63–5
    military fiscalism in, 56–7
    silver coins in, 48–9
    standard of living in, 54
    state institutions in, 54–6
    technological change in, 203–5
    translation patronage in, 198
mule, 98, 105–6, 155
muslins, 33–4, 130
    British tariffs on, 130–1, 145

European, 36–7, 108
Indian, 33–4
Musson, Albert Edward, 154, 220
Mysore library, 198–9
Mysore state, 207–8, 213

Naidu, Bundla Ramaswamy, 215
nails, 209
Naima, Mustafa, 125
Nantes, 141–2
Navigation Laws, 137, 234
Needham, Joseph, 189
Nef, John, 164, 166, 168
Netherlands, 95–6
Newton, Isaac, 188
North, Douglass, 8, 14, 52, 58, 262
North American market, 26, 136–7,
    140
Norway, 74
Nushka-i Dilkusha, 206

Oberkampf, Christoff-Philipp, 93, 142
O'Brien, Patrick, 68, 102, 130,
    133, 144
Ogden, James, 103
Oldknow, Samuel, 106, 110, 130, 146
Orientalism, 7
Orientalist writings, 264–5
*Origins of Industrial Capitalism in
    India*, 226
Ormrod, David, 137, 144
Osborne, Anne, 175–6, 179
Ottoman Empire, 115–25
    Anatolia, 122–3
    and Atlantic market, 137
    cotton industry in, 50, 123–5
    economic philosophy of, 131–3,
        145
    Egypt, 119–21
    and French trade, 118–19, 121, 124
    and Indian cottons, 115–19, 122–5
    labor in, 146
    and raw cotton exports, 119, 122
    silver outflows, 125
    state institutions in, 53, 55, 57, 137
    state policies, 125, 131–3, 143
    technical improvements in, 115
    trade deficits in, 125
    trade histories of, 116–17
    wool in, 132

Pamuk, Şevket, 125
Parthasarathi, Prasannan, 45
patent system, 216
Paterson, James, 181
pattern books, 33
pattern weaving, 204
Paul, Lewis, 107
Pelsaert, Francisco, 38, 54
perambulators, 242
Perdue, Peter, 55, 158
Perlin, Frank, 83–4
Persian, 193
Peyssonnel, Claude Charles de, 124
Phillimore, R. H., 257
Philosophical Transactions, 235
plows, 206
political competition, 55–6
Pollexfen, John, 32
Pollock, Sheldon, 193–4, 202
polyandry, 75
Pomeranz, Kenneth, 5, 8, 46, 61, 152, 162
Pondicherry, 228–9
population, 6
    balance of, 4, 51
    preventive/positive checks to, 71–2,
       75, 80
Portugal, 23
Prakash, Om, 22, 48
prefabricated buildings, 203
Prince, The, 53
printing
    on cloth, 90–5, 127–9, 138–40, 142
    text, 214–15
privateering, 167
Private Investment in India, 226
*Problem of Unbelief in the Sixteenth
    Century, The*, 8
Proceedings of the Royal Society, 235
property rights
    and agriculture, 66–71
    in Asia, 5
    and caste system, 58
    in Europe, 3–4
    and industrialization, 67–8
protectionism
    in Britain, 125–33, 145, 245, 267
    colonial trade policies, 244, 258
    in France, 138–9, 245–6
    and India, 236, 239, 252–3, 258
    and resource constraints, 246–7

Protestant Ethic, The, 81
Protestantism, 4, 80–2
provisioning, 131–3, 143
Prussia, 246, 248–51
Ptolemy, Claudius, 197

*Quarterly Journal of Science,
    Literature, and the Arts*, 235
Quataert, Donald, 118

railways, 250–1, 256
rainfall, 76–7
Raj, Kapil, 192, 202
Ranger, Terence, 264
rationality, 4, 6, 52, 80–4
Raveux, Olivier, 138
Raychaudhuri, Tapan, 38
Raymond, André, 120
reciprocal comparison, 8–9
Registry Act of 1815, 211, 234
religion, 81–2
Religion of India, The, 81
Relocating Modern Science, 192
resource endowments, 225, 246–7
revenue collection, 83–4
Rey, Claudius, 129
rice cultivation, 69–71, 77, 79
Richards, John, 157
Richardson, William, 242
Richthofen, Baron Ferdinand von,
    159, 172
Rise of the Western World, The, 58
Roberts, Lissa, 220–1
Robinson, Eric, 154, 220
rocketry, 213
Rouen, 148–50
Rowe, William, 159
Roxburgh, William, 217–18
Roy, Tirthankar, 225
Rule, John, 42
Rungta, Radhe Shyam, 241
Russia, 158

Said, Edward, 7
sailcloth, 132
salt, 61, 67
Samuel, Raphael, 156
Sangwan, Satpal, 234
Sanskrit learning, 193
Sarasvati Mahal Library, 200

Scandinavia, 158
Schaffer, Simon, 215, 220–1
Schwartz, Paul, 92
science
  early-modern, 190–1, 194–5
  and industrialization, 188, 219–20
  and technological development,
    219–21
scientific culture, 186, 188–9, 195.
  See also Indian science and
  technology
scientific revolution, 189–90
Selim III, Sultan, 118
Serfoji II, King, 200
Shammas, Carole, 35–6
Shapin, Steven, 190
shipbuilding, 204, 208–11, 221, 232–4
Shirazi, Mir Fathu'llah, 204
Shiue, Carol H., 62
siamoises, 148–9
Siddiqi, Asiya, 240
silks, 31, 37, 92
silver, 21–2
  in China, 46–7, 58
  in India, 46–9
  in Ottoman Empire, 125
  world production of, 46
Singh, Raja Jai, 196–8
Sivin, Nathan, 189
Sivramkrishna, Sashi, 45
skilled workers, 208
  in colonial India, 253
  in Indian industry, 241–4
  in Indian science and technology,
    216–19
  and knowledge transmission, 247–8
slave trade, 24, 140–2
Smith, Adam, 8, 51–2, 57–8, 66, 111,
  114, 261–2, 267, 269
Smith, Sir Thomas, 133, 144
Smith, William, 200
Smithian political economy, 84–5,
  109–14, 261–2
Society for the Encouragement of Arts,
  Manufactures and Commerce,
  103–4
Sokoloff, Kenneth L., 260
Solvyns, François Balthazar, 210
South America, 26
Southeast Asia, 30, 35

South India, 15, 40–1, 45
  account-keeping in, 82–3
  agricultural labor force, 70–1
  cotton consumption, 153
  food exports, 69
  iron works in, 235–9, 244
spinning, 41, 98, 100–2
  innovations, 98–100, 104, 106,
    108–9
  in nineteenth-century India, 227–9
  roller method of, 107
  spinning jenny, 98, 105, 109
Spirit of the Laws, 215
state enterprises, 249–51
state institutions, 13–14, 17
  British, 137
  China, 55, 57, 67
  and merchants, 67
  Mughal, 53–6
  Ottoman, 53, 55, 57, 137
  and political competition, 55–6
  and revenue collection, 83–4
state policy, 12–13. *See also* British
  colonial policies
  and agriculture, 206–7, 267
  British, 144–5
  Chinese, 173–6
  and coal, 164–8, 170–5
  and cotton industry, 125–31
  French, 249
  Indian science and technology, 187,
    195, 201, 206–7, 221, 255, 267
  and industrialization, 223–4, 251–2,
    259
  and iron, 168–70, 173
  Japanese, 177–80
  and knowledge transmission, 216,
    221, 247–9
  and labor, 146–7
  and market economy, 143–5, 259,
    261–2, 266–7
  Ottoman, 125, 131–3, 143
  and scientific culture, 187, 195
  and technological capability, 247–9
  and trade, 245–7
status quo bias, 14
steam power, 154–5, 161–2, 229–31
steamships, 233
Stewart, Charles, 198–9
Stiglitz, Joseph, 2

Strutt, Jedidiah, 95
Stuart, Charles, 213
Studer, Roman, 62
Styles, John, 32, 35, 130
Sugihara, Kaoru, 69
surveying, 192
survey of India, 242–3
Sykes, Joseph, 167
Syria, 119, 122

Tann, Jennifer, 230
taqavi (taccavi), 64, 69, 79
tariffs. *See* protectionism
Tavernier, Jean-Baptiste, 212
Taylor, Charles, 140
Taylor, James, 107
Taylor, Samuel, 97
technological innovation, 2–3
    armaments, 251
    British cotton industry, 90, 98–103,
        221
    challenge and response model, 98–9,
        101–2, 113
    and coal, 151–2
    and colonial power, 257
    and division of labor, 110–11
    and education, 260
    and European divergence, 189
    in France, 247–8
    in India, 15–16, 203–13
    and Indian cottons, 98, 104, 106–9
    and industrialization, 85
    and labor costs, 109
    and market forces, 111, 113–14
    in Ottoman Empire, 115
    and science, 219–20
    spinning, 98–100, 104, 106, 108–9,
        227–9
    and state policy, 247–9
    transmission of, 240, 247–9
    and West Africa trade, 108–9
    and yarn shortages, 109
Thirsk, Joan, 144, 169
Thomas, P. J., 93, 126
Thomas, Robert Paul, 14, 58
Timmins, Geoffrey, 102
Tipu Sultan, 198–9, 207–8, 231
Tod, James, 207
Totman, Conrad, 160, 179
Touchet, Samuel, 107

trade, 10, 13, 61. *See also* Atlantic
    market; market economy
    British, 112, 151–4, 267
    and China, 57–8
    and colonial policies, 244, 258
    cotton textiles, 23–7
    Indian, 13, 21–7, 239–40, 265–6
    Middle East, 117–18
    and state policy, 245–7
    West Africa, 95–8, 108–9
*Trade and Civilisation in the Indian
    Ocean*, 21
Traité sur les toiles peintes, 92
translations, 198–200
travel literature, 206
Treatise on Calico Printing, A, 92
tree planting, 178–9
Trevelyan, Charles Edward, 231, 252
Turkey red, 91, 96–7
Tversky, Amos, 14

Unbound Prometheus, The, 101
unemployment, 40
Unending Frontier, The, 157
United States, 155
university system, 215–16
Unwin, George, 146
Ure, Andrew, 101
useful knowledge, 213–19
    and printing, 214–15
    transmission of, 214–19

van Reede, Hendrik Adriaan, 191–92, 195
Varma, Vira Kerala, 191
Vasco de Gama, 137, 209
Veinstein, Gilles, 124
velvets, 150
Victoria, Queen, 225
von Tunzelmann, G. N., 155
Voth, Hans-Joachim, 42

Wadsworth, Alfred P., 101, 108
wages
    and consumption, 44–5
    Indian cotton industry, 34, 37–46
    and non-monetary perquisites, 42–3
    and skill levels, 43–4
Walker, George, 106
Wallerstein, Immanuel, 21
water cooling, 204

water frame, 95, 98, 105, 129
water power, 155
Watt, James, 230
Wealth and Poverty of Nations, 52
Wealth of Nations, 8, 51, 111, 267
weaving, 41, 59, 100–2, 204, 250
Weber, Max, 4, 8, 52, 80–2
West Africa, 24, 34
  and British exports, 134–6
  cotton trade with, 95–8, 108–9
  and French exports, 140–1
West Indies, 134, 140
widow remarriage, 75
Wilkinson, John, 248
Will, Pierre-Étienne, 173
William III, King, 31

Williams, Perry, 190
Wong, Roy Bin, 5, 8, 61, 173–4
wood, 2–3, 10–11
  forest management, 158, 177–80
  in India, 182
  scarcity of, 157–8
wool, 92, 132
woolen manufacturers, 127–8
working hours, 41–2
Woude, Ad van der, 66
Wrigley, E. A., 151, 158
Wujastyk, Dominik, 194

Yangzi region, 152, 162, 175–6, 179, 224
Young, H. A., 212, 254, 257